A New Vision for Missions

A New Vision for Missions

William Cameron Townsend, the Wycliffe Bible Translators, and the Culture of Early Evangelical Faith Missions, 1896–1945

William Lawrence Svelmoe

THE UNIVERSITY OF ALABAMA PRESS
Tuscaloosa

The University of Alabama Press
Tuscaloosa, Alabama 35487-0380

Manufactured in the United States of America

Typeface: Minion

∞

The paper on which this book is printed meets the minimum requirements of American National Standard for Information Sciences-Permanence of Paper for Printed Library Materials, ANSI Z39.48-1984.

Library of Congress Cataloging-in-Publication Data

Svelmoe, William Lawrence.
A new vision for missions : William Cameron Townsend, the Wycliffe Bible translators, and the culture of early evangelical faith missions, 1896–1945 / William Lawrence Svelmoe.
p. cm.
Includes bibliographical references (p.) and index.
ISBN 978-0-8173-1593-1 (cloth : alk. paper) — ISBN 978-0-8173-8065-6 (electronic) 1. Townsend, William Cameron, 1896–1982. 2. Wycliffe Bible Translators. 3. Summer Institute of Linguistics.
I. Title.
BV2372.T68S84 2008
266.0092—dc22
[B]

2008005571

Contents

Illustrations

Note to Reader

This is the story of William Cameron Townsend. To be strictly accurate, it's the story of his first forty-five years or so. When Uncle Cam (as he came to be known around the world) died in 1982, *Time* magazine referred to him as a "pioneering Protestant missionary" in an obituary in its "Milestones" section. Heads of state, educators, and Christian leaders from around the world sent letters and cables of condolence. Evangelist Billy Graham wrote, "No man in this century has . . . advance[d] the cause of Christian missions as [has] Cameron Townsend." Townsend achieved his greatest notoriety as the visionary founder of the Summer Institute of Linguistics and the Wycliffe Bible Translators, the largest, most innovative, and most controversial Protestant mission of the twentieth century.

The truth of the matter is, however, that I'm as interested in other things as I am in Townsend. His first wife, Elvira, is an intriguing case. I love Dr. Becker, and I only talk about him for a couple of paragraphs. Then there's R. D. Smith. If you see his demise coming, you're pretty sharp. I didn't. In short, I find missionaries fascinating. Whether for good or ill, they changed the world.

The title mentions faith missions. Some of you, diehard evangelicals of a certain generation, know what those are, or were. If the term means nothing to you, well, you'll know all about them by the time you finish this book. Understanding their culture is what the book is really about.

I also want my readers to get a sense of what it feels like to be an evangelical Protestant. Along with its heart, which has always been large, I'm searching for the evangelical mind. If you're an evangelical, I hope you see a bit of yourself in my subjects, your good self, and the self that makes you wince from time to time. If you're not an evangelical, I hope you at least learn a bit about what makes us tick.

That last line gave me away. I'm an evangelical myself, or at least I like evangelicals. At any rate, I grew up evangelical, and I'm still in the tent, or at least observing under the flap. I grew up in the jungle, in a house on stilts, with a grass roof, inhabited by far more rats, bats, bugs, snakes, and other creatures than human beings. My parents were missionaries, and I was along for the ride. In fact they were missionaries with the Wycliffe Bible Translators, the outfit Townsend founded. I can't remember if I ever met the great man, but we all knew who he was. I did meet Ken Pike (more on him later); I never understood a word he said, which is, I suspect, why he was a linguistic genius.

I loved my life. Missionaries were fun to grow up with. They were touched by an adventurous spirit. They tended to let their kids do wild things. They had great senses of humor, at least most of them did. They weren't all real smart, but then neither are a lot of us. Some were very smart. And a few, well, let's just say the jungle got to them. They were demon possessed, my parents thought. On the frontier normal rules don't apply. Just ask Mr. Kurtz.

I do not use the term "fundamentalist" very often in this book. Although most of my subjects were Protestant fundamentalists as historians use the term, the word has become so pejorative today that I prefer "conservative evangelical" or simply "evangelical." And Townsend, while fundamentalist in theology, certainly possessed little of the fundamentalist mood, as we will see.

Much of the research for this book was completed for a dissertation directed by George Marsden at the University of Notre Dame. Notre Dame was an ideal place to call home throughout my years of graduate study. George was a wise and generous mentor who taught me everything from American religion to golf and cross-country skiing. He and his wife, Lucie, continue to be both guides and friends.

Cal Hibbard, Cameron Townsend's personal secretary, oversaw the organization of the Townsend archives, located at the Jungle Aviation and Radio Service headquarters just outside of Waxhaw, North Carolina. His many years of labor have produced a goldmine for scholars who are interested in studying almost any aspect of mission work in the twentieth century. Cal's extraordinary knowledge of the archives, as well as his love for good food and zest for weekend road trips, made my months there very productive and enjoyable. While working at the archives, I spent the better part of five months living with Pat and Joanne Cochran. The Cochrans made research travel seem like going home, and I am deeply grateful for their hospitality. I cannot imagine feeling more at home in somebody else's house than I did there.

In Dallas, Steve and Jacqui Hohulin took me in for several weeks and made me feel like I was back at Nasuli, where Steve and I grew up in the Philippines. Tom Headland was the first in the Summer Institute of Linguistics to encourage my work regardless of its impact on the organization, and I have valued his support immensely. In Mexico City, Steve Marlett, David Córdova, Griselda Rivas, and Rebeca Rivas de López went out of their way to welcome and assist me during my five weeks there. I enjoyed one of the best meals of my life with the Rivas family.

The Central American Mission granted me access to their archives in Dallas. The day I ran across Dr. Becker's letters there was the highlight of my years of research. Dr. Becker and R. D. Smith, both of the CAM, were two of the great picaresque characters of the early history of faith missions. Reading their letters in that small room at CAM was a delight. I should add that the noon break at CAM was a charming experience of Southern hospitality and humor.

Captured by Cameron Townsend's vision, my parents, Gordon and Thelma Svelmoe, lived for thirty years with the Mansaka people in the Philippines, working under what were at times very difficult circumstances to learn an indigenous language and translate the Scriptures. Their choices ensured a wonderfully unusual childhood for my brothers and me. I wouldn't trade it for any other.

Lisa Svelmoe is all that a best friend and wife could be, living proof that young men, when blessed by a benevolent providence, *can* make good choices. An artist and writer herself, she knows what an isolating labor writing can be, and although we both can get wrapped up in our work, she has always kept us connected, refusing to settle for separate spheres. My admiration and love for Lisa and my parents knows no bounds, and I dedicate this book to them.

A New Vision for Missions

1
In Which Townsend Drops Out of College and Decides to Be a Missionary for a Year

1896–1917

> Limitation / Oh hateful word / That halts your aspiration / That downs your dreams / And brands your schemes / As filmy speculation / And says you shan't / Because you can't / In the face of limitation.
>
> —William Cameron Townsend, 1917

It is tempting to record that the man who would one day be called "the greatest missionary statesman of the twentieth century" first went to the mission field on a whim. While such an assertion would not be entirely accurate, it also would not be far from the truth. When the impossibly slight youth (with thin brown hair, protruding ears, and wearing a wool suit) bounded up the gangplank of the S.S. *Peru* on September 15, 1917, bound for Guatemala, he was not the typical evangelical Bible institute graduate burning with a long and zealously nurtured passion for the lost heathen. No, William Cameron Townsend came late to his interest in missions. When asked in college at a meeting of the Student Volunteer Movement why he wished to join the student missions organization, Townsend could not articulate a clear reply. Probably he joined at the urging of friends, and because the Student Volunteer band seemed to have more "enthusiasm," as Townsend put it, than did the ministerial students with whom he originally associated. That he embarked now for Guatemala had more to do with the restlessness of a young man bored with college and on the point of being dispatched into the mud of the European trenches, the challenge to leave the farm and gain significance in the wider world, and the nagging inner question of many a youth reared in a pious family, the question of whether he really had the goods spiritually.

The Townsend family, led by austere stone-deaf William Hammond Townsend, arrived in California in 1893. They came by way of Pennsylvania, Kansas, and Colorado, like so many others journeying to the Golden State in search of relief for lives tied to the land and to perennial poverty. They settled in the desert east of Los Angeles, close enough to feel the energy and the hope of the emerging giant by the sea, far enough away to be reminded, as the sand driven by the hot Santa Ana winds ground its way into the cracks of their bare farmhouse, that they were not yet there. Here, behind the faded curtain separating William and Molly's bedroom from the only other room in the house, William Cameron was born on July 9, 1896. He was the fifth child of an eventual six, and the first boy.[1] They called him Cameron or Cam to distinguish him from his father.

William was a solemn, scrupulously honest, hardworking tenant farmer. The Los Angeles grocers who purchased vegetables from the Townsend wagon knew him as "the honest deaf man," and they rarely bothered to carefully examine his produce. His plodding insistence that his children "finish one row before you start another" and his refusal to accept shoddy work instilled in them the work ethic that defined farm families for generation after generation. The adjectives that came to Cameron's mind when his father died in 1939 were "rugged" and "stalwart." "There was," he reflected, "no ostentation about him." If William had a weakness, it was his moodiness. Trapped in a world of silence, forever watching the conversations and laughter of others from a distance, William could sometimes be difficult to live with. His children remembered massaging his head in the evenings when his nerves bothered him, and trying to rapidly write down the gist of conversations in an attempt to include him in the daily flow of family and community life.[2]

William brought his dogged work ethic to his religion. He had wanted to be a minister before a lack of funds and his hearing loss forever closed that door. But he never lost the desire to keep the Sabbath holy and to read and expound upon Scripture. Early every morning, before beginning the never-ending round of chores inherent in farm life, he huddled by the stove and read three chapters of Scripture, five on the Sabbath. After breakfast he imparted biblical instruction to his assembled family and led them in prayer. During the years before his hearing completely left him, the children leaned close to his left ear and shouted out their memory verses and the correct order of the biblical books. He taught his children that their lives belonged to God "to use as he saw fit."[3] William liked to sing, and the children knew they laughed at their peril when their deaf father's voice cracked and twanged its way through the ancient hymns of the faith. On Sundays the family hitched up the buggy and plodded ten miles to gather with perhaps fifty other people to worship in a small, white, steepled, country Presbyterian church where the weekly tradition of sermon and sacrament provided a point of unity for the dispersed and often transient rural community.

Molly was a stocky, even-tempered woman who worked constantly to keep food on the table and her children outfitted, at least on Sunday, in decent clothes. Hospitable to a fault, she could always be counted on to invite the preacher over for dinner even if supplies were scarce. She dealt patiently with her deaf husband, listening politely in the evenings when he called her to hear a particularly profound portion of a sermon from the *Christian Herald*, or carefully writing out a joke one of the children repeated that had set the family to giggling.[4]

Despite all that Molly and William did, the family remained mired in poverty. In addition to William's deafness, he had a respiratory problem, which made breathing difficult, often preventing him from working. Throughout Cameron's youth the family lived at a subsistence level. The children worked hard alongside their parents, milking cows, growing pumpkins in the riverbed, picking walnuts and olives for nearby growers, selling their own vegetables door to door in Downey, or watermelons from a stand by the road. In their free time the boys fished in nearby streams and hunted rabbits in the hills. Eventually, an uncle took two of the girls to ease the burden on the family, as well as to give the girls an opportunity to get a year or two of college education.[5]

While the family was certainly fundamental in theology—they were disturbed by modernism, evolution, Sabbath breaking, cigarettes, and the saloon—by temperament they were not the sort to pick a fight or deny the benefits of the modern world. After patiently listening to a preacher archly put modern women in their place, Molly sighed, "Their bobbed hair might not be biblical, but it is very convenient." She refused to countenance easy dismissals of modern innovations as works of the devil. "Movies are here to stay," she lectured her children, "so it is up to good people to make them good." Despite the hardships of her life, Molly proclaimed her world "a fine old world with lots of fine people in it."[6]

The family was close, and early on seem to have united behind Cameron as their hope for a wider influence in the world. Being the first boy, he was doted on by his parents and sisters. He did not disappoint. He was slight of stature, not particularly gifted in book learning (although he excelled in grade school and high school), but full of ideas and, once his blood was up, doggedly determined to plow through all obstacles to succeed. One sister, reflecting on Townsend's boyhood, said, "If he thought something should be done, he was going to do it." He was a leader, the kind of kid who instinctively knew how to get people

1. The Townsend family: back row from left—Ethel, Paul, Cameron, Oney; front row—Mary, William, Molly, Lula. Courtesy Townsend Archives.

to follow, even if it required a little arm-twisting. His younger brother, Paul, who spent a good bit of his life doing Cameron's bidding, remembered that Cameron was always good at getting other people to do what he wanted. "It was kind of a laughing matter in the family that when he got to working on a person to do something, [they generally complied]."[7]

Cameron finished the eighth grade at the head of his class, and when trouble on the farm threatened to interrupt his education, his older sister Lula postponed her marriage to continue working to support Cameron's schooling. She lost her fiancé in the bargain. At his small rural high school Cameron earned seventy dollars a month hauling fifteen other country kids to school and back in a horse-drawn wagon, a four-hour daily round trip.[8] Somewhere he found the time to stand out on the debate team, edit the yearbook, act the lead in the senior play, win a championship in doubles tennis, date a Catholic girl (unheard of in most evangelical families), and once again graduate at the top of his class. The yearbook predicted he would one day take his place in national government as a senator from California. Photos from the period reveal a slight, neat youth, often with a hint of a grin, always with an intent, determined gaze.

When Townsend enrolled at Occidental College in 1914, the school was in the process of dedicating a new campus out in orchard and ranch land in the sparsely settled community of Eagle Rock. Several new two- and three-story buildings rose from the scrub-covered hills at the end of a long dirt road. It might not have been much to look at in 1914, but Occidental still prided itself on being "the College of the City of Los Angeles."

Founded in 1887 by a coalition of Presbyterian ministers and laymen (one of the first trustees was Lyman Stewart, an oil millionaire who also funded publication of *The Fundamentals* and the founding of the Bible Institute of Los Angeles [now Biola University]), the school, in order to promote formal academic freedom, voted to discontinue any direct connection with the Presbyterian Church four years before Townsend's arrival. Nevertheless, the college board was still made up of "evangelical Christian Church members," and the dissociation made very little practical difference. As yet no one wanted to make Occidental a secular institution. Two semesters of biblical literature classes were still required for graduation. The Presbyterian denomination continued to support the college, and graduates funneled into Presbyterian seminaries and to Presbyterian foreign mission boards. Most of the students became teachers or ministers. The Young Men's Christian Association (YMCA) was "an integral part of campus life and enjoyed the support of virtually all students." Seventy-five men attended on average, and "mission study" enlisted fifty. The Young Women's Christian Association (YWCA) was also active on campus, and both organizations received extensive coverage in *The Occidental,* the campus newspaper. As the yearbook, *La Encina,* noted, the organizations "served as an exhaust for the expenditure of the Christian energy and aspiration of the students." In addition, more than forty students (divided equally between men and women) were members of the Student Volunteer Movement (SVM), the influential international student missions association that had been challenging students to give their lives to mission work for almost three decades. According to John Mott, the movement's chief spokesman, this was the largest per capita percentage of SVM members in any college at that time.[9]

Still, Occidental was not a Bible institute. At a place like Moody Bible Institute (MBI) in Chicago, Christian and mission organizations did not see themselves as "exhaust" for politely draining off the excess zeal of young adherents. At MBI, missions and evangelism were the very heartbeat of the place, the raison d'être of their existence. At Occidental, *La Encina* noted that the YMCA "earnestly strives to stand for clean, wholesome living, and sanely and clearly to present Jesus Christ as the Savior of individual men." But this "sane and clear presentation" did not include overt evangelism or the kind of expressive religion practiced by less-educated Christians. The YMCA prided itself on attaining "some success in not parading our religious beliefs and experiences" (indeed they attributed increased student participation to this "success"), and their "Handbook" stated that in the college YMCA "there was no room for the hallelujah, amen, saintly, nor any of the kindred accessories of this type of Christianity." It concluded, "It is hard enough for a college student to take religious medicine without having to swallow 'sanctity pills.'"[10] Although closer to its Protestant heritage than many more-established colleges, Occidental was in the mainstream of the movement of traditional Christian colleges away from their roots. The campus climate was quickly becoming more liberal, adopting the rules of academic discourse; religion was becoming more genteel, its practice conforming to ideals of turn-of-the-century masculine character—self-sacrificing and heroic, but polite, civilized, not overly emotional or argumentatively verbal. While this phenomenon may go a long way toward explaining the eagerness of young men to join the Student Volunteers and prove themselves in the most physically challenging religious arena possible, the mission field, it also explains why such colleges lost their place of leadership in the missionary enterprise in the twentieth century to the Bible institutes and Bible colleges. After the goal of Christian character and civilization was swamped by the disillusion of World War I, organizations such as the YMCA and the SVM lost their way and their remarkable influence over college life as Protestantism itself lost its place at the center of American life. Ultimately, the "clean, wholesome living" and "sane" presentation of the "polite" Christ of liberal theology could not offer the motivation for the rigors of missionary life provided by the "sanctity pills" of "amen, saintly" evangelical Christianity.

When Cameron Townsend arrived as a freshman at Occidental, the twenty-five faculty members educated the more than three hundred students in a genteel Protestant "traditional cultural curriculum." Culture, citizenship, and Christianity were the "watch words" of the college, and secure in the fact that the "world [would] always be led by college men," the Occidental administration prided itself on producing the "perfect citizen," a "trichotomy of brawn, brain, and brotherhood."[11]

Entering college from a rural high school with the weight of his family's expectation and sacrifice on his shoulders, Townsend felt both the euphoria of entering a wider world and the inner question of just how he measured up.

There were 130 members of his freshman class, and it was easy for a country boy to be overwhelmed by the size of it all. In his freshman year he vigorously defended his upbringing on the farm in an essay for his English class. In California, Townsend claimed, farmers could no longer be recognized by their "'Uncle Samuel' beard and awkward appearance." Those were vestiges of "the stolid old agriculturist of Arkansas with his span of oxen and corn-cob pipe." Today farmers drove automobiles, wore clean shirts, and were politically active. A California farmer "assumed the bearing of his city brother" and was "a society man in the best sense of the term." Called "Skinny Townsend" by his friends, the slight youth felt his stature keenly in a culture where "brawn" was an integral facet of the perfect Occidental male. Like that American hero of the previous generation—Theodore Roosevelt—he worked vigorously to keep his body from becoming a limitation. He joined the wrestling team, played tennis, and got to bed every night by ten. In a formal essay for his English class, he reflected, "[S]uccess in any walk of life is as dependent upon the body as upon the inspiration. Genius . . . finds herself capable of doing vastly more when housed in a well made and well kept body."[12]

Townsend achieved some success on campus as a debater. Debate was second only to football at Occidental as a spectator sport. The campus newspaper gave debate matches extensive coverage, often in bold type on the front page. Townsend was one of more than fifty students who tried out yearly for the twelve positions on the debate team, but in what must have been a keen disappointment, never made the final cut. He managed, however, to become vice president of the Forum Debating Society, an elite debate club limited to fifteen members, in only his sophomore year. He was elected president of the society as a junior. In his junior year he also joined the Lowell Literary Society, was appointed the extension committee chairman for the YMCA, and had a small part in the junior play. He was apparently known around campus for his good humor, because the following ditty was inscribed beneath his class picture his junior year: "There's no one else in all the place, / With such a shining, morning face."[13]

Townsend worked part-time as a janitor at the college and received additional financial help from a ministerial scholarship provided by the Presbyterian Church. His parents were delighted with his seeming interest in the ministry, and his sisters and their husbands agreed to help William and Molly financially so that Cameron, as the oldest boy, would be relieved of that burden. In the spring of his freshman year, Townsend reported that he was preparing to be a preacher and expected to spend three years in "some seminary" after graduation. He also mentioned a slight interest in taking a medical course. But despite promising his mother that he would finish college and attend seminary,

Townsend's interest in the ministry seems to have been a passing fancy, probably more his family's dream than his; perhaps a very average grade in first-semester Greek encouraged him to set his sights elsewhere. He decided to major in history. Perhaps he still hoped, as he had in high school, to become a teacher. More probably, like many talented young people, he really did not know what he wanted to do. That he was still casting about for direction in his junior year of college is evidenced by the fact that a National Guard recruiter talked him and his best friend into joining up with the promise of free engineering training.[14]

Early in the spring of his freshman year, Townsend decided to visit a meeting of the Student Volunteers. He had been attending the infrequent meetings of a future ministers association, but found them boring. The young future preachers did not seem to have much fun or enthusiasm about them. The leader of the Student Volunteers began to ask newcomers why they were there, and Townsend grew increasingly nervous as he listened to the glowing "testimonies" of the other young men. Finally all eyes turned to him: "And why are you here?" Skinny Townsend, future president of a debate society, jumped up, blurted, "I don't know," and hastily sat down. He could hardly have admitted his real reason for attending: "You all seem to have more fun than the preachers." A month later Townsend provided only marginally better reasons for joining the group on his Student Volunteer application. He offered that he had "never studied the subject [of missions] to any extent." He hastily added, "However, I have read a number of pamphlets, and am now reading a life of David Livingstone." He reported being in a class that studied John Mott's *The Present World Situation,* but admitted, "I was very irregular in attendance owing to other work." He also offered that his association with other young people in the SVM who were "planning to go with Christ to the ends of the earth," as well as the well-publicized deaths of several missionaries in Africa, also "inspired [him] with the heroic in the decision." Enthusiastic or not, to join he had to sign the Student Volunteer pledge: "It is my purpose, if God permit, to become a foreign missionary." Although the pledge left plenty of wiggle room, the SVM bands worked hard to keep the dream alive in their members, and a remarkable 25 percent eventually served overseas.[15]

By the fall of his sophomore year, Townsend's interest in missions was strong enough that he wrote an idealistic essay in his English class urging American Christians to "give the money which you make above living expenses . . . to spread the gospel." Undoubtedly echoing lines he picked up from the Student Volunteers, he wrote, "You judge the vitality of a church by its interest in missions. . . . The greater need is where the greatest darkness is."[16] Sometime during his sophomore year he also read a biography of J. Hudson Taylor, founder of the China Inland Mission, whose story, along with that of George Müller, had more influence on evangelical missions and missionaries than any other in the late nineteenth and early twentieth centuries. Taylor's dynamic story of a life of faith lived in exotic foreign climes stirred many a young evangelical, and Townsend was no exception.

The turning point for Townsend seems to have come in the spring semester of his junior year, early in 1917. As is the case with many young people, a decision that was to last a lifetime was made after hearing an inspirational speaker. The speaker was John Mott, general secretary of the YMCA and globetrotting organizer for the Student Volunteer Movement. Two of Townsend's closest friends invited him to hear Mott. Mott was a powerful speaker whose passionate pleas to students around the world to "evangelize the world in this generation" enlisted thousands of young people in Christian missions. Mott pushed his listeners hard, arguing that "a man may well question whether he is living the Christian life . . . if he is indifferent to the needs of half of the human race." He painted the missionary task in heroic terms, mincing no words about the dangers of foreign lands, appealing to his young listeners' idealistic, manly virtues. Like other Victorians before him, he marshaled military metaphors—invasion, advance, occupation, strategy, crusade—and quoted Napoleon, as well as William James's call for a "moral equivalent of war." Like most Americans of his time, he believed that at the turn of the century the United States had been placed in a unique position to impact the world, and that it was the duty of Christian Americans to take advantage of the new world situation and modern methods of travel to spread the gospel and the benefits of civilization quickly around the globe. Inspired by the immense mobilization of manpower to fight World War I, Mott pushed harder than ever before, believing that he had been too soft on students and that they were capable of much more than the leaders of the SVM had realized. Townsend emerged from the meeting shaken. He was later to say, "I was impressed with how very little I had done to witness for my faith."[17]

Shortly thereafter, while still troubled by his lack of real experience of and commitment to God, Townsend and one of his friends who had invited him to hear Mott, Elbert (Robbie) Robinson, answered an advertisement seeking college students who were willing to spend a year in Guatemala selling Bibles. Robinson was an older student, a man of serious demeanor. He was well respected on campus, and the campus paper noted his eventual departure to Guatemala "with deep regret." He had served at various times as president of the Student Volunteers, president of the YMCA, and business manager for the yearbook. The ad Robinson and Townsend answered had been placed by the Bible

House of Los Angeles, a small outfit dedicated to the publication and distribution of Scripture portions in Spanish throughout Latin America, run by a cranky, overbearing, bantam rooster of a fundamentalist named R. D. Smith.[18] Smith was prim and fussy, with dark hair, a thick goatee, and circular reading glasses pinched on his nose. He was righteously dogmatic about matters of the faith and about most any other issue that might come up in conversation. He accepted the two young men eagerly; he was delighted to hear that Townsend had studied Spanish in college, although privately the diminutive fundamentalist suggested to Robinson that Townsend did not look capable of withstanding the strain of jungle trails.

And so it came about that Cameron Townsend, a twenty-year-old junior in college, found himself with disconcerting multiple commitments. He had committed to selling Bibles in Guatemala for the Bible House of Los Angeles (a place he had never heard of before answering the ad), shooting Germans for the National Guard in France, and (to his mother) finishing college and attending seminary. The story of how Townsend got out of two of his commitments has since become legend among his friends and followers. Sometime that spring, after the United States entered the war, Townsend visited R. D. Smith and told him that it appeared he would have to break his commitment to the Bible House, as his call-up seemed imminent. Smith asked Townsend to see if he could get a deferment and to visit a missionary from Guatemala who happened to be in the area, a Miss Stella Zimmerman. Zimmerman was not with the Bible House; she was with the Central American Mission. But Smith knew her well, as he too was on the board of that mission. Townsend and Robinson duly paid a visit to Zimmerman, a tough, gaunt woman about ten years Townsend's senior. Upon hearing of the men's commitment to joining the war, she exclaimed, "What cowards you are, going off to war where millions of other men will go and leaving God's work to women!" Stung by this challenge to his manhood, Robinson, somewhat of a "ladies man," turned to Townsend and said, "Well, Cameron, let's go to Guatemala." Townsend decided to ask for help from his history professor at Occidental, who was on the draft board. The professor, Robert Cleland, who was also a faculty adviser for the Student Volunteers, wrote a letter to the captain of Townsend's National Guard unit asking for Townsend's deferment on the basis of a "previous commitment to go to Central America."[19] Although Townsend's commitment to the National Guard was more than likely made before his commitment to the Bible House, the captain, upon reading the letter, agreed to a discharge, reportedly saying, "You'll do a lot more good selling Bibles in Central America than you would shooting Germans in France."

Townsend's mother was more difficult to convince; decades later he told an interviewer that she was "heartbroken" over his decision. She realized that once out of college for a year it would be very difficult to return, hence threatening his career in the ministry. But she knew that a tour in France also threatened a ministry career, perhaps permanently. So, upon obtaining her son's promise to return after one year to finish college, she agreed it was the best plan of action. Once again the family rallied around; Townsend's sisters and their husbands agreed to look after William and Molly, and Paul, who had also been discharged from the Guard, agreed to drop out of college and work to help support them.[20]

That summer Townsend's old National Guard unit shipped out to Europe. His best friend, Carroll Byram—one year ahead of Townsend in school, who, with Robinson, had invited Townsend to hear John Mott and had joined the Guard with him—was later killed in France. Townsend and Robinson spent the summer earning their passage money on a thousand-acre farm in central California. Townsend was in charge of irrigation, and both worked on the header wagon chopping the heads off of rye, wheat, and oats. The hours were long, but lazy and unhurried; as they worked, Townsend and Robinson tried to memorize Scripture verses in Spanish. Finally, on August 18, 1917, they boarded the train at Los Angeles bound for San Francisco. Bubbling over with youthful enthusiasm at the send-off his family and friends gave him, and thrilled that his parents had released him for his great adventure, Townsend recorded in his journal, "I've got the greatest folks God ever blest a fellow with. . . . Oh, it's great to have friends! May God help me to make more and to be as true as steel to them all. Adelante, now. Siempre Adelante [Onward, now. Ever Onward]. Eyes to the Front! Forward March."[21] In San Francisco Townsend and Robinson purchased passage to Guatemala on the S.S. *Peru* for $84.75 each, a 25 percent discount from the first-class rate because they were missionaries. On September 15, 1917, they hurried aboard ship eager to prove themselves on the ultimate battlefield for the evangelical Protestant, the foreign mission field.

It is easy in hindsight to see the choice Townsend made at this critical juncture of his life as somehow inevitable. Clearly, with all he was to accomplish—the notoriety he was to gain literally around the world, the impact he would have on thousands of future missionaries and, through them, hundreds of isolated ethnic groups—his decision can be seen in some ways as fortunate, even predetermined, or, for those who dislike missionary activity, calamitous. But for Townsend, a twenty-year-old junior at Occidental College, the choice was not nearly so obvious. In fact, in some ways, especially in 1917 with his country at war, it was improbable. To understand Townsend's decision, we have to attempt to explore his inner world during that spring semester at Occidental in 1917; we must take seriously the impact of a spiritual call on a young person's life; and finally we must understand that whereas in some religious persuasions the most natural outworking of a spiritual awakening might be to take up an ascetic or monastic life, or to devote oneself to the study of a set of Scriptures and to higher learning, within evangelicalism the most natural outworking of a spiritual awakening is a commitment to evangelism and, ultimately, to mission.

In the spring of 1917 there was little in Townsend's history that pointed to the Los Angeles Bible House and Guatemala as an inevitable destination. As we have seen, the Townsend family did not push Cameron toward missions, and his childhood interests did not give any indication of a bent toward future full-time ministry of any sort. Furthermore, Townsend himself later described the Presbyterian church where he had his membership during college as "lifeless," with a pastor who "wasn't much of a Bible teacher" and who had little interest in foreign missions. To this point in his young life, Townsend had never "shared his faith" with anyone, a critical rite of passage for any evangelical, and virtually inconceivable for a student at any of the numerous Bible institutes springing up around the country.[22] The campus culture at Occidental did not foster the fervent piety that was so familiar to the observer of evangelicalism. No doubt most of his friends were comfortably within the Protestant establishment, and their conversations, until that galvanizing spring of 1917, probably centered on the life of the college far more than on their own interior lives. Townsend was very involved at Occidental, taking full loads every semester in addition to working part-time and taking part in extracurricular activities. He must have seemed in many ways a typical college student.

Despite his involvement and accomplishments, Townsend's junior year found him restless and pressured. He confessed later to being "bored" with school. After excelling in grammar school and high school, his grades in college were merely decent, his grade point average fluctuating each semester between a B+ and a B–. He earned mostly A's in his Bible courses, A's and B's in his major courses (history), but struggled with the hard sciences and languages, earning B's and C's in zoology, Greek, and Spanish.[23] Townsend was discovering that the life of the mind did not hold much appeal for him. He wanted to do something! The problem that faced him as a college junior was that he still did not know exactly what he wanted to do. Adding to his discomfort was the burden of his family's expectations. Clearly they had all sacrificed a great deal to send him to school, and his mother was convinced he was going to become a minister. But Townsend's heart was not in the ministry. His own pastoral role models had not been challenging, and he was already sounding a note that would become popular with him throughout his career—that ministers were wasted in the United States, where too many of them spent their years feeding already overfed flocks. Furthermore, to someone bored with school, the prospect of three years of seminary after college must have seemed a dry and endless sentence. But Townsend appears to have been reluctant to communicate his feelings to a family that had sacrificed so much for him. Consequently, in the spring of 1917 he was in the frame of mind to seize opportunities that provided a way out of his predicament.

Paul Townsend's account of how Cameron was discharged from the National Guard is suggestive of Townsend's thinking. He remembered events quite differently from Cameron's account. Both boys had joined the California National Guard. When word came from the captain that they were going to be mustered into federal service, the captain offered to release one of the boys to stay home and care for their parents. Cameron seized on his prerogative as elder brother to insist that Paul be the one to stay with their parents, while Cameron joined the war effort. It's clear that he was ready to grasp any opportunity that would disrupt the dull track his life seemed to be taking. According to Paul, the very next day after their conversation with the captain, Cameron got word from the Los Angeles Bible House that they wanted to send him to Guatemala. When he informed the Guard of his appointment, the captain said, "Well, then I'd better change it around and let Paul stay in the Guard and then you can go down there. But if you go down there, you won't be with your parents. I was letting you off to be with your parents." After Cameron persuaded the captain that he had been "after this appointment a long time now," the captain went ahead and discharged both of the boys.[24]

Paul's story paints Cameron Townsend as a little more active in securing his release from the Guard than the traditional accounts have it, something not at all difficult to believe for anyone knowing Townsend, who was never one to let events dictate the course his life would take. At any rate, he did not abandon college and the ministry with any reluctance. Even the suggestion from some of his friends that his place was at home caring for his parents did not deter him. Still, having decided to become a missionary, why not finish school and go out with a Presbyterian board? He was at a college that funneled many of its graduates to Presbyterian missions. Furthermore, his mother may have accepted that decision with equanimity. It must have seemed the most logical and desirable course. Unfortunately, that choice meant finishing college and attending seminary, something Townsend simply could not stomach. More time wasted, more time with books. His restlessness, his eagerness to get away, to accomplish something, drove him to what must have seemed to many of his friends and family a hasty decision. For Townsend, the Bible House was a door to another world, and although he promised his mother he would return after one year to finish college, he must have hoped that a year abroad might cool his family's expectations. Whether or not those expectations cooled, the explosion of energy expressed in his journals and letters in the years ahead demonstrates that Townsend made the right decision for himself. Townsend was much happier doing something than preparing to do something.

"As long as I can remember I have believed." Late in his life, this was Townsend's own assessment of the beginnings of his spiritual journey.[25] Townsend seems to have acquired his faith as an almost seamless garment. He passed from childhood to young adulthood with no cuts or stains, no detours or opportunity for serious question. Occidental College, his friends, family, church, and a remarkably Christian society did not afford as many opportunities for serious question as does secular culture today. Not yet forced to be profoundly self-reflective, perhaps by personality not inclined to be so, his faith and theology took on a simplistic air—simple, unquestioning, but unwavering.

In his junior year of college, however, Townsend was still learning the language of faith. The words nestled within him as part of himself—comfortable, untested, largely unspoken. As we have seen, John Mott arrived on campus at a time when Townsend was restless and dissatisfied with the direction his life was taking. Mott's message acted on Townsend's restlessness; he suddenly knew that this agitation came from a lack of commitment to something outside of himself. He later said, "I was impressed with how very little I had done to witness for my faith." Yes, he had gone to church all of his life and attended family devotions; yes, he dallied with the idea of being a minister; yes, he attended meetings of the Student Volunteer Movement; yes, he read the stories of Hudson Taylor and thought that being a missionary would be a good thing; but as yet he had not acted. Mott's challenge brought all of these experiences suddenly and persuasively into stark relief. Townsend began to speak and to act on the language of faith that he had embodied for twenty years. He felt God leading him toward the mission field.

Evangelicals—in fact, many religious people—often speak of such leading. Those who approach religious people from a position of unbelief frequently find such language disconcerting, even deceptive. It is easy for the skeptic to see such language as merely providing an excuse for personal choice, at times even irresponsible action. Undoubtedly this is sometimes the case. Nevertheless, this language must be taken seriously if we have any hope of understanding the believer on his or her own terms.

How then does such leading operate in the life of the believer? Perhaps we can compare this aspect of Townsend's religious worldview to the worldview of a young man in love. Let us suppose that a young man has recently become convinced that a young woman returns the ardent affection he feels for her. He has no concrete proof. She has not verbally told him of her interest. Nevertheless, he is convinced. Perhaps he sat in a library trying to study, but his thoughts were absorbed with her. She entered the library, strolled down the rows of books, and as she passed our smitten young man, she fixed a dazzling smile upon him then passed on. Now, this sign from his love, whether or not it was empirically intended as a sign or can ever be proven to be such, can be absolutely galvanizing to the young man in love. It can lead him to take steps that previously he might never have dared to take. He has a feeling of infinite possibility. Even the most ardent skeptic does not call such a man insane. We accord lovers a certain space. *Ah,* we say, *he is in love.* In fact, we legitimize his feelings by acknowledging that, at least for him, his interpretation of events is possible, because it accords with his worldview. He has undergone a transformation in which previously innocuous actions now are laden with meaning. And when, as she walks across campus, the object of his affection lags behind her girlfriends, seemingly in a way that allows him to catch up to her, his worldview is confirmed and grows stronger.

The impressions of our young man are ultimately validated, of course, only if the young woman turns out to return his affection. He is then able to look back at his earlier experience and confirm that his interpretation of events was indeed correct. Ultimately, evangelicals confirm God's leading in the same manner. If indeed their efforts are met with success, they frequently look back at the circumstances of their lives and reinvest certain events with special meaning, vis-à-vis the supernatural hand of God on their lives. A desire of their heart is confirmed as the voice of God. A circumstance is validated as an obvious point where God intervened directly in human affairs in order to bring them to the point of success at which they now find themselves. This process, what we might call interpreting life backward, is an extremely important ritual in evangelical self-understanding, and when validated with success lends credence to their worldview.

Townsend's leading from God operated in a similar way. The broad challenge from John Mott, then the specific challenge from Miss Zimmerman, acted on his restlessness, his longing to do something, on all the years of Christian influence, to awaken within him the possibility that God might be speaking to him. He went home and, perhaps for one of the few times in his young life, prayed with a profound earnestness. He asked that if God wanted him to go to Guatemala as a missionary, God would somehow release him from his present obligations. Almost before he realized what happened, in a stunning turn of events, his captain in the Guard discharged him, declaring he would do more good in Guatemala than in France. Then his parents also gave him their blessing, concerned as they were about the possibility of his being drafted to serve in the war. However the skeptic might view these events, perhaps as natural and perfectly reasonable decisions, for Townsend they were galvanizing. All of his life had prepared him to activate this paradigm, a paradigm that saw God as alive and active in the world, delighting to answer the prayers of those devoted to him, skillfully and omnisciently working out the smallest details of their lives to fit into his overarching plan. Now suddenly God had placed his finger on Cameron Townsend, a twenty-year-old college junior in California. He was awakened to a feeling of infinite possibility, that the God of the universe was speaking to him and had a plan to use him in powerful ways. His journal literally exploded with joy. "We are feeling fine. Hallelujah, Hallelujah, Hallelujah! It's great to be in <u>THE WAY!</u> Now for a year perfectly consecrated to Him. Lord, grant it!"[26]

Evangelicals learn from their youth a piety without ambiguity, a language of visible certainty that deals with the invisible and the uncertain. Young evangelicals learn to interpret their world as they interpret their Bibles, always searching for the intention of the author behind the text, the text being the incidents and accidents of their lives. Life events from the profound to the ordinary can be seen as the affirming or disaffirming voice of God. Longings, desires, perhaps even whims, can be seen as the nudging of divinity. Eventually, as the young believer advances in the faith, learning to communicate with God as regularly as with a roommate, the language of certainty gives solidity and commitment to steps of faith. As Jim Elliot embarked for South America, where he was soon to become famous as one of the "Auca" martyrs, he wrote, "My going to Ecuador is God's counsel, as is my . . . refusal to be counseled by all who insist I should stay and stir up believers in the U.S. And how do I know it is His counsel? 'Yea, my heart instructeth me in the night seasons.' Oh how good! For I have known my heart is speaking to me for God!" This language of certainty runs throughout evangelical writings. As Townsend himself once wrote, "The devil reminded us that some of the tribes are very small. But the Lord reminded us that He had commanded us to go to 'every creature.' . . . 'Have I failed yet to supply the needs of this rapidly growing work?' the Lord answered." Far more than simply figures of speech (and quite apart from the question of whether or not the believer really dialogued that closely with God or the devil), this language functions as an agent for the internalizing and the propagation of a powerful and convincing piety that makes evangelicals a bold and confident bunch. This unambiguous piety and its language, as much as theological bickering or social constraint, may have contributed to the separation of evangelicals from other believers, drawing evangelicals into an exclusive community of faith.[27]

For the young believer it is as if every ray of sun on a cloudy day holds a specific message for him. Every twinge of conscience is the God of the universe taking an intimate interest in his spiritual formation. Standing behind every open door of opportunity is Christ himself beckoning her through. Every closed door represents an attempt by satanic forces to block what God is doing through her. It is heady. It is sustaining. It is a learned way of interpreting the world. Yet it is not crazy, unless all intuition and love is crazy. It is simply a belief system in action, and for those who believe, there is no headier wine. The presence of God in a believer's life is as tenuous as vapor and as tangible as love. The believer is certain of things of which it is not empirically possible to be certain. Regardless of how one thinks of it, this certainty must be taken seriously by those who study religion and its devotees if they hope to understand the religious person, and to accept him, even remotely, on his own terms.

Evangelism has been central to the evangelical movement at least since the rise of the Methodists and Baptists and the revivals of Charles Finney in the early 1800s, when the entire tenor of American Protestantism changed from Calvinism to a more democratic embrace of human free will in personal conversion. These denominations literally overran American Protestantism, relentlessly driving their ministers to greater evangelistic efforts, and making evangelism a primary obligation for *all* believers. As the nineteenth century progressed, evangelicals increasingly turned their eyes to those in foreign countries who had never heard the gospel. They established foreign mission boards to send Americans overseas as preachers, teachers, and doctors. In the late nineteenth and early twentieth centuries, influenced by continental theology and personal contact with intellectuals from other religions, some Protestants rejected the evangelical emphasis on personal salvation as available exclusively through the reception of the message of Jesus Christ. When the liberals, as they came to be called, began to make life uncomfortable for their conservative brethren within the historic denominations, some evangelicals left to form their own mission boards and eventually denominations. By the final third of the twentieth century, liberal Protestants essentially abandoned missions and evangelism, leaving the mission field increasingly to the conservative evangelicals. By 1980 conservative missionaries outnumbered liberals ten to one.[28] Throughout the twentieth century and into the twenty-first, evangelicals have continued to practice Christianity essentially as their forebears, the Methodists and Baptists, focusing their efforts on personal evangelism and missions, seeking to spread the Christian message throughout the world.

The devotional and evangelistic sides of evangelicalism have always gone hand in hand. During the late nineteenth century, new Bible institutes and faith missions seemed to pop up almost yearly. The two institutions grew up together, appealing to the same constituency, holding similar theological and educational views, and above all, focusing on the enduring evangelical quest to know and experience God. The Bible institutes nurtured a unique spiritual vision, and the faith missions provided the outlet for putting that vision to the test. That devotion and evangelism were intimately linked is seen in the description that the Moody Bible Institute, the crown jewel of evangelical Bible institutes, gave of itself. "Every effort is made to develop the spiritual life of each student," wrote the editor of the school's journal. "The devotional life has numerous encouragements in the many prayer services held and participated in by all." Alongside this spiritual development, the "leading feature" of the school was instruction in missions. The author noted that the "missionary spirit is never permitted to lag for a moment." In fact, the "air is filled with the passion for soul-saving." Mission leaders also recognized that the two went hand in hand. John Mott, in his classic mission text, wrote, "On the spirituality of the missionary more than upon any other one factor on the mission field depends the evangelization of the world."[29]

This devotional and evangelistic focus of evangelicalism has been underemphasized in the historical literature. Ever since the foundational work of George Marsden, the study of evangelicalism has been forever altered by the confluence of theological movements and social forces that merged in the rapidly secularizing culture of the late nineteenth and early twentieth centuries to produce within some evangelicals a "militant antimodernism."[30] While this study of what has been called fundamentalism has been critical to the understanding of evangelicalism in this century, historiography has suffered too often from fundamentalism creep to the point that evangelicalism, with its broad array of interests, has tended to be subsumed into fundamentalism, with its narrow focus and belligerent stance toward the world. The popular mind has often been unable to see the forest of evangelicalism through the great oak of fundamentalism.

Lost at times in this account is evangelicalism's view of itself, a view best articulated in its missionary enterprise. The missionary embodied evangelicalism's best dream of itself, playing a near-legendary role in its collective imagination as the embodiment of all that was best in the movement. The focus of historians and the public, however, has often been on the discontinuities produced by the fundamentalist-modernist controversies rather than the continuities within the broader evangelical movement, which stretch from the American Revolution to the present. And chief among these continuities has been the absolute centrality of evangelism, missions, and a devotional response to God. In studying missions we study the heart of the evangelical impulse.

With the centrality of evangelism and missions to evangelicalism, it is not surprising that the newly awakened Townsend felt called to missions. Evangelicals have always had strong theological motivations for evangelism and missions, stressing the requirement of obedience to the "Great Commission" of Jesus Christ in Matthew 28:18–20, and the lost condition of the heathen and their eventual permanent consignment to hell. But a romantic devotional call to an experience of God that was available nowhere else was perhaps even stronger than theological motivation. The various Holiness movements that profoundly impacted evangelical spirituality, from Wesleyan to Keswick, all emphasized that God's spirit filled Christians most completely when their lives were committed entirely to his service. Missionary biographies portrayed their subjects as spiritual heroes and their exploits in biblical terms. If the reader wanted to witness modern miracles, the mission field was the place to be. Authors engaged enthusiastically in creating a missionary mythology that acted powerfully on the imaginations of young people, beginning in Sunday school and then throughout their young adult years. *Moody Monthly,* the most prominent conservative evangelical journal in the early twentieth century, was filled with stirring accounts of God's intervention on the mission field. A. T. Pierson, in a book titled *The New Acts of the Apostles; or, the Marvels of Modern Missions,* wrote, "The modern missionary era has given birth to a royal race of giants; in fact, so mighty have been these men and women, so Herculean their labors, so heroic their achievements, that they seem rather to have made the age than the age them. . . . [T]he continents shake beneath their tread." According to Pierson, missionaries witnessed and engaged in mighty acts of the spirit, boldly going with God where no man or woman, at least since the New Testament era, had gone before.[31]

These visions influenced generations of evangelicals. Most who departed for the mission field left with a jumble of motivations imbibed throughout their lifetime. In 1940, before departing for South America, Dorothy Westrom VanKampen spoke of her missionary enthusiasm.

> Who can read the lives of such heroes of faith as Hudson Taylor . . . Adoniram Judson . . . Borden of Yale . . . without being stirred and challenged out of indifference and love of ease and plenty to a life of self-denial for Him. . . . I want to go out as a missionary to escape the danger of becoming satisfied with a life of ease and comfort; I want to go because South America needs Christ desperately; because Christ has commanded me to go; because He has been leading me in that direction and I believe I could not be in His will if I didn't go; because the love of Christ constrains me; and finally because He is coming soon and opportunities will cease.

Mixed throughout the theological rationale for missions one hears the unending romance of the call of Christ that echoed so persuasively in the hearts of earnest young believers. I go, Westrom VanKampen said, because there I will be in his will, there I will experience the spiritual intimacy, victories, and power of Hudson Taylor and Adoniram Judson, because there is "a place where thou canst touch the eyes of blinded men to instant perfect sight; There is a place where thou canst say, 'Arise!' to dying captives, bound in chains of night."[32]

In 1956, as Elisabeth Elliot found herself emotionally stripped of all the textbook rationale for missions after the death of her husband at the hands of the Waorani (Auca) Indians in Ecuador, she found relief in the foundational motivation for mission—the opportunity to know and experience God. "The crusading spirit, the thrill of reaching an unreached tribe, the passion for souls which is supposed to motivate some—all these faded out completely. I was forced back to the real reasons for missionary work—indeed, the real reasons for living at all. My husband Jim and the four men who had gone into Auca territory had one reason: they believed it was what God wanted them to do. . . . It is only in obeying God that we may know him. . . . I knew there was no other answer for me."[33]

The explosion of joy in Townsend's journal in 1917 came from precisely this anticipation—that in boarding a boat for Guatemala, he would experience God in ways he never could at home.

2
In Which Townsend Shares His Faith, Battles Roman Catholics, and Learns about Indians

1917–1918

> I just tell you folks all my dreams with the hope that it will not make you all as visionary as I am.
>
> —William Cameron Townsend

As the weathered steamer slowly beat its way down the coast, Townsend filled his journal with detailed descriptions of everything he saw and experienced. Throughout his life he journaled most often when exploring unfamiliar territory alone. He kept his journal religiously during his first year and a half in Guatemala. As his responsibilities grew (and the work became perhaps more routine), the journal lagged for more than a decade. He picked it up again when he traveled alone in Mexico in the early 1930s. Then once again the journal disappeared in a whirl of activity as he launched a new missionary enterprise there. Finally his writings picked up once again during his first trip to Peru in 1945, when, alone, he journeyed deep into the jungle to survey the forbidding topography by air and river, looking for a site to build a wilderness outpost. From the beginning of his missionary career, he adapted well to the unknown, to travel, to isolation, to adventure. In fact, the enjoyment of exploration springs from every page. In many ways these times of new beginning served in Townsend's life almost as vacations, initially a passport away from college and boredom, later a break from pressing responsibility as leader of a growing mission. Someone else could take care of home base for a while. Townsend was a pioneer, not a settler.

Townsend was a very inexperienced twenty-one-year-old on his initial voyage to Guatemala. His fellow passengers were by and large a scurvy lot of seasoned adventurers who passed the days gambling, fighting, and singing drunken songs. Townsend was fascinated by them, even as he dared not join them. "Vanity, vanity," he piously noted in his journal. The sailors relished the young American's gullibility. They dragged Townsend to the railing to point out "some large fish which have jaw-like fins with which they hold a person while they suck his blood." Townsend spent the bulk of his time preparing the only way he knew for the largely unknown experience that awaited him. He discovered that two years of Spanish in both high school and college still left him grasping to put comprehensible sentences together. He practiced the language by translating sermons from the *Christian Herald.* A young Guatemalan in the cabin next to him, with whom he frequently played checkers, corrected his work. He also read all he could about Guatemala, seeking to acquire some understanding of the country that would soon be his home. Having departed for Guatemala without any effective missionary or cross-cultural training whatsoever, he still mustered the courage to slip some gospel tracts to the waiters, perhaps leaving them on the table with a small tip, a classic evangelical soul-saving gambit. He had never mastered the art of turning every conversation to spiritual things, a discipline practiced diligently in evangelical Bible institutes. The young man was still a long way from achieving the boldness of renowned evangelist R. A. Torrey, who on one rough ocean voyage, with everyone else inside endeavoring to stay warm and dry, followed the captain around the deck "quot[ing] the Word of God, until a complete surrender was made."[1]

Eighteen days after departing San Francisco the freighter docked in Guatemala, and, staring intently at the thick coastal jungle, Townsend finally glimpsed the country in which he was to spend the next fifteen years. Guatemala, while remote in the consciousness of most Americans in the early 1900s, was a remarkably scenic country of enormous historic significance. Centuries earlier it had been the center of Mayan civilization, and the northern third of the country, while almost uninhabited now, was filled with spectacular Mayan ruins. In the highlands, which cut through the center of the country, one majestic volcanic peak gave way to another in regular succession. Some were still active. Lake Atitlán was the largest and most beautiful of the high mountain lakes that dotted the region. Most of the population in the country concentrated in the southwestern highlands about twenty-five miles from the coast at an altitude between three thousand and eight thousand feet, where the weather seemed locked in eternal spring. Cities here, such as Antigua and Guatemala City, were impressive centers of Spanish civilization. The twenty-mile stretch of coastal jungle through which travelers passed before beginning the climb to Guatemala City was a different country entirely. Hot, oppressively humid, and swarming with insects, the unhealthy climate combined with poor roads to make the area inhospitable to travelers. There were several large railroad towns on the coast, but the coastal population largely centered in hundreds of coffee (Guatemala's primary export) and sugar cane plantations, known as *fincas.*

The greater part of the population were Indians of Mayan descent, but the direction of the country was in the hands of the *ladinos,* those of mixed Spanish and Indian blood, particularly the wealthy coffee growers. The fortunes of the Indians waxed and waned under the leadership of various conservative and liberal governments. But in general, as throughout Latin America, the Indians were despised by *ladinos* and seen primarily as a source of cheap labor. The law permitted coffee growers to recruit Indians as laborers even against their will, and often after having their land confiscated for lack of paper titles. During the coffee harvest thousands of Indians from the highlands made their way to the coastal *fincas,* where they toiled for a subsistence wage. While not enslaved outright, elite opinion coupled with the current economic system ensured that Indians remained a perpetual underclass. The pseudoscience of *indigenismo,* theories developed throughout Latin America around the turn of the century, presumed Indian inferiority for various biological and historical reasons. *Indigenista* writers proposed that the Indian be civilized and incorporated into the national life of the country. This required that they give up their ethnic and communal loyalties (and land!) to be absorbed into the national life and economy.[2]

When Townsend entered Guatemala, the liberal dictator Manuel Estrada Cabrera was in power. It is dangerous to equate "liberal" and "conservative" in the Latin American setting with their meanings in North America. In general, liberal regimes throughout Latin America favored opening their countries to progressive influence. Progressive influence was understood as modern, Western, a devotion to enlightenment science, and Protestant as opposed to colonial, Spanish, a devotion to tradition, and Catholic. This primarily meant the construction of a capitalist economy (resulting in favorable deals for American and other foreign companies and individuals), modernizing infrastructure, creating at least the forms of democratic government, and the separation of church and state. The latter resulted, of course, in the disenfranchising of the Catholic Church. While this entailed a loss of lands and privileges for the Church, for the nation involved it often meant a wrenching dislocation from an institution that had long dominated cultural life. In many countries the Church controlled primary education, as well as religious life, and its influence in the lives of the people, particularly in rural areas, was not easily challenged. Despite their rhetoric of democratic development and equal opportunity, however, the reality of liberal regimes in Guatemala and throughout Latin America was often harsh dictatorships that clung to power by favoring local landowning elites and repressing the working classes, especially the Indians. Cabrera, for one, famous for his cruelty, was declared insane by Guatemala's Congress in 1920 and removed from power.[3]

One of the primary obstacles that threatened to thwart the liberal agenda was the lack of a sense of national identity among the many ethnic groups that made up the nation. The liberals desperately sought to foster a sense of nationhood in *all* the people. To do this they had to incorporate the Indians, who represented the majority of the population, into the project, if for no other reason than to avail themselves of their labor and land in building a productive capitalist export economy. It is in this context that the liberal caudillo Justo Rufino Barrios declared freedom of religion in Guatemala in 1873. This move, coupled with other anticlerical legislation, was designed to cripple the Catholic Church, the one institution that could compete most directly with the state for its citizens' allegiance. Liberals hoped that Protestant missionaries might act as civilizing agents for the Indians by establishing schools that were not under Catholic control. In addition, their plans for economic development required foreign Protestant investment, and few Protestants would invest in a country where their religion was outlawed.

Consequently, in 1882 Barrios personally persuaded the Presbyterian Board of Foreign Missions to dispatch the reluctant John Clark Hill to Guatemala. Hill established a school for the children of elites, where students were taught English, Christian living, and personal finance, among other things. Despite the fact that Barrios sent his own children there, the school was a failure, as the populace at large still despised Protestants. Edward Haymaker followed Hill. Inspired by the Social Gospel movement, he focused his work on the urban poor. Although he had more success, Guatemala attracted only a trickle of Presbyterian missionaries over the next several decades. Latin America simply had much lower cachet in American Protestant churches when compared to China or Africa, where the conversion of cannibals and other abject heathens in faraway romantic lands roused young hearts and opened wallets more readily than did competition with Spanish Catholics for America's next-door neighbor. In Guatemala conversions were few. Even if one was already a liberal agnostic or an Indian with a highly imperfect blend of indigenous and Catholic belief, it still entailed great risk to abandon the Catholic identity that so closely circumscribed virtually every aspect of life throughout Latin America.[4]

Toward the end of the nineteenth century other missions began to dispatch workers to Guatemala. The American Bible Society (ABS) established a base of operations for all of Central America in Guatemala in 1892. In 1896 the Central American Mission (CAM) sent its first missionary to Guatemala. Although he died within a few months, he was followed in 1899 by the Reverend Albert Bishop and his wife. Bishop would be a central and somewhat autocratic figure in Guatemalan Protestantism for the next thirty years. Within three years the CAM dispatched nine more missionaries, and by the time Townsend arrived in 1917, there were thirty-three working throughout Central America. The Nazarenes sent workers in 1901, and the Quakers established a permanent mission in 1906. In 1902, despite serious tensions between Haymaker and Bishop that paralleled later modernist-fundamentalist battles, the Presbyterians, the CAM, the Quakers, and the Nazarenes worked out a comity agreement in which they divided the country into manageable parcels, as no one mission could hope to cover all the territory. Guatemala City was divided equally between the Presbyterians and the CAM. (The Primitive Methodists entered into the agreement and received territory in 1914.) All the missions, not just the more liberal Presbyterians, both evangelized and operated schools, hospitals, presses, and other enterprises; all had established primary schools before Townsend arrived.[5]

As a Bible House colporteur, Townsend would peddle his tracts and Scripture portions across mission territorial boundaries, although he was directly supervised by Albert Bishop, the CAM patriarch. The Bible House of Los Angeles was an early result of the expansive "spiritual manifest destiny" felt by Protestants at the close of the Spanish-American War. It began as the vision of Lyman Stewart, millionaire oilman and supporter of numerous evangelical causes, who saw the outcome of the war as a challenge to Protestants to enter the door to Spanish Catholic countries that had long been closed. At a time when the glamorous mission fields were the supposedly more actively heathen continents of Africa and Asia, the Bible House and missions like the CAM sought to focus attention on the neglected fields closer to home. To do so they had to convince their supporters that people in these largely Catholic countries ("priest-ridden, Rome-blighted lands" was a common appellation) were "as much in need of the Gospel as any heathen in the world."[6] "To give the WORD OF GOD to Spanish-speaking and other Roman Catholic peoples" was the explicitly stated purpose for the mission's existence, and supporters were assured that Rome was the "most subtle and determined enemy of the Truth of God." In fact, mission literature stated that "the more faithful one may be to the Church of Rome . . . , the more sure is he of eternal perdition." Of course, as most conservative evangelicals (indeed, perhaps most Americans) at the time were decidedly anti-Catholic, the mission was largely preaching to the choir.

First organized as the Los Angeles Bible Institute in 1901, the organization was designed to aid missionaries as a school and publishing house. After two years the school was discontinued, and the institute became the Bible House of Los Angeles, which gave its full time to publishing Spanish-language gospels, gospel portions, and tracts. Although it later expanded into other languages, during Townsend's brief tenure the Bible House focused almost exclusively on Latin America and Spain. The mission shipped thousands of New Testaments, tracts, and collections of Scripture portions (all "underscored" with special attention paid to "the needs of Roman Catholic readers") to Latin America yearly. Most were used by established missionaries, but as we have seen, the Bible House supported a few of its own colporteurs. The mission's written policy was that all of its material was to be given away free of charge, although the board was opposed to "wasteful scatteration," but Townsend seems to have been encouraged from the beginning to sell the larger Scripture portions. For the first thirty years of its existence, the mission, as noted earlier, was run by R. D. Smith. Smith was well traveled and knowledgeable. He was on the boards of other missions, including the CAM, and he enjoyed the confidence of Lyman Stewart and other wealthy supporters.[7]

Missionary legend has it that upon first sighting Townsend and Robbie Robinson in Guatemala, one veteran missionary said to another, "Robinson will do fine, but that skinny Townsend won't last two months." Robinson was a dark, husky man already in his thirties, while Townsend was ten years his junior, of medium height, and weighing 130 pounds when he arrived in Guatemala. Photographs from the period suggest the astuteness of the observation. With a dark suit jacket draped over his skinny shoulders, his large hands dangling beneath the sleeves like some foreign appendage, his thin hair cut short above his ears, and his gentle (later bespectacled) gaze, he looked more like a grade school teacher, or perhaps a graduate student. When he spoke, his rolling Jimmy Stewart–like cadences revealed his country roots. However, what the veteran missionaries could not know then, but would realize within a very few months, was that although the young missionary may have seemed slow and somewhat helpless on the outside, his mind was working at a much faster clip. Townsend had an eager, even wild, imagination, and he never imagined an ordinary life filled with ordinary achievements. In addition, he was embarking upon a relationship with a God whom he believed had called him to this specific work, and he intended to make good on his chosen task. As he told his parents, "For the present and keeping an eye on the future, I am putting forth every effort to give a good report of myself."[8]

Townsend's education began as he slowly worked his way through customs.

Examining his baggage, which included twenty-six hundred pounds of literature carefully packed by R. D. Smith, a customs official conspiratorially whispered that he was "mighty glad" to see the tracts and gospel portions, as they would "enlighten the people." The Catholic Catechisms, he added, were "fanatical."[9] Thusly encouraged that they were at least on the side of officialdom, the two young missionaries caught a train for Guatemala City.

During the daylong journey, the train slowly made its way through the steaming jungle towns of the coast. Finally, after a three-hour lunch stop in Escuintla, the train began a labored climb into the mountains. Robinson and Townsend eagerly took in the hard blue mountain lakes and the rocky volcanic peaks of central Guatemala. It was dark when the train pulled in to Guatemala City, and the young men were glad to have jackets.

Stella Zimmerman, the CAM missionary who had challenged Townsend and Robinson so boldly to come to Guatemala, accompanied by the associate pastor from the CAM-founded Cinco Calles church, the largest Protestant church in Guatemala, met the young men at the Guatemala City train station. After hasty introductions, the *ladino* pastor whistled over an Indian to carry Townsend's heavy trunk. Townsend estimated that the Indian weighed one hundred pounds, and he knew his trunk was twice that. When he moved to assist the man, he was politely informed that such assistance to Indians was not the custom in Guatemala.[10]

Townsend and Robinson spent their first several weeks getting acquainted with the missionaries in the city. Everyone wanted the new recruits to come to dinner, and Townsend, whose love for food belied his slender frame, studiously recorded gastronomical matters in his journal. On their first Sunday in the city, the two were invited to lunch at the Allisons' after church. William Allison was the director of the Presbyterian mission in Guatemala. After lunch the young men were treated to the lovely piano playing and singing of Elvira Malmstrom, the Allisons' young secretary. Although short and rather plain, with her bright blue eyes, middle-class manners, and beautiful voice, Elvira made an impression on Robinson, but Townsend was more interested in Mr. Allison's history lesson. The senior Presbyterian missionary treated the new arrivals to a long lecture "pointing out the awful mistakes" of Roman Catholicism "both from a historical and present day standpoint." He recounted the history of the struggle of the liberal government of Guatemala against the Church, including the famous account of President Barrios's direct invitation to the Protestant John Clark Hill to come to Guatemala, a story that functioned for the small missionary community as an encouraging campfire tale when spirits sagged in what was still, for them, a precarious social situation.[11]

The bulk of the new arrivals' time was spent sightseeing, studying Spanish, and attending almost daily religious services. For Townsend it was a time for watching, listening, and learning. He filled his journal with eager cross-cultural observations. The Indians "resemble the Japanese very much, even to being slightly squint-eyed." One impressive man had "as . . . intelligent wide awake face as I've seen around here." At a baptismal service the men were "splendid looking fellows—stalwart and manly. Mr. Bishop says they are the best class of Indians he has seen." Townsend also noted how much more spiritual his life had suddenly become. For the young believer, thrust into an intense daily routine of focused attention on matters of the spirit, Bible studies were suddenly "much deeper than most of what we get in the States," and testimonies given publicly in meetings "were very spiritual and better than we have in many of the congregations at home." Townsend was delighted to learn that all Protestants were known as *evangélicos.* He naively felt that the title broke down denominational barriers, establishing real unity among Christians devoted to a common cause on the mission field. That this unity was, of course, far from the truth was to be one of the great disappointments of his life.[12]

Meeting the imperious Albert Bishop, field director of the CAM's Guatemala work since his arrival in 1899, was an eye-opening experience. Like R. D. Smith, Bishop was a fundamentalist's fundamentalist, a stuffy Victorian, "too pious to play" (as Lewis Sperry Chafer once noted), utterly committed to the mission, and filled with the confidence of someone who knows he is on the side of God in all matters theological. When the two recruits showed up a few minutes late to a church service, Bishop stared them down and ordered, "Don't let it happen again." Early in their stay, Bishop reinforced the cultural status of Indians in Guatemala. Perhaps noting the young man's sensitivity, Bishop drew Townsend aside and advised him not to get a pack mule for his journeys, but to walk and let the native worker carry the pack, which was not to exceed one hundred pounds. Townsend was not to help the Indian carry the load. Somewhat embarrassed, Townsend sheepishly recorded in his journal, "It sounds cruel, but he said that it would be the thing."[13]

Encouraged to sit in on a conference of CAM missionaries, Townsend eagerly soaked up the tales of hardship, victory, and defeat related by veteran missionaries. He was especially impressed by the female missionaries; when he looked around there seemed to be more than twice as many women as men. He sat with his mouth open as one stalwart single lady told of traveling fifteen hundred miles a year on the back of a mule over trails kept treacherous by the constant rain. She told of being trapped under her fallen mule, of sleeping in a

2. Albert Bishop and wife.
Courtesy Townsend Archives.

room with twenty-one male peasants, and of making do on twenty-five dollars a month. Other women spoke of equally rugged ministries, of preaching to audiences of up to three hundred people, and dodging mobs carrying "rocks, rubbish, offal of animals, sand, whistles, horns, and vile language." Thoroughly shaken, Townsend lamented in his journal, "When I bumped myself up against the other missionaries, I was so measly, measly small, that I almost wondered why God had brought me down here." Then, remembering the women, he angrily exclaimed, "An able-bodied man living comfortably at home in the States ought to be ashamed of himself when he reads of [their] work."[14]

Townsend was now experiencing firsthand what Stella Zimmerman had perhaps crudely suggested when she first met the two prospective Bible House recruits in the United States. When Zimmerman suggested that cowardly men were "leaving God's work to women," she expressed both the triumph and frustration of pious evangelical women who flooded the faith missions yet were always keenly aware that they operated outside of their respected roles. As one CAM missionary wrote, "We know that Honduras needs men, and we are told that we 'dear sisters' ought not to fill a man's place. But we weak women are constrained to do the work of men because the work is here and there are no men to do it." She concluded, "I would willingly let a man take this abuse—if he were here!" Although missions preferred single men or married couples, many single women enlisted, as it was one career to which an unmarried virtuous woman could aspire that included a real measure of self-reliance and adventure. Intrepid women flocked to the faith missions, which required no college or seminary training. The ratio of women to men in the CAM at the time was about three to one, and similar ratios could be found in other missions. This situation presented no problem for the Quakers, who allowed women to take part in all aspects of church work. In fact, single women usually headed up their station at Chiquimula. But it presented a serious problem for missions with a theology that did not permit women to take leading roles in church services and religious organizations. The CAM council explained their use of single women missionaries in this manner: "Shall the heathen go down to death and hell without the Gospel when sanctified women are offering to go and give them the Word of life when no man cares for their souls? We do not believe one woman who has ever preached the Gospel to the lost will hear aught from the Master but, 'Well done, good and faithful servant. Thou hast done what I planned for men to do, but they would not.' "[15]

The problem had been noticed as early as the 1870s, and mission leaders tried to find ways to stimulate male interest. Men, however, had many more options at home for service and leadership. The gender imbalance in missions was felt in the Bible institutes as well. In 1932 the director of the missions course at Moody Bible Institute declared that the "very decided indifference of the men students of the Institute to the claims of foreign service" was an "extremely serious" matter. "This is a situation which has obtained for many years and is common throughout the church," he wrote. "The Director is greatly disappointed that it should be evident in a place such as the Moody Bible Institute." An article in *Moody Monthly* titled "Needed: Men for Missions" asked in a bold headline, "Does God call only women to do the hardest jobs, or are men shirking their plain responsibility?" The article painted a picture of females in peril on the mission field. Everything from manual labor around the mission station, to foul language from "depraved Moslems," to violence-prone devil worshipers threatened their femininity. Like Stella Zimmerman, the author accused men of letting women do the really hard work, for which their "noble constitutions" were not fit, while men prepared for pastorates at home. "Be honest, men," he concluded. "God doesn't call five women to only one man!" The history of missions, however, clearly demonstrates that many women's constitutions were indeed quite fit for the most rigorous mission work, and throughout the twentieth century women continued to join evangelical missions in large numbers.[16]

When Albert Bishop initially asked Townsend and Robinson where they wanted to work, Robinson requested that he be permitted to work with the Indians. He had already decided to make missions his life work. Townsend, planning to stay for only one year, chose to work with *ladinos,* among whom he could perfect his Spanish. Bishop decided to take them both to Antigua; Robinson would then leave for Tecpan to work with Indians, while Townsend would begin to work in Antigua and surrounding towns.[17]

On October 17 the three missionaries boarded a mule-drawn stage for the trip to Antigua. There was only enough room for their personal belongings in the stage. Before Townsend could question how the bulk of their gear (including his four thousand tracts plus numerous New Testaments) would get to Antigua, he saw the ubiquitous Indian porters carefully loading their heavy packs onto their backs. Their gear would be carried the twenty-five miles. Rain pelted the stage, turning the road into a muddy quagmire. The mules strained at the harness, slogging steadily through the muck. Out his window, Townsend observed the panorama of highlands Guatemala, and always the Indians, with heavy loads on their backs, stepping aside to let the stage pass, then resuming their surefooted but laborious way through the mud. Townsend exclaimed to Robinson and Bishop at the amount of weight they carried great distances. "It is apparent," he recorded that night, "the Indian is Guatemala's beast of burden."[18]

Three days after arriving in the beautiful Spanish colonial city of Antigua, Bishop held a service in the small mission church. He vigorously challenged the members to boldly share their faith with their unbelieving neighbors. After the meeting all attending were urged to go into the streets to engage in "personal work," the euphemism for face-to-face evangelism. Townsend and Robinson followed the small congregation into the street. Bishop ordered the two of them to split up. The "need was too great," he said, to permit doubling up. Thus it came about that William Cameron Townsend, a young man with absolutely no training, other than the Spanish he had picked up in school and the Bible he had learned at home and church, first engaged in a cross-cultural missionary endeavor.

Townsend was in quite an emotional state. Anticipation mixed with abject terror, clogging his throat and making him short of breath. He was glad he was alone, because the thought of someone observing his first attempt at evangelism caused the blood to rush to his head. Up one cobblestone street and down another he went, oblivious to the history in the buildings around him. Finally

3. Weary Indians on mountain trail. Courtesy Townsend Archives.

he spotted a lone gentleman. He circled the man surreptitiously three times, because, as he later remembered, "my heart was palpitating so hard it kept me from speaking." Then, suddenly, he took the plunge. Introducing himself, he asked the surprised man in broken Spanish if he was certain his soul would go to heaven when he died. If Townsend understood the reply—and there is no guarantee that he did after only three weeks in country—the man "didn't know what his soul was and had merely a faint idea of heaven." Faced with this yawning conceptual and linguistic gulf, Townsend panicked and hurriedly excused himself from the conversation.

He decided to be more direct. He next approached a "polite young fellow" about his own age and asked him point-blank in Spanish, "Do you know *el Señor Jesus?*" which to Townsend meant, "Do you know the Lord Jesus?" but to this man on the street was an inquiry into whether he knew a Mr. *Jesus,* a common enough name in Latin America. The young man replied that he was a stranger in town, so unfortunately did not know where Mr. *Jesus* lived. This perfectly natural reply so confused and embarrassed Townsend that he gave up, went back to his room in despair, and prayed, "Lord, why have I come 2000 miles to make a fool of myself?"[19]

Two days after Townsend's initial experience in personal work, Robinson left for Tecpan and Bishop returned to Guatemala City. Townsend was utterly alone. It is not difficult to imagine the feeling behind the simple words Townsend wrote in his journal, "I was left alone with Spanish speaking brothers." From now on, until he learned Spanish fluently, every waking moment was a struggle simply to communicate.[20]

The next evening he conducted his first service. He sweated over a simple sermon in Spanish, carefully writing out each thought. Then he prepared sedulously through prayer. About twenty Indians showed up. After singing a few hymns—a frightful cacophony, he later remembered—he stood up to speak. "I peered into the semi-darkness alive with shapes and forms," he wrote late that night, "and where the light from the candle fell, eyes that beamed back at me. Outside the chapel, standing in the doorway, were figures of men who had come to hear but were afraid to come inside." Townsend read John 14 and then, after a prayer service, "took up a study on Salvation." Although he optimistically recorded in his journal that "[t]he Lord gave me a use of Spanish that was more than I had hoped for," he discovered later that the Indians, whose own Spanish was marginal, understood almost nothing of what he said. Yet a few returned every time he spoke and listened attentively. Perhaps the attraction of having a gringo among them was simply too much to pass up; perhaps they were too polite to stay away; perhaps their spiritual hunger was so acute that they genuinely hoped to glean some insight from this incomprehensible American; but whatever the case, their careful attention illustrates the problems and the possibilities inherent in the missionary enterprise. Townsend's white skin and the fear of those gathered in the shadows outside emphasize the foreignness of this message to those who for centuries had combined their native worship with the religion of their conquerors on the fringes of the Catholic world. Yet the few who gathered night after night inside in the candlelight remind us that for some this Yankee message brought hope that their lives, both material and spiritual, might change for the better.[21]

Townsend's native worker, assigned to carry his pack, turned out to be Francisco Díaz, an approximately thirty-five-year-old Cakchiquel Indian and recent convert. As a boy, Díaz had received a scholarship to study in a special Indian school in Guatemala City. Consequently, he knew Spanish better than most Indians. After just a few days of traveling together, the two became "fast friends."

Díaz agreed to give up farming his hillside plot after the fall harvest to become Townsend's assistant. They worked together for the majority of 1918. The Indian man carried the heavy pack of literature, cooked simple meals on the road, and did the bulk of the evangelizing in Indian communities. Townsend genuinely liked the older man, and recorded that he would "in all probability, become my mentor."[22]

On October 22 Townsend began his ministry as a Bible House colporteur. For the first month he worked in Antigua and surrounding towns, going door to door, giving away literature and attempting to engage everyone he met in a discussion about their personal salvation. His goal was to stop at every door in the towns he visited. He was accompanied by various Protestant converts, although, at least until Díaz joined him more or less full-time, he sometimes found them timid. Eventually Townsend expanded his travels to the farthest corners of Guatemala, and even ventured into Honduras and El Salvador. He would work like this for more than a year.

Townsend's daily life during his year with the Bible House in Guatemala was much like that of the Methodist circuit riders in the early nineteenth century, a rugged combination of brutal travel, spare lodging, subsistence eating, and constant repetition of the simple verities of the faith. Itinerant missionaries needed to be highly motivated self-starters. Yet Townsend seems never to have tired of it. He very rarely used an excuse to take a day off. Although he enjoyed visits to various mission stations, where friends and beds made living more comfortable, inevitably he quickly grew restless to return to the road. Commenting on the missionaries who worked in Guatemala City, he wrote, "We pity the folks that have to stay here all the time." There were plenty of people to work in the capital. The opportunities for evangelism were better in "the outer districts." It is truly astonishing how quickly he grew into the job. The refrain of utter pleasure in his journal becomes repetitious. Even a hermeneutic of suspicion eventually gives way to the genuine nature of his obvious enjoyment of the call—"All was beautiful without and joy within. And with every step, I thanked God for the joy of life and service."[23]

Mornings on the road usually began with an hour or so of devotions with Francisco Díaz. As the gringo and the one who ostensibly knew the Scriptures, Townsend usually took the lead in reading and commenting briefly on a select passage. At times they sang together, but always they prayed. After a simple breakfast, they packed their bags and set off. Early on, Díaz carried the heavier load as they walked from village to village, but Townsend, uncomfortable with this policy from the beginning, soon purchased a mule. At times he traveled

4. Townsend and Díaz beginning colportage tour, 1918. Courtesy Townsend Archives.

alone, inevitably puzzling and amusing Indians who observed an American walking and carrying his own luggage. Although rugged, the trails often led through stunning country, beauty that few North Americans had ever seen.[24]

Finding food along the trail was often an adventure. If they were lodged in a convert's home, the meals were free, if simple. But on the road they were at the mercy of people they met along the way. Someone usually agreed to provide for them, though often somewhat reluctantly because they were Protestants. The novelty of having an American in the house was perhaps too great to pass up. Townsend usually paid for his food or traded literature for tortillas. On occasion, perhaps mistaking him for a passing friar, people gave him alms. At times they went hungry, but often had plenty. Townsend, always hungry after a vigorous hike through mountains or jungle, found that in general he took to "native dishes like a duck to water." He could not handle their coffee, however, which he found too strong, and he sometimes grew tired of beans. Commenting on the meal prepared by one pastor's wife, he wrote, "I didn't have beans this noon! However, for supper I had them boiled with rice for the first course and beans covered with sour cream for the next and last course. I don't wonder that the pastor stays away from home most all the time." Another time he remarked, "[Beans] are good, but a fellow can even get too much pie!"[25]

The colporteurs searched for lodging in much the same way as for food. If they were fortunate they stayed with a local pastor or other convert, where they might drift off to sleep "to the music of someone reading the precious Word to a group in the next shanty." Otherwise they had to request permission to string their hammocks (Díaz slept on the floor) in the home of a stranger. On the *fincas* there was usually at least a shed where they could take cover. Often there was no choice other than making camp as best they could along the side of the road. Townsend soon discovered that comfort was a relative thing and learned to enjoy days when he found lodging in a "better class" of place. He described a "better class" of lodging in the following manner.

> The house is of adobe with dirt floors and has two rooms and a kitchen. Three dogs, three broods of chickens, and a calf live in the kitchen, and generally have pretty good success in their efforts to grab food out of the children's plates and off the stove. . . . I eat off of one table, the two older boys eat off of another, while the children and women folk sit on the dirt floor and eat out of the kettle. I have an unusually good bed made like a cot with ropes for springs and a straw mat and a cow hide for a mattress. The hens' nest underneath, however, keeps it lousy with mites[,] to say nothing of the bed bugs, fleas, and little ants which have me covered from head to foot with bites. Plenty of beans, cheese, plantains and tortillas, however, keep me in good spirits so that I sleep like a log.[26]

Townsend's primary daily responsibility, of course, was to spread the Word. Tract distribution is no measure of success, as they were given away free and easily discarded. But the sale of Scripture portions (Gospels and complete New Testaments), in as much as it signified greater interest and often a certain independence from the Catholic Church, serves as a better guide. Townsend did not sell many of these; selling nine New Testaments in one day was a success worth noting in his journal. A typical day probably saw Townsend sell from three to five New Testaments and perhaps a slightly larger number of gospel portions. As he probably gave a tract to anyone who would take it, he may have distributed anywhere from thirty to one hundred tracts per day, perhaps more. For Townsend and other Protestant missionaries, simply getting the Scripture into the hands of people who could read it represented a worthy goal. Protestants have always believed that the Scriptures alone provide a sure guide to salvation. Therefore, getting them into the hands of people who could and would read them was half the battle. At the point a person heard or read the message of salvation, they could be considered evangelized and the responsibility of the evangelist ended. For missions founded under the conviction that the return of

Christ was somehow influenced by the "preaching of the Gospel to all nations" (Matthew 24:14), this was an important measure of success.

Townsend's ultimate goal, of course, was to gain converts, not just to sell Scripture. While he firmly believed that the selling of a Testament was sowing a seed that would later bear fruit, he nevertheless hoped to reap that fruit himself. To do so required engaging the prospective converts in a conversation designed to persuade them of their need of salvation. Early on, Townsend's approach was quite direct. He recorded, "My practice has been to walk right into a yard and offer a tract to the Indian people[,] who, I've noticed, were often quite scared. Then I would quote John 3:16 and offer as much of an explanation as my limited command of Spanish would allow, then walk out." (After being bitten by a dog, he learned that it was a better practice to call out before entering a yard.) As he gained confidence and learned more Spanish, he developed more complex ways of interesting his conversation partners in his literature. For example, one of the booklets of gospel portions was illustrated, and Townsend found that if he interested someone in the pictures, he could relate the gospel story from picture to picture. If they showed interest, he then tried to either give them a booklet or sell them a more substantial portion. Of course, many were already familiar with the terms and basic constructs of Christianity and could be drawn into conversation from many angles. Both the *commandante* and the mayor of one village purchased New Testaments when Townsend interested them in the prophecies of the end times. One national pastor with whom Townsend worked had a more direct approach. He began "by saying that we had come in the Name of the Lord Jesus Christ to show them the way of salvation. . . . Everyone listened with interest." This direct appeal to authority could work in several ways. As Townsend reported, "One fellow asked Francisco if I was alright [*sic*], that what I said sounded like the truth. Frisco told him that it wasn't me that was talking, but the Lord. The man said, 'Well, we must be respectful then.' "[27]

Townsend gained his first convert after only a week on the road—an Indian by the name of Tiburcio Ordoñez. Townsend met him in a village saloon, an odd place perhaps for a young evangelical missionary to be. But Townsend was already an independent thinker, impatient with fundamentalist proprieties, apt to try almost anything if he thought it might work. And he was hunting for converts. Where better to find them? Inside the saloon, an Indian was drinking. Townsend discovered that the man knew a bit of Spanish, so he talked with him and offered him a New Testament. The Indian could not read, but purchased the small volume anyway, saying he had a neighbor who could read it to him. Townsend invited him to a service the following Sunday, probably at the church in San Antonio where he was staying. To his surprise, the man attended the service. Townsend preached for nearly forty-five minutes, a sermon he had laboriously translated from a book by the great nineteenth-century English preacher Charles Spurgeon. Although this early in his tenure he was still slaughtering Spanish "frightfully," at the end of his sermon when he asked if anyone wished to convert, Tiburcio Ordoñez, still intoxicated, wobbled to his feet and "confessed." He later promised to continue attending church. Townsend was naturally thrilled. Over the months that followed, as he traveled Guatemala, Townsend heard through the grapevine that Tiburcio had stopped drinking and was leading a committed evangelical life. Seven months later he heard from Díaz that Tiburcio showed up at church with a "black eye and a cut-up-face, and other marks of an encounter with a fanatical Catholic." Apparently Tiburcio's neighbors did not take his conversion lightly, and he was beaten up several times, even cut with machetes. Nevertheless, he seems to have clung to his new faith. Townsend recorded proudly, "I am sure that he would rather take a severe beating every day of his life than part with the salvation which he has in Christ Jesus."[28]

In late November 1917, after a month on the road, Townsend returned to Guatemala City for a conference. He had not seen Robinson, or any other American, for more than a month. Robinson was stunned with the change in his young friend. He remarked to Townsend that a month on his own evangelizing on the road had done more for him "than two years at college would have done." Giddy over Robinson's praise, in a burst of enthusiasm Townsend exclaimed that he would "like to give [his] life" to missionary work "if that were the Lord's plan."[29]

One day during the conference, Townsend was observing the Presbyterians' printing operation. That night he spoke to William Allison and informed the mission director that his press was running at only a tenth of capacity. He suggested that Allison ought to recruit a missionary printer from the United States to "work the plant to its full capacity," pointing out that a fully staffed plant on the field would save duty charges, transportation costs, and permit tracts to be "better fitted to the needs of the country." Allison was "heartily in favor" of the plan. Townsend sat up till one o'clock that night dashing off "a couple of letters in regard to the matter."[30]

As Townsend and Robinson packed their gear to head back onto the road after the conference, a wealthy Christian *ladino* noticed that Robinson had a mule, and he offered to loan Townsend his pony for the trip, as "it didn't look well to see one of [the men] riding and one walking." Townsend politely declined the offer, assuring the man that "it was alright [*sic*] for an American to [be seen walking.]"[31]

As Townsend's language skills increased, he found that often the first line of entree in his door-to-door evangelism was of necessity an attempt to explain how his beliefs were different from those of Roman Catholicism. American evangelicals despised and feared Roman Catholicism. It was the most dangerous heresy because of its earthly power and its close relation to Protestantism. Therein lay the danger; unfortunate millions were going to hell believing they were in reality Christians. The rhetoric from Protestant mission leaders was fierce. C. I. Scofield, founder of the CAM and author of the immensely popular *Scofield Reference Bible,* spoke derisively of "the profligate superstition which in Spanish America passes for Roman Catholicism. . . . The religion of the country is, speaking generally, the most debased form of Romanism to be found anywhere on the earth." Language such as this was common among American evangelicals in the early 1900s, and only intensified on the mission field, where Protestants found themselves an insignificant and often persecuted minority.[32]

In Latin America the hostility was mutual. If Protestantism still held a certain cultural hegemony in the early decades of the century in North America, its ties with the state had long been severed. Roman Catholicism's state connections had only recently been ruptured in some Latin countries, and its cultural hegemony had yet to be seriously challenged. Consequently, Protestants had to step lightly, even if their presence was looked upon with approval by liberal governments. In Guatemala tension was such that the cause for the devastating 1917 earthquake could still be attributed to God's judgment on the country for not driving out the *evangélicos.* Even as Albert Bishop gloated that "Catholicism will be at a disadvantage for [years] to come" because of the damage to the cathedrals in Guatemala City, he reported, "Much bitterness is manifested by the more fanatical because our home is still standing [and] our Mission building, while greatly damaged, is not so badly ruined as their Roman Temples." Absurd suspicions were not confined to the Catholics. When the CAM council discovered in 1921 that a prospective missionary who had failed her physical exam had been examined by a Catholic doctor in the United States, they immediately suspected foul play. The doctor was certainly "prejudiced," because he "was not in favor of missions to Catholic lands." Informed that this same doctor had given a clean bill of health to another CAM missionary, the council admitted that perhaps they had been too hasty, but then again the doctor may have simply "thought it sufficient to reject one of the two."[33]

As we have seen, practically from the moment he arrived in Guatemala,

Townsend was indoctrinated into the Protestant-versus-Catholic lore of the missions. In addition to William Allison's lecture on Catholicism, it seemed everyone those first few weeks was able to offer a tale of the triumph of the cause of Christ over Catholic superstition. An elderly widow sat Townsend down and recounted a hair-raising story of biblical proportions. A Good Friday procession, two hundred to three hundred strong, once stopped in front of the missionaries' home and challenged them to come out and worship the image of Christ. Her husband went out, but could not speak much Spanish. When the crowd began to threaten his life, his frightened wife, who had been listening from inside and understood Spanish well, asked the servant girl what they should do. The girl went out and "preached a regular gospel sermon" to the crowd. She rebuked them for hating the *evangélicos,* because Christ said we should love our enemies. It seemed the "ignorant servant girl" was granted "beautiful diction, keen logic," and an extraordinary grasp of Scripture on that fateful day. Eventually the priest moved the procession along when he saw "they were losing ground." Townsend appreciatively recorded in his journal, "The modern miracles on the mission field are certainly inspiring."[34]

Given this introduction, it is not surprising that Townsend's own early impressions followed a similar line. "Central American Catholicism as I have seen it so far, is too awful to describe," he wrote during his first month in Guatemala. "The ignorance and fanaticism [are] terrible." Another time he wrote, "They all profess to be Christians, but they know nothing of what the term should mean."[35]

The gospel presentation then boiled down to simple contrasts between the Catholic way and the Protestant way. Only three weeks after arriving, Townsend preached a gospel sermon, most likely in Antigua. He roughly sketched his ideas in English in his journal. Just as there were "laws of God found in nature," such as the seasons and day and night, there were also spiritual laws that needed to be observed to "live life by God's standard." The first "spiritual law" was the certainty of death as payment for sin. But through the death of Christ, humans are offered the "free gift" of salvation. The "free gift" was a natural starting point, as it seemed to contrast favorably with what was perceived to be the human effort required for salvation in the Catholic Church. For his second point, Townsend used the Mosaic injunction against the construction of idols (Exodus 20:4) and Christ's words to the Samaritan woman that God must be worshiped "in spirit and truth" (John 4:24) to contrast true Protestant worship with the false worship of Catholicism. His notes are stark but emphatic: "No images, penance, etc." Next he used Christ's warning of approaching persecution (Matthew 10:22) to caution his hearers that they "ought not to be with the crowd . . . and shouldn't expect to be popular." In Guatemala in 1917 this was a clear warning that to be Catholic was to "be with the crowd," while to join the unpopular Protestants was to find the "narrow way" that "leads to life" (Matthew 7:14).[36]

During door-to-door evangelism, Townsend returned again and again to the issues that most immediately and obviously distinguished the Protestants. Usually this meant an argument about worshiping images. Since a statue of Mary or a saint was in almost every home, Townsend had an immediate conversation starter. His journal contains numerous references to "long arguments about whether the images were saints or not and whether we really ought to worship Mary." A typical day included encounters such as the following.

> She said that she couldn't receive my popellitos (little tracts) because she had a god in her house. I told her that the God of the Heavens was the only true God and that He was an infinite Spirit. She said that she had a god of the heavens in her house and that she had to spend all of her spare money buying him candles. I don't see how Africa could be any darker.

> I got into an argument with the saloon . . . keeper about the images. He admitted that God is a Spirit, but claimed that the images were likenesses of him and that we could ask petitions of them. I told him that he would stand about as much chance of getting his petitions as he would of getting a political appointment by begging it of one of the pictures of President Estrada Cabrera, which hang in every town hall. As it is necessary to talk to the President in person, so it is necessary to talk to God in person.

Townsend seems to have eventually realized that this was not a particularly productive line of reasoning. He wrote of one encounter, "The mayor had been imbibing a little—enough to make him very agreeable. . . . He thought that I was simply wonderful until I began lecturing him about the monstrous image he had in his home. It is generally a poor plan to tackle them on this subject."[37]

Nevertheless, in a country where so many felt themselves already to be Christians and where Protestants were considered heretical, he found he had to engage these issues if he hoped to win converts. He even engaged priests in such discussions at times, with predictable results. After the earthquake in Guatemala City in December 1917, Townsend was talking with the priest of one of the "most famous churches" when the discussion inevitably turned to religion. Townsend immediately sought to highlight the major point of contention between Protestants and Catholics. He asked the priest how a person could be saved. The priest replied that it was necessary "to follow the Apostolic Roman Catholic Church." When Townsend disagreed, arguing that it was necessary "only to follow Christ to be saved," the cleric "got angry and using dirty Spanish said that to follow only Christ was like eating dung and then went into his house."[38]

Shortly before Christmas that first year in 1917, Townsend and Díaz stopped at a plantation and asked for a drink. The *finca* manager invited Townsend onto the porch for a pitcher of cold orange soft drink. Knowing his place, Díaz hung back, but Townsend called him to join them. When the manager returned, he was indignant and "with an imperious air" ordered the Indian off the porch. There is no record of how Townsend responded; probably he accepted the slight to his friend, even as it cut him deeply. He was troubled by the slights Díaz endured, although he lacked the self-confidence in the early months to rectify them. Such experiences, however, were integral to his education. He later recorded that the landowners were "very liberal with Americans[,] but they certainly believe in keeping the natives in the condition of slaves." Eventually, the slights became too much for Díaz and Townsend to bear. When Díaz became "self-conscious of his Indian garb," Townsend purchased him a set of *ladino* clothes so that he would not be immediately recognized as an Indian.

Francisco Díaz's influence on Townsend cannot be underestimated. Díaz became far more than a servant. Townsend wrote of him, "In every way Frisco is an equal colleague in my ministry, and in every way he is a prize. He is such a special friend to me. He always serves me willingly and cheerfully. He frequently gives me the needed inspiration to continue on. Our times of prayer and Bible study are especially precious." As Townsend's most intimate companion during his year as a colporteur, Díaz's stories, insights, and explanations provided the grid through which Townsend interpreted life in Guatemala.[39]

By late spring 1918, after six months together on the road, Townsend and Díaz were dreaming of starting a school for Indian children in San Antonio, Díaz's hometown. The school would be tuition free for the children of Indian converts. Díaz had kept the needs of his own people, the Cakchiquels, before Townsend around countless campfires and along miles of jungle trails. His hunger for the education of his children and his people motivated him to persuade Townsend that Indian converts from his hometown would support a missionary to teach their children. Díaz also hoped the missionary would teach the adults at night. Of course, he hoped Townsend would be that missionary. The prospect held great appeal for Townsend, who, after traveling with Díaz for so long, believed, contrary to popular opinion, that the Indians were a "vir-

5. Francisco Díaz. Courtesy Townsend Archives.

ile race and only need[ed] Christianity and some education to become a strong factor in these countries." "I may be overestimating their capacities," he told his brother, "but I think not." Townsend's opinion of the capacity of the Indians was undoubtedly based largely on a year spent with Díaz. He wrote, "[He is] an unsophisticated Indian man who [has] lived all his life in a society that makes it a practice to taunt and oppress the Indian. It is a society that considers it a disgrace for a Spanish-speaking person to be seen talking with an Indian as man to man, they being considered only an animal." And yet, "[W]hen I see how quickly Frisco learned and how eager he was to follow the Lord and do His will, and how many latent possibilities there are in him and his people, I am stirred even further to recognize the need among the [Cakchiquel] people." It was Townsend's close companionship with an Indian man that enabled him to step outside, at least partially, the prejudice that was subtly afflicting even his fellow missionaries.[40]

If Townsend had any prejudice at all, it was against the oppressors of the Indians, the *ladinos.* "The Indians make better missionaries than the ladinos," Townsend wrote. "They are a much hardier race, too. I can out rough it with any ladino I've met yet[,] but the Indians have me beat a mile." Then he added a few curious lines that suggest he may have picked up some of the racial theories that haunted Latin American *mestizos* themselves. "[Indians] haven't the immoral ancestry that the ladinos have," Townsend wrote. "Such a moral fiber develops finer Christians than do the ladinos, degenerated by generations of immorality."[41] At the turn of the century, elite Latin American *mestizos* were working hard to counter racial theories that valued racial purity over race mixing. Men such as José Vasconcelos in Mexico and José Martí in Cuba argued that in actuality race mixing brought together the strengths of several races, so Latin American *mestizos,* a combination of Spanish and Indian blood, were to be valued over pureblood Spaniards. Regardless of the theory, Indians were at the bottom of the race heap. Here Townsend both accepted and subverted the racial theories being discussed in Latin America at the time. Still, it would be dangerous to read too much into Townsend's comment. He was very young, no student of race theory, and no racist of any sort. He was a young idealistic man who was thoroughly disgusted with the treatment of Guatemalan Indians, and capable of lashing out at their major oppressors in a private letter to his family.

After a year of itinerating, Townsend one day met a Catholic woman he truly believed to be "saved." Under a journal entry wryly titled "A Saved Romanist," Townsend reported meeting a fairly well-to-do Catholic woman who had studied the Bible "considerably" and whom he believed "had a saving knowledge of Jesus Christ as her Lord and Saviour." This was a telling phrase for evangelicals, each word laden with meaning. In sum it meant that a person knew enough of the gospel story to understand that they were sinners and that their only hope of salvation was through faith in the salvific work of Christ on the cross. Once a person accepted this fact and "placed their trust" in Christ alone, they were considered saved. That this "saving knowledge" was of Christ as "Lord" as well as "Saviour" indicated the person was leading a life of at least outward obedience to Christian precepts as understood by evangelicals. This particular woman had some "expensive images" in her home, but Townsend was confident of her salvation, because she told him "she had them there only to serve as remembrances, and said that she worshiped in spirit and talked to God as to her spiritual Father. She lamented the fact that so many of the people of these countries worship the images instead of God."[42]

Such encounters, however, were few and far between. Townsend's work was often frustrated by the fact that even with the chronic shortage of priests, it seemed that everywhere he went the people had been prepared against him. (The only exception to this was in the coastal jungle, which might explain why he spent so much time working there despite the miserable conditions. The conditions were so bad there—intensely hot, humid, and insect-filled—that few priests bothered to make the trip. As many Indians gathered there yearly to harvest the coffee, Protestants saw it as a convenient place to conduct evangelistic trips.) From the middle-class matron who politely refused him, saying it "wasn't good to read that kind of literature," to the people who said it was a sin to read or even listen to *evangelista* propaganda, to villages like Dueñas, where he could trace his path through town by torn-up tracts, the colporteur found that the Catholic Church was usually one step ahead of him. While the average village dweller may not have been able to engage Townsend in nuanced theological debate, they all maintained basic Catholic practice and seemed to be well aware that the *evangélicos* threatened their standing with the Church. In addition, Townsend was told that the priests warned their parishioners that the evangelicals were "buying their souls for the devil." This was confirmed one day when he inadvertently provoked an uproar in a village after accidentally dropping a five-cent piece too close to an Indian's home. Passing by later, he observed a large and concerned crowd gathered. When the lady of the house spotted him, she insisted he take back the coin. Apparently she felt Townsend was attempting to purchase their souls by leaving money for the devil. At times someone who had purchased a Testament, but was then threatened by the local priest, returned it, and Townsend refunded the person's money. One nervous young man, after telling Townsend that the Testament was forbidden by the priest, finally purchased one anyway, remarking that he would read it at night, "when his mother didn't know anything about it." He made Townsend promise that he would not tell anyone about his purchase. A similar "sincere" young man purchased a Testament after Townsend encouraged him to "read it on the sly." If at the end of six months he "thought that it was a safer guide than the priest, he could then break off with the latter." If not, no one would be the wiser. Townsend concluded, "After satisfying him that the Book taught the Virgin Birth of Christ, he bought, but hid it away carefully."[43]

In May 1918 Townsend was working the coffee plantations on the coast. He had traversed much of Guatemala by this time and was a veteran of the Protestant-Catholic wars. Late one afternoon, he and Díaz wearily approached the hacienda on a large coffee plantation. They asked the owner for lodging and a meal, and the man kindly agreed. But over dinner the conversation turned hostile. The *finca* owner turned out to be a "hot headed Romanist." In a long, angry argument, their host raged against the "damned Protestants." Townsend responded vigorously. He was a fluent Spanish speaker by now, and he countered the man's every argument, using his superior biblical knowledge to squeeze the wealthy landowner time and again in the vice grip of good evangelical theological logic. Frustrated, their host accused Townsend of being a missionary only for what he got out of it. Perhaps Townsend's smartest reply would have been to simply remind the man who was the beggar and who was the host, but instead he piously replied, "Yes, the Lord has a Crown of Glory prepared for me which I will receive in that day." Thoroughly nonplussed, the man grunted, "Yes, the crown of the devil is what you will receive." Townsend quietly remarked, "And you, my friend, what will you receive?" His host stared at him in silence. The conversation ended.[44]

In a country where religious passions ran deep, and where conversion to a foreign religion was not an everyday occurrence, religious discussion did not always terminate with a polite decision to agree to disagree. More than once someone dispatched a "youngster" to follow Townsend shouting warnings about the coming of the *evangelistas.* Townsend found that this public warning usually meant "it was all off, for they're awfully afraid of their neighbors." Probably they feared punishment from the local priest if a neighbor reported their fraternization with an evangelical. "*La Virgen y nada más*" [The Virgin and nothing more] was a frequent rallying cry, with one woman telling him "to go to hell with [his] literature, that she believed only in the Virgin." Another woman gathered up tracts from her neighbors and burned them in front of him.[45]

The frustration undoubtedly felt by both parties in these exchanges was at least partly a result of the clash between a Western and a Hispanic approach to religion. Townsend wanted to engage in debate over the proper interpretation of scriptural passages and the correct theological approaches to God. Hispanic popular Catholicism, however, as Allan Figueroa Deck reminds us, "almost totally lacks rational articulation." Indeed, it "eschews the cognitive in its effort to appeal to the senses and the feelings." When Townsend wanted to argue Scripture, therefore, his frustrated Catholic listeners were left to insist over and over, "La Virgen y nada más."[46]

At times the opposition was physical. Very early in his sojourn an overeager Townsend offered a tract to an altar boy and was stoned for his efforts. "Fortunately," he reported, "none of them hit us, and it made me happy that we could partake in a little bit, at least, of what Paul and the early disciples experienced." Several times he and his companion were threatened with machetes, and at least once with a shotgun. In Iztapa an angry crowd gathered in the street, called them devils, and threatened to have them arrested. Eventually six soldiers arrived and dragged them to the mayor, who "more or less under the influence of liquor" ordered them thrown in jail. The soldiers apparently decided that was not such a good idea, and while they stalled, Townsend's companion managed to explain to the mayor's satisfaction what they were doing in the town. Eventually, Townsend wrote, the mayor settled down "with the application of a few

'Su Servidores' [Your Servants] and even took some tracts." "I suppose," he concluded, "that we should have visited him in the first place." At times the town leaders, if they were educated and in favor of raising the Indians out of their "superstition," were supportive. One even provided a military escort for the colporteurs. Through incidents like this, Townsend learned to check in with the authorities before beginning work in a district or town.[47]

Toward the end of his year with the Bible House, one hot August day Townsend was walking with a Catholic man down a country trail. As they walked they discussed Christian topics, and Townsend recorded that the man seemed quite "pious." Around a bend in the trail, they chanced upon some girls bathing in a creek. Townsend's companion nudged him, winked, and asked if he fancied one of the girls. Surprised and embarrassed, Townsend lit into the fellow—rode him "rough shod" was the way he later put it. They continued their journey in silence, the Protestant-Catholic rapprochement temporarily stilled.[48] Three days later Townsend came across another river, again with women bathing and men standing to the side, ogling. "All staunch Romanists," he noted that evening in his journal.[49]

On May 10, 1918, after eight months in Guatemala, Townsend sold 12 New Testaments in one day, his "best yet." On June 5, 1918, he sold 16 gospel portions. And in August 1918 Townsend posted by far his best numbers. He had worked his way to El Salvador at the time, and seemed to have hit on the key to opening doors. He recorded that "most everyone was wanting to buy, especially when I convinced them that I really believed in the Trinity and that Christ was born of a virgin (. . . the priests here spread the report that we don't believe in the Virgin)." Perhaps certain theological differences were best left unspoken. At any rate, on the fourth of August 1918 he sold 46 New Testaments and 16 Gospels. The next day he sold 25 more. The following day he sold the last of the 101 Testaments he had brought along, and was forced to order more. On August 10, with 63 Testaments and plenty of tracts, he set off on a three-week trip. He returned three days later having sold them all.[50]

How much was accomplished with Townsend's tract ministry we will ultimately never know, but lasting results were probably fairly negligible. As late as 1921, the illiteracy rate in Guatemala was still more than 86 percent, so few would have been able to read the tracts and Testaments with any real understanding. In addition, few of the large Indian population understood much Spanish. Twenty years later, in 1940, less than 1 percent of the population was Protestant. People certainly did not convert in large numbers during the time Townsend worked in Guatemala. It can be said with equal certainty, however, that this fact never bothered Townsend or other Protestant missionaries. If it is true that part of the Protestant ethos is an almost exclusive focus on the conversion of individuals, then it is equally true that the conversion of one individual provides enough motivation to keep missionaries at work. Today, however, Protestants make up more than one-third of the population in Guatemala, the highest percentage in Spanish America. While there are many political reasons for recent conversions, perhaps it can be said that the work of the early Protestant missionaries at least raised product awareness throughout the country, paving the way for the astonishing growth of Protestantism in recent decades. Perhaps in the very act of defining their otherness, and by weathering the resulting storm with a certain dignity, they manufactured a safe space that later generations felt free to inhabit.[51]

And Townsend? One gets the sense that he may have been as much a source of encouragement to believers as of genuine conversions among unbelievers. To have an American working alongside them, walking with them from town to town, was a source of entertainment if nothing else, something quite remarkable in their day-to-day lives. But Townsend was more than that. He displayed an infectious good cheer. He genuinely enjoyed the company of his companions, especially the Indians who were despised by so many of their own countrymen. Townsend saw them differently. He recorded in his journal, "They are beautiful Christians. . . . I [give] praises to God for the privilege of working among these people."[52]

Townsend traveled to Guatemala with the implicit understanding that it was God's will for him, and that in following God's wishes he would experience the presence of God in ways he never would at home. The development of Townsend's own faith may ultimately have been the most important aspect of his year with the Bible House. From his second day on the job, when he wrote, "I am learning to let the Spirit into my life more," his apprenticeship with the Bible House provided numerous opportunities to exercise his budding faith. Thrown upon his own resources, it was comforting to immerse himself in the daily practice of trust in God. He learned to think of God as his director, actively orchestrating the events of his life to accomplish God's own larger purpose. If he and Díaz got lost, they tried to figure out what God had planned for them. When the trail they subsequently found took them to a small town where a young man "accepted Christ," then they knew why they had gotten lost: "It was that this man could find his way to eternal life." If you prayed about everything, then everything that happened was God's will. This understanding kept them searching for signs of God, lest they miss some special event he had planned for them. Even disappointment could be a signal of his presence. If they prayed for a new mule but none was provided, then it might be God's will that they travel slowly, "working the towns on the way more thoroughly." The difficulty, of course, was knowing whether God or Satan was interrupting their plans, or, to complicate matters further, if God was using Satan to test them. These decisions could go either way, but in practice probably came down to how desperate they were to get to a certain desired end, or, to put it more spiritually, how convinced they were that it was God's plan for them to meet that goal. The pace of their travel was not of great importance, so the lack of a mule could be God's signal to work more thoroughly. But if they were scheduled to be somewhere that they really wanted to be, and one of them got sick, that was probably a sign of satanic activity.[53]

These decisions were made based on feelings and impressions, desires, dreams, maybe fears. It was certainly not an exact science. Once, Townsend "had a feeling" that God wanted him and Díaz to stay longer at a certain town, so when their mules wandered off, they took this as confirmation of God's plan. They stayed with "the man whom the Lord had put on my heart," who listened intently to the gospel but did not convert. Townsend, however, expected that eventually he would become a convert because of the special providence behind their extended stay. Townsend's "feeling," his notion that God had "put this man on my heart," was probably based simply on the fact that he had continued to think about him, probably wishing he had been able to spend more time evangelizing him or that he had expressed himself more clearly. Thus he was ready to interpret wandering mules as the hand of God at work. The continuing expectation that God was alive and intimately involved in working out his will in daily life was based on biblical stories that illustrated precisely such leading, and confirmed through constant post-event interpretation of how God must have worked. A tremendous boost to faith resulted when things worked out well as a consequence of a decision made on this basis. As stories such as this circulated through the community of believers, all learned to interpret events in their lives through this grid. It was a powerful comfort and incentive to holy living to believe that God was interested in your daily life and orchestrated events in your favor if you were seeking his will.

Though Townsend undoubtedly learned a great deal from missionaries such as Albert Bishop and R. D. Smith, it was the hours of personal Bible study on the road that taught him the basics of the faith. He religiously studied the Scofield Bible. He called it his "only text book." "I don't argue much with [Scofield]," Townsend once said.[54] For a year he studied the Bible every morning, and then spent the bulk of the rest of the day explaining Christian concepts in the simplest terms in a language he was still learning. Townsend never again pursued higher education, so this was his most formative religious training. His faith, as it developed, was simple, lacking nuance, but hearty, tough, and startlingly confident.

Townsend was at least nominally aware of the controversies over liberal theology that were enveloping the denominations in the United States. He advised his brother, still attending Occidental College after it hired a "higher critic" president, to "[s]tudy up on 'higher criticism' and hit it every chance you get. Don't let them pull you out on your 2 by 4 reason but stick to the Bible. They can't do anything with the Word of God." Ironically, the colporteur who spent many of his waking hours trying to reason Latin Catholics into conversion now flagellated reason as a threat to simple faith.[55]

Despite his simple faith and mistrust of liberals, Townsend traveled with and even conducted services with Mr. Humphrey, a Baptist missionary in El Salvador and a "New Theology man." The young missionary enjoyed the hospitality of the Humphreys, although he felt "rather uncomfortable," because there was no "spiritual fellowship." Townsend described one joint meeting at which nearly an entire town turned out.

> Humphrey had secured an old Catholic Bible from which he read a passage, after which we sang a duet, and then he told them to be good and join the religion which was most popular in the United States. I ended up with a little sermonette, telling them to get saved. There is so much interest in these parts that it is a shame not to give them a live gospel. Humphrey is awfully optimistic, but I haven't much hope for his work. He said that at first two hundred men would attend his meetings in San Miguel, but now after over a year, hardly a one comes out. Why should they want to be or how can they be good without being born again?

While traveling together Humphrey expanded on his beliefs, explaining to Townsend that "Paul was mistaken about Christ coming back," and that "we just had to be good and teach others to be good until all the world gets good and then that will be the reign of God on the earth." Humphrey thought the world was progressing rapidly toward that reign, while Townsend wondered how he could be so optimistic when he looked around Central America. Townsend remarked in his journal that while he didn't know for certain, he was "pretty sure" that Humphrey's theology was "of the devil."[56] Still, perhaps because of the influence of his practical parents, Townsend did not possess fundamentalism's knee-jerk tendency to dissociate from anything that smacked of unorthodoxy. If he could gain a larger hearing and enjoy some pleasant company by traveling with Humphrey, he was more than happy to do so.

In late spring 1918, with the time for his return to the United States and college approaching, Townsend sat down to write a difficult letter to his parents. "God has given me youthful vigor, faith and a challenge," he informed his folks. Then came the stunning, sweeping declaration that captured a yearlong growing vision and all the idealism of youth: "Therefore, I have decided to devote my life to the evangelization of the Indian peoples." In one sentence he swept away all the family's dreams and threw in his lot with the world's most despised people. There would be no college graduation. "I would never feel right in going to school when the world is so greatly in need of action." There would be no stateside pastorate. "The opportunities down here are simply wonderful. I could never settle down to a pastorate in the States," and then, leaving the door open a crack, "unless the Lord made it tremendously clear that He wanted me there." But he thought better of that and slammed the door completely: "And I don't anticipate that He will." Townsend was now dictating the terms of his life. From now on there would be only a single-minded commitment to native peoples.

Eventually his parents granted him permission to remain another year while expressing disappointment at not seeing him when they had hoped. His father wrote, "When you do God's will, you do mine, for I don't want you to do anything but His will. . . . I want you to be happy." Apparently concerned that the Guatemala experience was turning his boy too quickly into a man, he added, "Where you are, there is much to make you sad and serious. I was most afraid you couldn't be jolly and fun-loving anymore. I wouldn't want that."[57]

Townsend's plan—large, unwieldy, and idealistic—extended far beyond simple evangelism. He told his parents that he hoped to begin a ministry with Guatemalan Indians similar to the type of experiments done in North America to assist African Americans, "a Christian Tuskegee for Indians" he called it. He wanted to teach reading, writing, and arithmetic, agriculture and various other trades, along with the Bible. Such a school "would be an unequaled force in evangelizing the Indians of Central America and lifting them in the social scale." He noted that the school should be "interdenominational so that we could work among all missions."[58]

Díaz was delighted to learn of Townsend's decision, and together they began planning for the future of what Townsend called "our work." They decided to save all of their commission money (50 percent of total sales over $5.00 in any one month) to establish a fund for their Indian school. Díaz planned to teach the youngest children, who as yet spoke no Spanish, until they could secure a "professional teacher." Townsend ordered supplies from the United States, including seeds for the flower and vegetable garden Díaz planned as part of an agriculture class. By December others were getting interested in the work. Bishop promised the school a cow and her calf, several other missionaries contributed about $30, he and Díaz had saved almost $30 from their sales commissions, his folks and family had sent $47.50, and he had saved almost $100 of his own funds. Townsend was confident the school was ready to launch.[59]

Eager to find other ways to earn money to further his plans for the Indians, Townsend filled his letters home with wild schemes. He asked his brother-in-law to help him get an "agency" for Weck razors. He figured he could make a little on the side by selling razors to missionaries and wealthy *ladinos*. In addition, teaching Indians to shave "would be a real charitable work." He spent four pages of another letter spinning a detailed idea for an importing business. He planned to import hardware, corrugated iron, and barbed wire to sell to *finca* owners. He mused, "[It] sounds wild as usual but . . . may be workable." He dreamed about what could be done with better farming techniques, irrigation, and other improvements. He kept his father busy packaging the seeds of a variety of vegetables that he planned to introduce to Guatemala. In return he sent Guatemalan plants to California, hoping that if they grew there, his family might be able to make some extra money. He tried to convince his parents to move to Guatemala and invest in farmland. He requested a textbook on silver and gold mining from his folks, hoping to learn "how to prospect, and how to commence working a vein, etc.," and he warned his brother-in-law to "be ready to come down in case this mine turns out to be a bonanza."

Townsend failed to discover gold, but he did find some old bones in western Honduras, "a lower molar tooth of an extinct species of horse, Hipparion." Insatiably curious, with the interests of an amateur scientist, Townsend had seen a large tooth in the saddle bag of a national civil engineer, obtained directions from him to the hill where he found it, went there himself, and made what turned out to be a fairly significant discovery. He sent the bones to the Smithsonian Institution, whose representatives agreed he had found an important site and urged him to let experts handle the excavations. That Townsend did so was due more to his busy schedule than to their urging.[60]

Townsend's dream of giving his life to work with the Indians necessitated that he leave the Bible House. His most natural option was to join the Central American Mission, in whose territory lived most of the Cakchiquels, the tribe with whom Townsend wanted to work. In July 1918 he wrote to Albert

Bishop, director of CAM work in Guatemala, for advice. Bishop, who had already urged Townsend to join CAM, gave his "hearty approval" of Townsend's plans to work with the Indians, "seeing how God has used you for [their] salvation and enlightenment . . . and realizing that a very few missionaries have the qualifications and rearing that would make possible a successful work among these Indians."[61]

R. D. Smith also urged Townsend to make the move, even though it would mean losing him for the Bible House. Smith knew itinerating for the Bible House was a temporary position for anyone. If he was going to lose Townsend, better to lose him to the CAM, on whose council Smith sat. Referring to Townsend as a "royal good fellow," he personally brought Townsend to the attention of the CAM home secretary, Judge D. H. Scott. Smith shared a letter from Townsend in which, upon returning from his travels throughout Central America, the young man had analyzed the work of the CAM. Judge Scott was very impressed with Townsend's analysis, making copies for all the CAM council members, and calling it "by far the best synopsis of our C[entral] A[merican] work, given by an outsider that we have ever had." Scott remarked, "Every one of our Missionaries who have come in contact with him speak in the highest terms of him."[62] Skinny Townsend had convinced his doubters.

3

In Which the Reader Learns a Great Deal about Evangelicals and Faith Missions, While Townsend Takes a Wife, Builds a Cornstalk House, and Meets Some Important People

1919–1921

> [We have built] an Indian home in an Indian town, and though its inmates are white yet their hearts are chuck full of Indian-ward love.
>
> —William Cameron Townsend

On New Year's Day 1919, Townsend attended a dinner party at the home of the Allisons, the leaders of the Presbyterian mission. The Allisons were out of town, and the party was hosted by Elvira Malmstrom, William Allison's personal secretary. Where Robbie Robinson had fallen for Elvira almost a year and a half ago, this time Townsend was smitten. Elvira was the only game in town as far as young missionary women went, and after a year on the road Townsend fell hard. A few weeks later, back in Antigua, Townsend was stricken with malaria. Elvira traveled with another missionary couple to Antigua, where she ministered to Townsend regularly during his convalescence. He proposed marriage to her on Valentine's Day, and she accepted. Three days later he wrote to his parents, proudly crowing that he had "wooed and won (vini, vidi, vici)" her. He did not mention that he had claimed his victory over the older Robinson, who had sent a letter of proposal to Elvira at approximately the same time. Being absent, however, Robinson was not able to press his claim. Townsend also did not mention that he scarcely knew the girl. Young love knew nothing of such practical matters. For Townsend, she was "altogether lovely." After describing her unrelenting work ethic, he reassured his family, "You would think from this that she is one of the mannish girls but she isn't—she's just a delightfully girlish little girl." (In a later letter he promised his mother that Elvira "beat her picture a thousand to one.") Most important, she was "the most spiritual girl" he had ever known. "Her very presence draws one closer to the Lord," he wrote. "How I enjoy to study the Bible and pray with her! We are truly one in the Lord." In addition, she "love[d] the Indians, and . . . love[d] to tell people about her loving Jesus." Townsend summed up: "It was a work of the Lord pure and simple[,] and I have never had a minute's doubt as to His will in the matter." In evangelical circles such a pronouncement usually ends all debate, even if it fails to quiet all doubt.[1]

Elvira was four years Townsend's senior and had arrived in Guatemala several months before him. She had a business education, had been a secretary in Chicago, and came to Guatemala supported by Moody Church, one of America's most prominent evangelical churches. Fluent in Spanish, she regularly taught a girls' Bible class. Elvira came from a well-ordered middle-class Swedish home and was very close to her mother and brothers. She was intensely pious, but frail physically and emotionally. The earthquakes that regularly rocked the city terrified her. "I cried and cried and laughed until I was hysterical," she reported to her brother. Elvira was lonely in Guatemala. Her letters to her brothers were filled with desperate unhappiness. "You know of course how much I need to be loved," she wrote, "and if ever I hungered for love and appreciation it certainly has been these past months in Guatemala. . . . I think sometimes I was really spoiled being the only girl and guess you boys showered a whole lot of love on me that I miss so dreadfully here." Privately she longed to return home, and hoped that when the Allisons went home in 1919, they would take her along to be William's traveling secretary. "Mother and Dad Allison are so good to me," she moaned, "and I just do want to be happy."

As much as Elvira longed to return home, she was still doggedly determined to fulfill what she viewed as God's call on her life and be a good missionary, even as she was as ill equipped for the task as a missionary has ever been. Whenever her depression threatened to overwhelm her, she hiked to her "beautiful place," a deep ravine flanked by mountains. There, amid the tranquility of nature, she cried "like [she] never did at home," but eventually, she wrote, after I "cry and cry for a while I commence thinking of the wonderful things that God has made and how peaceful it all is, until I just ask God to make me that way in my own heart, fully trusting him, and knowing that He is always with me. . . . I do love Jesus so much and His presence with me is such a comfort." She vowed to remain at her post in Guatemala, where she felt she was doing God's will. "In spite of all the earthquakes in the world or anything else that may come," she vowed, "I love Guatemala and her people and I am anxious to see souls saved."[2]

Cameron Townsend had private misgivings about joining one of the established missions. He was not convinced that they would look with favor on his increasingly radical plans. Townsend knew that his vision, while still in its infancy, already went far beyond that of most evangelical missions in the area. Mission schools patterned themselves after North American institutions. Centered on a liberal arts education, every curriculum included English; in some schools instruction in the higher grades was exclusively in English. Other instruction was done in Spanish. Dress codes or uniforms proscribed Indian dress. In addition, the rationale for schools operated by the evangelical missions focused on education strictly as a means of promoting evangelism; Townsend knew that he and Díaz planned something very different. Townsend had the audacious idea that he would learn Cakchiquel and teach the Indians in their own tongue. He also feared that some of his "Indian Tuskegee" plans might stray beyond the evangelistic mandate of the missions.[3]

In the middle of January, Townsend visited the department governor, General José E. Barrios, son of the former president of Guatemala, to see about obtaining land for his school. The governor promised to help, saying he had "to keep the Romanists down as they deceive the people." In return for his help, Barrios asked Townsend to teach his own children a daily class on "morals (Bible, right living, etc.)." Townsend was distressed at the request. He had already agreed to teach English in the government school in Antigua, as well as in a few private homes, to bring in a little cash to fund his school. The additional responsibilities, however, threatened to keep him working for *ladinos* when he wanted to be with Indians. Unfortunately, he said, "as the wish of a governor in these countries is practically an order, I couldn't very well say no." He agreed to teach Barrios's children twice a week.[4]

Townsend's most significant initial hurdle came from the Indians themselves. Despite Díaz's assurances that the Indians in his hometown were supportive of the projected school, two of the more well off were nervous about the cost and concerned that a higher profile for the *evangélicos* might lead to more opposition. Their concern discouraged the others. For Townsend, this was merely a test of his faith. He badgered the two one-on-one, praying and cajoling. He related the biblical story of Gideon, who accomplished much with little, and read them the great chapter on faith, Hebrews 11. Unfortunately, the two men were not ready to "put on [their] spectacles of faith." They agreed, however, to permit Townsend and Díaz to proceed, and if all went well, they would reassess the plans at a later date.[5]

Sometime in March, Townsend and Díaz opened their school. None of the original children could read, but by August three could read "difficult passages of the Bible." The children were taught a Bible verse every day, in addition to geography, arithmetic, sewing, and manual training. "You would be surprised at their intelligence," wrote one interested observer.[6]

Since Elvira was with the Presbyterian mission and Cameron was now without a mission home, William Allison naturally felt Townsend should join their mission. He asked Townsend to apply, suggesting that an arrangement could be made despite his lack of seminary training, a necessary qualification for the traditional boards. Townsend considered the offer seriously; he scouted Presbyterian territory for several days on horseback, but he found that when he left Cakchiquel territory it felt too much like leaving home. The CAM offer began to look more and more attractive. In addition, perhaps aware of the Presbyterian courtship, the president of CAM, who happened to be traveling in Guatemala, gave him fifty dollars to buy a suit for his wedding. C. I. Scofield himself sent a Scofield Bible as a wedding present. (Scofield later sent Townsend some of his old clothes. Although the pants "went around [him] two or three times," he wore Scofield's trousers while carrying Scofield's Bible on evangelistic trips for Scofield's mission.) By May the decision had been made, and the applications were circulating among CAM council members. Judge Scott, CAM secretary, urged the council members to hurry up the Townsend-Malmstrom applications, as it was "not a case that require[d] much attention." The two young people were eagerly received as members of the CAM on June 9, 1919.[7]

When Judge Scott wrote that the Townsend-Malmstrom applications did not require much attention, he conveniently overlooked the elephant in the room—the issue of Elvira's health. One of the Presbyterian missionaries privately informed the mission that Elvira "was in no physical condition to marry." The CAM council took the information seriously enough to have Albert Bishop and council member Luther Rees discuss Elvira's condition with her physician in Guatemala. The doctor gave no reason why she could not marry and be appointed as a missionary. In addition, it was known that William Allison, Elvira's supervisor, was trying to recruit her and Cameron for the Presbyterian mission, and it was assumed, as he knew her best, that he would not do so if they were not both qualified for mission work. It appears, however, that the seriousness of Elvira's condition may have been kept from the CAM. Townsend later admitted that at the time of their engagement Elvira was in "very poor health."

Earthquakes, a bout with influenza, and "other things" had left "her nerves in bad shape." A month or so after their engagement she was advised by her fellow Presbyterian missionaries to return to the United States "for a good rest before marrying." She planned to do so, but a lack of funds resulted in the plans falling through. In June her doctor forbade her to marry before getting six months' rest at home. He finally gave his permission, "providing she be very careful about work for a long time." It appears that the doctor was less than candid with Bishop and Rees. How much Townsend himself knew is open to question.[8]

The couple married on July 9, 1919, Townsend's twenty-third birthday. Elvira was twenty-seven. Elvira's brother Carl, freshly discharged from the army, attended the wedding, and the next day the new couple and Carl journeyed to Antigua. Townsend had decided to locate in the town where his ministry with the Bible House began, where he first attempted to share the story of *Señor Jesus.* They spent their honeymoon fixing up their home and preaching in the town. One week later they departed on a weeklong evangelization trip with Carl. They covered eighty-five miles on mule back, held twelve services, and saw three professions of faith. They followed that up with a conference in Acatenango, where, in fifteen services over four days, they saw twelve confessions of faith and fifteen baptisms. Townsend preached, and Elvira played her portable organ and led the singing. Between 125 and 150 people turned out nightly. Elvira seemed to be catching Townsend's vision. "[T]he poor Indians," she wrote, "How we want to serve them and be a blessing to them, for they are so despised and downtrodden by everyone. They are indeed in need of just a little bit of love." By the time Carl left on August 13, Townsend had so thoroughly recruited him that he was determined to give his life to be a missionary in Guatemala.[9]

Over the next few months the young couple settled into their ministry with the church and school in Antigua. Elvira worked with the young women and established a small choral group that turned out to be "one of the chief attractions to the unconverted." They led two meetings on Sunday, prayer meeting on Monday, three Bible classes on Wednesday, a Thursday evening preaching service, and a class with the Sunday school teachers on Friday. Townsend also held services every Sunday in San Antonio and Santa Catarina, where there was an established Indian congregation of about eighty. He also worked with Albert Bishop, preaching at conferences and "working out a card system to organize all the congregations on the field."[10]

The Central American Mission, which the Townsends now joined, was a faith mission. As faith missions were one of the oddest, most dysfunctional, yet most enduring and, eventually, influential institutions ever established by evangelical

6. Cameron and Elvira, 1919. Courtesy Townsend Archives.

Protestants, it is worth our time to take a close look at the aptly named organizations, specifically the Central American Mission, with which the Townsends would be affiliated for the next thirteen years.

Faith missions emerged rapidly in the late nineteenth century from beneath the shadow of the great interdenominational and denominational boards that had carried the Protestant missionary enterprise forward since its inception early in the century. Beginning in the 1880s and 1890s and patterned after J. Hudson Taylor's China Inland Mission—the template for such things, where evangelicals were concerned—by World War I there were already at least forty independent evangelical missions either headquartered in the United States or deriving much of their support from Americans. Most of these were faith missions.[11]

Initially designed as complements to the traditional boards, by at least 1895 the faith missions were offering a competing and conflicting ideal for missionary service. These missions did not have their genesis in theological quarrels with liberalism as is often supposed. Many were formed long before the intense fundamentalist-liberal battles of the 1920s. Impatience was the driving emotional motivation, not theological cantankerousness. Premillennial theology stoked the imagination of many evangelicals who woke each morning to the sense of urgency that came with the territory when one lived in "the end times." Many evangelicals were eager to hasten the process of world evangelization and to launch missionary endeavors into areas untended by the denominations. In Latin America, for example, evangelicals grieved for an entire continent, which seemed to have been abandoned to the Catholics. The 1910 Edinburgh missions conference did not even list Latin America as a mission field, and few North American Protestants served there. The Central American Mission was created to fill this void.[12]

When evangelical missionary entrepreneurs wanted to occupy unevangelized fields, they often appealed first to the boards to send missionaries. When the boards turned them down, they grew irritated at the perceived lack of vision and frustrated with a bureaucracy that demanded adequate funding before embarking on a new enterprise. Such men turned to the faith principle of mission operation as an expedient way to achieve a desired end after other means of funding had been denied. Faith mission rhetoric granted mission founders the moral high ground as well as a means to found missions that would penetrate new territory while, at least theoretically, not competing with the boards for funding. If it was God's will to reach an unreached area, it was up to God to provide. It was the believer's responsibility to step out in faith, believing.

When Rowland Bingham, for example, could find no missionary society to commission him to go to the Sudan, he and two companions journeyed there on their own. After his companions perished in a quixotic attempt to walk to Sudan from Nigeria, Bingham returned for more recruits. He tried again to obtain board backing, this time from the Baptists, and only decided to form an interdenominational and independent faith mission when they also, perhaps understandably, refused. He founded the Sudan Interior Mission (SIM) in 1893.[13]

Once committed to a new course of action, it became easier to articulate the inadequacies of the traditional boards, and faith mission founders determined not to repeat any of the perceived errors of denominationalism. The Christian and Missionary Alliance (C&MA) was founded in 1887 as "an interdenominational movement not building up sectarianism, but . . . welcoming the cooperation of Christians and missionaries of every evangelical denomination without requiring the sacrifice of their convictions and denominational relationships." It was "a pioneer movement, not duplicating existing agencies but reaching out to the regions beyond and seeking to send the Gospel to the most destitute corners of this benighted world." The Scandinavian Alliance Mission was "nondenominational in character, working on an unchangeable principle never to become a church denomination, but welcoming interdenominational cooperation for the extension of the Gospel to heathen lands."[14] Such rhetoric was designed to signal the start of something new and better, while at the same time assuring the denominations that the new missions had no desire to compete with them for funds or manpower.

In order not to compete with the denominations for manpower, but at the same time to speed up the work of world evangelization, faith mission leaders dreamed of greatly expanding the missionary force by employing less-educated, but highly committed, candidates. In 1885 Arthur Tappan Pierson, influential editor of the *Missionary Review of the World,* feeling that "salvation was a higher priority than potential heresy caused by a lack of formal education," presented a paper to the Presbytery of Philadelphia arguing that seminary-trained men should lead and organize with "less-educated but sincere missionaries under them." The Presbyterians refused his suggestion.[15]

Most of the traditional boards required college and seminary education from missionary candidates. The ordination of the prospective missionary set him (and it was usually *him* as far as ordination and real leadership went) on a level with professionals in home ministry. As Arthur Judson Brown, whose book on missions was one of the standards on the subject in the early decades of the twentieth century, wrote, "[T]he standard of foreign missionary appointment is higher than that of the military and naval services." (Brown meant this as the sincerest compliment.) He went on, "[The boards] take only the picked men of the colleges and universities. [They] do not send the pale enthusiast or the romantic young lady to the foreign field, but the sturdy, practical, energetic man of affairs, the woman of poise and sense and character."[16]

At a time when only 1 percent of white males past college age were college graduates, when less than 30 percent of congressmen and only 60 percent of presidents had earned degrees, these requirements left a vast pool of potential recruits unavailable to the boards. Into this breech stepped the men who founded the faith missions. Men such as J. Hudson Taylor, Dwight Moody, A. B. Simpson, C. I. Scofield, and Rowland Bingham founded missions and their supporting agencies (chiefly Bible institutes) that were designed to quickly prepare devoted men *and women* of almost any educational background for evangelistic service. As Harold Cook, director of the missions course at Moody Bible Institute (MBI), later recollected, the genius of the faith missions was their mining of the "great resources of manpower among Christians of average schooling but of more than average devotion to Christ." "Average schooling" of the day, as we have seen, was average indeed. As the majority of Americans did not attend high school until the 1930s, the educational background of students entering

MBI and then funneling into the faith missions should not surprise us. In 1929 only 14.3 percent of MBI's students had graduated high school; only 41.6 percent had even attended.[17]

This light educational attainment was fine with faith mission leaders for two reasons. First, as Cook had noted, what the incoming students lacked in formal education, they more than made up in piety and devotion to missions. Most had been raised in evangelical families and had grown up in a subculture that, as Joel Carpenter put it, "saw evangelism as the all-consuming priority for the church." Most of the future missionaries arrived at the Bible institutes already committed to a missions career. From childhood they heard exciting missionary stories in church and Sunday school, at missions conferences, and from missionaries visiting in their homes. They read books put out by mission presses designed, as one Sunday school worker expressed it, to be "so full of thrilling adventure and stirring fact as to catch and hold the youthful reader and at the same time to draw him close to the Master in his loving purpose to save the world." They arrived at the Bible institutes utterly in awe of missionaries themselves. Speaking of a classroom visit by venerable missionary A. B. Simpson, but, in the overheated imagination of the young author, sounding more like a theophany, a student recorded, "One feels that he knows every thought and desire of the most wayward heart, yet his face and voice betray the fact that he has been caught up into the third Heaven and has seen things unlawful to utter. He comes to our level, but brings the glory of the Presence with him."[18]

It was this *spiritual* quality, in fact, that the faith missions most looked for in recruits, and, in their symbiotic relationship with the Bible institutes, counted on their sister organizations to provide. The manual of the Africa Inland Mission (AIM) recorded that "members of the Mission are accepted because of their desire and ability to win souls above all other requisites, and all else is secondary." Founded half a century later in 1942, the New Tribes Mission stated that it would "encourage, rather than discourage, potential candidates for foreign missionary service. They shall be chosen, not necessarily on scholastic acquirements, but upon evidence that they have a consistent passion for souls." The faith missions recognized that this "passion for souls" was a passion best fostered in a Bible institute. AIM required even Bible college graduates with a Bible major to attend at least one year at a Bible institute because of the "disciplining in the Christian life which is given in a Bible Institute beyond that that is secured in most colleges." The mission held so strictly to this policy that it endured a feud of several years' duration between Ralph Davis, AIM general secretary, and the fundamentalist patriarch Bob Jones, who was outraged that a graduate of Bob Jones College had been turned down until he obtained further training at a Bible institute. Jones threatened to send no more graduates to AIM unless the policy was changed. Jones declared AIM's policy a "waste of time" and therefore a "sin." "[W]e cannot encourage a sin when we know it is a sin," he groused to Davis. The mediation of Harry Ironside, pastor of Moody Church in Chicago, who served on both boards, was eventually required to resolve the dispute.[19]

Diplomas issued by the Bible institutes frequently carried the words "approved Christian character." The president of MBI assured an audience in Boston, "The words have come to carry a large degree of assurance that the person commended by them is able to practice the kind of Christian life he preaches, that he is able to live and work with other Christians, that he can bear the difficult things of life as a real Christian." To ensure the maintenance of this high standard, MBI officials annually took the school's spiritual pulse. The dean of education reported that the year 1919–1920 had been only average spiritually, but, he dryly understated, "[I]t is to be kept in mind that this average is high."[20]

The second reason faith mission leaders embraced Bible institute education was that the rigor and length of college and seminary education represented too great a risk for too little reward. A. T. Pierson remarked that long years in academia "not infrequently leave candidates with a chronic chill." Spiritual zeal could more easily be kept at a fever pitch if candidates were always just around the corner from the foreign field. At any rate, the desperate need for the gospel overseas precluded a selfish acquiring of useless knowledge at home. C. T. Studd, of the Heart of Africa Mission, argued that men wasted their time "clogging their heart and brains" with education while the "children of Africa" died "without God and without hope." Years of college and seminary were not required to tell the simple gospel story to lost souls. "Why confuse your brains by a serious and protracted study of the intricacies and contradictions of modern theology in order to be able to tell the story of Christ . . . in the simplest possible way?" Studd asked. Many times the missions were in such a hurry to get candidates to the field that the recruits were not even allowed to finish the two-year Bible institute course. Robert Ekvall enrolled at Nyack Bible Institute in the missions course, but since his mission was "in an awful hurry," he had to limit his training to one year. The director of the missions course at MBI complained, "The fact that these boards do not require graduation tends to make students take the shortest possible course acceptable to the board."[21]

It required money, however, to flood the foreign field with such eager, dedicated, but lightly educated recruits. Here faith mission leaders came up with an astonishingly quirky, audacious, counterintuitive, yet in some ways logically coherent solution. In short, they determined not to worry about money. They would, quite simply, send recruits overseas and let the Creator of all things concern himself with their sustenance. Hence the name "faith missions."

When Andrew Walls, the dean of the study of missions, dryly observed that "American religious culture had no *inhibitions* about money," he voiced a common criticism from overseas of American approaches to the funding of religious enterprise. Indeed, Christians from other cultures are often overwhelmed by the American religionist's devotion to sound business practice; to his judgment of a project's success through the tabulation of baptisms, converts, and services held; and to her instinctive attempt to solve problems with barrels full of omnipresent dollars.[22] However, Walls's comment is only partly true, especially when one considers that one could hardly find a group of Americans more conflicted about money than the early leaders of the faith missions, the missions that by and large dominated the missions enterprise in the twentieth century.

It is no accident that the faith missions blossomed at the same time that the traditional mission boards were turning over their fund-raising to professionals and embarking on what Valentin Rabe called "the use of unprecedented energy and innovations in fund raising," including "colossal denominational fund drives." John Mott, for example, preferred to raise funds from wealthy businessmen rather than trying to "nickel and dime it" with the average believer. Early on, even A. T. Pierson proposed that while "the supernatural basis for the successful evangelization of the world was the presence of Christ and the Great Commission, . . . the natural basis consisted of three great elements, 'Men, Money and Methods.'"[23] Such professional techniques were designed to stimulate interest in missions during a period when denominational leaders worried that the attention of the Christian public might be flagging.

Faith missions, although not specifically founded for this reason, gained a hearing at least partly because of a reaction against the bureaucratization of the boards, the denominations, the YMCA, and the Student Volunteer Movement. Many pious evangelicals were not particularly overjoyed to see the "cult of efficiency" make inroads into Christian organizations. For evangelicals, faithfulness to a soon-returning Lord was more important than any grand payoff promised by business methods—methods that smacked, at any rate, of the world's techniques. In this atmosphere it did not take long for the faith method to become a test of spirituality as the struggle with the boards became bitter, and business methods were portrayed as the natural and corrosive result of liberal theology. Pierson himself began to believe that pure missions should only accept "consecrated" money—that is, funds from true believers. Funds raised from wealthy businessmen seemed tainted, as their cash might have been gained by corrupt methods. Appeals to the rich, Pierson argued, "discount our faith, dishonor our Lord, and humiliate the Church; while they inflate the rich with self-righteous conceit and complacence as patrons of the cause of God."[24]

The roots of the faith method in Christian work go all the way back to the New Testament. Christ once sent out missionary teams, telling them not to take any money with them. They were to trust that they would be aided by those to whom they ministered (Matthew 10). Throughout the history of the church, mendicant friars traveled as missionaries, relying on the alms of the faithful for their support. The specific tradition of faith missions within evangelicalism, however, can be traced directly to George Müller and J. Hudson Taylor, the two men most responsible for popularizing faith methods.

George Müller was profoundly influenced by Anthony Norris Groves, a high churchman who, after an intensive study of the Bible, decided that Scripture alone was sufficient for spiritual growth, and that Christ was speaking literal truth when he said, "Sell all you have" (Luke 12:33), and, "Lay not up for yourselves treasures on earth" (Matthew 6:19). Groves promoted his views in a tract titled "Christian Devotedness." He went on to become one of the founding members of the Plymouth Brethren. Influenced by Groves, Müller joined the Brethren and decided to seek a "higher standard of devotedness." He left the London Society for Promoting Christianity among the Jews because he felt he should be guided by God alone in his activities and not by men. He then gave up his regular salary as a minister because it was based on pew rents. He lived on free-will offerings alone, refusing to discuss his needs with anyone.[25] Eventually, of course, Müller became justly famous for his large orphanages, which he ran on the faith basis. He refused to ask for financial support, relying on God to prompt Christians to give to his ministry. The stories of miraculous deliveries of food as the hungry orphans sat around an empty dinner table still resonate in the evangelical community.

Hudson Taylor's decision to conduct Christian ministry on the faith basis seems to have been a very personal decision stemming from a literal interpretation of Scripture. "I was led to feel that the [biblical] promises were very real," he recorded, "and that prayer was a sober matter-of-fact transacting business with God." A premillennialist, he decided to live as if Christ might return tomorrow. He gave away unneeded possessions and lived frugally. Determined to eventually become a missionary who lived by faith, Taylor began his now-famous "exercises" to strengthen his faith. He refused to remind his forgetful employer to pay his salary, enduring whatever hardship ensued with no complaint, simply praying and trusting God to jog the elderly doctor's memory. For Taylor, difficult circumstances led to more frequent prayer, which in turn resulted in a more profound relationship with God. "Not infrequently our God brings His people into difficulties on purpose that they may come to know Him as they could not otherwise do," he reasoned. "Are we not told to seek first the kingdom of God—not means to advance it—and that all these things shall be added to us? . . . I saw that the apostolic plan was not to raise ways and means, but to go and do the work, trusting in His sure Word."[26]

When Taylor founded his enormously influential China Inland Mission, he chose to operate it on the same basis. Mission policy stated that support would come only through the "freewill offerings of God's people." No member of the mission was "authorized to solicit funds on his own behalf or that of the Fellowship, and no announcement of material needs is authorized." Only God could be addressed openly about financial concerns, although missionaries were permitted to honestly answer direct questions about financial needs. The mission also refused to go into debt, as to do so indicated a lack of faith in God's eventual supply. Taylor continued to appeal for new missionaries regardless of whether funds were on hand for their support. Missionaries simply traveled to China trusting that God would supply their personal needs as well as those of the mission. Money received by the mission was shared by all equally, but this did not preclude individual gifts going directly to designated missionaries. Despite this seeming impractical policy, the CIM grew at a tremendous rate and became one of the most influential missions in the world by the end of the nineteenth century.[27]

Taylor and other faith mission pioneers saw the faith method as a way of ceding complete control of the enterprise to God himself, thus ensuring that God, not man, would receive the praise for any accomplishment. The faith basis of operation increased the spirituality of Christian workers who were forced to spend long hours on their knees looking to God alone for their basic provisions. When coupled with the drift of the denominational boards away from a singular focus on evangelism, their reliance on the gifts of possibly unregenerate church members (one supposes only genuinely converted people would contribute to a faith mission), their willingness to go into debt if need be to support missionaries, and their unwillingness to enter new fields unless financially viable, faith mission pioneers were able to argue that their missions, as Joel Carpenter reminded us, "made more efficient use of funds, cultivated greater spirituality among their missionaries, and were more aggressively evangelistic than the denominational mission societies."[28]

George Müller and Hudson Taylor built tremendously successful organizations while living out their at times harrowing vision. Müller's orphanages and Taylor's China Inland Mission were very high profile ministries within the evangelical world in the late nineteenth and early twentieth centuries. When faith mission leaders faced a question of missionary practice, they almost invariably asked, "What would the China Inland Mission do?" The council of the Central American Mission questioned CIM leaders about virtually every problem of significance that they faced. At times people on both sides of an issue supported their argument by referencing either a personal letter or public document of the CIM.

C. I. Scofield, renowned Bible teacher and author of the "guidebook to dispensationalism," the *Scofield Reference Bible,* first met Hudson Taylor at the Niagara Bible Conference. His friendship with Taylor aroused his interest in missions, and he began a scriptural study of the topic. He decided that Christ himself laid out a "Divine plan [for] missions" in Acts 1:8 when he instructed his disciples to be his witnesses in Jerusalem, then Judea and Samaria, then into the remote parts of the earth. Scofield noted that Christ's plan "contemplates the moving out by concentric circles from strategic centers, and—by implication at least—forbids the overpassing of unevangelized regions." While American churches, clearly in Scofield's mind the strategic center, had been sending missionaries to the remote parts of the earth, they had "strangely neglected [the] tempting and destitute field at their very doors." For Scofield, this field next door was Central America. Like most faith mission founders, he had no desire to multiply missionary agencies, but as he reported in the *Missionary Review of the World,* "[C]onference with some of the larger denominational boards made it evident that with the burdens already pressing upon them, they could give us no definite hope of an adequate Gospel invasion of this land." Consequently, in 1888 he shared his concern with Luther Rees, a Christian businessman and friend. On November 14, 1890, Scofield, Rees, and several other Dallas-area businessmen founded the Central American Mission. Rees was the mission's first president. Scofield was general secretary. Judge D. H. Scott soon joined as treasurer and conducted much of the mission business out of his office in Paris, Texas. The mission was interdenominational. It did not seek to "reproduce on mission grounds the divisions of Protestantism." The mission would focus its energy on evangelism, not education. Scofield believed that "evangelization of the world, not its civilization, is the true work of the church." It was, of course, a faith work. No salaries would be paid. There would be no personal or public solicitation of money, nor, in fact, of missionaries. In this way it was hoped that the CAM would not "invade the constituencies of the boards."[29]

Like many of his contemporary mission leaders, Scofield had an ambivalent view of U.S. economic power and influence in the world. He welcomed the access provided by American influence and transportation technology even as he dreaded the type of Americans that such influence and technology inevitably brought in their wake. He worried that because of the enormous resources of the region and its closeness to the United States, railroads would soon expand throughout the republics, bringing on their tracks a "sure influx of irreligious wealth-seekers." To Scofield, this presented a call for "the immediate evangelization of the country. The missionary should for once go before the trader."[30]

In 1890 the call went out for recruits to evangelize the "extremely degraded" Indian tribes. In an attempt to turn the eyes of the evangelical public from the more popular missionary destinations of China, India, and Africa, Scofield promised his readers, "Africa itself holds no more absolute heathen than these at our very threshold."[31] While the CAM was never able to replace the China Inland or the Africa Inland Missions in the eyes of young evangelicals, a few responses trickled in. In February 1891 the CAM's first missionaries, the McConnells, with their three small children, sailed for Costa Rica. They had no promised support and no knowledge of the land, the people, or the language, but they shared with all early faith missionaries an unquestioning faith in God and a passionate commitment to the cause of world evangelism.

The hair-raising experiences of the early faith missionaries and the enormity of the body count piled up over the years can make these ventures seem reckless, perhaps even criminally negligent, today. "Unacceptable losses" would no doubt be the phrase used by military commanders. Perhaps, however, such ventures suggest the potential that the heady mixture of evangelical spirituality and a Victorian emphasis on masculine endeavor and muscular Christianity had to inspire evangelicals to extraordinary effort and service. Evangelical teaching, especially that emanating from traveling Keswick evangelists, emphasized that spiritual power, once obtained from God through the baptism in the Holy Spirit, was to be utilized in total submission and active service, the yin and yang, the feminine and masculine, of potent spirituality. Missions represented the ultimate in both submission to God's will and service. In addition, living by faith could be a rather strenuous, even dangerous, life. As faith mission ideals became part of the whole package of the so-called higher Christian life, living by faith became a way of competing at the highest level of Christian experience. Such rugged self-denial and at times seemingly suicidal endeavor in the name of God resonated with Victorian culture in the same way as the exploits of Teddy Roosevelt, or of polar explorers who perished in handfuls in their attempts to reap glory atop the world. When the Oriental Missionary Society proclaimed they gave "no guarantee but God," they could count on appealing to young evangelicals who were seeking elite service.[32]

By the end of the first decade of CAM's existence, seventeen missionaries had departed the United States for Central America. Five had gained only a few words of Spanish before their fellow missionaries dug yet another hole in the mud as the final resting place for bodies yellowed and emaciated from disease, and yet another letter made its way by boat to Paris, Texas, telling of a "good and faithful servant" who had "gone to their eternal reward." Inevitably the letter boasted of the "sustaining faith" that had been "granted" to the surviving spouse or parent, and of their commitment to soldier on. The following chain of death and the inspiration it brought in its wake was typical of faith missionary activity around the world before the discovery of drugs such as quinine and penicillin: Clarence Wilbur, twenty-six years old and in country for sixteen months, dies of yellow fever. He is nursed by Laura Dillon in his illness. Six days after his death, she follows him to the grave, having contracted the disease while nursing him. Her husband, H. C. Dillon, wracked with grief, takes his two motherless children back home. While there he meets Albert Bishop, who is so stirred by Dillon's story that he quits his successful business and heads for Central America with his family. Dillon returns to Central America and conducts a pioneering survey, recording detailed information about the numerous tribes of Indians. At the conclusion of his survey he marries Margaret Neely. They have been married just a matter of months when Dillon dies at thirty-three years of age in a remote village in Honduras. Mrs. Dillon receives a letter from home with a check to finance her return. She returns the check and spends the rest of her life in the village where her husband died, eventually living to see hundreds of converts to Protestantism.

Alongside Margaret Dillon, the remnants of the seventeen CAM missionaries scattered themselves in a thin line across the Central American republics, hanging on in frequently desperate physical circumstances by sheer grit, commitment, and faith. By 1914, when Townsend entered college, the CAM supported twenty-seven missionaries on a total annual income of $10,800. No one was left in Costa Rica. William McConnell, the initial CAM pioneer, was dead of tuberculosis. Others had returned home sick. A few returned defeated, never able to adjust to their new lives. Guatemala was now the largest CAM field. It was occupied by five couples, including the Bishops, and one single woman. Two couples lived in El Salvador, and one couple and a single woman worked in Nicaragua. Two single ladies, Margaret Dillon and Laura Nelson (who lived and worked alone for nineteen years without returning home for furlough), were the entire CAM presence in Honduras. But despite fierce opposition from the Catholic Church, a few converts began to organize themselves into Protestant churches. Thirty indigenous churches with a combined membership of two thousand people affiliated with the mission.[33]

The CAM was not the only faith mission with such a mixed legacy of death and success. To read through the collection of nineteenth-century letters from China Inland Mission personnel now stored at the Billy Graham Center Archives in Wheaton, Illinois, is to be confronted with a litany of disease and death. It often seems to the reader as if the primary goal of each letter is to update the home office on who had died, who was sick, and to beg for more and stronger recruits. A majority of early missionaries to the Sudan either died or returned home as invalids, or simply from discouragement, within a matter of weeks or months. Yet Rowland Bingham doggedly recruited new workers until his fledgling mission managed to scratch out a few ongoing stations in the wilderness. The death of missionaries was such a common occurrence that the frugal Nazarene board once sent a letter to two of its sick missionaries, saying that since the members of the board "presume[d] you w[ould] already be dead" by the time the letter arrived, they would not send any salaries for that month. The missionaries recovered, although they probably went hungry.[34]

For many Victorian evangelicals, however, death and disease were badges of honor, not tokens of defeat. As A. T. Pierson passionately argued in the council of the Africa Inland Mission when they considered giving up because their entire first shipment of sixteen missionaries either died or quit, "Gentlemen, the hallmark of God on any work is death. God has given us that hallmark. Now is the time to go forward." Such sentiment was doubtlessly easier to conjure by home councils than by missionaries on the field. Karl Hummel, who served for many years in Central America before becoming general secretary of the CAM in the mid-1920s, reflected the judgment of a man with field experience when he admitted, "[M]en go the limit for dollars, and . . . we ought not be afraid to 'burn out' for God. It is a problem, [however], to know where to draw the line."[35]

When the Townsends first picked up their pens to fill out an application to the Central American Mission, they were immediately faced with the challenging reality of faith mission life. Practically the first question on the application read, "Do you understand that you are to trust the Lord for the supply of all your needs, and not rely upon the C.A.M. or any other human agency?" The mission wanted applicants to understand immediately the distinction between it and the traditional boards: the CAM would guarantee no salary. But immediately after that stark message, the candidate was seemingly assured that the faith basis truly worked. The application stated that the CAM "confidently expects to be enabled to support all who go out in its fellowship." Such a statement could not help but alleviate any anxiety the prospective missionary felt, at least so long as getting a regular paycheck ranked higher on their list of anxieties than dying of yellow fever. When a well-qualified female candidate pressed for more assurance that she would be supported from the mission's general fund, she was told that "the Mission could not promise full support from the General Fund, but that if she [was] trusting God for her support and willing to share, as the other Missionaries [did], what He sends," the mission saw no reason why she should not proceed to Costa Rica. As R. D. Smith argued, "If we are a Faith Mission . . . it seems to me that it would be lack of faith to refuse to send out workers who have . . . met our requirements." At least one faith board, the Inland South America Missionary Union, required candidates to have their first year's support either promised or in hand before they sailed. But for Smith and other faith mission pioneers, even that concession seemed no more "the part of faith than the methods usually followed by the denominational boards." "I am not exercising faith," Smith groused, "if I have a year's supply in hand." During months when funds were tight, however, he was willing to inform candidates that it might be some time before the mission could fund their passage. But even that concession bothered him. He worried that such a statement was "an admission of failure (lack of faith)" on the mission's part.[36]

The missions hoped, of course, that the missionary's friends and home church would undertake their support. While the missionary was not permitted to directly solicit such support, the announcement of her plans would be an occasion of some excitement among her friends and family. Her pastor could also choose to announce her departure from the pulpit. He might take up a one-time collection for her, or even commit a portion of the church mission budget toward her monthly support. The fact remained, however, that none of this was required of a new missionary. Few did anything remotely resembling the "deputation" tours, or "partnership development," familiar to evangelical missionaries today. Raising money has never been a pleasant prospect for missionaries, and it was much easier to simply rely on the mission to procure the necessary funds rather than do the work required to earn their own way. Few missionaries went out with anything remotely resembling even the promise of full support. For example, at one CAM mission station in 1933, three single women and one married couple had no regular monthly income from personal supporters. All of their money came from the mission's general fund. Three other single women and one married couple earned anywhere from fifteen to seventy-five dollars per month from personal supporters.[37] Faith missionaries nevertheless departed in high spirits, relying explicitly on God and implicitly on the mission council to keep them in food and clothes. Few were prepared for the sort of privation that awaited them on the field, even as many learned to bear up under it, if not endure it proudly, as a sign of God's special testing.

Where, then, did the money come from? Faith mission pioneers argued that funds were prayed in, arriving as God laid it upon the heart of a faithful believer to send the mission a check. Mission leaders implicitly recognized from the beginning that God's leading tended to be more effective when undergirded by a sound publicity department. They bitterly resisted acknowledging this simple fact in any explicit way, however, feeling that to do so would somehow invalidate their entire enterprise.

Despite their reluctance, the missions managed to get the word out about their ministries. Deputation was a fact of mission life, even if not explicitly required of individual missionaries. In general the missions tried to raise awareness about the mission as a whole rather than promote individual missionaries. They sent representatives to the mission rallies at Moody Church, Church of the Open Door in Los Angeles, and other large evangelical mega-churches. The mission secretary spoke at churches as often as funds permitted the travel. Extensive deputation trips were arranged for furloughed missionaries, especially for the most charismatic ones, despite the fact that this granted those already most likely to be well supported a platform to reach still more potential personal donors.

The rules were clear for the conduct of such meetings. Speakers could not openly solicit funds or even directly mention needs. They were simply to report on the ministry and close with a spiritual challenge of some sort. Pastors and the evangelical public understood the rules, of course, and could often be counted on to take an offering or quietly slip a ten-dollar bill into the missionary's pocket. Skilled fund-raisers knew how to work within the rules, skillfully showing but not telling, letting the prospective donors hear the urging of God behind the presentation of need. Leonard Livingston (L. L.) Legters, who later became Townsend's chief publicist and fund-raiser, once sent a wealthy woman to observe Townsend's work in Guatemala. He sent ahead strict instructions: "You warn every missionary of the Central American Mission, telling them not to in any way hint to her about where to put money, because if they do she will shut up like a clam. Just let her see all the needs, but do not in any way hint that there is a money need for these things." Legters fumed to Townsend that someone had ruined another of his projects by asking this woman directly for money, which "queered everything."[38] Donors wanted to feel they were responding to God, not to a human appeal. After the touring missionary used whatever money he needed to get to his next appointment, he sent the rest to the home office. Often he did little better than break even. Most of the money received from such publicity trips was placed in a general fund, from which every missionary drew his or her allotted quota, although gifts from family, friends, and home churches were channeled to the designated missionary. In theory, everyone prospered or suffered equally. In fact, because missionaries had varying degrees of personal support, the disparity in income between missionaries was often wide, which created a great deal of stress for all involved.

The *Central American Bulletin,* with a circulation of about thirty-five hundred when Townsend joined the mission, was CAM's primary ongoing means of publicity. An important part of every deputation trip was the securing of new addresses for the *Bulletin.* New recruits also chipped in the addresses of their family, friends, and home church. Each gift to the mission was followed up with a receipt and a *Bulletin* subscription. Every mission had such a journal, and faith rules applied here as well, although even the strictest faith missions found carefully worded ways to indicate their needs in print. It was important to ask for prayer that the need be met rather than to directly ask for the funds. "We would ask you to join us in prayer about getting a horse and buggy," Elvira Townsend wrote. "This would make it so much easier for us to visit our different Indian congregations." Giving directly could also be mentioned if the request was made indirectly. An invocation, for example, at the end of an article might say, "May God call some of you to go, others to give, and all to pray." If the editor was republishing an article from another source, he might get away with a more blatant suggestion. An editorial introduction to the article might read, "We found this small piece to be inspirational. We hope you agree." The article, titled, "How Much Shall I Give This Year to Missions?" suggested a series of New Year's resolutions, including the following—"Resolved: I do believe in greatly increasing the present number of our missionaries; therefore I will increase my former offerings to missionary work."[39]

A letter from R. D. Smith, the most conservative CAM council member, demonstrates how even those most fervently devoted to faith principles managed to make their needs known. Smith sent the letter to his personal constituency. The bracketed sentences indicate how his constituency might have heard the letter, how evangelicals who were familiar with the life of faith would have read the pitch between the lines.

> As you know, I have felt for a long time the Lord was calling me to go to South America. [I have been reminding you regularly of this call, and

> have only been waiting for God's timing, which will be indicated by the reception of your gifts designated for my trip.] Not until this year had any funds ever been provided for such a trip, but this year there have been received a number of personal gifts, some of them ear-marked "for the trip to South America." [Thank you for catching on.] I have not sufficient yet to make the entire trip . . . but I am quite confident that the Lord will not send His servant out and allow him to lack for any good thing. [I am departing in faith, trusting that you won't leave me hanging in Brazil.] I arose yesterday morning with the full assurance in my . . . heart about it, and all day long the Holy Spirit brought confirming Scriptures to my mind. [If you send in your gifts now, you can be assured you are doing the Lord's work and that your prompting was from the Spirit of God himself.] God has confirmed the leadings of His Holy Spirit to me, by solid Scripture and material gifts. It is such a comfort to know that the Lord Himself orders our path. [You can send your gifts with confidence, knowing that all the right procedures have been followed to ascertain God's will.] I especially want your help in prayer that I may be a blessing to the lonely, tired laborers for Christ. [Your money is being used in a great cause, the encouragement of missionaries.][40]

Although Townsend was far more educated than most faith missionaries and had not attended a Bible institute to acquire the requisite piety, he eagerly adopted faith mission principles, even if he never quite adapted to their practices. Even before joining the CAM, he sold off his life insurance, saying, "I don't like the principle of life insurance for a missionary, for the Lord has promised to take care of us and I don't doubt it for a moment." He learned to anticipate the leading of God by interpreting the divine financial weather vane—"Where God leads, there God feeds." Or as he put it in a letter to a donor, "When [God] wants us to make an advance, He will send money to do it." And then the logical, if disconcerting, flipside: "If He wants us to go more slowly, He will keep back the funds. We pray as definitely that God will keep back contributions for which His time has not come yet as we pray that He will send sufficient for our daily needs." While this may be difficult for readers today to believe, it was, as Townsend noted, "the policy of the CAM," and he tried to practice it. "We want entire dependence on God," he wrote, "and not on anyone's bank account." Of course, this was said to a donor who had just sent him fifteen hundred dollars. In a roundabout way, Townsend was paying her a high honor, letting her know that she had been providentially used of God in supporting whatever advance Townsend had in mind at the time.[41]

The divine financial weather vane had other practical uses. When the missionaries pushed for the purchase of a mission home to be used by furloughed missionaries, a member of the council wrote, "I believe that it would be wise for us to unitedly look to the Lord for a Mission home whenever He would have it, and He may lay it upon the heart of someone to provide a home whenever it is needed." The problem was that it was needed now, but nobody was willing to go out and raise funds for it. The financial weather vane allowed leaders to piously shelve projects that they were not enthusiastic about. As R. D. Smith opined, "These principles often keep God's servants from incurring expenses which He has not authorized, and keeps from that subtle danger common to all, of wanting enlargement, when the Lord would have us small."[42]

Although Townsend would not have expressed it this way, from the very beginning he had a problem with such faith methods. He had no intention of remaining small. With the needs so obvious and so great, he could not conceive of a God who intended anything but "enlargement." Furthermore, as much as he loved prayer, praying and waiting was not a favorite combination of activities for Townsend. Praying and twisting arms, now that might accomplish something.

Still, Townsend began his tenure with the CAM praying and making do with very little, like any other faith missionary. In the early years Townsend's work was largely funded through the mission's general fund, through gifts from Moody Church in Chicago (Elvira's home church) and Church of the Open Door in Los Angeles (which Townsend, realizing the importance of a large home church, joined in 1921), and through gifts from family and friends. They lived initially on about one hundred dollars a month.

At the end of 1919 Townsend and Díaz's school for the children of Indian believers completed its first term. Although the government examiner arrived drunk and demanded more brandy before he would examine the children, the military commander of the district ordered him to proceed. Before they left, the commission "praised the children highly." A number had learned to read, and all could quote Bible verses and sing hymns. They also displayed handmade baskets and handkerchiefs.[43]

Townsend was already scheming about the possibilities of Bible translation. He believed that without the Scriptures in their indigenous languages it would never be possible to "thoroughly evangelize" the Indians. Very early in 1919, before joining the CAM or marrying Elvira, Townsend had begun to study the Cakchiquel language. "It is going to be very difficult," he explained to his parents, "as it is not written and even the more intelligent Indians can not explain the grammar. I just learn expressions and when I get enough of them, I'll be able to figure out the grammatical rules." He figured it would require a year of "hard study" before he could make himself understood in any meaningful way.[44] When Elvira joined him in the project, she was more candid. "Do pray that we may quickly learn this awful language," she complained to Judge Scott.

Despite the success of the work in Antigua, Townsend was restless. He longed to live "right amongst our Indians," as he put it. Antigua was predominantly a *ladino* town. To immerse himself in the life of the Cakchiquels and learn their language, he knew he would have to move to the Indian town of San Antonio, a community with a reputation for being infested with malaria. To make matters more difficult, after centuries of exploitation the Indians were reluctant to sell property to anyone, least of all a gringo. It took Townsend the better part of half a year, but eventually he secured a small plot of land in the town. In January 1920 work began on a cornstalk hut on a piece of property with no running water. The Townsends built their future home for about one hundred dollars. "We don't ask for sympathy," Elvira wrote. "It's a privilege, and we are so glad that we are called to service among the Indians. We believe the Lord will take care of us."[45]

Townsend's eagerness to live and work with Indians would seem to fall naturally within the goals of the Central American Mission. After all, when C. I. Scofield initially founded the CAM, he did so out of a feeling of "peculiar responsibility" for the "aborigines." "The motive for this can scarcely require statement," Scofield argued. "It was deeply felt that the descendants of the interesting and lovable people who had received with guileless hospitality the discoverers whose advice was to bring to them centuries of unspeakable outrage, should be in a very especial manner the objects of solicitude to Christians laboring in those regions." Scofield found, however, that there was little information available about the Indians of Central America. "They entered so little into the political and economic life of the countries that even the respective governments felt but a languid interest in them," he complained.[46]

When Robert Arthington, a wealthy Englishman and "well-known friend of missions," offered to fund an expedition to gather information about Central American Indians, CAM missionary H. C. Dillon accepted the challenge. Between 1894 and 1896 Dillon spent more than ten thousand dollars of Arthington's money, traveling 4,872 miles—2,135 by rail and steamboat, 667 by sailboat, 210 by dugout canoe, 690 on the back of a mule, and 1,070 on foot. He carefully recorded the location and size of each tribe, as well as ethnographic impressions. Of the Guatemala Indians he wrote, "They are not very intelli-

7. Townsends' cornstalk house, 1923. Tomasa, Díaz's daughter, is in foreground. Courtesy Townsend Archives.

gent. Largely due, I think, to the fact that they carry such great loads on their heads and are kept as slaves." He was careful to make observations about Indian religious practice. "All are called Catholic, but in the main they have no idea of what it is," he reported. Dillon felt they had more faith in their images than in the priests, who "taxed [their] every movement in the Church . . . [and] encourage[d] drink and discourage[d] schools."[47]

After the expedition, Scofield proudly announced that the CAM could now send missionaries "direct . . . to any tribe," and could "inform such missionary as to their numbers, habits, language, degree of civilization, religion, and disposition toward white men . . . also the best route of travel . . . the prevalent characteristic diseases . . . what clothing and supplies should be carried . . . and the expense . . . of the journey and of support on the field." After a brief ethnographic description of each tribe, and after complaining of the "bestial whites" who taught the Indians "unspeakable vices," he wrote until it became a refrain, "There are . . . no missionaries among them. Who will go?"[48]

Nevertheless, despite the CAM's professed interest, it could be responsibly stated, as the Pioneer Mission Agency (PMA) later did, that by 1920 "the evangelization of the Indian in Latin America was largely a dormant matter." The statement requires several qualifications, however. First, the PMA was a Protestant organization, so it ignored Catholic efforts. Second, the PMA was greatly influenced by Cameron Townsend, for whom only indigenous-language work counted as true evangelization. When the PMA reported that they found only one mission station for the fourteen million Indians in Mexico, Guatemala, Salvador, and Honduras where "the Gospel was being taught to the Indians by a foreign missionary in their own tongue," the station to which they referred was Townsend's San Antonio. In the Amazon watershed the PMA found no indigenous-language work at all.[49]

Despite these qualifications, the PMA was essentially correct. The need to learn difficult indigenous languages had long been the primary roadblock to missionary work with Indians. When Scofield reported, "The language everywhere spoken is Spanish," he perpetuated an egregious misunderstanding. In actuality few of the Indians understood Spanish well at all. Unfortunately, few missionaries were willing to spend the time to learn their language, and fewer missions were willing to support such work even if willing missionaries were found. According to Virginia Garrard-Burnett, most missions in Guatemala declined to work in Indian languages because "of a general perception abroad that indigenous idioms were simple 'dialects' rather than true languages capable of conveying complex ideas and thought. From this perspective, to lend legitimacy to the unwritten indigenous vernacular through codification and use seemed . . . to border on the absurd." A Presbyterian missionary who, in 1913, tried to work with a Quiché-speaking congregation, was so opposed by his mission board that he resigned and accused his mission of being "unfriendly to the cause of the race." Townsend reported in 1921 that of the forty missionaries working in Guatemala only he and Elvira were ministering full-time in an Indian language. When Edward Haymaker, dean of the Presbyterian mission in Guatemala (he had been there since 1887), visited the Townsends' work in 1920, he was extremely enthusiastic. "If my life were to live over again . . . I should without hesitation devote myself to the Indians," he told Townsend. He indicated that he had "pled" with his board to start such a work, but to no avail. Haymaker noted that indigenous-language work was strategically smart, because Indians made up the largest segment of Guatemala's population. Besides, such work was simply the Christian thing to do. "Why should we be so ready to contribute and work for the evangelization of their cruel oppressors," Haymaker argued, "and have no word, no funds, no prayers, for the innocent helpless and cruelly wronged victims of the armed invasion and spoilation that marked their conquest in the 16th century?" He repeated Townsend's view that the Indians were generally of better character than *ladinos;* once converted, they stayed converted. He concluded, "I believe the work you are now getting started will be a veritable debacle of evangelism within a few years."[50]

The CAM position was that the most efficient way to evangelize Indians was through the conversion and subsequent training of Indians who knew Spanish. Garrard-Burnett argues that the CAM's reluctance to establish separate Indian work "perhaps reflects the fact that the missionaries, like many Guatemalans in the same period, considered 'Indianness' to be less an ethnic identity than a problematic social condition for which they had a remedy." The remedy was simply to assimilate the Indian population into the Spanish, a solution that resonated well with the agenda of most Latin American countries. There had long been laws on the books in Guatemala forbidding the publication of any texts in indigenous languages, or the use of Mayan tongues in schools or at public gatherings. Guatemalan *indigenismo* theorists believed that the only way to improve the lot of Indians was to see them absorbed culturally and even physically into *ladino* society.[51]

There are several reasons why Townsend, of all the missionaries in Central America, became passionately committed to Indian ministry despite the prevailing ideologies. We have already mentioned the time he spent during his first and most formative year in Guatemala with Francisco Díaz, his Cakchiquel traveling companion. As both a Protestant and an educated Spanish speaker, Díaz was well placed to articulate the benefits for indigenous groups of an education and Protestantism. As Townsend later recorded, Francisco "constantly spoke to me of his people and their hopeless condition, so that through him came the call of God to me to go and labor among them." Second, Townsend was single when he first arrived in Guatemala, which allowed him to fully immerse himself in Indian culture. He ate, slept, traveled, and worked intimately with them. Until he married Elvira, he spent very little of his time in Guatemala with Westerners at all. In so doing he was able to at least partially overcome his own prejudices and the stereotypes fed him by other expatriates, missionaries, and *ladinos.* "They are looked down upon by the Spanish speaking race as immoral and brutish and are treated accordingly," he reported, "but we consider them to be one of the great natural resources of the country." Third, Townsend was inspired by his college study of Booker T. Washington to believe that he could accomplish something similar with another downtrodden and enslaved people. Fourth, Townsend claimed to have been given special divine leading when, after praying for direction and then blindly opening Scripture and placing his finger on a passage, he alighted on Christ's parable in Luke 15 where a shepherd abandons his well-tended flock to find the one lost sheep. (The blind finger-drop technique has been indulged in by more than a few evangelicals looking for guidance over the years, but it is a technique usually admitted to only sheepishly, if admitted at all, and if unsuccessful, easily shrugged off.) Townsend's reading of the parable of the lost sheep empowered him with a sense of divine calling to the "one percent" who were overlooked by other Christian ministries. Finally, as Diane Langmore discovered in her study of missionaries in Papua, while initial reactions to foreign cultures can perhaps be predicted with some accuracy simply because of the common culture shared by the missionaries, over time people develop a unique response corresponding to "the mysteries of their own personalities."[52] Townsend reacted the way he did because he was sensitive to the people he considered his friends, and he was visionary enough to believe something could be done for them. If he succeeded, it was a tribute to his leadership abilities and sheer bullheadedness.

January 1920 found Cameron and Elvira working hard to make their little hut in San Antonio livable. Townsend was never much of a carpenter and with a total budget of $100 the going was slow. A young American working for the U.S. Agricultural Department befriended them and supplied enough corrugated iron to make a barn and a small room for their servant girl. They framed the house with rough timbers, built walls of cornstalks lashed with vines and lined with tule mats, laid on a roof of tile over bamboo cane, fashioned a ceiling of bamboo, and a floor of rough boards covered with mats. The house was divided into several rooms, a new concept for the Indians who were helping them. They moved in late in February with their cook; a lamb, four chickens, a turkey, two mules, and a calf were all either corralled or staked just outside. The newlyweds were bubbling over with good cheer. Townsend's family had sent him $170, with which they purchased a small buggy. They felt "very stylish" as their mule lugged them about town. In addition, a Christmas package had just arrived, and they giddily devoured raisins, walnuts, and candy, then brushed their teeth with new toothbrushes and "just the brand of tooth paste Elvira like[d] most." Elvira was particularly delighted that her husband's family had included some basic cosmetics, indicating that they did not think "as so many do that a missionary shouldn't use such things in her toilet, but should rather put on a long face and dress several years behind the fashions."[53]

Townsend was captivated by his new residence, as its location meant an opportunity to live more intimately with Indians. Nevertheless, it was a full year before the Indians began to trust him and his wife. The Townsends owed their eventual acceptance to a malaria epidemic that hit hard during the winter of 1920–1921. A woman in New York sent funds to purchase quinine, and Elvira visited as many as sixty homes per day, distributing medication. It was shortly after the epidemic eased that an Indian of San Antonio first addressed Townsend as "neighbor," an experience he never forgot. Only then were they permitted to buy property to erect a permanent mission station.[54]

Although Townsend was initially concerned with "the natural pride and arrogance of the San Antonio Indian which made work there difficult," he eventually decided the "arrogance" of the people was "an indication of strength of character which transferred into right channels by the Gospel would become an asset." He also thought it was a good sign that no *ladinos* were permitted to live there. He told a friend that in a town where Indians were oppressed by *ladinos,* his work would be among "semi-slaves, whereas in a purely Indian town [I] deal with men jealously defending their liberties."[55]

Sadly, as the Townsends moved into their new home, Francisco Díaz lay dying of malaria. His death was a tremendous loss to Townsend, although he appears to have said or written very little about it to anyone. He furiously soldiered on, as he would through even greater tragedies. The Townsends took in Díaz's daughter, Tomasa, who stayed with them until 1928, doing the bulk of the cooking and cleaning around the house.

Early in the summer of 1920 the Townsends vacationed for a month in Chiquimula at the mission established by the Quakers, also known as the Religious Society of Friends. Townsend was stunned by the expansive Friends compound and the extent of their ministry. The compound included "a nice commodious mission home"; a forty-student boys' school; a fifty-student girls' school (soon to be two hundred when a new building was completed); a farm; shops for woodworking, printing, and tinning; a brick kiln; a sawmill; a one-room hospital; and a site already laid out for a Bible school, a church, and a missionary rest home. All of this had been built in fourteen years. The center had been founded by two women on a twenty-dollar-per-month stipend, yet the mission's yearly income in 1920 was seventeen thousand dollars. Significantly, Townsend noted that most of the funds came "from channels other than the Friends' Board." He exulted, "How the Lord has replied to their faith! Can not as much be done for the Indians in 14 years?"[56]

Townsend was savvy enough to realize that the CAM council would see such a center as detracting from the mission's purported focus on evangelism only. After all, initially the young man had been reluctant to join the CAM for precisely this reason. Still, inspired by their visit to Chiquimula, in October 1920 the Townsends shared their vision with the council, couched, of course, as a directive from the Lord. The vision not only looked remarkably similar to that of the Friends, but it also appeared uncomfortably close to the mission centers built in the nineteenth century by denominations and boards whose methods were now beginning to be tainted by liberalism. The "center for Indian work" that the Townsends described included a home for "homeless and motherless Indian children," a "number of small, but model huts where the Indians could come to stay in times of conferences," a "Tabernacle" for services, a small school, and a library "with some reliable Indian believer in charge." The "model huts" would include shelves and other simple amenities so that Indians might be taught "how it becomes a Christian to live cleaner and neater and healthier." The Townsends longed for the San Antonio station to be a place that the "long neglected" Indians could always call "home," where "they would ever be welcome." In language she heard constantly from her husband, Elvira defended the dream: "I feel the Lord just dares us to ask big things of Him." She apologetically reassured the council that the center would be "only for His glory & honor & for the salvation of many thousands of hungering & thirsting Indians. We do not look for any big, beautiful buildings, only plain, cheap, rough, but durable little buildings, where Jesus may ever be glorified."[57]

As Townsend undoubtedly expected, the council was not thrilled with his vision; in fact, they did not initially engage the issues directly, because they could not get past his seeming endorsement of the Friends, a denomination the conservative evangelical council members did not feel predisposed to view with kindness. "I cannot tell you how much we regret their teaching and methods of work," Judge Scott grumbled, although he grudgingly concluded, "but if the Lord can endure it, I suppose we should do so cheerfully." But despite such intentions, endure it he could not, and from there his letter descended into complaints about convert stealing, an art at which he felt the Friends were especially adept. "I have not been real sure that he knows the Lord," Scott wrote of one Quaker missionary, "but he knows how to hustle for the converts of our Mission." Townsend was left struggling to defend his new friends, pointing out that they "surely know the Lord . . . tho they are far from understanding human nature." Though he regretted a few of their doctrinal quirks, he concluded, "We dearly love them and have precious communion with them."[58] A bitter realization began to dawn on the young man. The faith missions' commitment to "avoid sectarianism" and to "promote interdenominational cooperation" was only skin-deep. It was convenient rhetoric for the times, but evangelicals took their theology far too seriously to share their crayons with anyone who colored outside the lines. They were strict about that. Townsend's mistake was to put the welfare of the Indians ahead of theological punctiliousness.

Despite the council's hesitancy, the Townsends went on with their school. And to be fair to the council, they were not initially hostile to Townsend's endeavors, if perhaps made a bit uneasy by his larger dreams. Judge Scott "rejoice[d] in the opportunities . . . for reaching those people" through their school and their fledgling medical work. As long as Townsend could argue that his ministries led to evangelistic opportunities, the council, at least in 1920, was happy. Townsend could quite honestly reassure them that "we make all our efforts bend toward the evangelistic end." But for Townsend, as for many missionaries, almost any endeavor could be made to "bend toward the evangelistic end." As he wrote Judge Scott, "Of course we have a few schools and do some medical work, and some of us want to develop these two branches even more, but they are and always will be made only servants of the work of evangelization."[59]

In the summer of 1920 the Townsends spent several months in Patzum, a village with almost no Spanish speakers and where they spoke a purer Cakchiquel, in an attempt to make a serious start learning the language. They asked countless questions, recorded the answers, and then tried to deduce grammatical rules from the gathered material. Learning Cakchiquel would consume Townsend for the next decade through years of intermittent study as he struggled to grasp what he referred to as a "very orderly though highly complex grammatical structure which permits the conjugation of a single verb in a hundred thousand forms."[60]

By fall 1920 the school for the children of Indian converts had an enrollment of nineteen. The Townsends employed an Indian teacher, and she and Elvira began the fall semester waging warfare against "crawlers." The Indian girls cried pitifully as their lustrous black hair was shorn, but Elvira was not about to fight lice the Indian way, which involved a methodical barehanded hunt and the ingestion of the more sizable specimens. Visitors could be counted on to remark positively upon "seeing [the children] coming to school so neat and clean," and, rid of lice and hookworm, Elvira felt the children were better able to concentrate on their studies. Tomasa underwent a revolution in appearance. "When she came to us she was the dirtiest little creature you can imagine," Elvira boasted, but she was now "developing into a sweet, gentle little girl, neat and tidy."[61]

Most of the responsibility for classroom instruction fell on the teacher, who was half Indian and could speak the local dialect. The school opened with a kindergarten and first grade, then gradually added grades as the children progressed and the staff grew. Along with reading, writing, arithmetic, and memorizing Bible verses, the boys learned basic carpentry and basket and rope making. Elvira taught the girls to sew. An Indian woman gave them instruction in weaving. All the children worked in the garden. Before the orphanage/children's home was built, children from outlying towns were cared for in the homes of converts whenever possible. "Surely the Indian is worthy of a three to four year's schooling," Townsend argued in a promotional pamphlet. "It is our duty and privilege to help" them become better Christians and "better citizens."[62]

Townsend knew his expansive goals for the San Antonio station would require a lot more money than he and Elvira were getting through the mission and a bit of family and church support. He set to work finding creative ways to publicize his efforts. He instinctively understood that publicity went hand in hand with faith, and he was never ashamed to admit it. In the summer of 1920 he designed a leaflet on his fledgling Indian work, which the council permitted him to mail as an insert in the *Central American Bulletin.* He also sent several hundred copies to Moody Church, and dozens more to family and friends in Chicago and California, hoping they would go to work for him, publicizing and raising funds. "We feel that conditions should be brought before the people in the homeland in a larger way," he urged Judge Scott, who "heartily approve[d]" the idea, probably wishing more of his missionaries had similar initiative. That same summer Townsend designed his own letterhead, which proudly proclaimed, "THE SAN ANTONIO INDIAN MISSION STATION of the CENTRAL AMERICAN MISSION." The reader can probably guess which portion of the title was in larger type and set above the other. R. D. Smith, for one, was not pleased. To appease him, Townsend scissored off "San Antonio Indian Mission Station," so that "Central American Mission" predominated.[63]

Even as Townsend found ways to foster connections with small donors, whose regular contributions were key to a sustained income, from the beginning he demonstrated an instinctive feel for the cultivation of large donors, whose gifts made visionary projects possible. His earliest benefactor was a former Sunday school teacher of his who had come into a fair amount of money in her dotage. Mrs. Heim gave more than five thousand dollars toward construction of a clinic and boarding home in San Antonio. A notice placed in the *Bulletin* that he was looking for a nurse for his clinic put him in touch with Dr. Howard Kelly, one of the four original founders of Johns Hopkins Medical School. Kelly was a pioneer in the use of radium, a renowned surgeon and gynecologist, and author or coauthor of standard works on gynecology and urology. He was also a deeply pious evangelical, a member of the council of the China Inland Mission, who toured the country promoting Sabbatarianism, the very strict observance of the Sabbath. Kelly knew H. L. Mencken and persistently tried to convert him, inviting him to religious meetings and sending him tracts, thus thoroughly annoying the renowned curmudgeon. Kelly so exasperated Mencken on the train one day that Mencken recorded, "Three separate times I was on the point of jumping out of the train-window." He called Kelly "the most implacable Christian I ever knew, at least among educated men." One frustrated Kelly interviewer wrote that "for three hours—barring a short interruption to perform an operation—he talked to me of Christianity."[64] Kelly supported Townsend's work for the next several decades.

Elvira was having trouble keeping up with her work. She desperately needed a hernia operation in early 1920, and her doctor advised a year of rest. But there was simply too much work, and the missionary ethic tended to look askance at rest. Townsend's mother and sister visited R. D. Smith in California offering to finance their trip home "one way." They mentioned Elvira's need for an operation and claimed Cameron was "in a very bad shape" with malaria. The council, however, was under a great deal of pressure. Every letter from Central America seemed to tell of yet another broken-down missionary returning home. For every step forward they took two back. They suggested Elvira get her surgery in Guatemala at either the Presbyterian or the United Fruit Company hospital. "But we desire to leave this matter entirely in the hands of yourself and Mrs. Townsend," Smith noted, which was a bit disingenuous, as a few sentences before he had urged, "[T]he thing that is troubling us most of all is that if you leave just as the work is getting well under way, we know of no one who can take your place until it is better established." The council need not have worried, as Townsend had no intention of returning home. He wrote his parents making it clear that he did not have malaria, "at least to any noticeable extent," and that although they knew Elvira needed an operation, "as yet the Lord has not made it clear what we should do in the matter." So for now they would keep on working. Elvira bravely accompanied Cameron on his two-month sojourn in Patzum away from the semblance of a normal life she had manufactured in their cornstalk house in San Antonio. She rode mules and itinerated with him, an event that alarmed even the hardened Smith. He asked Judge Scott to caution Elvira about overdoing it. "I love their missionary spirit and am a firm believer . . . in giving one's self wholly and undeservedly to the natives but [they must take care of their health]."[65]

Despite Elvira's best efforts, she found it very difficult to adjust to Townsend's version of the missionary life. Elvira had been raised in a proper middle-class Swedish home in Chicago. She politely referred to her new husband as "Mr. Townsend" in many of her letters, and she undoubtedly expected Mr. Townsend, as much as he was able in a missionary setting, to look after her as a well-bred young woman deserved. But there was much about Guatemala and its Indians that she simply could not embrace. "Perhaps the hardest thing for me to bear up with is their awful way of living in filth and uncleanliness [as if] they are afraid of water," she once confessed. "But praise God," she hastily added, "that He shows us even through all the dirt, precious souls for whom Jesus died, and so even with all their 'live ones' we cannot help but embrace and love them." At times the reader gets the feeling that Elvira is trying to persuade herself that these things are true, that she is living up to the call to see "precious souls" through all the dirt and lice. Desperately struggling to construct the "mythic ideal" demanded of missionary prayer letters, Elvira wrote heart-touching, beautiful, and pious letters despite situations that must have been hell for her, a lifestyle that maddened her, intellectual demands that may well have been beyond her, and a husband who refused to coddle her. The signs of utter frustration are sprinkled throughout her letters, code words such as "filthy" people, "awful" language, "as hard as pulling teeth to get out of them the different forms of verbs." "I often have to get off alone as I see them in their poverty," she once wrote. All of this was couched in a language of prayer and compassion, but it is easy to see a woman struggling to cope. She was, in short, fast becoming a casualty of the faith mission method of operation. If a person felt God's call and somehow came up with the money to go overseas, who was the mission to deny that they were indeed a missionary?[66]

By the end of 1920, Townsend's devotion to Indians was beginning to take his ministry in surprising and sometimes uncomfortable directions. Initially, after Townsend organized a congregation of Indian converts in a given town, he placed them under the care of the local *ladino* pastor. When he passed that way again, however, he often found the congregation dispersed. When pressed, the Indians eventually explained that they would not attend services with the *ladinos*, because they were "laughed at" and "did not have a place there." Despite the fact that he taught the Indians "that as brothers [and] sisters in Christ, we are of one [and] the same family," he found that the ingrained prejudice on both sides was simply too difficult to overcome. "The feeling between ladino [and] Indian is very similar to that of the black and white races of the South," Elvira explained to Judge Scott. Eventually Townsend decided that to be successful he had to establish segregated Indian congregations led by Indian pastors and elders. His calling hardened; where once he worked with all, now he felt called to work exclusively with Indians, much as the apostle Paul turned away from Jews to devote his time to Gentiles. Townsend tried always to stay at the home of an Indian when traveling, despite the inevitable and more comfortable hospitality offered by the leading *ladino* converts. When *ladinos* asked him to lead a service, he politely explained that he was called to the Indians and that his time was for them. This approach began to win him the unusual confidence of the

Cakchiquels. Elvira proudly reported, "[T]he Indians are beginning to recognize us as really their own missionaries." Albert Bishop, who directed CAM's Guatemala work, appears to have initially gone along with Townsend's new method of organizing his ministry.[67]

An event of enormous importance for the development of Townsend's work among the Indians occurred in December of 1920, when Howard Dinwiddie and L. L. Legters first came to Guatemala to hold a series of meetings with Indian converts. Howard Dinwiddie carried himself with the grace of someone descended from a long line of Virginia aristocrats. His daughter later referred to him as "a real Southern gentleman." His great-great-grandfather was a brother of Robert Dinwiddie, governor of Virginia from 1751 to 1758. Dinwiddie's father was a professor at the University of Virginia, and later a Presbyterian minister and founder of two schools for boys. His mother was a poet. Howard was educated in private schools and at the University of Virginia. At twenty-one he began doing missionary work in the Virginia mountains. In 1903 he moved to New York City and worked for the Charity Organization Society, and later, from 1914 to 1917, he served as general inspector of the New York City Department of Public Charities. While in New York he became a Baptist, and in 1917 decided to devote himself exclusively to religious activities. He became secretary of the council of the Africa Inland Mission. He was one of the original eleven men who met in Philadelphia on March 31, 1917, to found the Interdenominational Foreign Missions Association. There he would have met Luther Rees of the CAM. In 1919 he moved to Philadelphia when he was appointed secretary of the American Keswick ministry, known as the Victorious Life Testimony. There he worked with Robert McQuilkin, dean of Columbia Bible College; Charles Trumbull, influential editor of the *Sunday School Times;* and J. Harvey Borton and Alice McClure Borton, who would later play significant roles in the Pioneer Mission Agency. Dinwiddie also served as co-secretary for Latin America of the Christian and Missionary Alliance and secretary of the Keswick Colony of Mercy for recovering alcoholics in New Jersey.[68] Dinwiddie was in his early forties when he first met Cameron Townsend.

L. L. Legters, Dinwiddie's polar opposite temperamentally, was born near Elmira, New York, in 1873, to a Dutch farmer known for his steely leadership as a foreman on road construction crews. In his twenties Legters attended Hope College in Michigan. He completed his education at the Dutch Reformed seminary in New Brunswick before becoming a missionary with the Dutch Reformed Church to the Indians of Oklahoma. The mission wanted the Indians to learn English, but, skeptical of this possibility, Legters learned to preach in an exaggerated sign language. The missionary who "acted out everything" became a popular figure with the Oklahoma Indians; legend has it that he conducted Geronimo's funeral at the great chief's personal request. He wrote a series of pamphlets and books about Indians, including "American Indian Stories Never Told Before," published by the Indian Mission of America. He dreamed of training Indian evangelists from tribes in the United States to go as missionaries to Indians in Latin America. Probably because of his "excessive zeal" for this project, he fought with the mission board, eventually resigning and taking up a pastorate in California.

Legters was a larger-than-life character—loud, frank, zealous, a tempestuous preacher who silenced squirming children with a glance. At his crusades he often selected surprised front-row sitters as targets for his questions and illustrations, thereby emptying the front rows on subsequent evenings of all but the most courageous devotees. He was "very outspoken" against sin, even as he battled his own hot temper and a "fondness for tobacco." One day, while hurrying to catch a train, a black man accidentally bumped into him on the sidewalk. "Like dynamite Mr. Legters' fist flew out and struck the Negro a heavy blow." As the train pulled out of the station, Legters squirmed, "deep in remorse," worrying "for hours how he could get in touch with the Negro and ask his pardon." At this point he heard of a Victorious Life conference to be held in Long Island, New York. He determined to attend "in quest of victory over the smoking habit, hot temper and worry." There, through messages by Robert McQuilkin, he "learned the secret of surrender and trust, which he expounded all the rest of his life with telling effect to defeated Christians." (Townsend later remembered that Legters immediately quit smoking and "began working on [his] temper, [which] didn't disappear immediately by a long shot but improved tremendously over the years.")[69]

Shortly thereafter Legters met Dinwiddie, who invited him to a conference in Alabama. There Legters publicly told of how he gained victory over smoking. Upon hearing his story, a businessman was inspired to give up his own habit. As a tribute, he handed Legters an envelope containing a five-hundred-dollar liberty bond, the amount he figured he would have spent on expensive cigars in the next year. Legters decided to use the money for the Indians. A few months later, the CAM missionaries in Guatemala invited the Victorious Life Testimony to send a speaker to their annual missions conference. Dinwiddie was chosen. Hearing of this, Townsend invited Dinwiddie to speak at "the first general conference to be held for Indians in Guatemala." Dinwiddie assented but informed Townsend that the man he really needed for his conference was Legters, who had experience in Indian work. Townsend cabled an invitation to Legters; the invitation was to speak at the conference and to survey the Guatemalan Indian field afterward. Legters used the liberty bond to make the trip, impulsively resigning his pastorate (at that time a Presbyterian Church in South Carolina) to do so.[70] Legters was almost fifty years old when he first met Townsend. And one could argue that one of the most significant meetings in the history of twentieth-century missions was fated when a hot-tempered preacher struck a black man who jostled him in a train station.

Dinwiddie and Legters traveled to Guatemala under assignment from America's Keswick, the Victorious Life Testimony, which regularly sent Keswick teachers around the globe to hold conferences for missionaries and their converts. Keswick spirituality had its general roots in Wesleyan Holiness theology and revivalism. Although it began in England, its specific genesis was the visit there in 1873 of Americans Robert Pearsall Smith and his wife, Hannah Whitall Smith. Hannah's book, *The Christian's Secret to the Happy Life,* was tremendously influential on popular evangelical spirituality. What an Englishman said of Pearsall Smith probably holds true for the entire movement. "I never gave Smith credit for much intelligence. It was his heart, not his head, which attracted me." Keswick theology, something of a misnomer in itself, is almost impossible to rationally articulate, but to earnest believers who had grown tired of the struggle to live a holy life, it promised "rest."[71]

The stated aim of a Victorious Life conference was "[t]o bring men and women into a life of fellowship with God, victory over sin, and fruit-bearing, through the presentation of the Bible message concerning the Life that is Christ." While the evangelicalism of the period was notorious for its arguments over theology, Victorious Life teaching was explicitly experientially oriented. The editors of a conference volume wrote, "The Conference began not first of all with a system of teaching which resulted in a life-experience, but with a life-experience which was followed by more or less accurate attempts to formulate a full explanation of it." Victorious Life leaders were not opposed to theological explanations, but were wary of the divisiveness that trying to explain such seemingly nebulous concepts and experiences could cause. They insisted that "after the last word that theology can speak has been spoken, there will remain the impossibility of the human intellect compassing in our logical systems the great truths of salvation." Robert McQuilkin, dean of Columbia Bible College, admitted that he had a lot of questions about the victorious life upon first hearing of it. But in order to receive the experience, he determined to abandon his theological questions. "This is a complete surrender," he wrote, "and I will surrender those questions, I will surrender my intellect."[72]

The "Say-So" meetings that traditionally closed Victorious Life conferences exemplified the experiential nature of the teaching. During these meetings people stood to testify to what God had done in their lives. But many could not point to any specific example of something God had actually done other than that they felt better, "had peace," or had ceased to worry. One was required to accept on faith that God was keeping his promise whether circumstances verified it or not. This "saying-so" was the key to the life of victory and peace. It was all very simple, really. For example, a man at the Whittier conference who was troubled with doubt and worry was asked repeatedly, "Is it true that God is supplying all your needs,—or is God a liar?" No other questions were permitted. As Robert McQuilkin recorded, "[H]e was forced to make the plain choice as to whether he believed God was supplying his needs. And on this simple statement he entered into the life of victory." One writer reported that at Charles Trumbull's meetings and counseling sessions, listeners were constantly brought "face to face with the question: Do I believe that Christ is meeting all my needs now?" Such meetings with Trumbull had the potential to be "joyously revolutionizing, when one learns by them to 'let go, and let God.'"[73]

At any rate, after the visit by Robert and Hannah Smith in 1873, a convention to promote their teaching was held at Keswick in England, and then every year thereafter, except for brief respites during the two world wars. Soon Keswick spirituality became closely linked with the faith missions. Hudson Taylor, who in 1869 had a higher life experience, and who had always believed that the way to increase the number of missionaries was to deepen the spiritual life of the church, saw the potential of the movement immediately. His pet name for the Keswick convention was "my happy hunting ground." By 1888, Keswick leaders decided that "consecration and the evangelization of the world ought to go together," and the convention began the regular sponsorship of missionary speakers. Soon the road to the main tent was lined with missionary barkers. Keswick's use of furloughed missionaries as speakers, and its offer to pay the way of any missionary wishing to attend, naturally brought many missionaries into the Keswick experience, which they then took with them to the field, further extending Keswick's influence and further cross-pollinating Keswick with missionary organizations. In 1889 Keswick began its "Mission to Missions," sending speakers around the world to missionary conferences and to national churches. The Student Volunteer Movement in England was closely linked to Keswick, and the SVM and the opening of evangelist Dwight L. Moody's Northfield platform to Keswick speakers deepened transatlantic connections. Both John Mott and Robert Speer, two of the SVM's most visible leaders, had close Keswick ties. The prominent faith mission pioneer A. T. Pierson had a Keswick experience, and soon he and Moody lieutenant R. A. Torrey, in typical American fashion, systematized the Keswick Plan into six simple steps, further broadening its appeal, especially to businessmen. When J. Harvey Borton, guided by

Charles Trumbull, followed the six steps into a victorious life, there "was no emotion about it. It was a cold-blooded transaction, just like a business transaction in my office." Keswick piety soon flooded American evangelicalism.[74]

From their beginning, the Victorious Life conferences in America were led largely by men who believed that "world-wide missions [were] the supreme duty of the Christian church." As one writer put it, "In every Victorious Life Conference the missionary passion of our Lord has had central place." More than one-quarter of the messages in a Victorious Life volume published in 1918 were brought by missionaries on specifically mission-related topics. Each conference featured daily mission study classes at 10:00 a.m. with titles such as "South American Problems," "The Moslem World," and "The Lure of Africa." Missions were presented at the conferences as perhaps the primary way of demonstrating full commitment to God, or as Charles Trumbull put it, "[T]he victorious life *is* the missionary life."[75] The teaching of the higher Christian life, cross-pollinated with the fervor of the missionary movement and fertilized by missionary leaders, had a profound impact on the development of the spiritual practice of evangelicalism. The *idea* of total consecration and the willingness to "lay all on the altar for God" that faith missions required, quite apart from whether one ever journeyed overseas or not, set the standard for commitment in evangelical spirituality, quite possibly the most significant impact on American religion of the entire missionary movement.

Working in a mission that was saturated with Keswick piety and that by 1928 would provide its missionaries with a Spanish translation of the Keswick classic *The Christian's Secret of a Happy Life*, Townsend was teaching basic Victorious Life principles to Indian converts long before Dinwiddie and Legters showed up. As Elvira recorded after one conference with Guatemalan believers in 1919, "It would have done your heart good to see the people weep and confess how much they lacked in their Christian lives, and how they were ready to 'let go and let God.'" The pithy sayings promoted in Victorious Life teaching appealed to Townsend's simple faith. He later admitted that when he came to Central America, he "didn't know beans about doctrine." And he never took the time for serious theological reflection, preferring to stake his life on a few basic principles. God was alive in the world. What God promised, he could be trusted to deliver. God wanted the Scripture brought to unevangelized tribal cultures. If he, Cameron Townsend, learned to "let go and let God" and "stepped out in faith," God would use him to reach that goal.[76]

Christmas 1920 found the Townsends, Dinwiddie, Legters, and Townsend's old friend Robbie Robinson all crowded into the Townsends' little house in San Antonio. Robinson had left Guatemala for a brief stint in the army and had returned with a new wife in tow, carrying no grudge over the loss of Elvira to his friend. "The corn stalks fairly bristled with folks," Townsend reported. Indian converts from congregations as far away as thirty miles gathered for the promised Victorious Life Bible Conference. The Christmas Eve program was "splendid," highlighted by Elvira's men's chorus, which, although lacking a bass section because Elvira could not sing low enough to teach them the part, "covered itself with glory." That weekend Dinwiddie and Legters led four meetings per day. More than sixty people underwent the Keswick experience, "surrender[ing] their lives entirely to the Lord," and sixteen "volunteered to go out and preach the Gospel . . . over the greater part of the territory."[77]

After the conference, Townsend took Dinwiddie and Legters on a tour of Indian towns and villages. Dinwiddie, an amateur scientist and member of the National Geographic Society, jotted down hourly barometer readings. His notes reveal a developing enthusiasm for Indians and demonstrate that he listened carefully to Townsend: "Economically: the prey of the white man, burden bearers of Guatemala, slaves of patrons, the victim of the rubber hunter, Morally: most virtuous race of earth."[78]

Late one January night, Townsend and Dinwiddie decided to climb a nearby volcano. Perhaps they wanted to view the sunrise from the stunning peak; perhaps they just wanted to talk. The hike turned into an all-night adventure. By the time they gratefully flopped down at the summit at 4:30 a.m., the two had formed an intimate bond. Townsend discovered a mentor who shared his passions and who would help carry his secrets. Dinwiddie would later say it was God himself who brought them together. "[M]any times I have longed for the privilege of just such a talk with one whom, under God, has been led to a vision so similar to my own," he later wrote to Townsend.[79] Townsend took to calling the older man "head Chief don Howard," and their frank, at times intense, yet good-humored correspondence remains a pleasure to read.

At some point that month, more than likely during their long night together, Townsend shared with Dinwiddie his darkest secret. His marriage to Elvira was a disaster that threatened all his dreams for the Indians. Although Elvira had been advised before the marriage to avoid becoming too involved in the work, because her "nerves" would not permit it, she "refused to lag behind," following Townsend wherever he went. Deeply insecure, she did not trust her husband out of her sight, became suspicious if he talked with another woman, and occasionally openly flirted with other men to arouse Townsend's jealousy. While it is impossible to pinpoint her first outburst, they likely began within the first six months of the marriage. By early 1921, perhaps exacerbated by the stresses of the conference, they were occurring almost daily. Elvira would fly into a rage, and would "absolutely lose control of herself," screaming at her husband and at times attacking him physically. Townsend attributed her outbursts to her "extreme nervousness."[80]

Now Dinwiddie and Legters met with the young couple for council. The deeply pious Elvira was utterly contrite. The two seasoned Keswick speakers led Elvira through the steps to the victorious life. Undoubtedly they spent a great deal of time praying together as Elvira learned to "let go and let God." She left the conference feeling she had indeed received victory. Elvira's "joy is without bounds as she rests from her own labors and just lets Him work for, in, and through her," Townsend noted. Undoubtedly feeling a good bit of relief himself, he concluded, "To all of which I add a hallelujah! It is so precious! This daily walk with Him."[81]

By the end of January the small group of Indian enthusiasts had decided to start a new mission devoted exclusively to the evangelism of the Indians. On January 23, 1921, the Townsends, Dinwiddie, Legters, Robinson, the Burgesses, the Tomses, the Treichlers, and a Miss Williams met at the town of Chichicastenango for several days to plan the focused evangelization of Indians throughout Guatemala. Most of those gathered were with the CAM, although the Burgesses and Miss Williams were Presbyterian missionaries, and Dinwiddie and Legters were visiting from Keswick. Paul Burgess, who had preached the Townsends' wedding sermon, was the most prominent missionary in the group. About ten years older than Townsend, Burgess, a member of the Socialist party while in seminary, had earned a PhD, spoke seven languages, and had studied for a year in Germany. In 1913 he had been appointed by the Presbyterian mission board to Guatemala, where he was bitten by the Indian bug, even as his many responsibilities did not permit him to devote his full energy to their cause. He was the kind of man who searched European libraries for the original copy of the *Popul Vuh* because he wanted the Quichés to learn of their ancient heritage. He eventually found it in the Newberry Library and published a Quiché-Spanish version in 1955. Before he retired he published more than four hundred articles and seventeen books, many in Spanish, including a church history, a biography of President Barrios in 1926, and an almanac patterned after *Poor Richard's Almanac.* The almanac landed him in jail, because he pointed out political faults of the Barrios administration. Eventually, with his wife, Dora, and several well-educated Quiché men doing most of the work, he oversaw the translation of a good portion of the New Testament into Quiché, completing the project in 1946.[82]

Anna Marie Dahlquist has written a good account of the conference in her book *Trailblazers for Translators.* For our purposes, it is important to note three key elements of the three-day meeting. First, despite Townsend's youth and inexperience, the entire group recognized him as an obvious leader. Townsend was a decade or two younger than most of the others present. He had been in Guatemala for only three years, and in the CAM for approximately a year and a half. Yet his voice is heard early and often and his influence felt throughout the entire affair. He led off the first session with a statement of his ever-expanding vision: "It is time for God to work in the evangelization of all the Indians of all Latin America in this generation." Remarkably, the conference decided to attend first to the Guatemalan Indians, then those of Mexico, and lastly South America, precisely the path Townsend was to travel over the next several decades.[83]

Second, the group focused from the beginning on Indian-language work. Dinwiddie argued that no group of people had ever been truly evangelized except in their own language. They were all aware that the government was not in favor of such work. Burgess noted the "importance of guarding against political trouble in doing Indian work." Townsend suggested creating translations with parallel readings in Spanish and the Indian language so that they could claim their intent was to help the Indians learn Spanish. Herbert Toms seems to have raised the most objections, wondering if it was not better to reach the tribal groups through Spanish-speaking Indians, especially if a language such as Cakchiquel had so many dialects that numerous translations would be needed. Undoubtedly at Townsend's instigation, Legters and Dinwiddie, as well as Burgess, all pushed for a consensus that translation work was needed, not simply Indian-focused evangelism. The group agreed that missionaries who were engaged in Spanish work simply did not have time to labor with Indians as well. Legters, again following Townsend's line, pointed out that the *ladino* and Indian work should be divided like Paul and Peter divided the Jews and Gentiles. They would need new recruits especially for this task. They decided that two missionaries were needed to work with each tribe, and that one of their major focuses would be training the Indians themselves to undertake the translations. The group figured that nine more couples would be needed to establish Indian work throughout Guatemala, including two couples to relieve the Tomses and Treichlers, who were now occupied in *ladino* work.[84]

Finally, although the group professed not to be eager to found a new organization, they were driven by a sense of inevitability to the founding of the Latin American Indian Mission (LAIM). Following accepted faith mission practice, the missionaries agreed that the new mission would occupy a field on its own only if established agencies refused to do so. The LAIM would cooperate with all "sound, evangelical societies" and would turn over its established work to such missions when they were ready to take over. Furthermore, the LAIM would be directed from the field. Dinwiddie, who clearly was held in great respect by all present, was elected unanimously as general director and executive secretary for the home council of the new mission. Legters was also asked to serve on the home council. When the group voted on officers for the field council, the balloting for chairman resulted in a tie between Burgess and Townsend. Burgess was chosen in a runoff. The new mission would be faith based—"The financial basis of the Mission shall be to depend utterly upon the infallible faithfulness of God"—and no debts would be incurred. The LAIM would be a full-orbed mission, not just a translation society. It was expected, at least initially, to employ Indian evangelists and carry on much as the CAM had been doing, with the proviso that it was to focus exclusively on Indians. Active members of the mission would go to the field under the LAIM. Members of established missions, such as Townsend, would be associate members and would get money from LAIM only if there was a surplus.[85]

After the euphoria of the conference died down, the group was left to ponder how their boards would take the news of the founding of a new mission by some of their most prominent missionaries. Legters, as impetuous and undiplomatic as ever, expected the new organization would not be well received and suggested associate members might not be associates for long, a comment that leaked out and caused a good bit of trouble for all involved. Mrs. Treichler was so nervous about the reception of the new mission that her report of the meetings to the CAM council neglected to mention that a new organization had been formed at all. Burgess was uncertain of his mission's reception and pondered the possibility that it might mean "severing relations with the Board." The Presbyterian board, more concerned with doctrine than anything else, was cautious, worried that Dinwiddie and Legters were "people who are laying particular stress upon the premillenium [*sic*] views." Although he did not recognize Dinwiddie and Legters, Stanley White, Presbyterian board secretary, warned Burgess, "[O]ur experience with men who lay stress upon the Victorious Life testimony has been in times past a very unsatisfactory one." Burgess, who had premillenarian sympathies, replied that Dinwiddie was a "scion of an old Virginia family" and a Baptist. "[E]ven the most eccentric premillenarian is infinitely far ahead of the Indian witch doctor," he cheekily replied. At any rate he had already learned to get along with "some pretty extreme premillenarians" in Guatemala and did not feel this association would lead to anything unsavory. Furthermore, Burgess sarcastically noted, the current Presbyterian method, putting "one lone missionary" in charge of seventy Spanish-speaking congregations, nine Spanish-speaking schools, and six Spanish-speaking evangelists and then telling him that "what time he has left over he can give to the Indians," simply was not working. After some haggling, Burgess's superiors informed him that they had no problem with his doing Indian work and belonging to the new organization as long as it did not "involve the board financially."[86]

Townsend was only a bit disingenuous when he reported the outcome of the meeting to Judge Scott. The realization that a new organization was needed was a "revelation to every one of us," he exclaimed. "We were driven more and more to prayer and the result was the organization of a body to undertake . . . the evangelization in their own tongues of the Indians of Latin America." He assured the council that his plans were "as free from any self seeking as any plan could possibly be." No one intended to leave his or her mission of "first allegiance." In fact, Townsend hoped for genuine cooperation among all the missions, old and new. He concluded, no doubt sincerely, "It is our prayer that our beloved C.A.M. may under God take first rank in pushing the Indian work here in Central America." As he began to list the "needs," however, the council, not for the first time, and certainly not for the last, must have felt the nervous tension that Townsend's dreams tended to produce in his listeners, at least those listeners charged with overseeing the financial health of an organization. Herbert Toms wanted to immediately begin Mam language study; a missionary couple was needed to take over his extensive Spanish-language work. The Treichlers wanted to leave their *ladino* ministry for work among the Quichés; a missionary couple was needed to take over their work. Townsend himself wanted a nurse and a schoolteacher for San Antonio to free him up for work among the Cakchiquels. In addition, he wanted the CAM to explore Honduras and Costa Rica to see what the needs were there. "I believe that if the fields were explored . . . and the facts made known in the homeland, that God could easily raise up these workers as well as their support," he confidently asserted. Then, utilizing the foundational logic of faith missions to spur his nervous superiors, he finished with a flourish. "May we pray that it may be thus and that if it is God's will to use the C.A.M. in this special way for the salvation of the Indians that we may in no way LIMIT HIM by our UNBELIEF."[87]

It was not just Townsend who was enthusiastic about Dinwiddie and Legters in early 1921. All of the missionaries greatly appreciated the ministry of the two skilled Bible teachers, and several encouraged the CAM council to take on Dinwiddie as the mission's full-time field superintendent. Albert Bishop, of all people, requested that Legters be placed on the council. Back in Paris, Texas, Judge Scott realized the mission needed a younger man to take over and give his full attention to the work. "I think well of Brother Dinwiddie," he advised the council, "and he may be the Lord's man to take this position, which is needed very much indeed." Even R. D. Smith, who had corresponded with Dinwiddie for several years, was not entirely opposed, although he was hardly enthusiastic. He grudgingly admitted that the missionaries felt the council was "not pushing the battle as aggressively as we should," and he was willing, "if we cannot do anything ourselves," to give a chance to the man the field personnel felt would "roll the old chariot along."[88]

As news of the creation of the LAIM trickled in, however, the council rapidly cooled. They felt there was no need for the new mission, as the CAM had "always emphasized the Indian work," a statement that betrayed the dramatic difference between the council's and Townsend's vision of such things. While they did not want to do anything that might "quench the zeal" of Dinwiddie and Legters, they also suddenly became concerned about the Victorious Life connections. Luther Rees had heard Robert McQuilkin speak several times and thought he was "quite immature." Scofield was "amused" by the whole movement, because its leaders "seemed to feel that they had made a discovery, while he had been teaching the truth as to victory for over thirty years." R. D. Smith breathlessly reported that the head of a Bible institute in Denver "felt [Charles Trumbull's] teaching was absolutely dangerous." And on top of that there were worrisome reports that Dinwiddie and Legters had been "quite friendly" with Pentecostals in Central America.[89]

R. D. Smith now blamed Dinwiddie for the creation of the new mission, believing that he, as the older and more experienced man, should have cautioned the young missionaries, namely Townsend and Robinson, to consult with headquarters before launching such an endeavor on their own. He was also worried that an organization with such aggressive plans would not remain on a faith basis, but intended to solicit funds and recruits. He uncharitably groused to Townsend that the people gathered at Chichicastenango had no "special ability" for such work. Townsend angrily retorted, "[W]e are all . . . fully conscious of lack of capacity on our part to in anyway qualify us for the big task we spoke of, only with one exception; we have the vision." "Undertake great things for God, and expect great things from God," he lectured his one-time mentor. He claimed to be more than willing to have other people take over the project, but hoped that the "foolhardiness" of the LAIM plotters might serve "to get other folks started."[90]

Unfortunately, enthusiasm on the field also cooled toward the new organization rather quickly. Albert Bishop soon rethought his position and at some point in April 1921 sent "seven criticisms" of the new mission to Judge Scott. Bishop was a strong separatist fundamentalist and may have been worried about associating with men in the Presbyterian mission who were not premillennialists. Legters's public statements that Burgess and Townsend were the only ones currently doing anything for the Indians did not help. Undoubtedly influenced by Townsend, Legters immediately began promoting the separation of the Indian and *ladino* work, specifically in an article in the *Sunday School Times.* With the issue suddenly splashed all over the evangelical world, Bishop testily asserted that Legters's ideas in the *Times* article were "blunders" and argued that "[t]o separate the Indian work from the Spanish . . . would be like picking woof and warp apart." Bishop was also disturbed, as were other missionaries, by Legters's wildly exaggerated claims, what Townsend called "ministerial statements." When fired with passion, Legters sometimes indulged in a bit of poetic license. Apparently the missionaries took umbrage when Legters referred in his article to "[f]ires from a thousand villages." "Well maybe there were a dozen villages!" Townsend retorted, "but . . . his vision was marvelous and we needed his help so I cultivated his friendship."[91]

Dinwiddie returned to the United States after the meeting and quickly proved to be an eloquent promoter of the new work. As he traveled the country, he spoke of the cry of the blood of dead Indians from the ground. "The impact of men of the white race upon the red man, the Indian, has been one of the bloodiest and most brutal pages of human history," he preached. White men were "parasites . . . drain[ing] the vitality" of the Indians and living off their labor. He told of Indians, "the most virtuous race on the earth," being raped, enslaved, and slaughtered by rubber hunters in the Amazon, and accused his fellow Christians of "pass[ing] by" Indians, just as the religious leaders passed by the beaten man in Christ's parable of the Good Samaritan. While thousands of missionaries journeyed to Africa and Asia, "to the red man, our brother, the original owner of our hemisphere, there were until recently only a handful of witnesses in all Latin America."[92]

Within two months of the Chichicastenango meeting, Dinwiddie raised support for seven native workers and forwarded the money to Robinson. In addition, two prospective missionary candidates were "in sight" and a supporter ready to link up with the first of them. A month later he had secured for the new mission the endorsement of Dr. Paul de Schweinitz, the missionary secretary of the Moravians in America, who held "a high place in the Foreign Missions Conference of North America," and of Samuel A. Moffett, a Presbyterian missionary to Korea since 1890, and popularizer of the so-called Nevius plan of indigenous church growth. By June, Dinwiddie had received pledges for the support of seventeen native workers and had the names of seventeen possible missionaries "who desire to go to work among the Indians of Guatemala." By mid-summer he had several nurses and a schoolteacher ready to embark to help Townsend in San Antonio.[93] By October 1921, Dinwiddie had resigned from any organization that did not have something to do with foreign missions and was committed to full-time mission promotion.

Legters, meanwhile, spent the three months after the Chichicastenango conference surveying Guatemala to assess where best to locate missionaries. For most of the rest of his life he spent several months every year on the field. The bulk of the year he traveled for the Victorious Life Testimony, always presenting the needs of the Indians in private conversation and from the platform wherever possible. Where Dinwiddie was eloquent and polished, Legters was irascible and passionate. Townsend once referred to Legters's speaking style as "a great bellowing." Still, in his own way Legters was just as effective as Dinwiddie. On one occasion he was invited to speak at a prayer meeting at the Church of the Open Door in Los Angeles. After using up most of the meeting taking prayer requests, at 8:45 the assistant pastor announced, "Now Mr. Legters has until 9:00 to tell us about the Indians of South America." Legters leaped up and said, "That is a perfect example of the deal the Indians have always received. I can't do it!" And he sat down. They gave him thirty minutes.[94]

Both Legters and Dinwiddie, while paying lip service to the faith basis for mission work, were more aggressive about recruiting both people and funds than were most faith workers. They were not shy about presenting the need and the requirement of God's people to meet that need. In a sense, for Legters and Dinwiddie the problem was one of primary motivation: Was your primary motivation the condition of the Indians or your commitment to faith mission protocol? They were unquestionably committed, at least initially, to both, but the perceived need of the Indians ultimately took precedence over commitments to a given way of mission operation. To put it simply, for a man like Legters, who truly believed that the flames of hell awaited those who did not hear the gospel, the question became one of faith principles versus the eternal destiny of thousands of Indians. Put that way, the choice was fairly obvious.

When Legters returned to the United States after his survey of Guatemala, he had a reluctant passenger with him. Unfortunately, her "victory," as most such victories were for Elvira, was short-lived. In March Townsend broke down and informed the mission that Elvira would be coming home to rest. Matters had reached a point where Elvira's public outbursts were hindering the work of the mission, or as Townsend put it, God's work in Guatemala was being hindered by God's own servants. He asked to speak to Judge Scott "very frankly" and proceeded to describe the hell his young marriage had become. "We have looked constantly to the Lord for relief," Townsend wrote, "and at times come wonderful periods of blessed communion" that were "joy beyond expression," but those times were "much less" now. Elvira sailed home with Legters on March 24, and Townsend would join her in the States at the end of summer. "[I]n her moments of calm in the Lord she is the sweetest girl I ever knew," he informed Scott, "but [she] must now be prayed out of her sad condition."[95]

From the beginning of their association Townsend pressured Dinwiddie to connect himself to the CAM. Dinwiddie kept an open mind, but he did not want to join up unless the CAM council truly adopted the Indian vision as their own. So far, other than Judge Scott's "personal Christ-like spirit," he had seen no indication of the council warming to the task. By July, Dinwiddie was even less convinced CAM was the place to start. Bishop's attack on the work, and the CAM council's seeming acceptance of his arguments without arranging to hear from him or Legters, disturbed him greatly. The council seemed to be dodging him, never able to find a time when they could meet. Dinwiddie found the inability of the council members to find a date on which they could all be in the same room "unexplainable." "It suggests to me," he complained to Townsend, "that the basis for confidence on the part of the Council is not strong enough for me to enter into full-time relationship with the Mission."[96]

That spring, Albert Bishop and Townsend met together to iron out the misunderstandings that had developed over the Indian and *ladino* issue. Turf wars were forming as Indian workers began to look to Townsend for leadership rather than to the *ladino* elders in the large Cinco Calles church in Guatemala City who had previously directed them. The two missionaries met with leaders of both communities, and together they decided that Bishop would oversee the *ladino* workers, and Townsend the Indians. For the most part, Indian workers would evangelize Indians, and *ladinos* would focus on *ladinos.* The two races would worship separately with their own pastors and elders. Technically, however, the workers would be considered co-pastors in one church, and the two groups would safeguard their "visible unity" by meeting regularly together in "union meetings" and Bible conferences. "Efficiency in winning souls and the edification of the believers was to be made paramount," reported Townsend. Townsend viewed this agreement with Bishop in almost mythic terms. In his eyes it "meant almost as much for the Indians as the dictum of the Council at Jerusalem meant for the Gentiles. The Indians can become good Christians now without becoming Ladinos or even subjugating themselves spiritually beneath the Ladinos. In this latter sense it was their emancipation act."[97]

Inspired by the Chichicastenango conference, Townsend began almost immediately to translate the book of Mark into Cakchiquel, despite the fact that it would be years yet before he considered himself fluent in the complex language. Mark was the most straightforward book of the New Testament grammatically, yet Townsend found it "the most delicate work" he ever did. Margarito Otzoy, a convert who had been "driven from his home on account of his new faith," and who was now living with the Townsends, assisted him. Townsend utilized three Spanish translations, two English, one Greek, one Latin (although he admitted that this was of little help, as he had forgotten his schoolboy Latin), and the Catholic translation of Mark into Quiché. Every difficult passage had to first be explained to Otzoy so that he in turn could help Townsend figure out how to word it in Cakchiquel. When Townsend wondered what to call the devil, Otzoy suggested a word used for a "little stink bug." Townsend did not think a stink-bug carried quite the right weight for "the enemy of our souls," and he struggled to find a better term.[98]

After a few months' work, Townsend was ready to publish the account of the death and resurrection of Christ from the last few chapters of Mark. There were two printing presses in Antigua. One quoted too high a price; the other was partly owned by the town's mayor, who was "anti-foreigner and suspicious." The mayor was not initially receptive to the printing proposal, and he angrily accused Townsend of "laboring for the liberation of the Indians." He felt "the Indian language should be stamped out rather than perpetuated in book form." Townsend showed him the parallel Spanish-Cakchiquel text and argued that such parallel translations would actually help the Indians learn Spanish. The mayor changed his mind and quoted Townsend a fair price once he was convinced that Townsend's work "would be an aid in promoting the national language" rather than "an encouragement for [the Indians] to retain their tribal speech."[99]

Many missionaries translated the Bible into foreign languages long before Townsend. They usually focused their efforts, however, on trade languages, and many worked to teach natives that language, while some even tried to teach natives English. Some rudimentary work was done in tribal languages, but it was rare and most likely not very well done. The Sudan Interior Mission claims that one of their early missionaries translated the four Gospels in his first few years on the field. Another finished his first Gospel within twelve months of arrival in the tribe. Such work could only have been very poor. The British and Foreign Bible Society advocated indigenous translation work. Their agent in Central America, F. Castells, urged translations for tribal groups but found little missionary interest. In 1897 he commissioned a translation of Mark into Quiché. The work was done by a Catholic professor of Mayan languages and published in 1898. Eventually the translation went through three editions and seven thousand copies. Castells also oversaw the translation of Mark into Cakchiquel. He published two thousand copies in 1902. In addition, the Spanish fathers developed some Cakchiquel grammar books, but in Townsend's time such work was probably available only in European libraries. Townsend became aware of Castells's translation of Mark into Cakchiquel in June 1921 as he worked on his own translation. He found the Indians could not understand much of it. He dismissed the work as being made by "some town secretary" who had gotten the grammatical forms all wrong.[100]

Townsend's initial work was also undoubtedly quite poor, and indeed has been judged as such by later members of his own mission. He had no more training than did any other missionary attempting such work at the time. Furthermore, in 1921 translation work was, for Townsend, just one part of an overall program of Indian evangelism that focused on close identification with the tribal groups. Working in indigenous languages in all aspects of mission work was the foundation of Townsend's effort on behalf of Indian groups almost from the inception of his time in Guatemala. Such a focus was his first serious challenge to the accepted methods of evangelical missions.

In all of this, Townsend was only following his own advice. In early personal notes that he titled "Methods of Reaching the Indians," he wrote, "Most educational material is impractical for Indians. . . . Study the situation in which the Indian lives (whole environment). . . . Don't try to teach them things that are outside the realm of the Indian's daily living. *Develop your own system or method rather than follow others.*"[101]

To fund his printing of Mark, Townsend wrote an article for the *Central American Bulletin.* It was carefully worded to appease faith mission sensibilities yet still let readers know he needed money. "The Lord is going to give someone the blessed privilege of paying for the printing of this translation," he announced, "and thus allow someone to have part in giving the words of the Lord to 150,000 people, in their own tongue."[102]

Townsend had been in Guatemala for just a little more than a year when he first voiced a desire to found "a training school for [Indian] workers, as there is none in all Central America." Such a school would train Indian pastors and evangelists. Some in the mission wanted him to continue sending Indians to Guatemala City to be educated in the *ladino* Bible institute. Townsend, however, clung to his vision for several reasons. First, the Indians simply did not understand sufficient Spanish to keep up with the rest of the class. Second, the cost of living was too high in Guatemala City. Third, he wanted to keep the Indians in an Indian atmosphere "so that there would be less danger of their being weaned away" from their own people to live like *ladinos* themselves. Fourth, a Bible institute in Indian country would provide the students opportunity to do evangelistic work in neighboring Indian communities, which, after all, was the task for which they were being trained.[103]

By August 1921, Townsend was holding Bible classes for Indian workers in a converted saloon. Twelve students from five different congregations attended the first session. After several weeks of teaching, students were sent out in twos on evangelism trips. This on-again, off-again schedule established the pattern for the Indian Bible institute throughout Townsend's tenure in Guatemala. Because of Townsend's language skills and the education level of the students, the teaching was on a very basic level, such that, Townsend reported to the council, "they would laugh at me at home or even in a ladino congregation here." Class often began with a student praying that the teacher would make his message very simple. Townsend routinely fielded questions on topics other than Scripture, such as, "Is the earth really round?"[104]

Despite his many other endeavors, Townsend continued to spend a good bit of his time on evangelistic trips. These trips were very similar to, if shorter than, the ones he took during his first year as an itinerant Scripture salesman for R. D. Smith's Bible House. Townsend's primary evangelistic work, however, was through the stable of national workers he employed. Often they were his own converts. He trained them, paid them ten dollars per month by connecting them with a donor in the United States, and directed their work. In 1921, after only two years with the CAM, eleven of the thirty-seven national evangelists and pastors employed by the mission in Guatemala worked under Townsend.[105] Most of his itinerant evangelists were Indians.

Dr. Howard Kelly supported several of Townsend's Indian evangelists. Kelly planned to spend the summer of 1921 touring Guatemala with Townsend, conducting clinics and evangelizing. Unfortunately, he broke his leg, so he sent in his place a young graduate of Johns Hopkins University, Dr. Potter, and Potter's mother, also an MD. Kelly equipped them with one thousand dollars worth of medicine. President Carlos Herrera granted them a personal interview and allowed them to bring in their equipment and medicine duty free. Dr. Potter traveled through the coastal *fincas* on an "evangelistic and medical campaign" while his mother manned the dispensary in San Antonio.[106]

Elvira, meanwhile, entered a hospital in Chicago on April 11 and spent the next six weeks there. She finally had her hernia repaired, although the doctor said that "was but a small part of her trouble." She had malaria in her system, which was treated with quinine. She reported that the Christian doctor caring for her told her that "had I not come now it is more than likely that I would have been useless both to God and man for the rest of my life." He ordered complete rest, and the nurses threatened to tape her mouth shut so that she would not tax herself talking about Guatemala and the Indians to visitors.[107]

While in the hospital Elvira received a great deal of spiritual advice. Cameron, Dinwiddie, the council, and others truly hoped the problem was physical (Dinwiddie called her condition "nervous invalidism"), but it remained terribly difficult for any of them to see her condition in anything other than spiritual terms. They filtered the problem through a Keswick lens. If you were struggling with a confounding habit over which you were not "getting victory," it was apt to be because you were not "letting go and letting God." Somehow the secret was to cease trying so hard and just let God work his inner transformation, or more precisely, to simply believe that God had already worked this transformation and to "rest" in that belief. Dinwiddie told Elvira that God had brought her to the United States not so much for her "physical deliverance" as that He wanted to bring her "into that sweeter and deeper intimacy of a new fellowship with Himself." Only when she was "utterly crushed in despair" and all of her ambition "to do anything or be anything" on her own was dead could Christ "work out in [her life] the fullness of His marvelous will." Given the attitude of those around her, Elvira had no choice but to view her problem in the same light. "For me to get well is to absolutely lose myself and let Jesus use me as a blessing to others," she wrote Judge Scott. This was extremely serious business. If Elvira failed to obtain victory over her emotions, she failed at the task at the center of her being as a Christian person, which was to trust God. All of which must have created an extremely painful internal struggle, even as her spiritual guides told her she was not to struggle, but to rest.[108]

At the same time her own spirituality was being questioned Elvira was finding life in the United States less than expected. Stunned at how little time even Christian folk spent in prayer and Bible reading, she bewailed the "awful coldness and indifference of the believers in the homeland." The flappers put her right over the top! "I was shocked beyond words to see the way those of my own sex dress," she exclaimed. "My! My! How much more sensible both in actions and in dress are our heathen women of Central America!"[109]

That summer she moved to California to stay with her husband's family. There a blood test found her in a "very anemic condition." She had a bowel infection, and a doctor started her on iron injections. R. D. Smith then took her to his personal doctor, who diagnosed a "leaky heart," a condition he considered "rather serious." Smith urged Elvira to rest and reported to the council, "This dear consecrated young woman is in grave danger of ending her life or becoming a confirmed invalid."[110]

Reading the letters today it is hard to escape the impression that the concern uppermost on everyone's mind was getting Elvira well so that Cameron could continue his work. Faith missionaries were always at a premium, but all of those concerned had now invested a great deal in the twenty-five-year-old. As Dinwiddie told Townsend, "[W]e must refuse by unbelief or any degree of assent to give ground to the assault of Satan upon her and through her upon you and the work to which God has called you." Certainly the most invested in his work was Cameron himself, who stood to lose the dreams of his life if something could not be done for Elvira. He was reluctant to leave the field at all, let alone to return to care for an invalid wife. Cameron assured the council, "God . . . can give her quietness in Him right away [i.e., without waiting for medical treatment] and how earnestly I pray that her eyes may be opened to it that our efficiency in his service may not be curtailed."[111]

That September, Howard Dinwiddie chaired a two-day "conference . . . for the Indian" in Philadelphia. Six denominations were represented, and invitations were sent to both Judge Scott and Luther Rees of the CAM, but neither attended. The CAM was represented by Frank Lange, who interviewed prospective missionaries for them, and Anna Gohrman, one of the CAM's most intrepid female missionaries. The conference resulted in the formation of a new organization, the "Indian Mission Committee of America," which essentially superseded the months-old Latin American Indian Mission. They sought to avoid offending other missions by calling themselves a committee rather than a mission. They chose not to use the term "Latin" America, so as not to offend the Indians, who "really have prior right in the territory in which they live." The Guatemala general council of the LAIM was now to become the Guatemala field committee of the Indian Mission Committee of America. The following were selected as the organization's first board members: Mr. J. Harvey Borton (Society of Friends and chairman of the Victorious Life Testimony), treasurer; his wife, Alice McClure Borton (Victorious Life Testimony staff); Howard Dinwiddie, general secretary; Dr. Howard Kelly; Dr. Thomas Moffett (secretary of the Indian work of the Presbyterian Board of Home Missions), chairman; Mrs. Alfred. R. Page (wife of a judge of the New York Supreme Court and active promoter of the Indian work of the Dutch Reformed Church in the United States), recording secretary; and L. L. Legters, field secretary.[112]

Twenty-two people attended the two-day conference. Gaining and then propagating information about Indian groups to the current boards was the stated purpose of the new organization, although the bylaws left room for direct Indian mission work "where the boards now functioning are not projecting or undertaking work for them." The letter announcing the formation of the new work stated, "The Indians of Central and South America and Mexico . . . are the most neglected people in the world with respect to evangelical mission work. The Indian field should be singled out as a racial problem requiring specialized service."[113]

In October 1921, Townsend returned to the United States to be with Elvira. It was his first trip home since he had quit college and boarded a boat for Guatemala four years ago. He returned via Mexico, something he had dreamed of doing for four years. Once again he picked up his diary, recording every detail of his trip; he was pioneering again, even if only for a few weeks. In a particularly vivid passage, he wrote of dropping gospel tracts out of the window of a train as it pulled away from the station. He watched one borne aloft on a sudden breeze and pictured it floating until coming to rest in the hands of a particularly needy person. Townsend, who earlier that year had written, "My heart just burns to get the pioneering part of the work done in this section so as to be able to go to a more needy field," was already dreaming of moving on from Guatemala. As if in preparation for that move, he made word lists as he traveled, comparing the indigenous languages and dialects. It would be a decade before he enjoyed himself in quite that manner again.[114]

As Townsend journeyed north by train, Dinwiddie and Legters traveled south. They were holed up in a steamship cabin on their way back to Guatemala founding their third Indian mission in less than a year. When the *Sunday School Times* announced the creation of the Indian Mission Committee of America in November, the CAM council referred to it as the "Dinwiddie-Legters Mission." In actuality, Dinwiddie and Legters had already decided that the Indian Mission Committee did not suit their purposes. Perhaps they felt the new enterprise was simply too unwieldy and its vision too large. It was both a mission and an information agency. What Legters and Dinwiddie needed was a streamlined organization that would funnel funds and manpower to Indian work around the globe. They wanted to channel those resources into existing missions, however, not take direct responsibility for their supervision themselves. They now created the Pioneer Mission Agency. The PMA would operate out of the offices of the Victorious Life Testimony, and would be controlled almost exclusively by the staff there. It was virtually the mission arm of the Keswick movement in America. Although Dinwiddie and Legters provided primary direction, the full board of directors was made up of the usual suspects: the Bortons, Charles Trumbull, W. H. Griffith Thomas, Howard Banks (associate editor of the *Sunday School Times*), and B. F. Culp (an elder in the Presbyterian Church USA, but brought into a Keswick experience by Trumbull). In their cabin Dinwiddie wrote out and Legters typed up a constitution and bylaws, which they subsequently mailed from Guatemala to the office in Philadelphia. The PMA was incorporated on October 26, 1921, almost a month before the article announcing the formation of the Indian Mission Committee ran in the *Sunday School Times.* The bylaws stated that the new mission would "help furnish the 'sinews of war' to other evangelical and missionary agencies . . . who will take the Gospel to the untouched fields."[115]

By the time Dinwiddie and Legters arrived in Guatemala that October, Townsend was back in the United States caring for Elvira, and they found that in Townsend's absence "the bottom seemed to have dropped out of the Indian work." No one was willing to set up meetings for them with Indians. The CAM council was not at all in favor of the team's second trip to Guatemala. They had tired of what they perceived to be exaggerated claims by Dinwiddie and Legters as to the significance of their travels, "which indicate that the results of thirty-one years' work in [Central America] is all due to their visits of two or three months." Luther Rees proposed that "in the interest of common honesty," they ought to complain to Charles Trumbull, who had been publishing accounts of the duo's adventures in the *Sunday School Times.* "Of course it must not be a personal matter," he added, "as the work is the Lord's and no one wants any credit, but we should protest against a false impression being made upon the people." Instead, the council aired their grievance in the *Central American Bulletin.* The article complained that "a wrong impression has been made as to the work that has been done in order to bring the Gospel to the benighted aborigines." It went on to recount all the work of the CAM for the Indians, and concluded that it would be a "gross injustice" to allow the impression to go unchallenged that the Indians of Central America had "just been discovered" and were "hearing the Gospel for the first time" from these "visiting brethren." In addition, the council came out strongly against the creation of a separate Indian mission organization. Even the normally sympathetic Judge Scott groused to R. D. Smith that he had "just about lost all . . . sympathy" for the pair's plans.[116]

Dinwiddie and Legters stayed in the Bishop home during the annual CAM conference in Guatemala City. Bishop was cool toward them and critical of Townsend in his absence. Even the Chichicastenango group gave them no succor. Robinson and Burgess were absent, the Treichlers were "unresponsive and distant," the Tomses were losing their enthusiasm, and the rest of the missionaries were preparing for a visit from evangelist Harry Strachan. Finally, the Burgesses hosted a second Indian conference in early February 1922. Only a handful of Indians and four missionaries—the Burgesses, Robinson, and Albert Hines, a Pentecostal missionary and friend of Burgess—showed up. The situation depressed Dinwiddie and permanently turned him against the notion of joining forces with the CAM and locating in Guatemala. He glumly wrote Townsend, "[F]or reasons not clear to me, there was a spirit of disaffection toward you . . . on the part of some, a spirit of skepticism as to the value of any such association as we had thought of at Chichicastenango." To make matters worse, the council gave him "not the slightest suggestion of any response" to Townsend's hope that he associate himself with the CAM.[117] Clearly the aggressiveness of Townsend's plans for the Indians was already beginning to create fault lines within the mission.

The LAIM was rapidly proving to be a bitter disappointment to Townsend. Only he and Burgess, of all the field personnel present in Chichicastenango, ever really committed to Indian work in Indian languages. The Treichlers never panned out as Indian workers. They caught the vision momentarily, but never had the capability for serious language work. They dropped out of the Indian picture within a year. In 1924 they resigned from the CAM because of Mrs. Treichler's "nerves," a condition similar to Elvira's. They were later reappointed briefly, although not without board resistance. In 1928 Legters found them quite hostile to separate Indian work. The Tomses were never able to relinquish their heavy involvement with their large educational enterprise in Huehuetenango. They had quite a going concern long before Townsend showed up, and they found it was not easy to abandon their work, especially if the alternate vision belonged primarily to someone else. They clung to the belief that the same person could look after both Indians and *ladinos,* or, as Townsend put it, Toms "thinks that we can make ladinos out of them and then reach them in Spanish."[118]

Meanwhile, Townsend was having a rough fall. Back in California, Elvira picked up where she left off in Guatemala. She refused to let Cameron out of her sight, even to pray or read the Bible. Once, while Townsend knelt in prayer, Elvira flew into the room and violently attacked him, kicking him repeatedly and screaming abuse. Her shrieks regularly roused the neighbors at night, and Townsend literally began to fear for his life.[119] In October the young couple visited the Smiths. Elvira pulled off the meeting with great aplomb, and Townsend kept his secrets to himself. Elvira demurely complained to Blanche Smith that Cameron "did not seem to realize the seriousness of her condition and was planning to return to the field without her, if necessary, within five months at the latest." This revelation prompted a lecture from R. D. Smith, who pointed out to Cameron that "his first duty was to get his wife well . . . whether it took six months or six years, [and] that God ha[d] established families before he did Missions." Elvira claimed to be "too weak to do any household work," a condition Blanche put down to her leaking heart.

A month later Mrs. Smith was wondering if she had made the correct diagnosis. Elvira insisted on accompanying Cameron wherever he went, despite her doctor's orders to the contrary. The older woman now wondered if this preference for being "out in the work" with Cameron was not due to "an unusual aversion to home duties." She suggested to Elvira that she learn how to cook, and to the council reported that Elvira was "very self-centered and lacking in womanliness."[120]

A few weeks later, everyone concerned was ready to forgo cooking for the moment and try a more drastic remedy. Stella Zimmerman's mother (Stella was the CAM missionary who first challenged Townsend and Robinson to go to Guatemala) happened to live in the area. She invited Elvira to spend a few days in her home. Elvira consented, under protest, after Cameron insisted and explained to her that she could not go back to Guatemala unless she was "delivered." Mrs. Zimmerman had the notion that Elvira was demon possessed, and the godly woman now spent several days fasting, praying, and attempting an exorcism, scenes perhaps best left to the imagination.[121]

Elvira was better for a week or two after the exorcism. She genuinely longed to return to Guatemala, so she made a valiant attempt to "get victory," but soon the spells returned worse than ever. As married life seemed to aggravate Elvira's trouble, Cameron was more than willing, even eager, to live apart, but Elvira would not permit it. As R. D. Smith was now overseas, Townsend's family desperately turned to Blanche Smith for advice, and this time Cameron "unburdened his heart." Blanche was appalled and angry. She was sure that had her husband known in October what she now discovered, he would have "dealt with [Elvira] along an entirely different line." But now she hardly knew what to tell them. She suggested placing Elvira in a sanitarium. Alone on Christmas Day, she reported to the council that when Elvira was "herself," she seemed to be "a sweet little Christian," but when she was "crossed in any way," she became violent. To Blanche it was either a case of "utterly uncontrolled temper or mental trouble or demon possession." She concluded, "It is hard to understand why the Lord permitted such a fine noble consecrated young chap to make such a serious mistake as he has seemingly made in the choice of a wife."[122]

Over the next few days Blanche did a bit of investigating. Mrs. Zimmerman informed her that Townsend had been "warned" by missionaries in Guatemala before he married but had ignored the advice. "He was very young," she sighed.

Elvira's doctor informed her that Elvira was "mentally unbalanced." He felt certain it was a problem inherited from her father, as reports were that he was "exactly like her in temperament." Her doctor, however, had never observed an outburst firsthand, although he had "deliberately tried to stir her up." Blanche checked out private sanitariums, but the Townsends would never be able to afford one. A state institution was a possibility, or perhaps a brain specialist. "Oh, it is such a sad case," Blanche moaned. "It would be easier to bury her."[123]

By the end of the year both the mission and Townsend were desperately looking for a way out of the mess. The council feared the work of one of their star missionaries was about to be destroyed, and Townsend, in turn, faced the possibility of his dreams dashed because of an invalid wife. The council thought Cameron might undertake some deputation for the mission while he was forced to be home, but they did not want Elvira to accompany him, because people expected their missionaries to be models of decorum and piety. A scene could cause real harm to the work. She could not return to the field for the same reason. Albert Bishop wrote emphatically from Guatemala, "[Elvira] writes that she has been liberated from Satan's power. She has repeatedly said the same thing here. *She must not come back to the field until there is certainty.*" Again displaying the mission's central concern, he continued, "Her coming, unless she has permanent victory along every line of her awful hindrances, would be the end of Mr. Townsend's great usefulness. . . . *I hope you know the truth about her awful actions in public in many parts of the field.*" The council wanted to leave her with "her people" in Chicago, "who understand her." Since Cameron's presence seemed to only aggravate the situation, they thought he should "feel free to go on with the work" in Guatemala. Townsend begged Luther Rees to let him return to the field, even as he acknowledged that this would cause trouble, because Elvira would insist on accompanying him. "I can only ask [God] to arrange it [and] then she will consent I trust," he wrote. Otherwise, he lamented, my life is "wrecked." Townsend welcomed the opportunity to leave her in the care of her family or even a sanitarium. He was only twenty-five and undoubtedly was completely overwhelmed by the entire situation. Cameron's brother, Paul, once remarked that in the "matter" of Elvira, Cameron was "as helpless as a child."[124]

Unfortunately for Townsend and the mission, Elvira's father, in a "very erratic and rabid" letter, "positively refuse[d]" to take her into his home. As no one had funds enough for a sanitarium, the situation was allowed to drift. In January, Townsend received a letter from the Guatemalan national he had left in charge in San Antonio saying he could not continue after February. At that point Cameron decided he simply had to return to Guatemala by March 1922.

Elvira seemed finally willing to let him return alone, but only if she joined him shortly thereafter. Blanche Smith warned Rees that he had better send her a strong letter, or she would simply jump on a boat and follow her husband. Cameron apparently was not much help in this regard. Smith reported, "Cameron is still very, very sanguine about her and I think has secretly entertained hopes that she could return to the Field in a few months. And I think you should set him right about this at once."[125]

4

In Which the Central American Mission Finds Trouble, Trouble Everywhere and Dr. Becker Makes a Brief but Memorable Appearance

1922–1924

> A long experience with missionaries has taught me that after all they are sometimes quite *human.*
>
> —R. D. Smith

New Year's Day 1922 found Howard Dinwiddie and L. L. Legters traveling in Central America. They would spend a total of five months there, leading Victorious Life conferences and encouraging missionaries. Legters took a side trip with Paul Burgess to survey Indian groups in Chiapas, Mexico, where they did not find a single missionary working with non-Spanish speakers.[1]

Townsend, meanwhile, was stewing in California, scheming to get back to Guatemala, while dodging the council's requests that he undertake deputation work for the CAM. The council seemed to have every argument on its side. Townsend was already in the States caring for his sick wife, and a few months spent traveling for the mission, which desperately needed funds, seemed the best and most logical use of his time, especially as he was a gifted fund-raiser. Luther Rees booked meetings in churches for him and placed a notice in the *Central American Bulletin* that Townsend was available to speak. But Townsend desperately wanted to return to Guatemala to oversee his fledgling work in San Antonio. He was understandably convinced this was God's will. He offered to return in the fall for deputation work, which he "would so like to do," knowing the council would never authorize the expense of such a trip just for deputation. "I'm sure that it is the thing to do. Shall I not go ahead [and] secure passage on . . . Mar[ch] 17?" Townsend asked Rees.[2]

Blanche Smith remonstrated with Townsend, arguing that by backing out and rushing back to the field he was "leaving Mr. Rees in the lurch." She told him that a few months at home building up the mission's constituency would mean more for him in the long run than a similar time spent at San Antonio. She concluded, "[I am] praying that you may have the Lord's own guidance about it, which you may have, if your will is entirely submissive to His," which was about as strong a suggestion as she dared deliver. Townsend offered to do some speaking on his way to New Orleans to catch a boat to Guatemala, but then a few days later reneged. He decided the time could best be spent in California learning how to use the new printing press he had "been led" to purchase. The leading was "confirmed" when "we presented [the options] to the Lord in prayer and He replied, by an offering of $145 from brethren in Redlands for this very purpose." Of course, the "brethren in Redlands" undoubtedly knew the course Townsend preferred to take and gave an offering accordingly. The confirmation was "conclusive" to Townsend, however. "Nothing came in for me to go East," he explained to Rees. "The door was closed." In addition, Elvira now "had guidance along the same line." When no word came back from the exasperated Rees within two weeks, Townsend went ahead and purchased his ticket. "I trust that your silence means consent to my returning direct to Guatemala this month," he wrote. "To me, God's leading has been very clear." Someone had recently offered to pay for his return voyage from California, not New Orleans, another "confirmation" of the Lord's leading. Rees, seeing he had no choice, gave up. "Under all the circumstances," he replied, "we have not felt that we could forbid your returning to the field as you plan, especially if the Lord opens the way for you to do so." He had hoped "that [Townsend] could take advantage of the many openings that have been made for [him]," but with that gentle rebuke let Townsend go. In faith mission culture the invocation of God's will was the final arbiter of dispute, and Townsend was convinced, as were most evangelical faith missionaries, that he understood God's will better than most. After all, the divine financial weather vane was swinging hard toward a boat for Guatemala. Mrs. Smith understood. "It seemed to me a matter about which he should have definite leading from the Lord and no one else could have it for him," she told Rees, even as she also agreed, "Cameron . . . is young . . . and impulsive, and it is always particularly hard for youth to wait."[3]

By the time Townsend left for Guatemala in March, a specialist had predicted Elvira's complete recovery and said she could soon return to her work.

The specialist was Dr. Brainerd, "the foremost authority on nervous and mental troubles" in Southern California. After several hours with the couple, Brainerd pronounced Elvira's troubles "emotional" rather than "mental." They stemmed from a "lack of self control" and could be overcome with "sufficient will power." Now that her physical ailments were "removed," Brainerd thought that as long as no more earthquakes hit Central America, Elvira would be fine.[4]

Perhaps Elvira felt liberated at being informed by a specialist that the responsibility for her actions rested largely upon her. At any rate, she was delighted with the opportunity to return to work. "While I realize that it is going to be difficult in living down the awful things in my life the past 2 1/2 years," she contritely informed the council, "yet I thank God that His love for me was so great that He would not let me go on in my own way, but truly chastised as a loving Father."[5]

With Dr. Brainerd's opinion to fall back on, Blanche Smith agreed in March that Elvira "certainly seem[ed] very much better." Elvira assured the council that God was keeping her "in quietness of heart and mind." Luther Rees was impressed, informing Cameron, now back in Guatemala, "We are very <u>much</u> pleased with the tone of her letters. She seems to be herself again and we owe our Father the praise for all this." Townsend was thrilled. "God has turned our darkness into day," he exclaimed to Dinwiddie.[6]

Townsend returned to a rapidly expanding station in San Antonio. A converted saloon had been turned into a chapel and dispensary. Townsend installed his new printing press, and soon, run by his translation assistant, Margarito Otzoy, it was churning out regular editions of the *Cakchiquel News,* Townsend's latest brainstorm, a newsletter for his supporters. Otzoy also printed their initial attempts at Bible translation. Children bustled about a thirty-by-twenty-five-foot schoolhouse and slept in two boarding rooms. As Indian converts from outlying areas began to send their children to school at San Antonio, more room was required to house them. Elvira recruited a friend of hers and a Moody Bible Institute student, Jennette Tallet, to run an orphanage/children's home. That spring Paul Townsend, Cameron's younger brother, and Paul's wife, Laura, arrived. For several years Cameron had been twisting Paul's arm to join the mission and bring his mechanical expertise to the San Antonio station. Paul brought a Model T with him, the first missionary automobile in Central America. A skilled handyman, Paul got right to work building the orphanage and a small clinic. Soon Signe Norrlin, a nurse, arrived to staff the little dispensary.

As Townsend's station expanded, the council sounded a cautious note but did not stand in his way, especially as Townsend kept assuring them that evangelism came first. The little clinic was necessary because, although a "well body without Christ amount[ed] to nothing," they had discovered that practicing a bit of medicine was "an effective way in getting [Indians] to hear the blessed old Story." The council, however, cautioned that medical and educational work were "apt to hamper" their ability to give their "energy without reserve to preaching Christ to every creature." Townsend agreed that the mission "should stick closely to its policy of keeping direct evangelization far in the front." He also agreed that it was difficult to walk the fine line between evangelism and social work, candidly noting, "This problem of just how much of the other things to do or plan to do has recently been my greatest problem."[7] But Townsend did not slow down. With his old Sunday school teacher, Louise Heim, eventually contributing seventy-five hundred dollars, the San Antonio station was soon the proud home of the Louise Heim Memorial Hospital, as well as a school and an orphanage bearing Heim's name, and a new print shop.

Historians speak of the faith missions' "single-minded emphasis on evangelization," because they have attended more closely to the rhetoric of home councils and conservative home constituencies than to the missionaries themselves. Faith mission theorist A. J. Gordon "explicitly rejected educational, industrial, or other 'civilizing' forms of mission work," feeling that Western education hindered, more than helped, evangelization. Many of the evangelical missions were founded on this basis. The Christian and Missionary Alliance, established in 1887, declared that it was "an evangelistic movement, not aiming to build up elaborate institutions, but to preach the Gospel immediately to every creature and give one chance for eternal life to every member of our fallen race." The council of the Africa Inland Mission announced to the Christian public, "In view of the many untouched millions, we feel called to do a thorough evangelistic work, rather than to build up strong educational centers." C. I. Scofield decreed that the purpose of the Central American Mission was "to carry the Gospel to every creature in Central America[, not] to plant Christian Institutions, or even churches. . . . The entire time of the missionaries, and all the funds contributed, are devoted to evangelization."[8]

By the turn of the century the "evangelism only" faith missions were having such an effect on the discussion about mission policy that Frank Ellinwood, secretary of the Board of Foreign Missions of the Presbyterian Church USA, felt he had to publicly refute arguments against the expenditure of missionary effort and funds on educational efforts. Ellinwood conceded that the number of conversions by the societies that reported a "great expenditure" on educational efforts "has seemed small as compared with the results gained by other societies devoted mainly to evangelistic work." He acknowledged that a "spirit of discontent with these results has sometimes manifested itself in the churches, and has been made a matter of criticism by the secular press, with invidious comparisons as to the relative 'cost of a convert.'" Ellinwood argued that although "these complaints have not been easy to meet," and he "most earnestly advocate[d] a great preponderance on the side of evangelistic work," missionaries still needed to lay a foundation for the future through education.[9]

Ellinwood's statement, while it indicates the power that the narrow focus on evangelism had to elicit a sympathetic public response, and vindicates the importance historians place on this aspect of faith missions, should also alert the careful reader to the fact that the choice between evangelism and education was perhaps not as stark as the common stereotype would indicate. As Ellinwood argued, he also would "most earnestly advocate a great preponderance on the side of evangelistic work." Mainline missionary leaders such as John Mott argued that evangelism was of utmost importance. Sounding like a CAM council member, Mott wrote, "The value of medical, educational, literary and all other forms of missionary activity, is measured by the extent to which they prepare the way for the Gospel message."[10] In fact, before and even during the battles between fundamentalists and modernists in the 1920s, the line between evangelistic and other forms of missionary work was quite fluid. It was perhaps as fluid for conservatives, despite their rhetoric, as it was for modernists. After the 1920s, the line hardened on the modernist side as the focus on traditional evangelism declined. Conservatives, meanwhile, continued even after the theological controversies to engage in educational and medical work, despite directors who attempted to sharply circumscribe such endeavors.

In the middle of the 1920s, at the height of the theological controversies, Dr. Robert Glover, missions professor at the Moody Bible Institute, still emphasized to his students the importance of all forms of mission work, evangelistic, educational, literary, medical, and industrial. While he acknowledged the "danger of becoming too busy and losing the preaching evangelistic touch," he nevertheless stressed that educational work "demands missionary money." "The question is—How far can we legitimately use missionary money to that end?" he asked, especially when "children abound like ants." He cited two "fruitful" models for educational work in his lectures: (1) "Begin the primary schools for the heathen with the object of making them evangelizing agencies, keeping the Gospel to the fore"; and (2) "Begin the primary schools only for the children of those who are already Christians." He also cited medical work as an ideal "opening wedge" for the gospel, and argued that industrial work was "necessary in some fields such as Africa and the Island World." All such work was wonderful as long as "the aim" was always kept in mind. Faith missionaries certainly kept the aim of evangelization firmly in mind, but that aim did not keep them from a genuine concern for people, which led naturally toward a commitment to extensive forms of social work for its own sake.[11]

When Townsend joined the CAM, the mission council was ambivalent about the education issue. On the one hand, CAM's founders definitely wanted the focus of the mission kept on "first things." In addition, they worried about the "inevitable expense of maintaining [educational and medical] institution[s]." As Luther Rees admonished Townsend, "We need to be very careful of starting [such] things unless we are sure that we are doing it in faith," which was faith mission speak for, "Are you sure God is behind this project and will keep money coming in for it?" On the other hand, the council recognized that most missionaries, when faced with endemic poverty and illiteracy, would inevitably act to alleviate the problem in some way. Though the council did not necessarily approve such action and did not want to run a charitable organization, as that would cost too much and might very well lead to the creation of phony converts, it recognized that to force the issue would be to alienate its field personnel. Rees warned a council member, "New missionaries especially become greatly burdened over the poverty of the people and feel that they must help them.... It is impossible to lay down an absolute rule stating that missionaries can relieve no cases of distress." The council found that missionaries who went to the field fully accepting the "evangelism only" dogma soon changed their views, sometimes radically. "At first the missionaries took quite a strong stand against this class of work," Rees reported, "but during the last two or three years nearly all the missionaries have come to feel that there is a need for at least primary schools in connection with the central stations."[12]

Therefore, as long as the funds for such work came from a missionary's personal constituency (i.e., not from the mission's general fund), and the missionary could reasonably argue that evangelism was the school's raison d'etre, the council looked the other way in tacit approval. Stella Zimmerman's school in Guatemala City was largely funded by her mother from California. Frank and Annie Toms, with their son, Herbert, ran a bustling center in Huehuetenango, complete with a large congregation and a school for approximately one hundred children. No general fund money was allocated for either school. Luther Rees articulated the council's position toward such efforts. "While we have ... given all to understand that this is not the work of our Mission, we have not felt that we could refuse to fellowship such work as is being done by [Zimmerman and Toms].... We are sure that none of our missionaries who have anything to do with supervising these schools have distracted in the least from the Gospel work we are doing." He assured an inquirer that the missionaries managed to slip Bible teaching even into math classes, thus avoiding "the maintenance of what is considered regular educational work."[13]

In April 1922, after Dinwiddie returned from Central America, Luther Rees and Thomas Jones finally met with him on behalf of the CAM council. They spent a weekend together and liked Dinwiddie's messages in church. Nothing was said, however, about Dinwiddie joining the mission, although Rees was not as opposed as he was before the face-to-face meeting. He was confident both Dinwiddie and Legters would be successful promoting the work in the discreet manner to which the CAM was accustomed. Clearly he had not yet met Legters! "Mr. Dinwiddie says that he never appeals for funds," he noted approvingly. "I think also he is going to be very careful about appealing for Missionaries."[14]

At San Antonio that summer, Townsend was working on promotional plans that were perhaps not quite as careful of faith mission sensibilities as Rees trusted Dinwiddie to be. He was hard at work on his memoirs, "A Thousand Trails in Central America," a story he was sure would be popular with the evangelical public.[15]

Townsend gained a kindred spirit on the home council when popular pastor and conference speaker Lewis Sperry Chafer was appointed general secretary of the CAM. Chafer had trained in music at Oberlin College and assisted in the music ministry at D. L. Moody's Northfield conferences. In 1901 he met C. I. Scofield, who became his mentor. Chafer left his music ministry to become a teacher for Scofield's Bible correspondence school and became popular on the Bible conference circuit. He pastored Scofield's former church in Dallas while serving as the CAM's general secretary. He later founded what would become Dallas Theological Seminary in 1924, where he served as president and professor of systematic theology until his death in 1952.[16]

Chafer was an executive of some polish when he came aboard in early 1922, and initially the council rejoiced for precisely this reason. He was someone with a wider ministry capable of enhancing the mission's profile and publicity. He moved quickly to get "new blood and live business strength in [the] body of directors." Chafer privately observed that the CAM had been criticized "far and wide" for its lack of a "progressive spirit or enterprise." He noted, "Those who have made this criticism,—and there are many,—were not asking us to do unspiritual or faithless things, but they were asking us to get this Mission before the public in a far more businesslike way than it has been done before." Chafer inherited a home office that for more than thirty years had never had any idea what its overhead costs were. Nobody knew how much it cost to publish the *Bulletin.* It took him two years to wrest control of the books from the pleasant but inept councilman who had previously kept them. Eventually, with the help of an accountant, he set up a system that kept track of "every detail in connection with the Mission." For the first time, the mission was able to keep monthly records of what each missionary received and how funds were spent.[17]

In late June, Townsend visited his friend Robbie Robinson at his home in Panajachel on the shores of Lake Atitlán. After lunch and a nap the two gingerly eased themselves into the high mountain lake for a swim. A few minutes later Robinson threw up his hands and sank beneath the surface. Townsend tried to grab him, but Robinson pulled them both to the bottom. Townsend managed to struggle free and gain the surface, but Robinson never came up. When Townsend finally managed to relocate the body with the help of some men in a canoe, an hour had passed. As the back of Robinson's head was bright red, the men figured he had died of a cerebral hemorrhage.

Nearly the whole town turned out for the funeral, as Robinson had become quite popular in his brief stay there. A month and a half later his young wife returned to the United States. For his part, the stunned Townsend wrote to Robinson's pastor, "My closest friend, the loving servant and hope of this needy Department, . . . silently sank to die in the waters he so dearly loved. It had been a perfect day of service, rest and fellowship, and to him it was a perfect end, an easy entrance into Glory."[18]

Back in Chicago, Elvira felt so good that the council encouraged her to take some meetings for the mission. She performed admirably at the Moody Church missions conference in June, where she spoke in two or three services and, in native dress, manned a literature table. Her Friday evening address on June 2, 1922, was published in the *Moody Monthly.* Shortly before returning to Guatemala, she candidly wrote to Rees, "What a year of trials, oh! so hard! It seems strange why I had to be put in such an embarrassing place [and] really humiliated by man to the very dust as it were,—but *now,* I praise Him for it all."[19]

Elvira arrived back in San Antonio in mid-July without incident. She had been gone one year and four months. The cornstalks had deteriorated a bit, but Cameron cleaned up the place and their Indian friends decorated the house, chapel, and school with palm fronds, flowers, and evergreens. Her welcome-home service attracted guests from eighteen miles around. She reentered the work energetically, even relieving Cameron of some of his duties, as he was still emotionally exhausted from Robinson's death. At times she went on evangelistic trips on her own or with one other female missionary.[20] Nevertheless, she had only been in Guatemala a month before Paul Townsend reported to R. D. Smith that Elvira was "back to her old ways again."

Townsend spent the summer wrangling fiercely with Dinwiddie long-distance over their competing goals for Dinwiddie's ministry. Townsend acknowledged that he tended to speak very frankly in spite of living in Latin American lands where politeness ruled. He also admitted he was "too apt to do other peoples' planning." Even so, that did not stop him from arguing vigorously that Dinwiddie ought to be in Guatemala using his talents to train Indians and to establish new Indian centers, and that he was reneging on his responsibility by not doing so. "I'm so in earnest about it that I'm hitting my hands together here at the typewriter," he wrote. At times he childishly threatened to pull out of the Chichicastenango plan entirely if Dinwiddie refused to spend more time in Guatemala. Eventually he would conclude with a line such as, "Of course this is just my way of feeling about it and I'm probably way off the track[,] but I'm just overly zealous for the Indians."

Dinwiddie, at this point the more mature man, would patiently explain, "One reason why I have not come to Central America to work among the Cakchiquels is that God has already given a man for that purpose, namely yourself." He reminded Townsend that there were numerous other Indian tribes, and that he felt called to find missionaries like Townsend who would go to them. He also, probably rightly, pointed out that if he had rushed right back to the field to "direct" the work there, the "suspicion and jealousy" already aroused in the CAM and Presbyterian boards "would have been fanned into flame[,] and the feeling would have reached such a height as to have made future co-operation practically impossible." By proceeding more judiciously, they at least had the chance of pulling off a successful inter-mission operation. Townsend was not mollified. "Don't worry about the Boards until they stop us from aggressive work here," he instructed Dinwiddie. Dinwiddie closed his letters with gentle admonishments. "I ask that you will love me and believe in me . . . even though you may think that I am now missing God's will for this moment."[21]

Townsend was a fabulous recruiter, as the steady flow of new missionaries into San Antonio indicated, but not always a good administrator. The man who later insisted that Billy Graham become a Bible translator, reasoning that there were plenty of people who could hold evangelistic crusades in the United States, did not always recognize the best use of a person's talents. He longed to have Dinwiddie working in Guatemala, where he could be directly involved with the Indians, but did not recognize that Dinwiddie would be more useful to him as a recruiter with a worldwide focus. Perhaps that can be attributed to the fact that Townsend's own vision at the time was circumscribed by Central America. He had not yet fixated on the "wild tribes" in South America. But then again, perhaps he just wanted his chosen mentor closer to him in time of trouble. Regardless, that fall Dinwiddie took off for Puerto Rico to continue spreading the Indian word.

Townsend spent the fall on evangelistic trips. His team continued to work at translating Mark and John. As far as Townsend knew, this would be the first translation of John into an Indian dialect in Guatemala. A check of Townsend's schedule during the period reveals that his Indian assistants, Margarito Otzoy and Brigido Zuñiga, must have completed a large portion of the work. Elvira also assisted in the translation.[22]

By January 1923 the possibilities for Indian work in Guatemala seemed to be on an upturn. The Burgesses had been permitted by the Presbyterian board to undertake Indian work, including Bible translation. At Dinwiddie's encouragement, a Mr. Peck would soon arrive under the Presbyterian board to work with the Mam Indians. A Philadelphia School of the Bible student heard Legters speak and came to Guatemala with his wife to work with the Treichlers. Another couple, the Murcells, applied to the CAM to do Indian work with the Del Norte Indians under Frank and Annie Toms.[23]

In March, however, Dinwiddie referred four single women to the CAM for appointment to work with the Pipil Indians in El Salvador. If accepted by the CAM, Dinwiddie offered to personally raise their support. Unfortunately, the CAM council did not believe single women should engage in such pioneer Indian work. Chafer felt sure "that the entrance into an unevangelized tribe of Indians will have to be made by some man who is called and equipped for the work." Once a missionary couple had begun the work, the single women would have "a splendid opportunity for a cooperative work" in the tribe. Chafer remarked that the CAM had recently "sent out a disproportionate number of unmarried young ladies" as compared to men, and, he claimed, "It is rather difficult to place very many more young ladies on the field until we have brought up the list of men missionaries to the point that is needed for efficiency." Other proposed recruits met similar roadblocks. Legters recruited a Hispanic man, born in Spain and raised in Puerto Rico, but at that time the CAM would not send out Hispanics as missionaries. They would only allot them "native worker" status. The young Spaniard refused to go out under those conditions. Another candidate, a Moody Bible Institute graduate, was disqualified because at thirty-eight he was too old. Others were turned down over doctrinal issues.[24]

For these and other reasons, the Pioneer Mission Agency and the CAM never established a productive working relationship. Problems were bound to develop when two different agencies attempted to guide missionary candidates. As the businesslike Chafer argued, "We must have a boundary line at which point the authority of one society ends and the other begins." Unfortunately, that boundary line was often difficult to find. For Dinwiddie and Legters, the greater tragedy would be if the Indian need were not met because of interagency conflict and turf warfare. Dinwiddie bluntly informed Chafer that the Presbyterians, Friends, Baptists, and Moravians would all welcome "a supply of men and means for pioneer work." If the CAM did not "feel free to be used as a channel," the PMA would direct workers and funds elsewhere, or even create a new channel where needed.[25] Unfortunately for both parties, the conditions were not right for a genuine meshing of their effort. The CAM council was simply too suspicious of a whole array of possible doctrinal failures to work easily with a more broad-minded group. And perhaps even more significantly, the personalities involved did not fit together. Consequently, Dinwiddie and Legters continued to work closely with Townsend, but efforts to associate them with the CAM were largely stifled.

Dinwiddie spent the rest of 1923 on the road. In the spring he presented the need of the South American Indian to churches in England, Ireland, and Scotland. From June through December he held Victorious Life conferences and surveyed Indian tribes in Peru and Ecuador.

In San Antonio that spring two teachers instructed forty-five children in a two-room schoolhouse. Twenty-one children from nine surrounding towns boarded in the children's home. More than one hundred people showed up regularly for Sunday services in the chapel. The cornstalk house now had six rooms and housed the two schoolteachers as well as the Beckers, an older doctor and his wife. Dr. Becker had given up medicine for his first love, evangelism. The children's home was "running very smoothly." The Louise Heim hospital was not yet finished, but Signe Norrlin was already "treating a great many sick folks." Paul and Laura Townsend were "getting onto the swing of things very well."[26]

Jennette Tallet, Elvira's friend from Moody Bible Institute who had joined the small band to run the children's home, and about whom Townsend once remarked that she had an "independent disposition," had already deserted San Antonio for Guatemala City. She decided during a trip to the city to stay there, abandoning the children's home in San Antonio with no advance notice, essentially telling the San Antonio missionaries to send the children home or look after them themselves. With no one with genuine authority on the field to oversee things, she simply switched "assignments." "Strong" letters were exchanged, and Signe Norrlin, the nurse, who was forced to take over her responsibilities, "had a long cry over it," but what could Townsend do when Tallet "ha[d] it pretty direct from the Lord that she should stay" in Guatemala City. Indeed, it is hard to blame Tallet. She was very young. She came to Guatemala entirely unprepared for what awaited her, was given no time to learn Spanish before she was thrown into the work in a rural Indian village caring for almost two dozen children, not one of whom could communicate with her through anything more than hand gestures. That she now decided to stay in Guatemala City to "study Spanish" should have surprised no one, least of all Townsend, who was no stranger to getting independent notions "pretty direct from the Lord." Such obstinate ideas were either an exercise of great faith or a display of an "independent disposition"; it all depended where you sat at the moment.[27]

In March 1923, after several council members visited the field, where they received an earful of such problems, they appointed Townsend "director of all missionary activities" both at San Antonio and Panajachel, Robinson's old station on Lake Atitlán. Both stations now had a number of missionaries and a host of interpersonal problems. It was all Townsend could do to uphold Chafer's desire that he keep "a sweet confidence and fellowship existing between the missionaries," especially as it was one of Townsend's "tendencies to fail to exercise a strong word of authority where it [was] needed."[28]

In June of that same year, the Cameron Townsends, Paul Townsends, Signe Norrlin, the Beckers, and Archer Anderson, newly arrived to help Cameron in the Indian Bible institute, organized themselves into the "Cakchiquel Department" of the CAM.[29] With Cameron spending more and more time in Panajachel with the newly relocated Indian Bible institute, it often fell to Paul Townsend to run the station at San Antonio. He had been in Guatemala for one year.

Situations such as that caused by Jennette Tallet were not unusual in faith missions, which tended to have a very inefficient governance structure. When Hudson Taylor made the China Council, located in Shanghai, the "supreme governing body" of the China Inland Mission (CIM), at the time, it was the "only major mission to be directed from the field rather than by a board in the homeland."[30] The traditional boards hired missionaries essentially as employees and directed the work from offices in New England. The faith missions, which tended to mimic the CIM in all things, tried to follow the example of Taylor, but absent a strong-minded founder who remained overseas, for most the issue of institutional control was vigorously contested deep into the twentieth century. For men like Cameron Townsend, the contest revolved around vision and adaptability. Would faith missions be run from home by well-meaning but part-time council members who often had never set foot overseas and tended to be frustratingly doctrinaire, or were they to be run primarily by the missionaries themselves, admittedly lightly educated and often distressingly young, but nevertheless full-time field personnel able to learn from and adapt quickly to local needs?

When C. I. Scofield wrote of his new mission, "No office-rent or clerk-hire is paid, the work being gladly done by the members of the council," he outlined for the Christian public one of the primary arguments for the existence of a new kind of mission. Faith missions, run by committed council members donating their own time and funds, promised to be remarkably *efficient,* able to send virtually every penny contributed directly to the field. What he did not know was that he also summed up what threatened to become a fatal flaw in the method of the new missions, just one of several points where the *ideal* of faith worked against the development of the missions into smoothly functioning organizations.[31] As the Central American Mission grew in the early decades of the century, the operation of the mission by a group of pious hobbyists proved drastically *inefficient.*

Unlike the CIM, launched overseas by a field missionary, the CAM was founded by a group of interested pastors and businessmen in Dallas, where, from the beginning, authority was vested in a small group of council members. In the early years there simply was not much for them to do. The minutes of early council meetings reveal a small group of faithful men gathering to read and answer a few letters. Most of their time was spent praying together. In the early years, with council members centered primarily in the Dallas area, they met only once or twice a year, conducting most business through the mail.

As the mission grew, the method by which the council operated changed very little. As it proved virtually impossible to find council members who were willing to live by the faith basis and give their full attention to mission administration, the council added pastors and Christian laymen with an interest in missions. Unfortunately, few of these men lived in Texas. During Townsend's tenure, three council members lived in Texas, and one each in Chicago, Cleveland, Philadelphia, Los Angeles, and Portland. As each member paid his own way to meetings, getting everyone together even once a year was virtually impossible. The men exchanged letters for months in what was usually a vain attempt to find an appropriate meeting date. For those who could attend the meeting, funds had to be secured, often through the arrangement of speaking engagements along their travel route and in the Dallas area.

The daily business of the mission was conducted by Judge D. H. Scott, the mission treasurer, until Lewis Sperry Chafer became general secretary in 1922. Both men gave only part-time to mission affairs. Until 1925, when Karl Hummel, already a full-time CAM missionary, took over the position of general secretary, no one in the United States had given his or her full attention to the mission for thirty-five years. The general secretary, at Chafer's instigation, was assisted by an executive council made up of the Dallas-area council members. But neither the general secretary nor the executive council could make a decision of any importance without the vote of the entire council, which could take months, even years, to secure. Letters made their tortuously slow journey from city to city. As each council member weighed in on the topic at hand, often with sharply divergent points of view, the secretary was left with a perplexing array of opinions and usually found himself no closer to a solution than when he first solicited the council's advice. As Karl Hummel once complained, "I hesitate to try and get any action by mail[,] for the viewpoints are usually so varied that I never know what course to take." Such uncertainty required yet another round of letters, in which the secretary laid out the various opinions and tried to move the members closer to agreement. As conservative evangelical pastors tended to have rather strong opinions, the process of closure on an issue often necessitated multiple rounds of letters. Meanwhile, missionaries on the field waited for months to hear of a decision in their case, and often, with leadership so far away, simply acted as they saw fit. As Hummel warned the council, "We can not blame the missionaries for becoming restless and at times going ahead on their own initiative when so many months are lost in reaching decisions."[32]

Another inevitable result of this situation was that the candidating process often required months to complete. It took two months for an application to make the rounds between council members. Then the council started asking questions of the applicant, and the lengthy process began again. "Applicants are naturally getting restless," Hummel advised the council in 1927, but there was little anyone could do without a complete revision of the process. When Paul and Laura Townsend applied to the CAM in December 1921, there were conflicting medical reports on Laura's health. It was March 1922 before the council decided, after an exchange of letters, that one of them needed to meet directly with the couple. As the Townsends lived in California, R. D. Smith was the logical council member to conduct the interview. Unfortunately, he was out of the country and would not return for several more months. They were finally interviewed in July 1922. As the council required unanimous decisions on a candidate, sometimes one cranky council member could hold up an application or see a worthy candidate rejected. The CAM lost at least one prospective missionary couple because of "months of delay in answering their application . . . for which they did not understand the reason."[33]

By the early 1920s, Judge Scott, who had conducted most of the mission's business for the thirty years of its existence, realized a change needed to be made. Although he found it "impossible" to convince Luther Rees, mission president from its founding, that the "Mission [was] any larger than it was twenty years ago," Scott was well aware that the work needed "a man strong and active, in body, mind and spirit, to do the things that a Superintendent should do."[34]

As we have seen, when Lewis Sperry Chafer joined the council in 1922, after Scott and Scofield both died in 1921, he seemed the man for the job and he was appointed general secretary. For Chafer, the worst thing that could be said about someone was that their doctrine was unorthodox or that they were "very untidy and disorganized." Chafer argued that the CAM needed to thoroughly review and update its organization. He organized an executive committee that he hoped would be able to "get together . . . as often as demanded." He pushed council members to visit Central America. "[W]e should go down there and have a heart-to-heart talk with every missionary personally," he argued. "There is no modern business house which would think of trying to do business with its representatives and not keep very close to them in personal touch."[35]

In early 1923, Chafer, Rees, and mission treasurer Thomas Jones visited Central America together. Chafer returned from the field enthusiastic and ready to press on with the promotion of the work. "[O]ur work is top heavy," he reported, "in that the field has run way beyond the home backing or the understanding of the Council. We have little realized the mighty work that is forging on there[,] and I do not wonder that missionaries have not understood why the Council has not visited them or taken more pains to get informed." He felt the "imperative and instant need" for one hundred thousand dollars "to put the present machinery we have into working condition" and for fifty new missionaries "as fast as they can be secured under the hand of God. We must have such a new departure in home publicity that we will gain four friends for the mission to one we have at this time." In order to meet that goal, Chafer argued for a full-time secretary who would visit the field every year and devote considerable time to promotion. He concluded, "Our Central American Mission has outgrown the day when it can be conducted at home as a mere side line to someone's business undertakings."[36]

By the summer of 1923 Chafer was hard at work putting the home office in order. He was astonished to find that the mission had operated for thirty years "without so much as filing cases or any system that is modern and accurate." He labored to get the office "systematized and organized" so that he might "really tak[e] care of things in a businesslike way." Chafer had a much larger ministry than any of the other council members, so he was able to promote the work to a wide audience. He found that as he spoke to "thousands of people," most "had never heard of the Central American Mission." He spoke at Moody Bible Institute's commencement and before six hundred to seven hundred students in Dr. Glover's missionary classes. His aggressive promotion began to pay off. "We are receiving a splendid list of applicants," he enthused.[37]

Townsend was enthusiastic about Chafer's leadership. He expected the home council to be primarily a recruiting and fund-raising body anyway, and in Chafer he thought he had found the man to attend to those functions more aggressively. He hounded Chafer to secure eight new missionaries for his Cakchiquel station and one hundred in all of Central America! "That's a nice little task for us to hand you," Townsend wrote, "but really we're expecting you to get them. God's limits are those we put upon Him and none others." And indeed, Chafer did manage to get CAM finances in better shape. In December 1923 he reported "a decided relief in the financial situation, so that we have sent not only the usual amount, but in most instances considerable additional, which I hope will not be resented on the part of the missionaries."[38]

When Chafer returned from his trip to Central America, he was thrilled with the educational programs he had observed at the various mission stations. He discussed with the council the idea of making a public "pronouncement" as to the mission's "exact policy with regard to educational work." He was not, as one might expect, planning to criticize such work. "I think the Central American Mission could bear . . . testimony that we have been swept off our feet and carried forward in this matter of education," he wrote, "and while a year ago I was positively unreconciled to such a program, I found myself heart and soul committed to it when I reached the Central American field." He therefore planned a statement that would "assure our constituency of the reason for taking this position."[39]

The abrupt departure of Jennette Tallet, the treatment by the council of Dinwiddie and Legters, the tensions developing in Guatemala over Townsend's radical plans for the Indians, along with the general inefficiencies of the home council began to stir within Townsend a desire to see more authority invested with some type of field organization. Despite the fact that the council had recently appointed him director of San Antonio and Panajachel, he now agitated for a plan whereby the field missionaries would essentially direct themselves. The precipitating action was the circulation of a proposed mission constitution that had been drafted by the council as part of Chafer's efforts to place the mission on a sounder footing. The constitution placed "final authority" in the mission with the home council. In October 1923 Townsend lodged a "formal protest" with Chafer, a protest made, he said, "after much prayer and study of the problem and one from which I can not conscientiously retract."[40]

Chafer, who had great admiration for Townsend, never intended the new constitution to be inflammatory. "It is the thought of the Council that our relation to the missionaries is contained largely in the meaning of the word Council," he wrote to Townsend. "Nevertheless, we all agree that there must be sometime, somewhere, a final word spoken, and it had been the attitude of the Missionaries who have gone to the field to concede this to the Council." It was precisely this "final word," however, that Townsend was not willing to yield. He argued for field councils of missionaries in each country that would have the "final word" in "all matters touching the native church and the planning of the work in general." An addendum to this plan reveals his ultimate personal agenda and concern. "[W]e Indian missionaries would like to have a special Indian organization of our own while cooperating in the general Guatemala group," he told Chafer. The home council would allocate missionaries, direct American workers, and create general mission policies.[41]

At Chafer's direction, R. D. Smith investigated how other faith missions were organized. After checking with the China Inland Mission and other mission leaders, Smith was convinced that the CAM had "struck a happy medium between the plan of administration by the big Boards and the other extreme of having an autocratic Director as in the CIM." When the CIM suggested to Smith that someone from the council needed to meet more than once a year with the field missionaries, Smith, in a telling statement, pronounced such an idea extravagant. They "evidently d[id] not know that the Mission has an Executive Committee here at home which meets at intervals of less than three months to deal with matters which are constantly coming up," Smith grumbled.[42]

To mollify Townsend, the council attempted to get one of its own members to take a full-time field secretary position. No one was interested. Then the council considered Townsend for the position. They decided he was still too young. And besides, as R. D. Smith argued, "Do we want a man in such a responsible position whose wife is what Mrs. Cam is?" Rees, however, liked the idea. "As to field secretary, I do not see how any one of our missionaries except Cameron would fill the bill," he said.[43] Although pushed aside by other controversies in 1923 and 1924, the struggle for control of the CAM was just beginning.

Townsend first began to think of moving his Indian Bible institute to Panajachel in 1922 after Robinson drowned. The mission station was now unoccupied, and it seemed the perfect setting in a small town on stunning Lake Atitlán. It would be a wonderful place to live. Dinwiddie donated three hundred dollars to help him relocate. When the council appointed him director of San Antonio and Panajachel during its visit in the spring of 1923, Townsend enacted his plan. He relocated to Panajachel along with the new missionary, Archer Anderson, a graduate of the Philadelphia School of the Bible, who had been sent to manage the Indian Bible institute. Anderson was young and immature, but loved evangelism and seemed to have a real flair for teaching. After just a few lessons in Spanish he began conducting evangelization trips. Although Indian workers did most of the speaking, at times Anderson went alone. He played his flute to gather a crowd, then sang Spanish hymns without really knowing what he was singing. On Wednesday morning, March 14, 1923, seven students attended the first classes in the new Indian Workers' Training School of the Central American Mission in Panajachel, soon to be renamed the Robinson Bible Institute (RBI) in honor of Townsend's friend. Townsend was confident that once word of mouth got around, he would not "be able to take care of the bunch that will want to enter." For the next several years, the Townsends paid the men who came to the institute, as it was the only way they could support their families and feed themselves while in class. Townsend taught one class himself, while Anderson taught three classes, with Townsend interpreting for him. A quick study, Anderson was teaching alone by August. Weekends were spent evangelizing the local towns around the lake.[44]

The curriculum was based on the Scofield correspondence course. A typical schedule might look as follows.

9:00–9:30 a.m.: Morning devotions
9:30–10:20: Book study of Exodus or Romans
10:30–11:20: Chapter summary of Luke or John
2:00–2:50 p.m.: Doctrine—conversion, eternity and faith, atonement, or the church
3:00–3:50: Spanish study—An hour a day was given to reading, spelling, and Spanish study. Townsend felt the students had to learn Spanish, as there was not yet enough Scripture in Cakchiquel.[45]

Eleven men attended the second term, fifteen the third, and seventeen the fourth. Terms ran for one month, with the institute operating every other month. Anderson was enthusiastic. "One of the Indians got 100 in his doctrine exam," he exclaimed. Still, "some of the men do not understand very much Spanish and what they need is for me to teach in the Cakchiquel itself."[46]

Townsend quickly fell in love with his new home on the lake. With typical enthusiasm, he suggested the mission build a conference and recreation grounds at Panajachel that could be used by all the boards in Guatemala. Unfortunately, many of the missionaries took the comity agreements very seriously, because they did not want themselves or their converts to be forced to confront Christians of suspect faith. Beautiful Lake Atitlán was in CAM territory, and some CAM missionaries wanted Panajachel kept only for themselves. Townsend, however, could not countenance "hog[ging] . . . from [other boards] a beautiful place which the Lord has given [the CAM]." He complained to Chafer, "I may not be well enough taught on separation[,] but I can't understand why I should hold aloof from fellowshipping in recreation [and] conference with brethren just because they believe differently on non-essentials . . . and I would like to know the Biblical reasons why I should." If Townsend expected sympathy from Chafer, he was in for a surprise. Chafer agreed that while fellowship with the Presbyterians might just be possible, such a project, if it included Pentecostals, Friends, or Adventists, would lead to "the most unpleasant discord." "They would give you no peace day or night," he lectured. "It is impossible for you to have any such fellowship with these strange people. It is not a matter of theory. It has been tried hundreds of times and always utterly fails."[47]

In March, as Townsend traveled back and forth between San Antonio and Panajachel, Elvira was back in the hospital in Guatemala City being treated by Dr. Ainslie, a Presbyterian missionary. On April 26 Ainslie removed one of her ovaries and half of the other. He ordered a year's rest, and Townsend arranged for her to stay in a boardinghouse in Guatemala City. Ainslie appears to have provided Townsend with some marital counseling as well. "Dr. Ainslie has opened our eyes as to my culpability in not knowing how to care for my wife," he reported to Chafer. He decided that for too long he had put his work before Elvira. "I have not ceded Scriptural authority as head of the house," he added in case the biblical literalist Chafer was concerned, "but my wife does know that after the Lord she comes first in my life."[48]

Elvira was soon up and about and once again reporting that she felt "like a new person." Against doctor's orders, she moved back to San Antonio to be at least intermittently with her husband. The ever-hopeful missionaries trusted once again that God had "at last heard our prayers on her behalf." Paul Townsend, however, was skeptical. "If [Cameron] has the strength," he wrote their parents, "to keep the work up and live with her until something happens to set him at liberty[,] he will be O.K."[49] What that "something" might be he did not speculate.

Though the daily inefficiencies of the council's method of operation were a profound irritant to missionaries on the field, a controversy that exploded in the council during Chafer's tenure as general secretary illustrates the issue at the heart of the struggle for control of the mission. For Townsend and other like-minded missionaries, the primary question was whether a mission run by well-meaning but distant, part-time, and ultimately unknowledgeable councilmen could summon the vision and adaptability required to position an organization to aggressively grow and meet the remarkably fluid challenges on the field.

Baptism had been a divisive issue from the beginning of American foreign missions, ever since Adoniram Judson sailed with the American Board of Commissioners for Foreign Missions, changed his views on baptism en route, and founded the Baptist Board for Foreign Missions in 1814. If faith missions were to be truly interdenominational, questions surrounding the mode of baptism would have to be settled right up front. Like most early faith mission leaders, Scofield did not want to reproduce Western sectarian disputes on the field, at least theoretically. Although the CAM drew missionaries from Presbyterian, Congregational, and Baptist churches, there was no thought of organizing such churches on the field. The CAM permitted each male missionary to baptize as he wished, and tried to locate missionaries with similar views on the subject, where they could work with like-minded individuals. Approximately one-third of CAM territory practiced baptism by immersion. No missionary was permitted to dissuade a new convert from choosing his or her own preferred method of baptism. In addition, no missionary was permitted to found a church that excluded from membership anyone baptized by a method not practiced by that church. As Chafer argued, "Whatever is done through adjustment to satisfy the conscience of missionaries shall be done in such a way as to provoke the least possible notice on the part of the native Christians."[50]

In 1923, when the baptism controversy began in the council, not one CAM missionary believed that mode of baptism was an issue over which separation should be practiced in Central America. They had no desire to see such arguments become issues of contention among their converts, many of whom had already paid a steep price in the loss of family and friends when they converted to Protestantism. Nevertheless, for William Pettingill, the Baptist dean of the

Philadelphia School of the Bible and CAM council member, the issue proved too doctrinally provocative to drop. In the summer of 1923 he proposed that the council "extend the freedom to missionaries of forming exclusion churches if they so wish." Pettingill's rhetoric ingenuously made his narrow position seem the broader way. He clothed intolerance in the language of tolerance. "It seems to me . . . utterly wrong to put a yoke upon the churches and prescribe as to the conditions under which they may receive persons into full membership," he argued. "My plea is for liberty on the part of the churches to do about this matter what they will, in obedience to their own interpretation of the Word of God." In other words, it was wrong for the council to set itself up "as a center of authority over the churches" by forcing them to be inclusive if they wished to be exclusive. Pettingill darkly warned that if the council did not go along with him, "the effect will be to warn every future Baptist candidate for appointment that he need not apply; for no Baptist who is a Baptist from conviction (and there are such) will consent to an enforced relationship in local church membership which is contrary to his convictions as to Bible teaching." Even Chafer, as doctrinaire as they came in the 1920s, saw the folly of Pettingill's position. He sarcastically replied, "[I]t is simply a question of whether we are depriving people of their liberty when we ask them to be liberal."[51]

Here was the crux of the issue. Pettingill, thinking like a fundamentalist fighting doctrinal battles in Philadelphia, worried about strict interpretations of doctrine and about the recruitment of missionaries who adhered to that doctrine. Missionaries on the field realized that such an argument would never become an issue for new converts in Central America unless it was imposed or encouraged by the outside, and most were willing to agree that in the larger quest for souls in a foreign land, mode of baptism was a secondary issue. Immersed in such contexts, evangelicals on the foreign field tended to move beyond their more rigid brethren at home to focus on what they considered the essentials of salvation. For Pettingill, however, mode of baptism was a *primary* issue of conscience, and it did not matter that it was *his* conscience, not those of the Central American converts or missionaries.

Frank Toms, a fairly hard-line immersionist himself, summed up the argument of the missionaries in a letter to the council.

> To me this is a very sad affair. Especially at this time when the agitation between the Modernists and Fundamentalists is so acute and when all are hoping that those who stand for the Truth will come out from the denominations and unite in a common testimony and fellowship on things that are fundamental. What hope can there be of any success of such a

> movement when those who are leaders in the movement and recognized teachers of the Word, and who have the ear of the people, shall insist on the same things that have caused the former splits among the Lord's children? Is it possible that we are not willing, at least for the sake of united testimony for the Truth, to put secondary things and things not fundamental to salvation, in the <u>second</u> place? What good can possibly come from magnifying these differences in ceremonies and governments on the Mission field? It can only bring to these simple believers confusion and misunderstandings that cannot be explained,—even as they have in our own land.[52]

The argument raged all that fall and into the following spring, with Pettingill winning some council members to his side. Both sides appealed to the China Inland Mission, as was their wont in such disputes. The CIM supported Chafer, coming down on the side of open membership. Chafer also polled other mission secretaries. Everyone with whom Chafer corresponded agreed that field missionaries should be flexible on such issues, including the AIM, South Africa General Mission, and the Bolivian Indian Mission.[53]

Nevertheless, by July, Baptist churches were getting wind of the affair and threatening withdrawal of support. One hysterical letter to Chafer began, "Recently . . . word has come to us that the Council recently voted and will so instruct the missionaries that baptism by immersion is immaterial." Worse, Pettingill's threatened resignation was beginning to unsettle some of the missionaries, for whom Pettingill, as Chafer admitted, was "the teacher they most love and cherish," and who would never think "of holding any doctrinal position . . . opposed to [his] view."[54]

The problem profoundly irritated Townsend, especially since, as R. D. Smith admitted in a letter to him, "The 'joke' about this whole affair is that the controversy has arisen in the Council, not on the Field." Townsend, who felt "very clearly that the biblical mode was by pouring," worked closely with the Robinson Bible Institute's Archer Anderson, a young Pettingill disciple, who would only immerse. The two had agreed to leave method of baptism up to the new converts and had managed to work together fairly harmoniously. As we have seen, Townsend believed fervently in the ideal of a united Christian church on the mission field. He desperately longed to avoid the denominational divisions of churches in the United States. As he wrote to Rees, "[W]e look forward to never having but one undenominational, evangelical church in each town." Now the council was fighting about an issue that Townsend thought should have been left to the missionaries, who knew the situation on the field much more intimately. Townsend grew even more upset as Pettingill's obstinacy began to threaten the delicate arrangement he had with Anderson. Anderson and another missionary couple talked of resigning and founding an independent work if Pettingill resigned.[55]

Townsend worked hard to patch over the situation, and by spring of 1924 felt he had solved the problem. Both he and Anderson wrote brief arguments for their preferred mode of baptism, which candidates for baptism had the privilege of reading before deciding how they wanted to proceed. Townsend's five single-spaced and closely reasoned pages in favor of pouring ended on an irenic note. "This is my belief," he wrote, "but many brethren whom I love with all my heart believe otherwise. Not until we get to heaven can we know who was right. Meanwhile . . . the reader . . . should [also] consider the arguments of the immersionists and should then select the form which seems to him most Biblical, but never should he belittle the beloved brethren who hold other opinions."[56]

"I think that the subject is settled once [and] for all here," Townsend reported to Chafer in March 1924. Chafer, wiser and more seasoned in doctrinal battles, advised Townsend that his exuberance was naive. "You say you got it settled," he wrote. "My impression is you just got started, so far as history can make a suggestion." Chafer proved to be right. With Pettingill having released the doctrinal cat from its bag, it refused to slink graciously back into hiding. Both Townsend and Anderson betrayed their youth, as each privately toted up the numbers of converts choosing their method of baptism. Townsend, by far the more powerful and established personality in that section of Guatemala, easily outstripped Anderson, which ultimately, as we will see, contributed to Anderson's leaving to work in a more hospitable clime.[57]

Although Pettingill eventually resigned, the controversy he caused in the CAM ignited Townsend's passion for more direct control of the mission by its field missionaries. In addition, Anderson's abrupt departure provoked Townsend to consider a field organization with real teeth that could keep missionaries at their assigned task, despite what they might feel about God's leading. He began to wonder if an organization might not hear God's voice more clearly than an individual.

There were moments when the rage that possessed Elvira terrified the entire mission compound. The council was deluged with alarming letters from frightened missionaries all during the summer and fall of 1923.

One day the young nurse, Signe Norrlin, heard screams coming from the Townsend home. Rushing to the cornstalk house, Norrlin saw frightened Indians, including quite a number of children from the children's home, gathered outside, listening. Naturally concerned, she decided to enter the home to try to intercede. "I cannot write the words I heard and the sight I saw," she reported to Chafer. "I would only like to tell you that personally the Lord only knows what I have seen and heard these past four months, even had to get up at night and separate them when they were fighting. With 20 children and servants in the house!"[58]

Fannie Becker, the elderly doctor's wife, informed Luther Rees that she could not "endure [Elvira] any longer." Mrs. Becker remembered seeing Indian workers running from the house at the onset of "an insane attack of Elvira which caused quite a scandal." After the commotion died down, a distraught Townsend confided in Mrs. Becker that he felt his "public" ministry in San Antonio was over. Too much damage had been done. The only way he might continue was if Elvira would agree to return to the United States and permit Cameron to remain in Guatemala. But they both knew such an idea was grasping at straws. Even as they discussed the issue, Elvira continued to "accuse" Townsend and "justify herself." Mrs. Becker begged the council to take action. With Elvira's "awful example and testimony," she concluded, "what influence can she possibly have over the unsaved or how can she lift up a standard before these humble believers?' "[59]

Paul Townsend was deeply concerned about the effect all of this was having on his brother, who seemed helpless to cope with his older, domineering wife. Several years earlier, when his marriage to Elvira was just beginning to wear on him, an older female missionary reported to the council, "Cameron looks frail, but his faith and trust are unwavering and truly sublime. One feels always that the boy is a host in himself." But by 1923 Townsend was reaching the end of his rope. Paul's long, candid, and painful letter to Chafer illustrates the deeper concerns of all in the CAM, the effect Elvira's behavior was having on Townsend and his rapidly expanding role in the mission. It also reveals how Townsend was coping, or not coping, with the situation.

> Many times during the past months I have felt that I should write to you and tell you about Elvira[,] but it is hard for a fellow to talk about his brother's wife in the way I feel it my duty to do. The merest reference to her before Cameron makes him pale and cuts him deeply. . . . The worst thing we have to contend with is her lying tongue. She is continually making trouble between missionaries by telling untruths or only part truths about them. We do not know when to believe her. . . .
>
> She is so jealous of Cameron that he cannot talk with any of the women

> missionaries without causing trouble. While they were in the States she objected to Cameron being with his sisters or mother without her being present. Mother said that during Cameron's entire visit she did not have as much as fifteen minutes alone with him[,] and when Elvira was present she was determined to do most of the talking. . . . I think she is crazy and the folks in the American Hospital seem to feel much the same. . . . Mr. Bishop's word as well as your own[,] I believe[,] was "cussedness[,]" but I would like to be generous and call it insanity. One thing peculiar is that when we are around her for a little while we get nervous and positively sick. Everywhere I go I hear of Elvira's actions. The believers are watching to see if the operation will make a change and so are others. It is common talk and the example of their family life is horrible. I have been asked many times the question, "How are Elvira and Cameron?" and the questioner has smiled in a knowing way and even laughed out loud. The operation has made no difference; she is worse now if anything. They fight or rather she nags half the night so that all in the house can hear them. She uses profanity at times and makes scenes before others just to make Cameron give in to her. When she has these spells she will stop at nothing to get her will. Now Cameron cannot keep up much longer. He looks like a corpse yet he will do nothing. He feels that it is his duty to live as he is until the Lord comes or she is changed. I do not.

A month later he was equally as candid. "It probably seems that I have it 'in' for my sister-in-law and I will say that I certainly have. Seeing Cameron in his terribly run-down condition last night and this morning was enough to just about break a fellow up. . . . [W]hat could Cameron be if he were not handicapped so in his work? . . . Oh, I do hope that something can be done to put Elvira where she belongs."[60]

The council was entirely flummoxed, with no good idea how to respond. R. D. Smith called it "one of the saddest things that has ever happened in the history of our work." They could not drop her as one of their missionaries, because they would then lose Cameron as well. They also worried about the trouble Elvira might cause them with the Moody Church, one of the largest missions-supporting churches in the country. Chafer feared she would "use her powers to make us out in the wrong." They decided once more to appeal to Elvira directly. Luther Rees was selected for the task. Again the problem was addressed in theological and spiritual terms. They simply had no other way in which to cope with it. "I have recently been wondering whether you appreciate the fearful responsibility resting upon you and the possibilities in your life either for or against the work of the gospel in Central America," he began. He went on to inform her that they had heard that her "condition" was "still causing considerable embarrassment in the work." "There is a difference of opinion as to the extent to which you are responsible for your actions," he lectured. "It seems to me that Satan is getting the victory in your life." He tried to be gentle. "It is not in my heart to scold. I cannot know the conflicts and trials that beset you." He closed with Keswick-inflected pieties. "But [God] knows and I do plead with you to let Him give you the victory. Don't pity yourself, because of infirmities even, but rather glory in them, that His power may rest upon you." Then, a little more sternly, "It is true that He alone can work. But there is to be on our part a definite yielding of ourselves to Him."[61]

"I sincerely thank you for this sweet, fatherly message," Elvira demurely responded, "and I am so glad it has come in the absence of my dear husband, so that he shall never know about it, for I think it would break his heart." She insisted that her life before coming to the mission field "had always been in harmony with [her] testimony," and that she could get along with anybody. She seemed genuinely grieved. "I do not mention these things to boast or to justify myself in the least, for I know as well as does my Lord Whom I have seriously grieved, that I am not worthy of a single word of commendation in my actions ever since my marriage." She tried to explain her actions, saying that in her home in Chicago, "I never knew anything . . . but the most scrupulous neatness and everything most inviting, and that with limited means and economy." Since coming to the field she had been forced "to fight in order to live in a fashion that is at all appealing." Indicating that perhaps a cornstalk house in an Indian village had not been the best choice for her, she explained, "I cannot stand dirt and disorder and unsystematic living, and I never have been able to see that because we are missionaries that we should be made to live a life of sacrifice along that line, in our own homes." She candidly confessed, "Naturally therefore I have asked for things that would tend to just such a home, and not getting them, I began to nag until just such a bitter spirit is mine at times that I just do not know what to do." She paid her husband, who once confessed to living and working in "slip-shod" fashion, a backhanded compliment: "I have spent a good bit of time in the home of his folks[,] so I know and realize that it is in a very, very different way that he has been brought up from me and he is not to blame." She concluded by promising once again to try to "let go and let God." Unaware of any medical science that could help her, and believing it to be a spiritual problem, where else could she turn? Her desperation to overcome her emotions and her genuine desire to live up to the missionary ideal mingle in her plaintive and agonized promises.

> And now it is for me to yield to God, and say yes! yes! even though it will be without just the kind of a home-life that I long for. This spirit has developed into pride and selfishness which cannot and must not rule this life, for which my own dear mother has so earnestly prayed and given me for His service. My life must possess the fruit of the Spirit and I know God offers it to me. Last year it was fairly a haven of rest to be at home with mother and to enjoy the home that is so dear to me, but God has called me to service on the battlefield, and woe is me if I can only live a sweet life when all is agreeable. No! His grace is sufficient. I do yield my life, my all to Him and trust Him to do the rest. . . . I am not worthy to be called a child of God and much less a messenger of His. But oh! how I love to witness for Him and long to be used of Him.[62]

Rees, always in Cameron's corner, was inclined to give the couple one more chance to remain in active service. "I think that the fact that she knows the Council is watching her case will do much toward [changing] her behavior," he told Chafer. Chafer, however, was more realistic. He knew the chances of her truly changing were remote, so he asked Townsend to leave San Antonio and Panajachel and take a home somewhere, preferably Guatemala City, far enough away from any mission center that any embarrassment caused by Elvira could not be linked to the mission. Chafer thought such a home would be a perfect setting to quietly carry on his translation work.[63]

If Townsend had been so inclined he might have seen Chafer's suggestion as the hand of God freeing him from all extraneous labor to devote himself totally to his translation work. A year or so later he might, in fact, have seen it that way. At the time, however, Townsend loved the house on the lake in Panajachel and longed to remain there. After Bible translation, the Robinson Bible Institute was his favorite endeavor. He begged Chafer to permit him to stay. "I feel like a 'castaway' with my fingers slipping from the longed-for crown," he pled. He promised that Elvira had been "crying to God for victory" and that she was much better. She was currently boarding at the Ainslie home "while the Dr. studies her case." Townsend noted that Ainslie was "quite hopeful of locating her trouble soon." He even talked of his parents coming to Guatemala to "make me a home [and] take care of Elvira."[64]

Dr. Ainslie had indeed placed Elvira under observation in his home. The agreement with the mission was that he would care for her for six months, and at the end of that period would give the council his professional judgment as to her condition. If at that point she had "not been relieved of her outbursts of temper and her opposition to her husband," Ainslie was "prepared to give medical testimony to her inability to serve as a missionary." Elvira, however, refused to serve out her six months.

Somehow Townsend managed to continue his work. In August 1923 the Indian workers began running the Gospel of John off the little press in the Townsend home. After they printed John, Townsend decided to finish the whole New Testament before doing any more printing. He wanted to wait until they completed a good translation of the entire Testament rather than publish early versions that would need extensive revision. In addition, his early translation efforts had aroused opposition from *ladinos,* and even from a few Indian converts who knew Spanish and maintained their positions in church leadership through the ignorance of the Scripture on the part of the majority. Several council members and Guatemala missionaries were also critical of this expenditure of his time. R. D. Smith, for one, discouraged his translation work, thinking it took too much time away from the supervision of the larger work. They fought about it sharply later when Townsend was home in the summer of 1925, eventually necessitating mutual apologies. Townsend had strong supporters among some council members and missionaries as well. Chafer was delighted with the Gospel of John in parallel columns that Townsend sent. "This is an amazing piece of work," he exclaimed. Albert Bishop was also "filled with wonder and delight." Still, Townsend hoped to take the work underground for a few years to mute criticism.[65]

The work was slow, however, as Townsend had numerous other responsibilities. By late 1923 Townsend's love for his translation work was causing internal conflicts over his priorities. With Elvira sick again, he thought of taking a year's leave of absence in the United States (a notion normally abhorrent to him) to help her and try to "regain [his] old time pep." He wanted to take his two translation helpers with him. He told Chafer, "One thing I can't think of giving up is my language work." While some missionaries believed his priority ought to be managing the San Antonio station, Laura Townsend, resigned to Cameron's departure, remarked to her folks, "He said he would go crazy if he didn't get to translating pretty soon[,] so I guess there is no hopes of keeping him out here." Eventually, with Elvira hospitalized under Ainslie's care in Guatemala City, Townsend moved full-time to Panajachel. He turned the work at the RBI over to Archer Anderson so that he could focus on translation. By May 1924 he seems to have begun spending considerable time translating again.[66]

By late 1923, with Dinwiddie apparently committed to a permanent Indian-promoting globetrotting ministry, letters between him and Townsend were few and far between. Although he essentially left Townsend behind, their mutual esteem never abated. The CAM council, on the other hand, was thoroughly sick of all things Dinwiddie. "Explore, *Explore*, EXPLORE! Mark my word, he will be off to Persia or Tibet next," laughed R. D. Smith. He remarked sarcastically to Chafer, "When I read [Dinwiddie's] articles I am so often reminded of what Josh Billing said, 'I am getting tired of knowing so many things that are not true.'" Of a Dinwiddie trip to the Amazon, Chafer groaned, "I suspect that we will be deluged with marvels and wonders when he gets back to civilization." When Dinwiddie came to Los Angeles for meetings, Smith reported that he was to be housed next door to the furloughing Albert Bishop. "Poor Brother Bishop," he remarked, "I fear his nerves will go on a rampage."[67]

In 1924 the Cakchiquel Department of the Central American Mission consisted of three stations. San Antonio was the site of the Louise Heim Indian hospital, Louise Heim Indian children's home, a school for children of converts, and the printing press for publication of "gospel literature" in Indian languages. The Panajachel station consisted of the Robinson Bible Institute for Indian workers, and the Bible translation work carried on in the Townsend home. A station in San Lucas had a small clinic. The special Cakchiquel Department letterhead proclaimed, "All stations give first place to evangelistic work."

Paul and Laura Townsend and the rest of the San Antonio team were struggling to keep up. The hospital now boarded eight patients, and a new addition promised still more room. The children's home housed fifty students, twice as many as capacity. Ninety turned up regularly for classes. "The kids are over running us with head and body lice and we are waging a war on them," sighed Laura to her parents. "We are boiling everything we can and are fumigating the rooms." Fortunately, the children were fairly self-sufficient. They did "all of the real work such as cleaning, dish washing and most of the cooking." Alicia de León, the "native matron," was "very competent" and shouldered a good bit of the responsibility. Annie Esdon and Lavanchie Barrows, two hardworking farm girls, had arrived the year before to replace Jennette Tallet. Together they oversaw a daily schedule that began at 5:30 a.m. when the wake-up gong sounded. By 6:00 everyone was at work. The girls made tortillas while the boys chopped wood, ground corn, swept, and cleaned. The older boys tended the garden. At 7:00 everyone gathered for breakfast. School began at 8:00, with class sessions running from 8:00 to 11:30 a.m. and 1:30 to 4:00 p.m. Dinner was served at 5:30. At 7:00 all assembled for singing and prayers, followed by bed for the young ones and homework for the older children. The *Cakchiquel News* reported, "About seventy percent of the children enter the school with the express pur-

8. Carl Malmstrom and wife, Cameron and Elvira beside Panajachel home on Lake Atitlán. Courtesy Townsend Archives.

pose of preparing [to be] pastors and Church workers."[68] As these were small children, who could hardly have been realistically expected at their age to have chosen their life's vocation, this statement of purpose seems transparently a sop to their supporters and the CAM council. It reflects the tension Townsend felt between the declared purpose of the mission and the broad program that he now oversaw.

A sample income report from 1924 shows the Townsend monthly income at $225, which included $10 and $11 from individual donors, $6 from an individual to help support a native evangelist, $125 from Church of the Open Door, and $73 from the CAM general fund. By the end of the year, the Townsends' personal funds climbed to more than $300 per month after Chafer put Cameron in touch with a well-to-do Scottish industrialist who began sending Townsend $1,350 every year. Chafer could have chosen to connect this man with virtually any of the CAM missionaries, although the industrialist was "not an immersionist and would not care to support an immersionist propaganda." Townsend was a particular favorite of Chafer's, although the entire council recognized that the twenty-eight-year-old was quite possibly already their most accomplished and ambitious missionary, if also at times their most troublesome. In the tradition of passing additional talents to those who already possessed much, Chafer sent the money to Townsend, saying that the support "would be a matter of peculiar fellowship between yourself and Mr. Nairn."[69]

Townsend was not content to remain even at that level of generous support, however. He continued to publicize his needs in that elastic area at the edge of what faith missions considered proper. Townsend utilized the *Central American Bulletin* heavily, knowing that the time spent writing rich, descriptive letters to the home secretary would pay off if his letters were chosen for publication. In the *CAB* Townsend sometimes presented his needs directly, particularly during Chafer's years as CAM general secretary, even managing to slip dollar figures into his notices. "What do you think of Miss Barrows running a school for about ninety children out of $50.00 a month?" read a typical letter. "She is mighty happy in doing it, but . . . she is in great need of a new building. . . . Several thousand dollars are needed to construct a school building and a separate girls' dormitory, and equip them properly."[70]

In the *Cakchiquel News,* which he personally printed and mailed to supporters, Townsend regularly flouted faith rules by the end of 1924, mentioning financial needs in dollar amounts in virtually every issue. He rationalized his change in philosophy by arguing that supporters were losing blessings because they were uninformed of opportunities for service. In a tangled thicket of rationalization, he wrote:

> How many more opportunities would there have been for service if Christian, praying people had known of this work so that they could have helped? . . . There is someone who would have been happy in this work with us who is now very unhappy because he or she is not getting the best God has for him or her. . . . We . . . will not try to tell anyone how to invest either time or money but from now on we will have a little space in The Cakchiquel News dedicated to the telling of what seems to us to be rare investments. They will be told briefly so as not to mislead anyone by human sympathies. We believe that truly "great minds run in the same channel" because they are all yielded to the guidance of the Holy Spirit.

Townsend went on to note that five dollars per month would support a child at home and school, fifty dollars would repair the floor in the children's dining room, and twenty-five dollars would keep the Model T running. He presented a long list of other needs both large and small, including a motorboat and an electric plant, which would "increase efficiency and lessen costs." (Both boat and electric plant eventually became realities.) When he ran out of funds to finish a new chapel, he wrote, "The congregation has done all it can and they are now looking toward the north for help to complete the building." He reported that five hundred dollars would finish the project.[71]

Townsend was consumed with other promotional projects as well. In 1924 he wrote a thirty-eight-page biography of Antonio Bac, one of his favorite Indian workers. Although he was unsuccessful in getting it published, the booklet wound up in abridged form in a book put out by the Moody Bible Institute Colportage Association titled *Souls Set Free,* which contained missionary stories from several fields. He wrote articles for the most popular evangelical magazines, including *The King's Business, The Sunday School Times, Moody Monthly,* and *The Christian Herald,* and urged the council to run ads in the same. He also wrote a thirty-two-page booklet called "The Guatemalan Indian" and ordered three thousand copies. The last several pages were devoted to an explicit mention of financial needs. A missionary could be supported for fifty dollars per month, a "Spirit-filled native preacher" for ten to thirty-five dollars per month depending on location and size of family, and an orphan educated for three to five dollars per month. In addition, twenty thousand dollars was needed for a mission building in San Salvador; other buildings were needed at various centers for one thousand to five thousand dollars. "A proposed central Bible Institute also affords a splendid opportunity for investment." The council, perhaps turning a blind eye as Townsend's work prospered, sponsored the booklet. Someone with a sense of humor noted on the last page, "The Mission was born and has reached its present thriving state through prayer and today solicits neither missionaries nor funds except at the Throne of Grace."[72]

Some of Townsend's fund-raising schemes were quirky, demonstrating his eagerness to think outside the norm. He ordered 150 copies of a book on Indians after getting a special deal from the author. He talked his folks into selling them, with the profit going to his work. He tried to talk Chafer into hawking them in the *Bulletin,* but Chafer refused, saying such a scheme was contrary to "our whole basis of work."[73]

The Cakchiquel Department of the CAM focused its ministry primarily on Indian evangelism and founding Indian churches. Albert Bishop and the Cinco Calles elders continued to oversee the *ladino* evangelists and churches. When Bishop was invalided home in 1924, however, the situation rapidly deteriorated into a nasty struggle over theology, vision, and turf.

Fred Lincoln, a CAM missionary since 1911, took over the supervision of the *ladino* work in Bishop's absence. That summer a prominent *ladino* pastor, Don Arturo Borja, complained to Lincoln that Townsend refused to place his Indian workers and congregations in Borja's area under Borja's leadership. Borja, who was reported to have informed the CAM that it was "money thrown away" to build schools for Indians, claimed to have been "used of God" to raise up four Indian congregations. Townsend retorted, "AS USUAL HE GIVES no credit to the Indian pastors who did most all the work." Borja argued that Townsend's divisions had "resulted in spiritual loss to the Indians." He suggested that in each town there be a "Ladino Pastor and an Indian Preacher." Townsend replied, "If you knew Don Arturo better, you would understand that he means that the preacher be under the pastor." For his part, Borja claimed to be taking the high road, telling Paul Townsend that Cameron's plan was "diametrically opposed to the word of God and to justice." "If this is my crime," he said, "I am willing to die for it, and I believe the hand of the Omnipotent is with me."[74]

Townsend told Lincoln that he had developed the Indian work "with two ends constantly in view; unity and efficiency, with no thought of personal ambition." Nevertheless, within the larger unity, it was necessary to have a distinct and largely separate Indian work, or the Indians would be neglected and all the missionaries would go into Spanish-language ministry. Townsend insisted that experience demonstrated that unified church meetings with dual translators simply did not work. If Indians predominated at the service, *ladinos* stayed away, and vice versa. The problem was doubly difficult in evangelistic services. It was well and good to preach unity to converts, but you could not expect unconverted Indians to enter a service where *ladinos* predominated. Townsend likened his plan to the First Mexican Presbyterian Church of Los Angeles, which, although an autonomous church in many ways, was still governed by the Presbytery of Los Angeles. Townsend felt that any objections to this method of organization were "due almost in every case to desire upon the part of certain Ladinos that the Indians continue in subservience to them." He asked Lincoln to request the *ladino* workers to "quit dabbling in the affairs of the Indian congregations in a bossy way" and to exhort them "to look upon the Indian pastors as their equals." He suggested a united meeting for communion once a month with alternating leadership and location to stress the point of equality as well as unity. He concluded, "As the Indian is gradually assimilated in the Ladino population and the need of specialized effort ceases to exist, the organizations could gradually be amalgamated, but this will be many, many years to come."[75]

The problem, of course, was one of emphasis. From the beginning, where Townsend spoke of unity but emphasized equality, Bishop spoke of equality but emphasized unity. For Bishop, theological considerations were primary—the church was to be one body. For Townsend, practical considerations were primary—race prejudice was a fact of life; Indians would not attend worship and would never develop leadership ability if forced to gather with people they thought despised them. Bishop had agreed with the separate chapel approach, but he wanted "union meetings" several times a week, not once a month, and he wanted a board of elders over both chapels, with elders chosen from each congregation. "Just like Jew and Gentile came together, so should Indian and ladino," Bishop told Townsend. Fred Lincoln agreed. He felt Townsend was fostering prejudice by dividing the work. He wanted the two groups to be forced together to deal with the issue. He accused Townsend of dividing the work without proper consultation.[76] Ultimately, despite what seemed a great deal of common ground, the dispute refused to go away. Townsend and Lincoln had different constituencies. Townsend primarily listened to the concerns of the Indians. Lincoln primarily listened to the concerns of the *ladino* elders.

For Townsend, there was too much at stake to allow any encroachment on his methods or territory. He felt he had developed an entirely new method of working with Indians that *ladinos* simply could not duplicate. Townsend eloquently argued against the common wisdom that held that "you must resort to force and to sternness to get any place with the Indian." "Certainly it is the easiest way here where everyone treats him sternly," he argued, "but I am becoming more and more convinced that it is the wrong way." Treated in that fashion, Indians would show respect and act humble, but would always treat you as an outsider, "as . . . one who enters not at all into the sphere of his soul." But when treated gently, Townsend argued, you would develop "a Christian who is strong in his soul and thinks for himself rather than simply submitting in humble ignorance as previously under the other system." Even Christian *ladinos,* Townsend felt, lacked "completely the necessary sympathy and understanding" of Indians to ever treat them in any way other than as inferiors.[77]

In the spring of 1924, after Elvira prematurely checked herself out of Dr. Ainslie's care, Townsend took his wife to Panajachel. In doing so, he expressly violated Chafer's instructions to keep Elvira far enough away from any mission station that she would have no opportunity to embarrass the CAM further. Townsend argued that Chafer's instructions were that Elvira was not to be permitted *directly in* any mission station. As the house on Lake Atitlán was a mile from town and the Robinson Bible Institute, he considered that Elvira would not be *in* the station. Townsend was like a child eagerly trying to convince his father to let him keep playing past curfew. "Oh, Mr. Chafer, it's wonderful here. I'm getting to feel like a kid again," he wrote. "You would like to see me running my horse at a gallop jumping ditches . . . just for fun. . . . I want to go forward. Things have never been brighter." He tried a little humor. "If you feel that we have disobeyed, I can only trust that the dictates of the Council may not be as unchangeable as those of the Medes & the Persians."[78]

The house was, however, where Archer Anderson was staying. Chafer had assured Anderson that Elvira would not be coming to Panajachel, and Anderson was surprised to find her there when he got back from a trip to Huehuetenango. He dashed off a letter to Chafer. "I thought that you saw that it is really at the peril of the work here that she comes." He refused to live in the same house with her and moved into a room at the RBI. A month later Anderson threatened to resign from the mission. He suggested that the council was lax in its responsibility to deal with Elvira ("tolerating sin" was how he put it), because Cameron was viewed as too important to antagonize. "You gave me your word that Elvira would not be permitted to be in Panajachel," he fumed piously to Chafer. "For my own spiritual life I will leave."

Anderson may have been sincere in his feelings, and in truth, he had reason to worry. But it must be remembered that he was very young, and had recently been challenged by Paul Townsend for "flirting" openly with Elvira in an unseemly fashion. Perhaps guilt added to his vehemence. Pride and ambition probably played more directly into the mess created in the following months, however. Anderson sensed an opportunity to increase his own authority at the RBI at the expense of Cameron's. The reader may remember that Anderson was upset when most new converts in the area chose Townsend's method of baptism over his. Townsend clearly was "the man" as far as the Indians were concerned, and Anderson apparently felt his secondary status keenly. Indeed, secondary status was the only status open for competition for missionaries in Townsend's orbit. Paul Townsend felt it, too, though with less regret. He mentioned once that the Indians rarely listened to him unless he began by invoking the name of "don Guillermo" (Cameron). "Some seem to think that because I am his brother I ought to have something to say[,] and others seem to think that since I am *only* his brother, what I say is of no value unless I say 'don Guillermo says so.'" At least Paul was rather used to it. "I feel that since God has placed me here I must stay[,] even if it is only to play second fiddle to Cameron all my life."[79]

Anderson was right, of course, that the council was inclined to extend Townsend every opportunity to continue his work on the field. Like the star player on a baseball team, different rules seemed to apply. But in reality, anyone willing to be as stubborn as Townsend could get away with virtually any flaunting of the council's authority. Naturally those with a sizable personal constituency had a good bit more leeway. Chafer was not happy that Cameron and Elvira had returned to Panajachel, but agreed to let them stay if Elvira would stay away from the RBI and not cause any public trouble. "It certainly is going to be a serious condition if word reaches us that a bad testimony is being created in any mission field," he warned Townsend. "We must depend upon you to protect our hard-earned work by the most definite and drastic stand on your part." In words that probably did not mollify him, Chafer explained to Anderson, "[Townsend] is one of our most valuable missionaries and we are hoping some arrangement can be made which will not drive him wholly from the field."[80]

Despite the council's and Townsend's best intentions, the situation at Panajachel deteriorated rapidly. Elvira's presence exacerbated the differences of opinion between Townsend and Anderson over how best to engage in Indian work. The RBI became the focal point of contention as Anderson privately plotted with the Treichlers and the Tomses to move the school to Huehuetenango. When Townsend realized what was happening, he refused to let the students leave. He accused Anderson of attempting to "steal the affections of the men." Things got so bad that Townsend requested that the council send funds for the institute directly to him, bypassing Anderson. The situation profoundly discouraged Luther Rees. "We are going through deep waters," he scrawled in the margins of a letter from Townsend, "and those we love are causing it."[81]

The problem eventually forced the council's hand. Most of the Guatemala missionaries took Anderson's side in the dispute, or at least requested that Elvira be removed from all contact with the work. Even the San Antonio missionaries, Townsend's closest coworkers, supported her removal. Chafer once again asked Townsend to remove from Panajachel, even as he expressed full support and love for him. "We would gladly do anything in our power to make matters easier for you," he wrote. "But we have more interests than one to consider at the present time."[82]

The reception of this letter may have been the low point of Townsend's years in Guatemala. He bitterly announced to Anderson that since the council had taken Anderson's side in the dispute, he would resign. He refused to leave Panajachel, however. He vowed to build his own home beside the lake and continue the translation work as well as the direction of the Cakchiquel workers. "For three months we have had a happy home," he told Anderson, "and I don't propose that you and the mission should rob us of it." He once again appealed to God as his guide. "My sympathetic Savior has shown me that it is the only thing that I can do and save my home and our usefulness for the work. I have given of my very best to the mission and to you[,] and since I receive a helping hand from neither of you[,] I feel perfectly free to work out my own salvation."[83]

Anderson fired back the very next day. In a letter not designed to regain

Townsend's friendship, Anderson lectured, "When you came out here you did it in open rebellion to the council. I have prayed that the Lord would take this rebelliousness out of you[,] for it hurts to see you in this condition." Then, playing a card only selectively played by faith missionaries through the years: "For, Cam, the Word of God teaches us that we should submit ourselves to those who have the rule over us."[84]

Backed into a corner, and perhaps having thought through the consequences of his threat, two days later Townsend tried once again to make peace. "Andy, we have planned and dreamed together," he begged. "Won't you take back your ultimatum to the Council and let's go ahead and show what real brotherly unity is? I beseech you, Andy, by the memories of blessed fellowship in the past."[85]

Before officially resigning, Townsend made one last attempt to sway the council. Another missionary, on Townsend's behalf, collected statements from the fourteen Indian students currently at Panajachel. Each solemnly swore they knew nothing of a "bad testimony" concerning Elvira. The statements provide a remarkable, if brief, glimpse into the relationship the Townsends had forged over the years with the Cakchiquels. "I have known [Cameron] for six years, and with all my heart I can say that I have not found one defect in him. In my congregation I have not heard nothing about any scandal concerning Mrs. Townsend," wrote one. "This is the work of the enemy. I love her in the Lord," said another. Others said similar things: "They have been like a father and mother to us." "What I know is that he has a love for the Indians." Many said they knew Elvira had been "sick," the explanation undoubtedly provided them by Cameron. Margarito Otzoy, their closest translation helper, who spent considerable time in their home, was the only one who claimed to have directly witnessed an "outbreak." "Regarding his wife[,] I have been told of her illness that caused her outbreaks," he said. "Once I heard what seemed to be a quarrel, and immediately I rose up and left with Mr. Townsend. I did not know what was wrong. I asked Mr. Townsend but he told me nothing. I have heard of another outbreak. I myself love Mrs. Townsend in the Lord and believe the believers in San Antonio love her too."[86]

In addition to the testimonials, and in a remarkable reversal of typical roles, Townsend asked the Indian workers "to do what they could to bring about peace" by writing to either Anderson or Chafer. Antonio Bac, the Indian evangelist whose biography Townsend wrote and tried to publish, wrote a neutral letter to Chafer, and eight men cosigned it. He referred to Townsend as "the missionary," and Anderson as "the professor." "We all affirm that we have no feeling against any of our foreign, American brothers and especially neither against our missionaries nor against our professor," he wrote. "But now we have come to know of trouble between them, the missionary and the professor. The reason is very clear. Through [them] we have received great blessings and for this reason, the Enemy wants to destroy us." He concluded, "We want . . . peace real soon." Townsend triumphantly forwarded the letter and testimonials to the council, remarking, "The Indian workers whom Mr. Anderson claimed to be protecting from our 'terrible testimony' stand with us to a man." Furthermore, he claimed the Indians had promised that if he left, they would leave also. "God has given me a ministry among the Cakchiquel Indians," he concluded, "and I must continue to carry it forward."[87]

A Presbyterian minister who spent ten days with Anderson traveling to Indian congregations, then three weeks in Panajachel with the Townsends, chimed in. He wrote to Chafer to contribute a "disinterested outsider's view." The letter was more than likely solicited by Townsend, so is perhaps of limited value. It does, however, confirm reports from other sources, and demonstrates Townsend's enormous persuasive powers. The traveling minister reported that the antagonists were of "two distinct types." Townsend was "a most unselfish, an exceedingly modest, an unusually accommodating and most successful missionary whom everybody loves and respects for his years of unselfish work among the Indians." Anderson, however, had "not met the marks of modesty shown by Mr. Townsend, but is rather egotistical and bold . . . [and had demonstrated a] most unchristian attitude towards the Townsends." After all, "What was to hinder him from busying himself with his school, which by the way is really Cameron's school, and from allowing the Townsends in isolation to work out their own domestic problems and continue their translation of the New Testament?" He concluded, "Of course no married man can think well of a young man who tries to give advice or interfere with another's domestic relations."[88]

The situation grew even more confused, because Luther Rees and Chafer, the two most prominent men in the council, held different viewpoints on the matter. Rees was inclined to support Townsend, claiming that as senior missionary at Panajachel he had the right to stay there as long as Elvira made no public scenes. The case reminded Rees of John Wesley, who, he said, "accomplished so much in spite of the eccentricities and opposition of his wife." In spiritual terms, Rees did not want to see Satan use Elvira to drive Cameron from the field. Chafer, influenced by R. D. Smith, got the Elvira situation tangled up with the battle for authority in the mission. He felt he simply had to stand by his earlier directive to Townsend or risk placing the authority of the council in jeopardy. He declared to Rees, "I have pressed [Cameron] to this to the limit and he <u>must</u> do as he is told. . . . I saw too much of the tendency down there to ignore the Council and set up a missionary government[,] and Cam was leading in that propaganda." Chafer was also adamant, however, that Townsend and Anderson settle their differences. To Townsend he wrote, "You two boys have got to get together and pray this out and get back into love and fellowship. . . . You are older in years and experience[,] and you know how to dig out the roots of bitterness and return to blessing. May I not expect you to do this for the honor of Christ and the defeat of Satan."[89]

News of Townsend's bitter letter to Anderson and resignation threat reached Chafer as he boarded a boat for Europe. He fired off a note to Luther Rees as his ship pulled away from the dock and sent it back with the pilot. He begged Rees to go immediately to Guatemala to straighten things out, saying he would go himself if he did not have prior commitments in Europe. He warned Rees, "Remember this is not Cam's real self. He is driven and pressed by a crazy woman and doubtless needs a friend." He added, as if it was some consolation, "Conditions are even more disturbed in other missions. The [Africa Inland Mission] is near a crash. It is Satan's final smash."[90]

As usual, R. D. Smith toed a harder line. The mentor turned on his protégé. He was in favor of calling Townsend's bluff, and told Rees he did not think he should go to the field, as it would set a bad precedent for the council to appear too disturbed over the "resignation threat of a headstrong missionary." "Mrs. Townsend has been an absolute dead-weight and worse in our Mission for several years," he harrumphed, "and we have ample proof that he has not been able to stand up against her will, so that much as I regret losing him[,] I really feel that if they had not resigned we should have had to have dismissed them before very long."[91]

Rees, now freed of Chafer's oversight, immediately cabled Townsend: "Don't resign. Await Committee's decision." He refused to forward Chafer's final letter to Townsend, fearing it would "irritate" him. He argued for dealing "very cautiously with one who has been so wonderfully used of God during his connection with the Central American Mission,—and that with a 'crazy woman,' as you call her, on his hands." Rees went so far as to remind the council of what the future King David said when encouraged to attack King Saul. David warned his soldiers, "Do not destroy him, for who can stretch out his hands against the Lord's anointed and be without guilt?" It is difficult to imagine a more strongly worded statement of respect for the life and work of a young man not yet thirty years old.[92]

The executive committee now backed Rees, professing to not understand what could have been on Chafer's mind when he asked Townsend to leave Panajachel. The committee, of course, was made up of the few council members who lived in the Dallas area. With Chafer gone, Rees in effect had them in his pocket. Both R. D. Smith and William Pettingill favored Chafer's position, but living a great distance from Dallas, they were easily cut out of the loop. Rees restored Townsend to full authority over Panajachel and, by extension, Archer Anderson. He concluded, "I am so glad to learn that Elvira is feeling better and is gaining in flesh and that you are both so hopeful. Why should you not be? As Brother Powell said in our meeting, 'We have been praying for this, and why should we not expect it?' "[93]

In the meantime, Paul Townsend had journeyed to Panajachel to try to make peace. Apparently he was successful, because before Rees's letter reached the field, Anderson and Cameron had settled their differences. Townsend used the settlement to further his other ambition—namely, to see more authority vested in the missionaries themselves. In a letter signed by Elvira, Archer, Paul, and himself, Cameron reported that an agreement had been drawn up that settled the matter. The Townsends would stay at Panajachel; they promised to leave if a reoccurrence "of such conditions as existed in San Antonio" developed. Elvira would stay out of public work until the council gave her permission to return. Anderson would withdraw his ultimatum and continue to work at the RBI every other month, spending the off month working at a different location. The letter noted, "We agree to forget this whole matter and hope that the council will do likewise." In a clear rebuke to the home council, Townsend added, "Hereafter any question of dispute will be brought before the Cakchiquel Department organization before it is presented to the home council. In an emergency the General Secretary of this organization has the power to make a temporary decision which is binding until the following meeting of the organization." Anderson added privately to Rees, "I do believe that Cam and I are knit closer together than we have ever been. . . . I fear that I may have resorted to some 'mud throwing' at Cam in the correspondence that has been ours. I have asked his pardon and now want to get it all straightened up with you folks."[94]

For the next several months nothing but good news came out of Panajachel. Even R. D. Smith was inclined to be hopeful. "What you tell me about conditions in C[ameron] T[ownsend's] Station . . . greatly cheers my heart[,] and I think I have had more faith since reading your letter for Elvira than I have ever had before," he told Rees. "I hope my lack of faith has not held back the blessing which I am sure she needs." On several occasions Elvira discreetly mentioned to Rees that she was still burdened with too many houseguests. "I would not even mention the fact to you if I had a cook and other servants, but this of course is between you and me," she complained. Still, she undoubtedly found her home and its surroundings at Panajachel much more agreeable than San Antonio. "We have a real BEAUTIFUL home," she confided to Rees. "I do not know if you can fully appreciate what it means to me to have a REAL home after living in filth and dirt and disorder for those years in a HUT in San Antonio." During Anderson's final three months in Panajachel, he boarded with the Townsends without incident. Soon, however, discouraged by the difficulty of learning Cakchiquel, he "lost the Indian vision" and left in October 1924, four months after his rapprochement with Townsend, to begin a "mixed school" with Frank and Annie Toms. "He is wonderfully gifted" was Townsend's epitaph, but "he'll never do much for the Indians . . . unless he learns their language. It's IMPOSSIBLE."[95]

Dr. Becker, who had lived with his wife, Fannie, for several years with the Townsends in their cornstalk hut, was not much help at the San Antonio clinic. He had thrown over medical practice for his new passion, evangelism. For the past year, he had been experimenting with an exciting new method for reaching the Indians with the gospel. He was now ready to announce to his superiors in Texas that he had unearthed "the quickest and least expensive method of evangelization . . . to date." This momentous discovery was the megaphone. "It multiplies the efficiency of the missionary . . . many fold," he boasted, "as by it the largest town can be evangelized in a few minutes, or remote settlements reached without difficulty of hard walking." He found that the best time to "attack" a town with the megaphone gospel was at 5:00 a.m., when people were still in their homes. In this manner he evangelized San Lucas "from the mountain above the town," preaching to an "invisible audience of Indians." He felt certain that "the message reached many ears a long way off." He discovered that for the most part "people . . . listened with respectful attention," with one man reportedly saying, "It must be the truth that the Evangelistas preach, because God is now telling the same thing to us from Heaven." But in Patzum the villagers "got together some tin cans and made quite a noise to try to drown the Gospel message[,] but it was in vain." In Pakip, where they preached from atop a large rock on the ground of a Protestant farmer, the people "shouted at a distance." Someone fired a shotgun, but "the bullet only whizzed above [their] heads." A gun exploded in the hands of another would-be shooter in a different town "so that no harm was done." Despite the inherent dangers, Dr. Becker was confident that as "faith cometh by hearing . . . the message [will certainly] bear fruit in their lives." He reported that many Indians had been reached with the megaphone gospel, rendering them thus "without excuse." Townsend was not entirely enthusiastic about his colleague's megaphone adventures, much later wryly dismissing Becker's megaphone ministry by remarking that the good doctor "did not find the Indian mind very receptive to this form of approach."[96]

Elvira. Dr. Becker. Mrs. Treichler. Jennette Tallet. Were they eccentric? Cussedly independent? Psychologically troubled? Regardless, how did one small mission wind up with such a high percentage of odd folks patrolling its territory? One could as well ask, how did the faith missions keep anybody out? The answers lie in that odd nexus between faith mission ideals and faith mission practice.

Faced with the prospect of sending out missionaries with virtually no promised support to countries where living conditions for Westerners were fierce, if not suicidal, faith mission leaders desperately needed to recruit extremely committed men and women, if one can use the term "recruit" at all when speaking of such missions. The term must be used guardedly. The more conservative missions felt about active recruiting the same way they felt about soliciting funds. To actively recruit would be to display a lack of trust that God would supply the necessary missionaries in his time. When the CAM council was encouraged to recruit one promising young man, they replied, "We would not feel at liberty to be the first to raise the question of his entering our Mission; as you know[,] it is opposed to our policy to ask anyone to become a member of our Mission."[97] In general, however, their methods of application, such as they were, were designed to ensure that they obtained very faithful missionaries.

The faith missions preferred candidates from the Bible institutes or from reputable evangelical churches, where they could trust the word of a known pastor or institute executive as to the spiritual credentials of the applicant. Beyond that they relied on a short application form and often a brief interview with a council member to determine a candidate's fitness. The CAM application form was only two pages long. The most important question was dealt with immediately: "Do you understand that you are to trust the Lord for the supply of all your needs, and not rely upon the C.A.M. or any other human agency?" Twenty-seven brief questions followed, such as, "Are you in debt?" "Are you a total abstainer from stimulants and tobacco?" "Are you willing to hazard your life in unhealthy localities . . . to reach the unsaved?" Only three lines were designated for the applicant to describe his or her conversion, a topic that would be explored in great detail in the candidate's interview. They were required to endorse the CAM doctrinal statement, which was fairly standard within conservative evangelicalism. When candidates were interviewed, however, they were advised "of the dispensational *and* Calvinistic position of the mission" (emphasis mine), and were not appointed unless they were "in harmony with such teachings." As Luther Rees explained, "Although we would receive into the fellowship of our local churches, any who were sound on the fundamentals, we would not appoint as missionaries, those who did not hold with us on dispensational questions. . . . I am satisfied that the missionaries of the China Inland Mission are Calvinists and Premillennialists." Men were asked specifically about how they preferred to administer baptism and if they could perform the rite another way if requested. There was room to describe what kind of Christian service they had done and "with what result." Three lines were designated to explain their reasons for seeking missionary service. The only question truly pertinent to cross-cultural living, other than whether they were willing to hazard their life, was a request to know if they had ever studied a foreign language. Beyond that, a medical exam was required, as well as two or three references.[98]

If the candidate seemed acceptable from his application, the mission endeavored to have him meet with a member of the council. This could be difficult, especially if the candidate did not live conveniently close. Candidates were often poor and could not afford to travel to meet with a council member. The mission used trusted "referees" in such circumstances. It was not impossible for a missionary to be sent to Central America without ever meeting with a member of the mission. This problem was exacerbated for the council, because missionaries on the field often did their own recruiting among their friends and acquaintances. Townsend was one of the worst offenders in this regard. At times people Townsend had recruited would show up in Dallas to join the mission before the council knew anything about them. In 1924 the council discovered that a woman whose services they had politely declined had already been installed by Townsend "in service at San Antonio." (One of the problems the council apparently had with this woman was that she liked to wear pants, which perhaps scandalized the natives. Townsend made her promise not to "wear her breeches around San Antonio and Antigua.") At other times missionaries who arrived in Guatemala with a particular assignment soon asked the council to let them join Townsend's Indian work. Townsend's protestations of innocence rarely convinced his superiors. "I want to explain that I didn't once think of Miss Barrows for San Antonio until she first spoke of her desire to get into Indian work," he innocently reported. "I haven't been proselyting." Such activity led R. D. Smith to wring his hands in frustration. "I feel we ought to do something about our missionaries accepting for work in our CAM stations people . . . with whom the Council has had no correspondence," he griped. "We must have some kind of understanding with our missionaries that they, as well as ourselves, <u>are members of an organization</u> and that it is <u>for us</u> as a Council to decide who shall work in connection with the CAM stations,—not the missionary."[99]

The council members used the candidate interview to determine the applicant's spiritual fitness for missionary work. R. D. Smith's report on his interview with Paul and Laura Townsend demonstrates well the focus of a typical interview. Paul was twenty-one and Laura eighteen at the time. "I found that both of them are sadly lacking in knowledge of God's Word," he reported. "She doesn't know it at all. . . . When I asked her what reason she had for thinking she was a Christian, she was simply nonplused, and could no more have answered that question than she could have written a book on astronomy." Worse, she appeared to have nothing to say about "soul-winning" or "the lost condition of the heathen." Smith advised them to attend the Bible Institute of Los Angeles (Biola) for two years. Two years later, although the young couple appeared to be no more ready for missionary work than before, they were dispatched to Guatemala. The council's suggestion of yet another year at Biola was overruled, because Paul was desperately needed to help his brother on the field. "I think Paul will continue to learn & develop after reaching the field," Smith rationalized. Apparently, whether his young wife was missionary material or not mattered little.[100]

If a candidate's spiritual qualities seemed acceptable to the mission council, and the candidate was healthy, she was usually accepted and dispatched to the field as quickly as possible. Very little, if any, additional training was provided. Gladys Wright, who went to Africa with the Africa Inland Mission in the late 1920s, remembered only a booklet sent from the mission to help her start on the language. In addition, experienced missionaries onboard ship gave her some advice. Paul Stough (AIM 1928) remembered that no special studies were required. "We appeared before a Chicago committee . . . and they examined us as far as our biblical knowledge was concerned, and that was all that was necessary." No orientation was provided. It was 1953 before AIM established a candidate school, a twelve-day orientation session. In 1955 an AIM missionary wrote a mission handbook and sent it to the general secretary, because he felt its need "quite strongly" after his own experience as a candidate. The CAM did not have a candidate school until 1951. The school provided two weeks of training in field conditions. The China Inland Mission had homes scattered around the country where candidates lived while preparing to go overseas. There they were observed by CIM personnel, and judgment was passed on the quality of their personal and spiritual lives. Any demonstration of an uncooperative spirit, a lack of submission, or other of the seven deadly sins could prove fatal to an applicant.[101] This much observation by mission personnel was unusual, however. Most of the faith missions simply relied on the Bible institutes to do the bulk of their screening and training for them.

That the faith missions eventually prospered would seem to be a tribute to the quality of missionaries recruited through this process. There is no question that the level of piety and commitment of their recruits was generally very high. Indeed, the very risks involved in the missionary life seemed to attract the most devoted evangelicals. Yet faith mission leaders themselves recognized that there were problems inherent in the recruiting system. Lewis Sperry Chafer voiced a common, if private, complaint of mission leaders when he admitted in a candid moment that the CAM "would be benefitted by a much higher standard of missionary timber." Unfortunately, this high standard was simply an "ideal," and, he continued, "Very few such are applying at the present time[,] and it seems to be a case of taking the best we can get."[102]

Faith mission executives learned that piety did not necessarily guarantee intelligence, tact, or maturity. In fact, some of the rules by which they recruited worked against more mature candidates. The faith mission recruitment process naturally selected individuals who were highly motivated and believed they had clear direction from God to pursue an extremely rigorous life. Evangelical piety stressed the individual leading of God's spirit, and missionary candidates heard his voice more clearly than most. As David Sandgren noted about AIM, its selection process led to the mission sending to East Africa "a group of strong-willed individuals who felt themselves personally directed by God and answerable only to Him." Such candidates did not necessarily take direction, or even suggestion, well. C. T. Studd, the famous British cricket player turned missionary, is an amusing example of a missionary so convinced of his direct connection with God that he could work with no one. Desiring only Jesus as his captain, he bounced from board to board, each of them eager to have the famous sports figure as a member, but each of them quickly regretting their decision as he wreaked havoc on the field. Studd even found it difficult to remain in the missions he founded himself. He enticed new recruits by telling them that they would be "free to be guided by the Holy Spirit," but once on the field added the following stipulation: "The Holy Spirit never guided a man to be disobedient to his superior officer."[103] C. T. apparently had a blind spot or two.

Long-range planning could be difficult when missionaries shifted locations at the leading of God rather than at the direction of the home council. When Archer Anderson decided on his own to leave his assignment in Panajachel for Huehuetenango, Chafer tried to persuade him to stay by arguing that his work had been "blessed" in Panajachel, an indication that God had "placed his seal" upon that endeavor. This argument, of course, could become circular. When, in frustration, Chafer asked for proof that Anderson's move was God's will, the young missionary's reply was eminently logical. "You say that God has blessed me here. I thank Him for the gracious way He has worked," Anderson wrote. "But, as I see it, we cannot be led by past blessings. He blessed me here[,] for I have been in His will for me. He now calls me to Huehuetenango. Were I to be disobedient to that call He would quickly remove the blessing which I have enjoyed. Whereas, by following step by step in His path He will continue to bless me." He concluded, "If peace and joy are any sign of having done His will, [then] I am doubly sure . . . that I have [made the correct] move." In 1924 after a small run of abrupt missionary decisions to abandon assigned posts for other fields, a female missionary asked the council's permission to return home to be married. Chafer sarcastically remarked to Rees, "Perhaps we will need a pulmotor to revive us after having been consulted to this extent on a matter of this kind. Why not come directly home and tell us about it afterward?" In short, what was said of one CAM missionary could as well have been said of many faith missionaries. "Some feel that she is not stable, but rather visionary. She gets a sudden conviction as to what the Lord's will is for her, and then, in the midst of that, she may suddenly change all plans upon receiving further light."[104]

The question of institutional control was filled with complex pitfalls for faith missions. How did you institutionalize the leading of God? Faith missions had been founded as an antidote to the "cult of efficiency" and the businesslike methods that dominated the traditional boards. They implicitly resisted bureaucratic control. God would lead; God would supply. An early policy of AIM stated that administrators could not override an individual's "leading." "No officer of the Mission has any authority to force his personal ideas upon his fellow workers," recorded the astonishing document. "Particularly is large freedom given to each head of a station[,] who may shape the character of the work on his station, but all other workers are also free to choose as far as possible the station where they can work with greater liberty, and if not happy, may be changed to another point." A CAM council member argued, "Often, more harm results from too much than from too little government. . . . Our great need is for missionaries who do not need superintending—other than by the Holy Spirit." Or as another councilman said in the midst of a dispute with a Guatemala missionary about mission procedure, "Who am I that the Holy Spirit should place me in right channels and allow Toms to go in wrong ways?"[105] In such an atmosphere, mission leaders found it very difficult to actually lead and were forced to become adept at putting out the fires caused by individual missionaries creating their own policies under the superintending of the Spirit on the field. A historian determined to write providential history, upon observing the Guatemala missionaries chasing the divine will from station to station, would have a difficult time indeed making sense of the Spirit's intent; perhaps this is why providential history is best written over centuries rather than decades.

Perhaps of greatest ultimate consequence, however, at least for indigenous people groups, was the fact that cross-cultural and language training were virtually nonexistent for prospective missionaries. As AIM's own historian candidly admits, in the early years missionaries were "deliberately chosen . . . for their zeal and godliness rather than their schooling and skills; so they could boast few linguistic talents." Willis Hotchkiss, the last survivor among those who initially went with Peter Scott to Africa, reflected late in life on the "astonishing patience of the natives in the face of [his] abysmal ignorance." He described himself as a "baby in toyland, smashing things in joyous abandon . . . serenely unconscious of the absurd figure I cut in the eyes of those whom I had come to teach."[106] As we have seen, the missions relied almost entirely on the Bible institutes to train their missionaries. But the institutes provided little in the way of cross-cultural training. They were founded to teach students the Bible under the presupposition that if a Christian worker *in any land* knew the Bible well and knew which passages to apply to any given situation, the Word of God "would not return void"; the need would be met, the soul saved. Despite a few embarrassing false starts, and the eventual development of a "missionary track" in institute education, the fundamental presupposition never changed. The most important thing for any Christian worker to know was the Scriptures.

When Moody Bible Institute in 1910 declared itself the best missionary training school in the country and stated that instruction in missions was "the leading feature" of the school, this did not mean that students spent the bulk of their time studying what today we would think of as mission-related topics. It simply meant that the thorough biblical instruction provided by MBI was a "sufficient guarantee" that the student of missions would receive "the fullest information as to the spiritual needs of man . . . and the perfect provision to meet them." The only cross-cultural training students received was when they happened to run across a person from another ethnic group on an evangelism trip. The few required missions courses were education by inspiration. The entire second year of Dr. Robert Glover's general missions course was primarily made up of weekly inspirational messages, his own and those of numerous guest speakers. Out of the eleven class meetings in the fall of 1925 (missions courses were only one unit), five of which were led by guest speakers, eight were simply Bible studies or sermons with a missionary theme and challenge. The other three were reports from various mission fields. Whether consciously or unconsciously, missionary leaders felt that getting students committed to the foreign field was most of the battle. The practical training a prospective missionary acquired was a few basic guidelines from professors who had been on the field and whatever information they could glean from visiting missionaries and the numerous missionary biographies that lined the shelves of the library. Any value placed by the missions professors on the importance of understanding other cultures and of contextualizing the message was undermined by the bulk of the program, which emphasized the fundamental tenet of evangelism: the preaching of the simple Word by a consecrated messenger bears fruit. The world into which the seed was sown must adapt to the seed, not vice versa. Dr. Glover told his students to train themselves in native thought so that they could use illustrations that would be familiar to their audience. But he then told the students to use the pedagogic principles they had learned at MBI and concluded, "The catechetical method is good to get their attention." Many missionaries taught natives around the world directly from their MBI notes.[107] Under such conditions, and with the faith boards providing little additional training, any success achieved by early faith missionaries can be attributed to dogged determination and ability by some to adapt quickly to local conditions and learn from those they were attempting to convert.

When R. D. Smith wrote of Paul and Laura Townsend that "their youth impresses one forcibly," he voiced yet another problem inherent in faith mission recruitment. Because of health concerns, and a perceived wisdom declaring that older candidates would have difficulty learning a foreign language, faith missions were of the opinion that "a candidate above thirty years of age is likely to prove a liability rather than an asset." Consequently, they tended to discourage older applicants. Unfortunately, this meant their missionaries tended to be very young, lightly educated, and often still maturing. When twenty-two-year-old, immature, uneducated, but strong-willed missionaries were thrown into a situation for which they were largely unprepared, the result was often not very edifying. If the mission was fortunate, they got somewhat eccentric workers who presented no problem for the home council or their fellow missionaries. One single woman with CAM carried out a prodigious evangelistic ministry, even while her years of living alone made her a challenge to deal with. She was reported to have "prayed the Lord to make her homely so that the men of Honduras would not bother her."[108] (Photographs from the period reveal that God was gracious.) The sweet-spirited, megaphone-wielding Dr. Becker probably did no permanent damage, even as he undoubtedly did no real good.

Unfortunately, the stress of missionary life on immature young people often caused a great deal of interpersonal strife on the field. When Karl Hummel remarked, "If we would call home every ill-tempered missionary from the field today, we would close half our stations," he was exaggerating, but not by much.[109] The stress seemed especially hard on women. The CAM council dealt constantly with problems caused by women with "nervous conditions," which served as a euphemism for anything ranging from extreme irritability to dangerous mental illness. Elvira, of course, was the worst offender in this regard. That the council would have to order one of their own missionaries to stay one mile away from any mission station offers absurd testimony to the difficulties to which such recruitment policies could lead. But Elvira was not alone; steady reports of women with "nervous conditions" kept the council busy throughout the 1920s.

Once the candidate reached the field, it was virtually impossible for the mission to rid itself of them. The council could only station them somewhere by themselves, where they would not hinder other missionaries, and hope they failed so miserably that they would return home of their own accord. Several nervous CAM wives eventually left their husbands to return home, where they spread rumors about their husband's living situation. Of course, when nervous women were invalided home, someone had to care for them. If their families were unable or unwilling, they turned to the mission to pay their bills. Field missionaries at times faced difficult dilemmas with such women. Paul Townsend had more than Elvira to deal with. He wrote of another nervous woman, "She herself is now talking of returning to the States[,] but we are all afraid to talk to her about it for fear she will decide not to go. If she thought we wished it[,] she would refuse to go[,] I am sure. . . . She hates me . . . and when I am about she all but swears at the believers or anyone else who may be present."[110]

Men, of course, were not immune to nervous conditions. Chafer reported on one man who fought with other missionaries over territorial boundaries, accused the council of withholding his money, and generally believed the worst in any situation. "He is so overwrought and sensitive and temperamental, and looking so constantly for impositions to be heaped upon him, that he is in hot water continually. I do not think he has ever been in any other frame of mind than that of personal offense over something," Chafer groaned. "[He] is increasingly unsettled in his mind . . . a desperate character [with] broken nerves . . . an impossible missionary."[111] But missionaries did not require the excuse of a nervous condition to fight over territory, doctrine, method of baptism, or other missions issues, and the council kept busy mediating disputes throughout Townsend's tenure.

The frequency with which such accounts turn up in archives certainly speaks to the difficulty of life on the field. But more important for our study, such accounts bring into question a recruiting process that tended to rubber-stamp virtually every application that God purportedly dropped in the council's lap. If at first glance the missionary was spiritual enough, the council overlooked a great deal of potential problems. A CAM council member unconsciously indicted its candidacy procedures when he recorded his agreement "about the desirability of sending first class men to Central America." He was skeptical, however, about the possibility. "I am afraid that we may not know first class men when we see them," he wrote. "Sometimes we are greatly disappointed in men whom we suppose to be first class, and on the other hand, greatly surprised by men whom we thought to be second class. The only safe thing to do is to be in prayer and then follow as the Lord may lead." In faith missions, where God's will was often determined by cash flow, the Lord's leading as to a missionary's candidacy was likely to be judged by financial support. As Luther Rees argued, "I have felt that if one was called as a missionary to a certain field, the Lord would signify that fact by providing funds for outfit and passage." An unmarried woman with a "nervous condition" was approved for appointment because she "seemed to pray herself out into the field." In faith mission language this meant that her financial support had been promised. Given such proof of the direction of God's will, who were the mission leaders to question God and turn her down?[112]

Recruiting techniques such as this, which favored willingness, desire, and spirituality over other attributes, provided an unintentional bonanza, however, for female candidates. The missions clearly preferred men, but usually sent out quite a few more women. In 1925 thirty-seven of the CAM's fifty-two missionaries were women. "With regard to sending out so many women, I am sure we are subject to what seems to be the leading of God. We have the women and we do not have the men," Chafer reported. "It is possible that God will use ladies on the field if the men are not available. However, I feel we have about reached the limit at the present time." Chafer's statement reveals both the possibilities and the limitations for women in evangelical circles at the time. Paul Townsend, as was his wont, put the situation more colorfully. "If you get a man to send[,] don't forget me," he begged. "I like the girls[,] but even I get tired of them when there is 'nothing else but.' "[113]

By the second decade of the twentieth century, faith mission leaders were beginning to privately voice concerns about the quality of their recruits. In a private letter to his council, which eventually circulated through other faith mission councils, the general director of AIM pleaded for better-equipped missionaries. He wrote, "The partial or complete failure of many missionaries on the field compels me to call attention again to . . . lessons which need to be deeply taught to new candidates." But despite all they had learned, it was difficult for faith mission leaders to understand these deficiencies in anything other than spiritual terms. AIM's director called for missionaries for whom evangelism was the "master-passion" of their life. Personality failures were spoken of in code. "Habitual victory [in personal life] is a necessary qualification," he wrote, meaning most probably that he hoped to find candidates who knew how to get along, who manifested a little love, patience, and grace.[114]

From the beginning of his tenure as leader of the CAM, Lewis Sperry Chafer was concerned about the problems of sending out "immature missionaries." "I wish we could find more thoroughly equipped missionaries," he wrote to Townsend.[115] But for Chafer, as for the AIM council, maturity tended to be defined in theological terms. If a candidate knew the Scriptures well, there was at least a presumption that he or she would live accordingly.

Nevertheless, by the mid-1920s the CAM council was making a conscious effort to screen candidates more diligently. R. D. Smith and Chafer interviewed a young couple and reported to the council that they "were not particularly impressed," despite the fact they were "undoubtedly dear consecrated Christians." Smith reported that the couple was "decidedly lacking in force and strength of character, and following out our plan of seeking a higher grade of missionaries[,] I told Mr. Chafer that I could not conscientiously vote for their acceptance. A chain is no stronger than its weakest link, neither is a Mission." That Smith expected resistance from other council members at his refusal to endorse the candidacy of such "consecrated Christians" is clear from his concluding sentence. "Other faith missions," he reported, "are also feeling this same thing, that the standards must be raised. We ought to pray for one another that true heavenly wisdom be granted and that both missionaries and councilmen be willing to follow it."[116]

Despite their best intentions, however, the recruiting process improved only in fits and starts. At the end of the decade the problem of missionary quality had not improved. As the financial situation worsened with the onslaught of the Great Depression, the importance of selecting successful candidates intensified. Karl Hummel noted that now the council would be "hesitant about appointing anyone who does not show a real gift for leadership." "We have had so many sad experiences of rushing appointments, that I think it is too risky a thing to encourage," he noted. "The few weeks necessary for deliberate consideration could hardly be considered as lost time." That Hummel felt it necessary to plead for a "few weeks" to consider a candidate's appointment speaks volumes about faith mission candidacy procedures.[117]

In general, however, the hunger for recruits simply overwhelmed the need for improved screening and training. Applicants were too few and far between to be turned down for anything short of some type of theological or spiritual disqualification. And the number of quality applicants was not likely to improve when the council refused to engage in active recruitment. What was said of a missionary in 1919 was true of many in the next several decades. Of this missionary, Judge Scott wrote that he was "a great big-hearted, rather ignorant Christian, not well posted in the Word or the Language, but having an overwhelming desire for the salvation of souls, and with me . . . this covers a multitude of other faults." Unfortunately, the mission did not ascertain even this much about him before sending him out. Consequently, they placed this simple man in charge of the entire work in Nicaragua. Only after he failed miserably on the field did they find the proper place for him as a Bible and tract distributor.[118]

In 1935 the CAM council asked Kenneth Grubb for his opinion of their work in Central America. Grubb was an Anglican layman and missionary explorer, who had traveled extensively throughout Latin America on behalf of the Worldwide Evangelization Crusade and the World Dominion Press. It was reported of Grubb that he "did not find personal relations easy. By temperament he was a loner, an authoritarian who found it difficult to suffer fools gladly." He was characteristically blunt in his assessment of CAM's work. "Almost all of [the missionaries] are of conspicuous Christian devotion," he reported. "Some, [however], could have profited by better preparation in any of the Institutes devoted to the purpose." Then, tellingly, "This comes out not so much in their capacities as in their ability to get on, or not to get on, with each other." Grubb concluded with a gentle but nevertheless devastating indictment of faith mission procedure: "The sending out of missionaries is not, to my mind, a necessary policy for a faith mission. I do not see any point in multiplying missionaries if those on the field lack means to fulfill their mission. One good man used to the full is better than many second rate ones."[119]

Elvira had a "bad spell" that December. "I finally was able to put a stop to it by resorting to unpleasant measures," Townsend dutifully reported to Chafer, "but all has gone on beautifully since. I really don't think that any harm was done." What those "measures" were he did not say. Perhaps, as R. D. Smith constantly urged, he was learning to be "head of his house." His Indian co-translators "saw too much," Townsend admitted, "but God gave me grace before them. . . . However, what I had expected wouldn't happen did happen and I am ready to bear the consequences. May God direct!" At this point, Chafer was not inclined to be legalistic. He informed Townsend that he would "say nothing" in Texas so long as Townsend kept him closely informed of Elvira's behavior.[120]

5

In Which Council Members Sail to Guatemala to Save the Mission, Mrs. Townsend Makes Some Practical Suggestions, and R. D. Smith Has Some Surprise Visitors

1925–1928

> It is useless to try to make the public believe that we are a Faith Mission, if when we are tested we rush to the public with information to that effect. Or when a missionary wants . . . something . . . , he is to write to his friends (and even strangers) about it.
>
> —R. D. Smith

In the spring of 1925 the Central American Mission was in the process of self-destructing. The arguments that threatened to blow the CAM apart centered on just what kind of mission it would be. Who was in charge? What was the mission's mandate? And would certain missionaries be permitted to focus exclusively on Indians? Cameron Townsend was the fuse igniting each of these explosive issues.

Ever since Chafer returned from his trip to Central America in the summer of 1923 fired up over the possibilities of the missionaries' educational endeavors, the CAM had struggled mightily over the issue of extra-evangelistic work. More precisely, the struggle centered on just what could properly be termed evangelistic. At the two poles of the contest were council members who were concerned about a constituency whose antennae had been sensitized to the issue because of the theological struggles in the denominations, and field missionaries who had grown increasingly enamored with all manner of social endeavor.

The power struggle in the CAM focused on the mission stations constructed by Cameron Townsend and by Frank and Herbert Toms. When the elder Toms first came to the field in 1902, he believed wholeheartedly in the "evangelism only" gospel. But as he later reported to R. D. Smith, he soon found that "often [those] i[n] the homeland don't understand conditions on the field." In 1920, about the same time Townsend launched his dream project for the Indians, the Toms family started a school for the children of new converts. From the beginning, however, they agreed to take in other children. They soon found the percentage of unconverted children increasing. This delighted the Tomses, "who took it as a blessing from God, and as a great opportunity for saving souls," or as one missionary reported to the council, "The school is his bait." Frank Toms, who had been a prosperous businessman before going into the ministry, and who had developed perhaps the largest constituency of any CAM missionary, soon built the school into the crown jewel of a thriving center in Huehuetenango. Some considered it the CAM's "most substantial work."[1]

When Chafer returned to the United States thrilled with the educational centers established by the Tomses and the Townsends, he ran headlong into a constituency that was fast losing its appetite for any endeavor that smacked of liberalism. With influential journals such as the *Moody Monthly* carrying articles complaining of money wasted on "sidelines while the all-important work of direct evangelization goes undeveloped," many CAM supporters were opposed to missionary schools altogether. A year after his enthusiastic vow to craft a statement in support of such efforts, Chafer was backpedaling vigorously. In November 1924 he called a council meeting to determine the attitude of the mission toward educational and hospital work by its field missionaries. "We are getting into deep water," he complained, "between a constituency that is not committed to this kind of thing and some ambitious missionaries who seem to think of little else." To R. D. Smith he grumbled, "If we do not take some kind of stand very soon, the enthusiasm of some of our missionaries is going to run us into a very embarrassing position." That "embarrassing position" threatened to undermine the faith basis of the work. The council feared that educational institutions would be difficult to finance and would lead the mission away from its founding principles. "This is one of the penalties of setting up an institution. One is compelled to finance it[,] and this becomes, always, a nightmare, and quiet faith often gives way to noisy clamor for more funds."[2]

As the discussion within the mission commenced, both sides were willing to be conciliatory. Herbert Toms admitted that "the school work absorbs about all we have to give," and his father agreed that in his reaction to his initial stance opposed to any form of educational work, he had perhaps "erred going to an opposite extreme." Chafer wrote an article defending at least a limited amount of education work and circulated it in the council for approval. In the article he went so far as to say that anyone opposed to work other than evangelism was engaging in a form of prejudice. Furthermore, when the council questioned the China Inland Mission as to its policy regarding educational work, they discovered that where originally the CIM "kept aloof from all educational programs," it had now "become convinced that [it was] God's program for [them] from [now] on," and the mission was planning to establish schools in connection with every mission station. Even more surprising, CIM schools permitted the enrollment of unbelievers to reach 25 percent. Chafer found the same change in position to be true of other faith missions as well.[3]

The situation seemed to call for proceeding slowly, but feeling the pressure of its constituency and goaded by R. D. Smith and other of its most conservative members, the council acted dramatically in January 1925. "The feeling that we must 'do something' prevailed," Luther Rees later admitted. The full council passed a dramatic resolution against the educational program undertaken by the Tomses, their so-called educational evangelism. Townsend escaped the initial thrust of the council's ire, because at least as far as the council knew, he enrolled only the children of converts. The council's rationale, however, would soon encompass his schools as well. The council argued that educational programs were too expensive, would "concentrate Missionaries[,] thus reducing direct evangelization," and were "very subject to degeneration." The last was a reference to both the enrollment of unbelievers and the hiring of "unsaved" schoolteachers. The resolution, coming in the middle of the Tomses' school year and granting them, as they supposed, "no chance for discussion or appeal," aroused the Huehuetenango station. All the missionaries located there cabled back, "If resolution is published all resign." Karl Hummel, a career field missionary, who took Chafer's place as general secretary when Chafer resigned in early 1925, managed to talk the executive committee into postponing the publication of the council resolution until the matter could be resolved.[4]

The debate raged for the next six months before petering out in an uneasy acceptance of the status quo. Conservatives on the council were outraged that the executive committee had set aside a statement agreed upon by the full body. As often happened, the issue got tangled up with questions of organizational authority and spirituality. Who was really hearing from God? "It looks as though Mr. Toms had much more the courage of his convictions than the Council," raged Frank Gillingham, "and seems to be a confession that the Council was <u>not</u>

led of God or guided by Him in passing the Resolution." He wanted the resolution published, and "if that [brought] resignations, accept them."[5]

Uppermost in R. D. Smith's mind was the reaction of the CAM constituency. "I for one do not think the CAM wants to enter upon extensive school work as an evangelizing agency," he argued. "I do not think it was the intention of the founders or early Missionaries, nor the wish of the present constituency." Gillingham agreed. "The Field Staff does not seem to bother about Council's responsibilities toward our constituency," he charged. "The Toms and Townsends . . . seem to be the real leaders in this trouble," and then, with paranoia taking over, "To me the reading between the lines is very clear that the Townsends (both W. C. and Paul), and the Toms are really earnestly seeking a good valid excuse to pull out of the CAM and join another Mission: probably already selected." He concluded with the hope that the CAM would soon "get back wholeheartedly and unitedly into our only and proper work of evangelizing."[6]

The cooler heads of Karl Hummel and Luther Rees eventually prevailed. They argued that the schools in Guatemala were genuinely evangelistic agencies and as such should be permitted by the council. "There is no evasion of the gospel appeal in any part of the school life. Conversions are frequent and genuine," argued Rees. Even some of the "unsaved" schoolteachers the Tomses had been forced to employ because of a lack of Protestant teachers had eventually been "saved." Rees felt sure that Toms would "have no sympathy whatever with the <u>ordinary</u> denominational schools."[7]

Ultimately, however, the issue came down to the fact that the council was powerless to control missionaries who secured most of their own funding. In addition, when all operated by the direct leading of God, it was simply very difficult to judge who had heard the voice of the Lord most clearly. Rees admitted that "very little, if any[,] money" had ever been sent to the Tomses out of the general fund. "I am confident that he has brought much more to the mission than he has taken from it, as many of his supporters have become helpers in the general work," Rees wrote. "It should also be borne in mind that the valuable properties in San Antonio have been purchased and erected by direct gifts to Cameron Townsend." Ernest Powell, who together with Luther Rees had been on the council since 1890, had the last word.

> Mr. Toms had built up a large work before any one ever questioned his plans. I feel safe in saying if Toms has done wrong it has been done in ignorance and God will forgive him. I am not so sure of the action of the Council. . . . I am willing to hold my thoughts in regard to schools

> in abeyance until more evidence comes in. . . . I am willing to listen to Brother Toms, or any man of God who has the missionary spirit and the decades of experience on the field that Brother Toms has. . . . Who am I that the Holy Spirit should place me in right channels and allow Toms to go in wrong ways?[8]

In the end, then, the contest was won by the missionaries, who, through their threatened resignations, forced the council to back down. Despite the taint given to social work in the struggles between liberals and fundamentalists at home, conservative evangelical missionaries on the field hardly skipped a beat, continuing, until the Depression slowed them somewhat, to construct schools, hospitals, orphanages, and even, as we shall see, coffee-curing plants.

The issue of where ultimate authority in the mission lay had simmered since the early 1920s with Townsend periodically stoking the flames, agitating for a missionary field organization with real power. Ironically, Townsend argued for more authority on the field even as at times—such as in 1924, with Panajachel in an uproar over Elvira's presence, and San Antonio rife with warring factions—Chafer begged Townsend to exercise more authority. "The Council is depending upon you to be the head in the San Antonio station," Chafer had once begged Townsend, "and it is necessary for someone to get these warring factions together and make them empty out all the bitterness that is there and be reconciled . . . or else we shall have to take hold of the work with some decisive hand as a Council."[9]

Now, with the mission already in an uproar over its educational programs, the issue of authority boiled over. Townsend lit the fire. The past year had been very difficult for him. On account of his incorrigible wife, the council had banished him from mission stations he had himself founded. A dispute over baptism among council members had riled the field missionaries and threatened the fragile understanding he had with Archer Anderson. He felt his vision for the Indians threatened by council members who made decisions based on a few letters rather than on a deep immersion in the work. He also felt his plans threatened by field missionaries who acted independently, relying on God alone for direction, to the hindrance of the overall work. Several missionaries to whom he had committed responsibility for the Indian work had left him when they felt God's leading to another sphere of service. "This policy of 'every man for himself' (& I might add, 'the devil take the hindermost') has lasted too long[,] and we'll never have a strong mission until it is remedied," Townsend complained. "A field organization with authority to act . . . will unify our work. . . .

We are now like a sheep without a shepherd or rather an army without a general & no teamwork (mixed metaphor but you will understand.)"[10]

Conservative council members had never appreciated Townsend's broaching of this subject. As Smith argued, "There cannot be two heads in one work, and therefore we cannot and must not give the Field organization executive powers." Smith saw no reason why the missionaries could not form a field organization for prayer and fellowship, as long as it was clearly understood that "such an organization could never have administrative powers which would conflict with those of the Council." For Smith, submission to authority was ultimately a spiritual issue. "If [the missionaries] would only stop and consider," he wrote, "they would surely see that it is 'the backslider who is filled with his own ways' and that it is good for all of us to be under authority. Poor humanity cannot stand anything else." He added, "I will especially pray that the Lord may help . . . to get Cameron Townsend straightened out." Privately, he dismissed Townsend as "one of those people who are always wanting to organize something,—and generally they want to be the leading factor in the organization." What Smith never understood was that Townsend's organizations were symptoms of something far deeper; they were slaves to his passions, and thus deserved to be taken very seriously indeed.[11]

After several hours with Smith and Pettingill, Chafer adopted their line. "Both of these men feel strongly that there must be more order among the missionaries and I heartily agree," he told Rees. He adopted a fatherly line. "It is no time to be too easy with these boys for their good and the good of the mission. I saw too much of the tendency down there to ignore the Council and set up a missionary government[,]and 'Cam' was leading in that propaganda."[12]

Now, in early 1925, with threats of resignations flying about over the education issue, Townsend tossed his own threat on the pile over the authority issue. "My conviction is too strong as regards the matter for me to do otherwise," he told Chafer. "If I am heard I shall be very happy, if not, I shall continue preaching the gospel to the Indians wherever He calls me and as long as He feeds me[,] and Elvira says that she will stick by me."[13] This was a serious threat to the CAM, as the council well knew that Townsend was one of their biggest stars with a large ministry and wide and aggressive publicity. The council agreed to create a field organization by which each republic or district would be represented at an annual conference. The field conference would draft recommendations that would then be submitted to the council for action. The final authority, however, still rested with the council at home.

Townsend did not see this step as an adequate concession. He wrote a very candid, and frankly inflammatory, letter that again threatened his resignation.

It would be "unwise" to give the council the final word, he argued. He thought the council was trying to create something new in mission history. Ultimate authority in the traditional boards was invested in the denominational constituency, which elected its representatives to a home council, which in turn directed the mission. The China Inland Mission was directed by a missionary who gave his full time and "first interest" to the mission. Townsend accused the CAM council of keeping final authority when they were neither elected representatives nor full-time missionaries. Your "first interest [is not] with the Mission you direct," he charged, "nor have many of you been missionaries to thoroughly understand the work, nor do you know the peculiar qualities and needs of the people of Central America." In addition, the distance at which they were located made it impossible to make quick decisions. He was willing to let the council control finances, direct the work at home, and decide doctrinal issues, but he was not willing to "concede to you the right to dictate in those matters which pertain purely to the field." He was amazed they did not at least give the suggested missionary council the right to make provisional decisions. "Your complete distrust of us and your perfect confidence in yourselves surprises me," he concluded.[14]

The problems for the council went deeper than just Townsend and Toms. Paul Townsend assured Smith that "the same position is being held by many other missionaries in the CAM. The others are not speaking out as Cameron is[,] but they are planning just the same." He informed Smith that the missionaries wanted an organization that "would make decisions and would be final for us in spite of the Council." Paul also suggested the missionaries be given input into the selection of council members, claiming the missionaries did not appreciate ceding "ultimate authority" to "unknown" quantities. An exasperated Smith replied, "Do you really consider yourself sufficiently informed concerning men here at home . . . to vote intelligently as to whether they should be on our Council or not?" Which was, of course, precisely the Townsends' point about the council's knowledge of the field.[15]

Karl Hummel, who had taken over the general secretary position as Townsend's bombshell landed at headquarters, inherited what had now become an explosive situation. He had barely unpacked his pencil sharpener before his inbox was deluged by a ticker-tape parade of resignation letters from both missionaries and council members. It helped that he was himself a field missionary, and one for whom Townsend had great respect. "Dearest Cameron," he wrote, "I think we had better be slow in passing judgment on these questions." Hummel argued that the CAM was organized on as good a basis as other faith missions. In fact, the Africa Inland Mission had a field director but was "in an awful state for that very reason." Four new men had recently joined the CAM council, and Hummel counseled patience. "Perhaps you will think I am a backslidden missionary and have joined the Council," he wrote Townsend. "Such is not the case. The new men on the Council are men of broad vision, and final authority must be placed in somebody's hands. I think we can well afford to let the matter rest where it is until some issue comes up which demands the position you now take."[16] This was good advice. In practice the council did not often cross the will of the missionaries, and actually were utterly helpless to do so, as Townsend well knew. Townsend almost always got his way, even if it took a great deal of argument to get it.

Unfortunately for all concerned, Townsend's rhetoric proved too much for R. D. Smith. When he decided to address Townsend directly on the issue, personal feeling got the best of both men, and the situation escalated to a surprising level. Smith asked Townsend whether he could name "a single Missionary Society which is thriving and going ahead, governed by such a plan as you propose." Clearly for Smith, who served on the boards of several faith missions, this was a rhetorical question. Smith made a scriptural argument for submission, suggesting, in what could be considered a cheap shot, that Townsend, more than anyone, ought to understand its importance, given his domestic situation. "Just as thousands of homes are being wrecked because the wife refuses to take her Scriptural place, so many a dear Missionary is in danger of becoming quite headstrong and getting out of God's plan for his life." Smith, in fact, privately blamed the entire situation on Elvira. "In the case of Brother Townsend, I am inclined to think that this virus would not have gotten into his veins if it had not been for his wife," he reported to the council. "In fact it is not hard to imagine that she tells him just what to write. . . . Cam is suffering the logical results of having yielded, after all these years, to her uncontrolled temper."[17]

Smith also suggested that Townsend's threatened resignation betokened his ungratefulness for all the CAM had done for him, and that if he resigned, his future as a missionary would be destroyed. Speaking as "an older man," Smith warned that Townsend was at "perhaps one of the greatest crises of [his] life[,] where a mis-step would prove fatal to [his] future usefulness." "It is very well to resign from a Mission after it has taken you into its family and . . . expended . . . both time and money to help you during the first five or ten years of your missionary life," he said, "but do you think that if the great Head of the Church were sitting with you there in your own home, that He would advise you to do so?"[18]

Townsend took Smith's bait. "The man is the head of the home just as you say," he sarcastically replied, "but do you think that the wife would be benefitted much by his headship if the latter were a thousand miles away?" He resented being accused of "resisting oversight." "I am willing to obey what He may lead the majority of my fellow-missionaries to direct me," he argued in a statement destined to be tested in the years ahead, "but the theory that He can show His will more perfectly to a group of men several of whom have never seen C[entral] A[merica], who can with difficulty meet more than once a year and who are separated by 1,000 miles from the matters they are supposed to decide savors too much of the Papal theory to suit me."[19] It was the ultimate insult.

Smith lost patience with his one-time protégé. "Allow me to remind you, my dear Brother," he snapped at Townsend, "that some of us were engaged in these duties long before you went to the Field." To the council, Smith groused that Townsend's letters were "impertinent." After receiving a letter "even more snappy than the previous ones," he exclaimed that he was "almost ashamed to show it to my fellow members on the Council." He questioned Townsend's current spiritual state. "I have been burdened by a sense that he was not living as near to the Lord as usual." In Smith's view, it was time for a showdown. "Either those two men [Townsend and Toms] are going to run the Council, or the Council is going to have to deal somewhat drastically with them," he huffed. "They may be putting up simply a good <u>bluff,</u> . . . but . . . it is necessary for one side or the other to yield, and for the other side to be recognized as the final authority in the Mission." Most of the council members felt similarly. Declaring that "Mr. Townsend . . . evidences an even more intolerant spirit than Mr. Toms," new council member Frank Gillingham charged that "things ha[d] gotten out of the Council's control. Council . . . <u>cannot</u> shirk its present responsibility to hold and <u>to exercise</u> full and final authority," he urged. "The Mission was not conceived or started by a Hudson Taylor or any man as a Missionary, but by Dr. Scofield and the Brethren associated with him as the first Council, and has always been in the control of the Council."[20]

In a statement not particularly well suited to easing tensions, Smith and Gillingham accused the field missionaries of allowing Satan to "direct [their] thought" away from "the one objective of preaching the Gospel . . . to an unspiritual discussion regarding authority in the organization." While they agreed to permit the missionaries to form an organization that would "give advice and help" wherever the council "need[ed] the advice growing out of the experience of the Missionaries," they insisted that "the discharge of those functions which determine the scope and character of the Mission . . . shall continue with the Council of the Central American Mission."[21]

In private Smith was even less accommodating. His blood was up, and now he wanted to force the issue "to a head." He told Hummel to ask the Townsends and Tomses "for a written acknowledgment that they recognize that the Council is the 'Final Authority,' whether pertaining to questions of administration here at home or matters on the Field," even if it "cost the Mission six or eight workers." He concluded with his own grand flourish. "If the Toms-Townsend ideas about these things prevail and the Council becomes a mere Collection Agency, I shall be obliged to resign from the Council."[22]

Luther Rees had to laugh. "The council a mere collection agency?!" He reminded Smith that the Townsends and Tomses brought in most of their money on their own. He told Smith the council should be happy that the two energetic center builders had not "call[ed] our attention to the real situation and remind[ed] us that we were a pretty poor collecting agency as far as they were concerned." Indeed, without the presence of Luther Rees and Karl Hummel, the CAM most likely would not have escaped the situation without the resignations of a number of missionaries and/or councilmen. Although, with the passing of Scofield, he was now the longest-tenured council member, Luther Rees never seemed to let his personal investment in the mission get the best of his feelings. He always saw the best in people and trusted the field personnel. Now he feared the loss of key missionaries and counseled a conciliatory approach. "I will be greatly humiliated if the Central American Mission cannot hold such men as F. G. Toms and Cameron Townsend," he admitted to Hummel. Rees argued for the elimination of the reference to "Final Authority" if it antagonized the missionaries. "A field organization which would have to submit everything to the Home Council would be of no practical value," he urged the council. "I would suggest that the missionaries submit a plan for field organization. We should wait to see what authority they want before we undertake to restrict them." He concluded, "I have confidence in Frank Toms and Cameron Townsend. God has been pleased to greatly use them. . . . I am writing this hoping it may help my brethren to know them better."[23]

Hummel, as a career missionary now on the council, was perhaps the only person who could have negotiated a way through the rhetorical minefield. He urged key council members to travel to Central America for a face-to-face meeting with the field missionaries. He mollified R. D. Smith by agreeing that "Cameron's demands [were] unreasonable," but then urged him to give the missionaries "more say than they have [had] in the past." He argued that the missionaries should be given the "power to act," not just to propose. All the missionaries would agree, he said, that it takes far too much time to get action from the council on issues of importance. Hummel dryly remarked that he had written the council in 1919 requesting power of attorney so that he could arrange property matters in Nicaragua, "and two months ago I myself wrote out that power and sent it to the field." He also agreed that the missionaries simply knew the situation on the field better than the council.[24]

By late spring in 1925 there seemed to be grounds for hoping, as Gillingham reported to Hummel, "that some method may be found of smoothing out the difficulties here and, as the Chinese say, 'Save our faces,' both Council's and Bro. Townsend's." Some of the newer council members were desperately seeking a way out of what had become a fiasco, and were contemplating resignation if an accommodation was not found. Perhaps most important, Townsend had been forced to return to the United States because of Elvira's health. Temporarily on the sidelines, he had time to relax and consider the council's point of view. He confessed to Hummel that he had gotten "into a rut on the field . . . where we over emphasize our own problems and just can't see the other fellow's view point." "At least that is true of myself," he admitted. "I'm sure that I can be dealt with here in the States better than I could while fixed in my own little grove in Panajachel," and added, "I think that you get me." He rescinded his resignation threat and apologized to the council. "My motives straight through have been the best[,] though at times, in my efforts to be frank I have sacrificed courtesy[,] and for this I beg your pardon."[25]

Townsend's mood was undoubtedly helped by the fact that the council finally recognized his plan of organization for his Indian work, approving the "Articles of Organization of the Cakchiquel Department of the Central American Mission" in late April 1925. The council had actually intended to authorize the Cakchiquel Department long ago, but had simply forgotten to ratify the "Articles." Rees did not even know it had been submitted to the council for ratification. When he went back through Townsend's correspondence, he noted that Townsend had repeatedly asked for recognition of the Cakchiquel Department. "On learning that it was in the files," he told Townsend, "it was produced and we were glad to ratify and commend it. I am sure there has been no purpose on the part of any member of the Council to ignore the Cakchiquel organization, but I can well see how you may have felt about it. It was simply overlooked."[26]

The council finally suggested that Luther Rees go to Guatemala to calm the waters and settle the matter. "Send a man who has sympathy for them," argued an elderly councilman, "one who will get their view point . . . beg their pardon for our failure to get their idea; show love, peace, longsuffering, gentleness." Rees did indeed seem to be the man for the job, although eventually others would go in his stead. "I do not have the remotest fear that these brethren are going to usurp authority which properly belongs to the council," he admonished a conservative councilman. "Let us not anticipate that they will."[27]

Before the delegation from the council could board the boat for Guatemala, the tense standoff between Townsend and Fred Lincoln over the separation of the Indian work from the *ladino* erupted into a nasty shouting match, thereby placing yet another urgent matter on the agenda of the visiting councilmen.

Behind the scenes, at least, the council seemed to favor Townsend's position in the matter. Luther Rees wrote a remarkably even-handed position paper on the issue for the rest of the council in May 1925. In part it read:

> We are not in Central America to settle the race question, but rather to preach the gospel to every creature. In carrying on the work, race prejudice cannot be ignored. The ideal would be that the brethren should dwell together in unity; that the Indian and Ladino should forget all racial differences and lay aside all prejudices; that the Ladino should avoid giving offence to Indian, but if he does, that the Indian should take it in all humility. But in practice, we do not find such ideal conditions; nor can we expect them in dealing with mere babes in Christ. We must face conditions as they are.... I do not think the Mission should insist that the races must work and worship together. Often, it is cowardly to seek the line of least resistance, but not so in the work of the gospel. We are rather to remove every hindrance to the acceptance of Christ by the lost. If race prejudice is in the way, avoid it. Don't compel the Indian to identify himself with a church in control of those whom he thinks count themselves his superiors. Although the Ladinos may be willing to give full recognition to the Indians, the latter may not be able to appropriate grace enough to forget past treatment. We cannot force them into a spiritual attitude. They must grow into it. Where the races are working harmoniously in local churches, they should not be disturbed. But if the minority, whether Indian or Ladino, desires to separate and to work for and among its own race, the Mission should not interfere.[28]

The council unknowingly complicated the problem when they officially recognized Townsend's Cakchiquel Department as an integral division within the CAM. On May 26, emboldened by their newfound status, the San Antonio missionaries drew up a resolution outlining their plan of work with the Indians and sent it off to Lincoln and other missionaries working with *ladinos* in their section. The two-page resolution codified Townsend's policies of Indian work.

In Cameron's absence, Paul Townsend wrote the resolution, the most important points of which are outlined below.

> Whereas there has been a good bit of misunderstanding upon the part of the missionaries and native pastors engaged in Ladino work attributing to the Cakchiquel Department a schismatic tendency . . . We hereby set forth the following as our program for the carrying on of work among the Cakchiquel Indians and cordially invite our fellow missionaries to submit their criticisms. The Cakchiquel Department has found:—1. That if there is to be adequate growth in the work . . . regular services must be held and personal work done in the Cakchiquel language; 2. That this can best be done by Indian pastors and evangelists, since almost none of the Ladino workers have a sufficient knowledge of Cakchiquel and also because of differences in race, customs, and mode of thinking; 3. . . . the Indian workers should not be under the Ladino workers but rather co-pastors with same, each responsible together with his board of elders for the welfare of his department of the congregation—i.e. the believers of his own race, and for the evangelization of the unsaved among his people; 4. . . . a separate place of meeting for each department of the congregation should be established which would also give the unconverted of each race an opportunity to attend services in their own language without raising the old question of race prejudice which is so strong among the unconverted; 5. That those missionaries who feel called to specialize on Indian work . . . be allowed to give their whole energies as far as possible to this work . . . and that the matter be explained to the Ladino believers so that they will not be demanding the attention of the Indian missionaries nor vice versa; 6. That to manifest the unity of the congregation before the world, to enjoy Christian fellowship and to eradicate race prejudice among believers, union meetings should be held at least once a month.[29]

Paul and the other San Antonio workers probably considered that most of these issues had already been settled and hoped that the resolutions would serve as a gentle reminder to those who had begun to complain. They certainly did not anticipate the conflict their resolutions touched off. Fred Lincoln fired back, in essence accusing the Cakchiquel Department of trying to steal members from churches that belonged under the supervision of the Cinco Calles church in Guatemala City, arguing that he and others believed "such a program uncalled for, unbiblical and not calculated to produce the best results for the work in general." He concluded, "We cannot believe that in recognizing the

Cakchiquel Department it was the purpose of the Council to give your group of Missionaries an arbitrary right to change the program of development of a field from the first under the direction of another center and this without consultation, agreement and cooperation of the other Missionaries concerned."[30]

The San Antonio missionaries, of course, considered that there *had been* a previous agreement between Cameron Townsend and Albert Bishop, and naturally took offense at Lincoln's tone. The dispute, which in its essence had the possibility for a truly high-minded discussion of missionary method, rapidly degenerated into charges and countercharges of dishonesty and greed. Old grudges surfaced, missionaries from all over Guatemala lined up on opposite sides, testimonials were secured from *ladinos* and Indians as well as from Paul Burgess and others, until the council was faced, yet again, with a blizzard of resignations from both sides.

Paul Townsend was placed in a very difficult position in the resulting conflict. With Cameron in the United States, Paul was forced to lead the Cakchiquel Department before he was ready, a fact he readily acknowledged. "Every responsibility has been forced upon me," he told Karl Hummel. "I would have liked to have kept a back seat, but there was no chance unless I proved spineless and didn't care." Besides, he always struggled with the feeling that he was Cameron's lackey. That he reacted as fiercely as he did in this conflict may have been in part a way to prove that he held the position on his own, not just because he was Cameron's brother. He complained to Hummel, "It . . . is not very pleasant to be always 'second fiddle' or 'follow-up man' to one's own brother even if he is the finest fellow in the world. . . . I would if possible, without going against my convictions, disagree with Cameron just to show you folks that I don't follow him for any other reason than for my convictions." Then, not wanting the council to think he was just acting the typical ornery fundamentalist, he concluded, "Please don't let anyone think I got my disposition from attending BIOLA."[31]

At its most low-minded, the dispute aroused latent jealousies over the prominence of Townsend's work. Some of the older missionaries had grown a bit peeved at the relative latecomer to Guatemala with the deft fund-raising gift, who had built a station of some prominence in only a few years. In 1925 the Townsends often had upward of one thousand dollars pass through their hands every month, during a period when some single missionaries were struggling along on thirty to forty dollars of monthly income. This figure was a tribute to the large ministry the Townsends had built and included their personal support, support for native evangelists, funds to maintain buildings and run the Robinson Bible Institute, as well as the San Antonio station, which included a school, orphanage, and clinic. From May to October 1925 the Townsends received roughly thirty-three hundred dollars outside of the regular mission channels and specified for Indian evangelization. This represented an increase of more than 200 percent from what they had received during the same period just the year before.[32]

Paul was not sympathetic when the San Antonio station was accused of "extravagance." "It is not our fault that San Antonio has received more publicity than [your station]," Paul wrote to one disgruntled veteran. "Your jealousy might better lead to harder efforts on your own part to secure publicity." Both sides enlisted the nationals in the dispute, which created less-than-edifying missionary moments. At one point, Paul angrily accused Don Arturo Borja, the prominent *ladino* pastor whose complaints a year ago kicked off the dispute, of spreading rumors that the missionary women at San Antonio were "lost women that had to flee from the United States."[33]

At its most high-minded, the dispute produced statements such as the position paper written by Luther Rees and the testimonials submitted by Paul Burgess, W. F. Jordan of the American Bible Society, and Edward Haymaker, dean of the Presbyterian mission in Guatemala. Burgess, a missionary of unusual education and vision, as well as vast experience working with both Indians and *ladinos*, wrote, "I am absolutely convinced that Indian and Ladino work should be carried on separately to attain the best results. There is every reason here for the separate work for these two peoples that there is in the United States for separate Churches for Negroes and whites, with the additional factor of language weighing for separation here." "But the matter is not theoretical," he went on. "It is a simple matter of fact. . . . If the Church is a Ladino Church, a few Indians, who wish to turn Ladino, may be hangers on[,] but they will make no vital contribution to the evangelization of their own people[,] and if the Indians carry the responsibilities of the Church[,] even the most spiritual Ladino believers will maintain only a nominal relation to it."[34]

Paul Townsend also compared the situation to the racial conditions in the United States, if more bluntly than Burgess. "Would you who are not agreeing with us wish to tell the Scofield Memorial Church that they must . . . join the nearest Negro Church[,] making one congregation? That would be ideal but unwise." Luther Rees made a similar argument. "I am surprised that missionaries from this country and especially from the South, should oppose a separate work for the Indians," he told R. D. Smith. "The northern churches (Pre[sbyterian] and Meth[odist]) working in the South, have come to see that it is best for the Negro to have separate churches[,] and they even have separate conferences and Presbyteries."[35]

W. F. Jordan of the American Bible Society had seen the Townsends' work personally and written about it in journals such as the *Christian Herald.* He was astonished at the dispute. "Surely you are joking when you say that there are those on the field who object to specialized Indian work," he exclaimed. "To me, after a visit to Guatemala the need is too patent to require any defense whatever. . . . The Indian and ladino live in altogether different worlds of thought, experience and outlook on life. It is only by going to them, living among them and becoming one of them as Cameron has done that the Gospel can be made a reality to them." Obviously influenced by Townsend, Edward Haymaker was even stronger. "The Indian is the staunchest and most religious and strategically valuable race of the two," he wrote. "If the Ladinos are evangelized, the Indians will not necessarily follow. If the Indians are evangelized, the Ladino must follow or be eliminated, for the Indian will then control." He considered it absurd to try to reach Indians in Spanish, even if it did "help the Government unify the nation."[36]

Paul Townsend forwarded the weighty testimonials to the council, but feeling the pressure from established missionaries such as Lincoln and from the Cinco Calles elders, leaders of their largest indigenous church, the council ordered the Cakchiquel Department to "refrain from any further division of congregations" for the time being. Once again the home office was inundated with threatened resignations, beginning with Townsend's. Cameron was furious. He fumed to Karl Hummel, "You might as well ask me to quit Indian work as to demand that the Indian believers [and] workers be made subject to the other race." To Luther Rees, he complained, "I gave my life for the Indians [and] not to be worn out by endless discussions."[37] Sick of the fighting, and without Cameron around to take the heat for him, Paul threatened resignation also.

The San Antonio letters were followed by a letter from the missionaries who opposed the Cakchiquel Department, stating that they were ready to resign en masse over the issue. The signatures included those of Townsend's old Panajachel partner, Archer Anderson; Frank Toms and his wife, Annie; the woman who initially helped recruit Townsend to the Bible House, Stella Zimmerman; and Jennette Tallet, Elvira's friend and recruit, who had fled the San Antonio station a few years earlier when she found the work not to her liking. The Cinco Calles national church leaders felt very strongly about the issue also. "They will not accept the Townsend policy," reported a Guatemala City missionary. "Our protest . . . means the voice of <u>all</u> the Guatemala division of work and workers apart from the Cakchiquel Department itself. It means that we will stand together <u>in</u> or <u>out</u> of the Mission." She concluded with a stinging threat. "Unless you brethren of the council take a definite stand and revoke your permission and recognition of this movement by not later than the middle of December . . . we will act on our own responsibility."[38]

Two factors eventually rescued the mission from disaster. First, in late October, after months of heated wrangling, and with resignations piling up around him, Karl Hummel sent a panicked message to the council. "The situation is more serious than words can express," he wrote. "Unless the Council can very quickly agree on a delegation and send it forth[,] I fear our Guatemala work will be torn to pieces." Fortunately, the council agreed with him. Second, Cameron Townsend, with newfound perspective after months of rest in the United States, realized he had himself caused some of the problem, even if from good motives. He decided he did not want to see all of his effort go to waste and chose to be conciliatory. He wrote to Hummel, "Out of love and deep appreciation to Mr. Rees and others of the Council and in hopes of relieving somewhat the tension on the field, I want to state that whatever the proposed delegation to the field may decide regarding the Ladino-Indian situation I will stand by the CAM."[39] Given the depth of his feeling on the issue, it was a truly remarkable concession.

Townsend was never unsympathetic to the argument that Indian groups ultimately needed to learn Spanish if they were ever to assimilate to the broader culture. He often justified his opposition to the plans of Latin American governments and missionaries by arguing that his way was actually the *best* way to ensure the eventual assimilation of the Indians. Townsend later promoted bilingual education throughout Latin America and the United States, arguing that if someone learned to read first in their own language, it would then be easier to teach them to read Spanish (or English). There is no reason to conclude that Townsend did not genuinely believe that it would be better in the long run for Indian groups to learn Spanish and assimilate into *ladino* culture. He later wrote, "Bilingual instruction comes to [the Indian's] aid . . . and gives him a bridge . . . to cross over from his perfect knowledge of one beautiful language to a more-or-less perfect knowledge of another and more important beautiful language, the national tongue. . . . If the great Indian race could be taught to read today[,] there would be a new Indian world tomorrow, and day-after-tomorrow that world and our world would be blended into one." In the context of arguing that funds ought to be spent in more "needy" areas, he once wrote of an Indian tribe in El Salvador, "Those Indians are fifty years ahead [in the process of assimilation] of our Indians here in most every way[,] and I hope that within 75 years . . . very little Cakchiquel will still be talked in Guatemala."[40]

Yet at the same time, he clearly valorized Indian culture over that of the *la-*

dinos. If Indians must assimilate to *ladino* culture, it was so they might protect themselves and advance themselves economically and in social standing, not because *ladino* culture was inherently better. In some ways, at least at this point in his life, he did not understand the implications of his own work. He clearly sought to restore cultural pride to Indian groups, but, influenced no doubt by the goals of the cultural elite in Latin America as well as of most missionaries, saw their ultimate advancement in the framework of adaptation to the broader Spanish culture. But he insisted that such adaptation, when it finally arrived, be constructed on the basis of equality, not inferiority. And clearly, for Townsend, Christianity had a role to play in leveling the playing field between the races. Townsend knew that total assimilation was a process of decades or even centuries. He seized on the rationale behind bilingual education as a convenient argument to win the support of Latin American governments for his primary goal, which was to teach Indians to read their own language so that they could truly understand the translated Scriptures.

In December, Karl Hummel, new council member Herbert Mackenzie, and the Townsends sailed for Guatemala. One week later they were joined by Dr. Robert Glover, missions professor at Moody Bible Institute and veteran China missionary, who had just published a book on missions. On New Years Day 1926 in Guatemala City, the party met with virtually all of the CAM missionaries assigned to Guatemala. They spent the weekend listening to devotional messages and attending prayer meetings, probably a good strategy given the heightened state of emotions between the San Antonio and Guatemala City factions. Between the devotional meetings, the delegation conducted personal interviews with all involved in the *ladino*-Indian controversy. After working through the bitter feelings, the delegation addressed policy adjustments. Essentially, all parties agreed to disagree. Policy was put in place "on the basis of a division of territory," which left the "various missionaries free to pursue different policies and methods within the several districts," with perhaps a good degree of uniformity now that hurt feelings were patched over. Only afterward did they meet with the native workers and explain the decision to them. The nationals had no part in constructing the new policy.[41]

Under the new agreement Townsend was now responsible for *both* the Indian and *ladino* work in his assigned territory. The same went for the Guatemala City missionaries. Each governed their territory as they wished. The plan added a lot of responsibility to Townsend's already full plate, but he had won, at least for the Cakchiquels in his district, a certain amount of autonomy in the church.[42]

At least initially all went well. Don Arturo Borja, chief among the displeased *ladino* pastors, was content. Hummel thought it a good idea to let him supervise the Indian pastor in his town, Tecpan, provided he would recognize the Indian as co-pastor in other towns in that district. Since Borja knew a good bit of Cakchiquel, Townsend agreed. Soon even Borja was advocating separate chapels. "True peace and fellowship reigns in all these congregations," he announced to Townsend. In April 1926 Townsend gleefully reported to Hummel, "The Indian-ladino trouble is buried so deep it doesn't even stink—at least I don't smell anything."[43]

When R. R. Gregory, the Central American representative of the American Bible Society, wrote Townsend about his impressions of the CAM in the midst of all these controversies, he put his finger on a problem at the core of the very idea of a faith mission: the need to bring some form of institutional control to missions founded on the principle that institutional control was somehow antithetical to faith. "One of the outstanding impressions during my thirteen weeks in Central America was the utter lack of co-operation in the Central American Mission," Gregory told Townsend. "Each one was working at his own little field as it were independent of the other missionary of the same Mission. It seemed to me as if I was dealing with so many different mission bodies instead of one whose central office was in Dallas. It seems to me for real efficient work this should be remedied."[44]

The council delegation also worked on this problem. They installed a field organization in Guatemala, an annual conference of all missionaries, and an executive committee to direct the work between conferences. Karl Hummel then went on to the other republics to establish similar organizations there as well. The conference recommended that a full-time field superintendent be appointed over the whole work. This would greatly diminish the daily work of the home council, as most decisions would be handled on the field and much of the correspondence directed through the field secretary and field committees. The report to the full council concluded with thanks to God "that He has brought the Mission through this recent crisis so safely and happily. We trust that the needed lessons may have been learned by all concerned."[45]

In early 1926 the CAM's remedies seemed to be working well. Townsend reported to Hummel, "The field organization is proving a great blessing to me [and] I think to most all. The fellowship is glorious." Even the council's most conservative curmudgeon saw the benefits of a more businesslike organization. "Recently I have come to see that it is very similar to the 'growing pains' of a child who takes a sudden spurt upward," wrote R. D. Smith. "I suppose every

Mission has had to face the crisis of emerging from a small, family, go-as-you-please affair, to a well regulated organization."[46]

The council, however, was slow to implement all it had learned. Five years later, in 1931, Karl Hummel reported that although the field organization in Guatemala was "functioning very well" and should have been "started years ago," a field secretary "to link up the work in the five Republics" was still a real need. "The more the direction of the work can be handled on the field, the better it will be," he told the council. Nevertheless, it was 1949 before the CAM appointed a field secretary over all of Central America.[47]

Townsend spent a good portion of 1925 in the United States. One would expect that someone like Townsend, with such passionate convictions, would be a tower of strength, but in fact Townsend could be quite fragile, both emotionally and physically. He did not handle conflict well. Elvira reported that at times "the least disturbance . . . sent Cameron to bed, oftentimes just a letter from the Mission or some individual." By May 1925 Townsend was on the verge of collapse. He had been declining for several months and decided to return to California for a rest when he found it difficult to complete the journey from Panajachel to San Antonio. The strain of living with Elvira as well as his argument with the council over authority, and his struggle to separate the Indian work from the *ladino*, all undoubtedly contributed. Paul Townsend blamed his brother's incapacitation on the conflict between the Guatemala missionaries. He angrily charged Stella Zimmerman, "Whoever helped out in the criticism of W. C. Townsend and wife is guilty before God of the present sickness of that servant of God. If they had prayed in place of criticizing he would still be here."[48]

Cameron left Elvira behind. She managed to carry on for two months without him, fairly remarkable in itself, before sending him several threatening cables demanding his return. When the council balked at his returning before he was completely well, she joined him in California, a welcome trade-off as far as Paul was concerned. "Her going has relieved us of a strain[,] and although we do have more work, the relief is more than a recompense," he told Hummel. Once in California, Elvira demanded they go to Chicago to see her family and friends. Townsend asked if there were any meetings the council wanted him to take on the way. R. D. Smith disapproved. "It seems preposterous to send such a woman out to represent the Mission and urge people to be fully surrendered to the Lord. I do not think the Lord or the Mission needs that kind of help." Nevertheless, they journeyed to Dallas, where both spoke at the Scofield church several times, before going on to Chicago. In Chicago they met with a new council member, who reported that Cameron appeared to be "a nervous wreck."[49] The couple remained in the United States recuperating until returning to Guatemala with the delegation from the council in December.

It was a year of transition for Lewis Sperry Chafer. Chafer's aggressive promotion of the CAM ran headlong into faith mission ideals. The rest of the council resisted his progressive ideas. His attempts to modernize the work of the office were hindered by the territoriality of council members whose feelings he had hurt when he rather abruptly seized control of office business affairs upon first coming on board. Council members who often had been instrumental in the recruitment of various missionaries continued to correspond with their favorites, at times making decisions about which Chafer had no input or even knowledge. Upon his return from a trip to Europe in 1924 he found that the plans he had made "for the prosecution of the office work were reversed and taken practically out of [his] hands." The subsequent council meeting was stormy, "most unpleasant to us all," as various council members expressed resentment at losing their job or authority to Chafer's businesslike streamlining of the office.[50]

Chafer grew increasingly frustrated at his inability to act decisively on behalf of the mission, as the approval of the council was required before major decisions. He begged Rees to spend some time in Dallas so that they could get some work done. "I am greatly distressed that we do not get anything done in connection with the Council," he wrote. "The whole country is before us and we must take some kind of new step forward." It took so long to make decisions on some applications that Chafer, out of embarrassment, suggested to a few that it would be better if they withdrew their applications and tried somewhere else. It was no easier to make decisions that concerned CAM's own missionaries. About one he wrote, "It is a pity to leave that poor woman in distress looking to us for advice and we taking our time to get together when it may be convenient."[51]

Conservative council members were very critical of Chafer's fund-raising strategies, which seemed to compromise faith ideals. They complained that Chafer's attempts to build up the support base of individual missionaries by connecting them directly with supporters amounted to too direct and aggressive solicitation for a faith mission. Chafer's fund-raising methods in the *Bulletin* also raised their ire. "I see no objection to saying that there is . . . need of a building in San Salvador in which to hold meetings," one member wrote, "but [we must] say nothing of the amount desired, but simply ask them to pray that this need be supplied."[52]

In early 1925 Chafer resigned the general secretary position to devote his full time to what became Dallas Theological Seminary. He remained on the council, and Karl Hummel, a CAM field missionary of real ability, was called to the position. Although Hummel had more interpersonal ability than Chafer, and consequently did not hurt as many feelings, he would often echo Chafer's frustrations in the years ahead.

In May 1925, utterly worn out and about to return home to recover his health, Townsend wrote what turned out to be a farewell letter to Howard Dinwiddie. It was their first contact in some time, and Townsend was feeling abandoned by the man he considered a mentor and soul mate. "I suppose that you have little time now to think about little C[entral] Amer[ica]," he complained. Dinwiddie had indeed been extremely busy. The Pioneer Mission Agency files are filled with reports on Indian tribes from all over the continent, primarily collected by Dinwiddie and Legters. Traveling with Arthur Tylee, who, along with his two-year-old daughter and a nurse, would be murdered in 1930 by Nambikuara Indians, Legters surveyed the Amazon basin for six months in 1924. Dinwiddie spent the spring of 1925 in Argentina and Chile. Their surveys had turned up the need for at least seventy-five men if all the Indian tribes were to be reached. By mid-1924 nine had been recruited and funded through the PMA. According to Dinwiddie, the number of Indian believers in Guatemala since he had visited in 1920 had leaped from a "few hundred" to "approximately three thousand," largely accomplished through Indian-to-Indian evangelism, a remarkable fact if true. A number of the Indian evangelists were supported by funds channeled through the PMA. Consequently, Dinwiddie reassured Townsend, "You are greatly mistaken to think that I have little time to think of Central America." In his travels he had spread the word that Townsend's work in Central America was a blueprint for what could be done for Indians. "I do not understand all the [whys] and wherefores of the change in the relationship between you and me," he told Townsend, but assured him of his continued love and respect.[53]

In late 1925 Dinwiddie visited the mission stations of the North East India General Mission. He planned to survey unexplored regions of India, but he died there of enteric fever on the morning of Sunday, December 27, 1925, and was buried in Aijal. "His vision of the mission fields of the world and of the untouched regions was almost unique in our generation," reported the PMA in its eulogy, a bit of hyperbole Dinwiddie would have loved. "Will you not pray that God may clearly indicate the leader upon whose shoulders Mr. Dinwiddie's mantle should fall, and under whose direction the pioneer missionary work in the untouched regions of the world may go forward in preparation for His coming?"[54]

Dinwiddie's mantle fell on Leonard Legters. In January 1925 Legters got in touch with Townsend after his five months in the interior of South America. Legters's admiration for the young man was immediately apparent. "How I wished time after time, that you were not in Guatemala, but in South America. . . . I wished that you could be 100 men, and be in 100 different places," he enthused. Legters requested information he could use on a planned six-month speaking tour "to find men and money to man Indian work." He also longed to publish books on the topic.[55]

Before launching his tour, Legters had lunch with R. D. Smith. Smith's report of the luncheon indicates that the CAM council would feel about Legters as they had long felt about Dinwiddie. The following is Smith's report to the CAM council of his meeting with Legters.

> Yesterday I had lunch with Mr. Legters, famous 'Indian expert.' I endeavored to learn all I could from him and incidentally to impress upon him some of my own views concerning Mission policies,—particularly along the line of the Golden Rule. Mr. Legters is giving six months of his time to deputation work for the Inland South America Missionary Union. But his one line of talk is 'Indians[,]' and he told me that his object in helping that Mission was to help only the part of it which is engaged in Indian work. . . . He said to me,—'You have a good man in the CAM whom I should like to get a hold of.' I inquired who it was and he said, 'Cameron Townsend.' . . . Another thing which he told me[,] and which is one of the most foolish things I have heard, is that Mr. Dinwiddie, who leaves next month for Argentina and Chile . . . has for his errand down there the removal of the Alliance Missionaries in those two Republics away up to Ecuador and Southern Colombia!!!!!! . . . He says that Mr. Dinwiddie thinks there are too many Missionaries in Argentina and Chile,—whee!!!!!!!! Well, brethren, I almost had to fan myself after that interview,—to think of two men going about the world posing as Mission specialists and proposing such foolish plans.[56]

The council never took Legters and Dinwiddie seriously; consequently, their failure to harness the tremendous passion, energy, and influence of these two men for the benefit of their mission remains one of the council's greatest failures of the 1920s. Townsend would make no such mistake.

R. D. Smith, in a remarkably prescient, if unduly paranoid, moment, sensed the direction Townsend was heading as early as 1925, shortly after Townsend and Legters began a close correspondence. First the paranoid: with Townsend invalided home that summer and traveling the country undertaking deputa-

9. L. L. Legters. Courtesy Townsend Archives.

tion for the mission, Smith warned the council that Cameron and Elvira were really "out for themselves, not the CAM." "I . . . think that the Central American Mission is of very little consequence to them," he wrote. "I think we may just as well prepare ourselves to expect their resignations[,] for I quite believe that they contemplate leaving the Mission when it suits their convenience to do so." Then the prescient: "And do not be surprised if later you learn that Cameron and Legters have linked up together for Indian work . . . Cameron to be the leader on the Field and Legters carrying the home end of the work." And then the paranoid again: "I have no doubt they have been in correspondence and are to meet in the East before Mr. Legters goes to Central America."[57]

Townsend's translation efforts continued at a slow but steady pace. In December 1924 he and his assistants finished the first revision of Luke. In February 1925 he reported to Chafer that he was "getting things down to a system." He genuinely enjoyed the work, remarking to Dinwiddie that his ambition was to translate the Bible into three Indian languages. There were numerous interruptions, of course, and with the new organizational plan, he had several stations and quite a few workers to oversee. He lost most of 1926 to such work. But Paul seemed to be holding his own managing the San Antonio station, and the Robinson Bible Institute required less of his time. From 1924 to 1929 Townsend procured help wherever he could to keep the RBI operating. The Burgesses taught during the spring 1925 session; Ed Haymaker took over another; and a Presbyterian missionary from Mexico who knew Townsend from college also donated a month. "I don't know what we would do if it were not for the help of the Presbyterian missionaries," Townsend told Karl Hummel. By 1928 three missions were cooperating to staff the institute: the CAM, the Presbyterians, and the Primitive Methodists. All the missions in the territory sent their Indian students there. From time to time Legters dropped in to lend a hand, once holding a "Cakchiquel Keswick Conference." Townsend hoped to one day see indigenous Keswick conferences "with the missionaries attending, not as paternal leaders, but as unofficial brethren and observant auditors." In 1930 he even managed to talk prominent radio evangelist Charles Fuller into teaching some classes at the RBI and speaking at the conference in connection with graduation. "He is a very fine man and intensely interested in missionary work," Townsend recounted.[58]

With the arrival on the field of Carl Malmstrom, Elvira's brother, the translation work picked up. Cameron had vigorously recruited Carl when he visited Guatemala to attend their wedding, and now, seven years later, that recruitment paid off. Carl located at Panajachel and relieved Townsend of more of his duties, including, in December 1927, the superintendency of the Cakchiquel Department. "The translation work is booming," Townsend reported in March 1927. It must be reemphasized, however, that the work "boomed" largely because of the efforts of Indian translators. "Many other matters have demanded our attention, so that heretofore we have done well to get one week out of each month for translation work," Elvira reported. "However, native helpers are engaged in this work constantly." For example, out of the first 273 days of 1927, the Townsends were away from home 140. The Indians were able to work much more regularly.[59]

In June 1927 the team finished a first draft of the New Testament except for Revelation, although Townsend realized it needed a great deal of revision. Some of the Gospels had already been revised half a dozen times or more. They had published nothing in the five years since they self-published John, and Townsend was growing impatient. Under the leadership of Brigido Zuñiga, the team had just about completed the second revision, but Townsend felt he had to be with them for the last several revisions. "It has dragged on too long and must be finished," Townsend told Legters.[60]

Many missionaries still opposed his translation work, arguing that Indians could better be reached in Spanish. By 1927 Townsend had lost patience with such arguments, calling them "good for old missionaries or lazy ones who don't want to go to the effort of learning a new language."[61]

Legters spent most of 1926 on a second trip through the Amazon. He met with numerous Indian tribes, categorizing them, taking notes on their language, and filling pages with florid descriptions. "Physically they are a marvelous people, not in size but in bodily development . . . sleek and agile, broad shouldered and with narrow hips, reminding one of a racehorse," Legters enthused. "It was a pleasure to watch the beautiful rhythmic movements of their nude bodies unhampered by any clothing." There was a dark side to Legters's reports, however. He acknowledged the problem of exploitation by "frontiersmen." "What the gold seekers and adventurers were to us, the rubber men are to them," he reported. One man told Legters how with "modern arms, imported from the United States," he and his men had wiped out entire villages, clearing the land for rubber workers.[62] Missionaries were often the first to bring such news to the attention of the public.

The stimulation of Legters's report was too much for Townsend, who read it with a "burning heart." "How I would like to go!" he exclaimed.[63] By 1926 Townsend was already restless, bogged down with administrative work, eager to be out on the road again blazing a trail where no missionaries had gone before. Now Townsend had his eye on the legendary Lacandone tribe on the border between Guatemala and Mexico. The Lacandones were reported to be particularly "wild" and dangerous, and Townsend longed to be the first to enter their territory with the gospel. That winter Legters tried to interest the CAM in expanding into Mexico. The territory nominally belonged to the Northern Presbyterian Mission Board, but Legters thought he could persuade them to let the CAM undertake Indian work there. The council was favorable as long as they entered from the Guatemala side, and as long as Legters supplied the men and money—a no-risk proposition for them, to be sure. Legters, Burgess, and Townsend made a few exploratory surveys, but nothing permanent came of it.[64]

In 1925 A. E. Forbes, a coffee, tea, and spice importer from St. Louis, Missouri, sent Townsend fifteen hundred dollars to support a missionary couple in Indian work. In 1927 Townsend, who was endeavoring to work around faith mission constraints and make his orphanage and school self-supporting, suggested that Forbes help him set up a coffee-curing plant that would be run by workers from his school. Forbes would buy the cured coffee from Townsend, with the profit going to the orphanage. Indians in the community would also benefit, as, with the help of Forbes, Townsend would be able to pay more for their raw coffee than they were getting from local plantation owners, who, Townsend complained, purchased coffee "for a song." Townsend loved working with businessmen, who generally had little patience for faith mission propriety. It must have been refreshing for Townsend to receive letters from Forbes like one in 1927 that cut directly to the chase. "You must be nearly out of funds by this time," Forbes stated. "Please let me know."

By September 1927 Forbes had contributed forty-five hundred dollars to Townsend's cooperative. Evidence is sketchy, but the venture seems to have had mixed results. With another one thousand-plus dollars from Forbes, Paul Townsend, much more mechanically inclined than Cameron, expected to have the plant up and running by the fall of 1928. By September Paul was sending monthly reports to Forbes. By the summer of 1930 Forbes seems to have been discouraged with the project, but in 1932 Elvira reported to Hummel, "In spite of hard times, the Forbes Tea and Coffee Co. have just sent in $1,000 with which to buy coffee and ship, so these are busy days buying in coffee[,] and Cameron is working hard to get the machinery in good shape. . . . We trust that the coffee deal will mean a good profit this year as it did last, so as to be able to keep our little Indian school 'agoing.'"[65] Forbes was still sending money to Townsend as late as 1935.

While Townsend was doing well by faith mission standards, the rest of the mission was suffering. The CAM had grown steadily, if slowly, during Townsend's tenure. In 1920 the CAM supported forty-four missionaries with a combined income of $50,888. That works out to roughly $1,100 per missionary for the year, but that is a highly misleading figure. Some missionaries got more money on the side from personal supporters. Many got much less, as the disparity in income was wide. In addition, some missionaries supported native evangelists, subsidized churches, and operated clinics, schools, and orphanages, all from mission income. In 1930 the CAM supported seventy missionaries, and almost double that number of native evangelists, on an income of $77,407, still roughly $1,100 per missionary for the year. In addition, somewhere close to $1,000 per month went directly from donors to the field, bypassing the general fund. By 1935 the CAM had founded 63 churches and counted 13,700 baptized converts in Central America, certainly another valid measure of success.[66]

A closer look, however, reveals that for at least one-half of Townsend's tenure, the CAM was in real financial trouble. Beginning in at least the winter of 1924 and continuing well into the Depression years, CAM missionaries lived on a monthly income well below quota. Quotas were established according to missionary budgets, and these budgets were already "reduced down to actual necessities." In general, single workers required from $50 to $75 and married workers from $100 to $125 per month. During the fiscal year from June 1925 to June 1926 the CAM on average sent about 75 percent of what was required to its missionaries. Individual months varied from 100 percent in April 1926 down to 47 percent in June of the same year. By that October the mission was in serious shape. "It seems to me that we must have a time of heart-searching and prayer to find out what is wrong if we expect to continue the work of the Central American

Mission," Hummel informed the council. "Last month, September, we sent a 45% remittance, the lowest, I believe, that has ever been sent. In August it was 50%.... In September a great number of lady workers received exactly $22.50 from this office. We of course are always in hopes that they will receive some gifts direct, but their monthly reports reveal that some of them have hardly ever received such gifts." In May 1927 the mission was only able to send 30 percent of quota to its missionaries. Some donors had stopped giving; others had died or suffered financial reverses. In November 1927 Hummel reported, "For the past few months we have sent more or less 50% remittances." Matters were so desperate that Hummel suggested recalling missionaries who did not have personal supporters, cutting off all funds to national evangelists and churches, and "depart[ing] sufficiently from our faith basis to lay the exact situation before our constituency." The problem deepened month after month, year after year, but little was done, and little changed. In November 1929 Hummel was still writing about the "continued shortage." With the Depression just beginning, there was no relief in sight.[67]

For at least 150 years, ever since dramatic stories of God's provision in response to prayer for George Müller's orphanages and Hudson Taylor's China Inland Mission first circulated, evangelicals have believed that the great faith missions (the CIM, the Africa Inland Mission, the Sudan Interior Mission, the Central American Mission, the Wycliffe Bible Translators, and dozens of others) operated successfully on the faith basis—that simply through fervent prayer, without active solicitation or publication of needs, God supplied the financial needs of the missionaries. Mission history offers countless stories in proof of this thesis. But such anecdotal stories tease more than enlighten. How did such a process really work on an institutional, not anecdotal, basis? Did faith missions really work by faith? Although the definition of *work* is certainly open to debate, the story of the CAM reveals that however we define it, by the definition of the missionaries themselves, the faith basis did not work. It simply did not bring in enough money.

Alvyn Austin has argued that the first great faith mission, the China Inland Mission, operated quite successfully on the faith basis. Austin documents large sums of money poring into CIM coffers during the 1920s and 1930s, precisely the period in which the Central American Mission struggled terribly to fund their missionaries. The CIM statistics reveal, in Austin's words, "the financial underpinnings of one of the great inspirational moments of the twentieth century." God (again in Austin's words) "manifestly blessed the CIM ... moving people to give through prayer alone ... staggering amounts of money." Austin, however, records his own frustration at the "aura of secrecy" that surrounded the mission and how the archives were purged, at Hudson Taylor's orders, of anything "which might prove an embarrassment" to the mission. The biggest secret, Austin reports, was money, and nothing remains in the archives that does not substantiate the accounts written by Taylor. Taylor boasted that no one in the mission was ever "hindered in work by lack of funds; no one has ever suffered in health from this cause; no one has ever left the Mission on this ground, or has remained dissatisfied on this score, to my knowledge."[68] A remarkable claim! None of these statements could be said about the Central American Mission, as their uncensored archives amply illustrate.

The Central American Mission represents the flip side of the faith mission coin. The China Inland Mission was heads. It was the first mission founded on the faith basis. It had an enormously charismatic founder and other very gifted leaders. It had a gigantic publicity machine, which made the daring faith quest of its missionaries common knowledge in the home of every worthy evangelical in America, Canada, and Britain. It had the sexy mission field; Americans had long had a love affair with China. But the true test of faith mission principles lies on the opposite side of the coin. What was life like there, where missionaries of equal piety and faith labored for lesser-known missions with less-charismatic founders in less-celebrated parts of the world? For a historian, the question must be approached pragmatically. Did the reality of life on the field live up to the promise of the faith life as idealized by George Müller and Hudson Taylor? Were other organizations, which copied their method of operation, able to repeat their record of remarkable success? The problem for the other faith missions was how to capture the imagination of a public that was enamored with the CIM. The Central American Mission had the additional problem of interesting people in Central America when the more traditional and more romantic mission destinations were China, Africa, and India. Would God prove equally as faithful in the experience of these missions? Or perhaps more to the point, was the true variable God's faithfulness or an efficient and businesslike publicity machine?

As CAM council members cast about to explain their drastic financial straits, the one thing they refused to do was to doubt God. "God has not failed—He never can fail," Hummel wrote to the CAM missionaries. "It seems hard to understand why [finances are so low,] but we can't doubt Him nor His love for us." If God could not fail, and if the method itself was not faulty, then the problem must lie elsewhere. What was certain was that somehow God was behind it all, and there was a definite reason for the difficulties. As R. D. Smith said, "[God] does not afflict willingly,—here again there is a cause." Perhaps sin was the cause. "Purge away any hindrances," Hummel implored the missionaries, and then added pragmatically, "If you have failed to acknowledge gifts from donors[,] please write them." Perhaps they did not have enough faith when they prayed. Perhaps God was displeased that some missionaries were "content to receive and use so much more money than their fellow Missionaries have." For R. D. Smith, shortness of funds meant that God was testing and trying the mission "with a view to larger blessings and heavier responsibilities later,—to find out whether we really do have any faith or not." It was up to the mission to discover what God meant to teach through the trial. Smith rather uncharitably concluded that it was "our dear workers on the Field" who needed "chastening and testing," although he also worried that "some of the Lord's stewards in this country are deliberately saying Him nay, when the Holy Spirit prompts them to give to the Mission." At any rate, he hoped that God would continue "keep[ing] right after us until we acknowledge our fault and do what He wants us to."[69]

The reason mission leaders searched for spiritual solutions to what seems a material problem was that with the faith basis, God had become so intimately associated with money that they were incapable of viewing financial issues through anything other than a spiritual lens. The problem became absolutely critical, because with God linked so closely to money, financial failure threatened to impugn the very honor of God. In a letter that circulated among the financially stressed missions, the general director of the Africa Inland Mission wrote to his council of "the danger in wavering or doubt, of fatal failure to self, to life and to dependent friends, and all the danger of great dishonor to God in a failing experience." He continued, "Ten-thousand times better never join a faith Mission than to 'trust' and fail to get. Of course those who fail to get never did trust or they would not have failed to receive. Better never profess to trust than to dishonor God by appearing to do so and by doubt or sin compel Him to withhold."[70]

This inability to question the method has persisted over the years for the same reason. The feeling lingers among missionaries and in the broader evangelical community that to question the faith method of operation somehow questions God's faithfulness. Despite a dismal record of failure during the early years of the Africa Inland Mission, an AIM missionary wrote, "How can it be possible that for a period of nearly thirty years a large number of individual workers . . . should unite on the one principle of absolute dependence on God and not one, as far as we are aware, fail at any time to have all his needs supplied?"[71] Such a statement demonstrates either selective amnesia or a selective definition of "having one's needs supplied." To question whether early faith missionaries truly had their needs met threatens the very foundation of missionary, even evangelical, piety, that God is faithful to answer the earnest prayers of his people, regardless of whether God ever suggested or approved such a means of operation.

Financial failure also threatened the very reason for the missions' existence. If you believed, as did R. D. Smith, that "a Faith Mission, as also its Missionaries, must not assume financial obligations without being sure that the Lord is undertaking the responsibility, AND if this is so, there will never be any lack, for God is able and does supply," then financial "lack" meant God must not be directing the affairs of the mission.[72] God must have been interested in something upon which the CAM council had not yet put its finger! Few missionaries were willing to question themselves that pointedly, but the haunting fear that God did not approve their ministry surely lurked behind many of their impassioned prayers.

By the mid-1920s, with the CAM council discovering that the faith basis grew more difficult as the mission expanded, Karl Hummel, for one, was willing to argue that "some of our policies are self-imposed, rather than Scriptural requirements." In June 1926, after several years of financial privation, Hummel suggested that it might be time to send a letter to CAM donors "stating the situation in a straightforward manner," that unless more funds were raised they might have to release national evangelists, maybe even missionaries. "Would such a letter be contrary to our faith policy?" he wondered. He followed that question with a clarification that signaled a subtle, but nevertheless dramatic, shift in his thinking. "Or rather," he asked, "would it be displeasing to the Lord?" There was precedent for such a letter. The Inland South America Missionary Union, which required one year's support before sending out missionaries, published the following notice in 1924: "[Our] missionaries . . . are going to be short in their allowances because of the insufficiency of the General Missionary Fund. . . . The missionary allowance at best is small[,] and then when it is cut down it would seem impossible to live upon. Will you not join us in prayer that the needs of these self-sacrificing, devout missionaries may be supplied?"[73]

Most council members were favorable to the proposal, if somewhat nervous about it. They still wanted the letter focused on prayer, not a financial appeal. As one wrote, "I still believe that a monthly prayer letter addressed to our prayer helpers sent *for the purpose of securing prayer fellowship* is quite in harmony with Bible illustrations of faith. . . . The thought is that the Lord's people generally need to be informed of facts in order that [they] may intelligently let their request be made known unto God."[74]

Smith, however, was bitterly opposed. He argued that such efforts must "not go the length of appealing for money; or (and this is the more important) that in our own hearts it is not God plus publicity, which is a fatal snare to faith." He went on to insist, "It would be a terrific loss for the CAM to lose its testimony about being able to trust God in time of need." For Smith, even "the private clientele of the individual Missionary" could easily become "a snare to that Missionary." In the rawest statement of the faith credo, he argued, "If [the missionary] did not have any clientele to whom to write about his need, he would simply trust God, go along with his work, and his needs would be supplied; but having friends whom he knows will probably respond to his statement of need, he consciously or unconsciously leans upon them instead of upon Jehovah-Jireh."[75]

Hummel, who engaged Smith most directly in the debate, could not see any inconsistency between making public the mission's needs and still trusting God to supply them. In essence he accused Smith of being akin to a faith healer who always sought divine healing rather than submitting to a visit to a physician. "[Why] relegate the remedies that God has put into the world to the devil's territory," he argued. "If one of God's dear servants needs $50.00 with which to buy a mule, thus enabling him to preach the Gospel in some distant station . . . , must we demand that God reveal that need to some one of His servants by a special revelation? I well realize that God very often does this, but I see no grounds for our limiting Him to such a plan." In another letter he indicated that some of the council members were ready to make a declaration of independence of sorts from the China Inland Mission. "I disagree with those who say that a work is not of faith simply because it does not measure up to the experience of George Müller and Hudson Taylor," he wrote. "God's callings are infinitely variant even in the life of faith."[76]

Finally, in May 1927, a year after Hummel broached the subject, the council voted that "a bi-monthly letter [should] be sent to our prayer helpers 'stating definite needs.'" Hummel wrote the carefully worded letter, which read in part:

> Dear Prayer-Helper: After waiting upon the Lord for several days, we feel led to seek your prayer fellowship in the very pressing need that our Mission faces. We have hesitated somewhat in sending such information for fear of being misunderstood, but on the other hand it has been pointed out that the friends of the CAM are due to know exactly what the needs are so that they may pray intelligently. To meet adequately this current

> month's expenses, we still need almost $3,500.00. . . . Thus far this month the incoming gifts have fallen off to a degree that we have never before experienced. It has brought us to our knees in prayer and humiliation, but as yet the need remains unmet. Will you not join with us in very definite prayer for this need? Pray too that the Lord may search our hearts and remove any hindrances. Perhaps it is His will that we suffer. Pray that we may have grace to do it as unto Him. The thought of retrenching has entered our minds, but we have not felt that God would have us do that. . . . Between $5,500.00 and $6,000.00 are needed monthly for general expenses.[77]

Perhaps signaling their desperation, every council member responded favorably except Smith, who cabled, "Letter you drafted is splendid if considered as from a mission not committed to faith basis." The council decided to send the letter only to "a select number" of their constituency, to which Smith sarcastically replied, "Be sure not to omit any of the rich folks,—we all agree they are very select."[78] Smith resigned shortly thereafter. Apparently the "select number" failed to respond, as the letter, apologetically worded and only tentatively followed up, produced few results.

Still, once having crossed this watershed, the CAM continued to send out carefully worded letters that explicitly mentioned needs in dollar figures, even as they continued to betray a certain uneasiness with the procedure. The letters were sent only to CAM's most consistent supporters. Clearly they did not want the wider Christian public to think they had departed from the faith basis.

When funds stayed tight despite the more explicit appeals, the CAM experimented with the "pro rata" plan between 1927 and 1930. The pro rata plan was a dramatic attempt to ease the burden on undersupported missionaries by requiring that *all* missionary support, even that designated for specific missionaries or work, come through the home office, where it was split up and divided among all the missionaries equally. Most faith missions at one time or another experimented with some form of this plan, including the China Inland Mission, Sudan Interior Mission, the Ceylon and India General Mission, and the South Africa General Mission.[79]

Both those for and against the plan, and it should be easy to figure out how the sides lined up, argued according to faith mission logic. The mission councils, and the missionaries with lean bank accounts, offered three points in its favor. First, everyone was placed on the faith basis equally. "If full support is guaranteed to certain ones they need exercise no faith." Second, "Not every successful and faithful missionary has the gift for building up a constituency in the homeland." And third, it had a certain spiritual ring to it, making it seem somehow the more Christian thing to do.

As might be expected, Townsend was against the plan, although he appears to have gone along with it as an experiment. He, along with other missionaries with relatively healthy bank accounts, offered three points against it. First, the plan would become a "poor crutch to weak faith." Or as Townsend scrawled across the back of Hummel's letter when he first heard the idea, "Missionaries [would be] tempted to depend on a share of the already meager allowances designated to other missionaries rather than on the Lord." Second, it effectively removed one of the faith missions' core operating principles, the financial weather vane. Paul Townsend made this argument. "To me the pro-rata plan removes the only advantage the faith mission has over a denominational mission. . . . We are forcing God to support any part of the work that may not be in accord with his will in order for him to meet the needs of that which <u>is</u> in his will." Finally, donors might not support the plan, as they would lose that direct connection with an individual that was the foundation of so much missionary giving. Regardless, the plan was soon abandoned when it did not lead to an increase in receipts. As the pro rata epitaph, Hummel wrote, "Policies that are not workable, no matter how idealistic they might be, certainly ought to be gone into very thoroughly and[,] if necessary, changed." It was a statement that echoed the thinking mission leaders were doing about the entire faith basis of mission operation.[80]

When R. D. Smith insisted that "God plus publicity" was a "fatal snare to faith," he touched the issue at the very heart of the faith enterprise, at least as it was idealized in evangelical popular culture. Perhaps, then, the most significant watershed crossed by faith mission executives and missionaries was when they began to openly articulate that publicity and the aggressive building of a large constituency was an integral part of the fiscal process, even for a mission operating on the faith basis.

Struggling missionaries recognized this first, as they compared firsthand their own income and the size of their ministry to that of Townsend and others who had built up large, well-funded institutions. But locked into a system that came to seem ordained by God, some missionaries found no way around the faith system other than to question their own fitness for the work. In 1921 CAM missionary Leroy McConnell was desperate. Given a position of responsibility in Central America, he never seemed to have enough money, and the work languished. He prayed and prayed, but year after year his financial support remained stagnant. "It has led me up to a critical point in a mental battle which has been going on for some years," he informed the council. "I find after these years of trial that the policy and manner of managing the [CAM] demands a certain class of men with special backing in the homeland and a special gift for procuring supporters for the aggressive pushing forward of the work." McConnell did not feel he was of this "class of man," and he was upset that the home council seemed reluctant to undertake the task for him. He argued, "What Paul says about salvation, 'how shall they believe in Him of whom they have not heard' applies equally well to the support of missionary work." He begged the council to do something more than pray to bring in the necessary funds, perhaps to start a special fund for promotion, travel, and literature. He concluded, "If you say the trouble is that I have little faith, the result is the same, for a man should not attempt to hold a place of responsibility on a higher plane of faith than he possesses."[81]

Four years later McConnell was still desperately hanging on, just barely getting by on extremely limited support. "The incentive for faith and the ambition for the extension of the work has been greatly suffocated in me," he lamented to the council. "The faith part of our Mission means that [the Councilmen] assume no responsibilities outside of the distribution of funds. As the responsibility is assumed by the Missionary[,] he should have a constituency of his own procured through faith, work and prayer. But that is a special gift and only those having it should be in charge of important Fields of the CAM." McConnell received no sympathy from R. D. Smith. "These statements," he groused, "reveal a Missionary <u>uninstructed</u> in what it means to live by faith. He says in effect that God alone is not sufficient, but that God <u>plus a constituency</u> is necessary." Shortly thereafter, McConnell left the mission.[82]

By the end of the decade, faith missions were getting the message from other sources as well. The chair of the missions committee at Moody Church told Townsend that the CAM needed to do more deputation work. There was no replacement for publicity. The issue came to a head because some men had been waiting at MBI for up to two years to go to the field, but the faith missions had no funds to send them.[83]

Karl Hummel and others like him were thinking along those same lines. As Hummel told Townsend, "Of all the faith missions, I think the CIM is the most spiritual. Their experiences regarding answered prayer are simply amazing. . . . Nevertheless, they are the most active and the best organized in their deputation activities of any mission." In this remarkably candid statement, Hummel implicitly admitted that there was more than likely a direct causal connection between publicity and "answered prayer." Hummel was certainly correct about the publicity efforts of the China Inland Mission. In addition to *China's Millions,* the American publication of the mission, with a circulation of twenty thousand, the CIM printed "nearly 300 titles between the years 1926–1952. Many would be considered 'best-sellers' in today's market."[84] In a sense, what Hummel and other faith mission leaders learned in the 1920s, and what men like Townsend understood instinctively, was that it was wonderful to have great faith, but even better if every evangelical in the country *knew* you had great faith. If a farmer had a sack of potatoes he felt led to give away, chances are he would leave it on the doorstep of the man he knew was running an orphanage by faith rather than with the poor family with equal faith of whom he had never heard. That he left the sack of potatoes on the doorstep without announcing his call only fostered the legend.

Townsend's mother, always practical, had never been convinced that the faith basis was a sound method of operation. To go out with a denomination seemed "the best and most business like way to work." Looking about at her friends, she complained that "so many of them know so little about the undenominational boards. They *hear* very little about them, and a great many of our most generous givers do but little reading." How could her pious friends send money to missions they had never heard of? In addition, she felt that denominational missionaries seemed "more level headed." They seemed to "pull together" better than the faith missionaries. She had what seemed to her a sensible settlement to all the CAM's financial problems. "How much more you people could accomplish at San Antonio if you had the Pres[byterian] Board back of you," she noted. "It seems to me that if the CAM are handicapped and see that the Lord's work would be advanced more rapidly, it would be the Christ-like thing to do to give that territory over to them, you folks with it. I don't believe you would have any less faith in God, but just more faith in your backing."[85]

Cameron and Elvira remained in the CAM, where the financial situation remained difficult. With the arrival of the Great Depression, the outlook turned, if possible, grimmer than ever before. January 1933 had the lowest January income in CAM history. "The prosperity that was just around the corner is still there," Hummel told Townsend, "but it looks like that corner is a long way off." The reception of a five-hundred-dollar check was an occasion for a shout of joy and a little dance in the home office.[86]

Despite all they had learned, the method of operation in the home office still emphasized faith over more pragmatic solutions. After two consecutive months in the summer of 1933 in which the mission's general fund contributed not one penny of support to the field, Miss Spain, the office secretary, was wondering what "word of advice" to send the missionaries. The word came back from one council member that what was needed was "a real season of prayer." Perhaps they had not yet learned to "pray things through." "I am asking today that the Lord would send in funds enabling you to send checks to these who must be really suffering," he concluded. "I still believe God will provide but He surely is testing us. God grant that if he is finding in any of us the hindrance that He may remove it or us."[87]

Such was the hold of faith ideology on missionaries and the evangelical public that it would take many more years before a new generation of leaders shifted the faith basis of operation toward a more expansive definition of faith, which included aggressive publicity and other methods learned from the business world. Still, the resignation of men like R. D. Smith from the CAM, and of Charles Hurlburt from the AIM, who was forced out as Africa director after he bitterly protested AIM's decision to publish specific needs, can be seen as a crossing of the Rubicon, the first admission, however tacit, that the strict faith principle simply did not work.[88]

The student of missions history knows, of course, that the independent evangelical missions eventually carried the day in the twentieth century. Most of the large Protestant mission societies today come from the faith mission tradition. In that sense, then, the faith missions were remarkably successful. But the fact remains that the faith missions no longer operate by faith, as anybody on a missionary prayer letter list well knows. The independent evangelical missions have very professional fund-raising operations, and few missionaries go overseas without their entire yearly quota committed in perpetuity through promises from friends, family, and churches. Partnership development is the new euphemism for deputation, and missionary partners know they can count on regular reports on the needs of their favorite missionary, and in truth, few would probably wish it otherwise. Some missions still tip their hat to the old ways by publishing percentages of the need still unmet rather than stating dollar amounts. But if a missionary is asked about such a technique, she is more apt to defend that method as a means of distinguishing herself and her mission from the televangelists than she is to reference the faith mission tradition. Many of the current generation of missionaries have forgotten, if they ever knew, the history behind the movement they enter.

When Willis Hotchkiss—the last man not dead or invalided home from the group that initially went with Peter Scott to Africa to found the Africa Inland Mission—finally returned to America, he was completely disillusioned with the faith basis of operation. His fledgling home council had left him alone and starving in Africa, reduced to threatening with his gun the natives he had come to save to keep them away from his limited food supply. Yet five years later Hotchkiss returned to Africa with another faith mission.[89] Hotchkiss was a tribute to both the dysfunctionality of the faith basis of operation and the tremendous grip it held on the imagination of the American and British public. If the idea that one could operate a mission successfully on a strict faith basis was always a somewhat fanciful notion—and the judgment of history must be that it was—it was at least a noble conceit, one that resonated deeply with evangelical spirituality and Victorian notions of honor and self-sacrifice and inspired hundreds and eventually thousands of individuals and churches to dedicate their lives to something beyond themselves. It was a conceit that carried struggling organizations through extremely difficult times, until a new generation of leaders adapted modern business methods to the faith basis and began to recruit and train a higher caliber of missionary. Faith missions survived, then, despite the faith basis of operation, and they thrived only after either implicitly or explicitly abandoning the strict faith method of operation, which was, after all, at least as far as we know, not God's idea in the first place. In short, faith missions carried the day in the twentieth century because they became in essence independent evangelical boards, adapting the more businesslike methods of the traditional boards that they so despised to their own peculiar religious sensibility.

With the CAM struggling financially in the latter part of the decade and stubbornly resistant to methodological change, L. L. Legters became a very important person in Cameron Townsend's life. Legters knew how to play by faith rules but at the same time was more than willing to stretch those rules to their semantic limits. He regularly connected Townsend with new supporters—"This is a group that it will pay you to cultivate"—and forwarded money at every opportunity. Legters worked outside of faith boundaries when Townsend could not, approaching businessmen for him to directly solicit aid. When Townsend had a project on his heart, he nagged Legters constantly to help him, asking him to try to "interest some Christian capitalist in the project." There is ample evidence that Legters was not shy in doing so, undoubtedly one of the reasons Townsend's ministry flourished at a time when most CAM missionaries and projects were suffering severe financial shortages. Townsend shrugged his shoulders when his fellow missionaries complained about Legters's methods. "It got them no place and diverted his support," he later remarked. "Storekeepers find that it pays to take the attitude that 'the customer is always right.'"[90] And godly businessmen were always right as far as Townsend was concerned. Their money and his vision made a perfect match. It was Legters's job to loosen them from that money and channel it to Townsend and his Indians.

Legters was adamantine in his support of Townsend and in his relentless quest for money and men for Indian work. When his wife was diagnosed with cancer, he decided it was his duty to remain in the United States till she got well. That did not mean, of course, that he stayed at home. He traveled the country recruiting for Indian work, reporting his wife's progress to Townsend as he received it from her via letter! By the end of 1927 Legters had money designated to support work with almost every Indian tribe in Guatemala, and prospective missionaries for some. He also had obtained consent from boards working in Mexico to let the CAM work with Indian tribes there. He badgered Townsend to expand his work. Even though he was at this point channeling men and money all over Latin America, he saw Townsend as his primary resource. "I think Cameron the most valuable Indian worker in the field today," he told Karl Hummel. "There is no man in America like him." He wanted to create with Townsend a "plan of advance" to systematically reach all the Indians of Latin America. In Legters's mind this program would begin by sending every prospective Indian missionary he could recruit to train with Townsend in Guatemala.[91]

As he had with Dinwiddie, Townsend worked hard to get Legters tied closely to the CAM, but the CAM council continued to view him as a loose cannon, and indeed, it must be granted that in some ways he was just that. Legters was known to write directly to missionaries inviting them to take a new post. He once asked an Indian worker to travel with him to Mexico as his interpreter. Unfortunately, the Indian was the right-hand man of one of the missionaries, which of course irritated the missionary to no end. The council recognized the possibilities in linking up with him, but in short he frightened them. In 1927 Townsend asked the council to invite Legters to Dallas for a face-to-face meeting, hoping they would respond to his "enthusiasm and ability at arousing interest." Karl Hummel was sympathetic, reporting to R. D. Smith, "I can say that Mr. Legters now has a very deep interest in our work and has put forth much effort to help us. . . . Mr. Legters is apt to be very forward[,] but at the same time he is burdened for the lost like very few men." But Legters's frontier style did not resonate in cosmopolitan Dallas, and the CAM continued to hold him at arm's length.[92]

Three years after the great education versus evangelism controversy in the mission, Townsend himself was feeling the pressures inherent in running a large educational work. By 1928 the number of kindergarten children from "unbelieving homes" outnumbered those from the homes of converts. The women in charge of the San Antonio school refused to limit the number of such children, because they coveted the "brightest and best" students. The council's warning seemed to be coming true. "As long as an evangelizing school is in the hands of godly soul winners . . . , it can be a mighty power for evangelization," Hummel warned. "But when it gets to be controlled by just Christian educators, it suffers the fate of the denominational mission school generally." The cause of evangelism had been subjugated to the promotion of the interests of the "best and brightest" regardless of faith. While this policy undoubtedly made for a more rewarding atmosphere for the teachers, it left Townsend in a precarious position. He originally intended the schools to be for the children of believers. Now he found himself worried about his own constituency, which had contributed so much for the schools, as well as wondering how long he could keep the still restless council at bay. "The entire Council is opposed to schools run on that basis," he warned one of his teachers. "A good many friends advised against it saying that we cannot afford to put missionaries into the class room when missionaries are so few. . . . I replied that natives would do the teaching merely under missionary supervision." Two missionary women now taught full-time in the school. Sounding like a council member, Townsend argued that this was "not good missionary economy." He wondered if perhaps he should not give up on the whole project and stop "interesting contributors" in the school. "This letter sounds blue," he concluded, "but it's just because of having to give up a pet hobby." Townsend, of course, did not abandon his "hobby." Hummel assured him that even though the current council was not in favor of making "evangelistic schools" part of mission policy, they were "satisfied to let [such schools] go on" as long as they kept reporting that "many, many souls . . . have been won to the Lord."[93]

The conflict between evangelism and social ministries continued to be a potential battleground for mission boards as long as the evangelical ethos remained saturated with a sense of urgency. Driven to a sense of haste by premillennial theology and the horrific vision of millions dying without Christ, evangelicals struggled valiantly to evangelize the world in their own particular generation. Although field missionaries undoubtedly agreed with a need for haste, they often found that the contexts into which they plunged demanded their attention to earthly realities. When Harry and Susan Strachan founded the Latin American Mission, they intended to focus their energies on evangelistic campaigns. They found, however, that they could not ignore the plight of the children on the streets of San José, Costa Rica. After a six-year struggle over their own priorities, they launched a hospital and a home for needy children. When Legters reported on his survey of "wild" Indian tribes in the Amazon basin, he argued for the necessity of both types of endeavor. "The man entering the Indian work should be of great adaptability," he declared. "The one who goes . . . should be able . . . to minister to their physical needs, in time begin a school, and teach the older men better means of agriculture. . . . Before and above it all, he must bring them the Good News of God." The struggle to follow such advice while maintaining a sense of urgency about evangelism is reflected in a statement released by the men who launched the New Tribes Mission in 1942. "We pledge ourselves," they wrote, "to refrain from doing even the good things if they do not contribute to the most important thing, namely, reaching the last unevangelized tribe in our generation."[94]

By the late 1920s Elvira ceased to be a continuous topic of conversation, and her outbursts appear to have become more irregular, although there are certainly indications that she continued to present a problem. In 1928 Paul Townsend remarked to Hummel that he "would like to spank a certain sister-in-law." It appears her jealousy was keeping Cameron from dealing personally with issues raised by the female missionaries at San Antonio. Still, she seemed to be doing better. Perhaps the presence of her brother on the field helped her feel more at home. Perhaps with age she was better able to control her temper. Perhaps she was learning the secret of "letting go and letting God."

Plagued by "lack of pep" at high altitude, Townsend designed a "sea-level tent," a place to sleep that would keep the air at sea-level pressure. Townsend's plan called for a small air compressor, an airtight tent, a glass window, and a telephone for conversations with the outside. The pep tent scheme consumed several letters between Townsend and Karl Hummel in 1928 before it died a natural death.[95]

In May 1928 Mr. Gregory of the American Bible Society (ABS) suggested the Townsends return to the United States to finish the translation, a suggestion that Cameron embraced, believing it was the only course of action that would get him far enough away from his quotidian responsibilities to permit full-time work on what was now an all-consuming pet project. The ABS even offered to pay for the support of the two Indian translators so that Townsend could take them with him. The proposed move caused real division. Paul Townsend and Carl Malmstrom were supportive. Frank Toms and the field committee, however, were very much against his taking Indians to the United States. They feared the move would "risk . . . irreparable spiritual injury to your . . . humble

Indian helpers, [when they come in] contact in the States with nominal Christianity." They worried that the Indians would become too Americanized and would never fit in again among their own people. The council agreed, and wondered why he could not simply go into seclusion at Panajachel.[96]

Townsend initially agreed to go along with the rather vehement wishes of his fellow missionaries, perhaps because he did not have the funds to carry out the project. By the end of July the Townsends had resigned themselves to continuing the work in Panajachel. However, when a cable arrived from America's Keswick offering to house them there, Townsend interpreted that as God's leading to go ahead with his original plan. He argued that simply because the subject had come up again, he "was forced to the conclusion" that God was leading him to complete the translation in the United States. "I concluded after a great deal of prayer and indecision that there was an urge within me which must come from God," he explained to Hummel in impeccable evangelical and faith mission logic. "Since then I've had peace of heart and feel that I can trust Him to take care of the Indians and over-rule the other objections which have been raised." It seemed that God was once again pulling rank over the mission's authoritative bodies, including the field committee that Townsend himself had fought bitterly to create, at least in part as a check on just such behavior. "In view of the many advisers against [taking the Indians to the States], it would seem to be unwise, but there must be reasons all unknown to us which causes God to call us," he argued. "I have prayed Him to close the way if it were not His directive will[,] but He has rather opened it."[97]

By early September 1928 the Townsends were housed in Santa Ana, California, on the opposite coast from America's Keswick, spending five hours a day translating. When he was not working, Cameron exercised in his father's garden and visited with friends and relatives. Trinidad Bac, one of Townsend's Indian assistants, happily reported that he had successfully preached (with Townsend translating) in some American churches. "All the brethren here . . . are very pleased with me," he wrote. "Indeed, these brethren (Americans) are not proud, because they are ready to listen to a common man like me." By the end of March 1929 they were translating the seventh chapter of Revelation. All that remained was to revise Acts and then make a final review of the entire New Testament. Bac was homesick, but young Joe Chicol was "having a wonderful time." He was learning English and did not appear "in any particular hurry about getting back to Guatemala." He was in a hurry, however, to finish the translation, because he had decided he wanted to go to college in America.[98]

Perhaps the real reason for Townsend's desire to return to the United States was that it seemed a way for him to begin the weaning process from the CAM.

By spring 1928 Townsend's vision had expanded far beyond Guatemala and Central America. He later admitted that it was Legters's photographs from his Amazon explorations that moved him to want to work with the "wild tribes" of South America. He notified Carl Malmstrom, who had been granted the superintendency of the Cakchiquel Department while Townsend was in the United States finishing the translation, that he would not take the position back when he returned to Guatemala. As soon as he finished the translation he intended to "go to a new tribe." In fact, he had a plan to evangelize all the Latin American Indians "in this generation." The essential points in the plan were (1) "friends in the homeland like Mr. Legters to raise support in finances and prayer and to secure competent young missionaries"; (2) a Bible institute in Guatemala to train Indian workers; and (3) a mobile force of missionaries who would join forces with the trained Indian workers, open up new territory, work there until "the native church . . . could take care of itself," and then head off again for a new field.[99]

Townsend neglected to mention one of the factors that by this time was driving his vision for reaching the Indians of Latin America. In 1926 a U.S. government survey team flew to Guatemala to conduct an aerial survey of the country. Townsend apparently had some contact with the team, and the idea of the airplane captured his fancy. This was a vision worthy of a master visionary, and Townsend was immediately hooked. He attempted to interest one of his earliest supporters, Dr. Howard Kelly, in funding the project. "I wrote Dr. Kelly about a visionary idea I had for evangelizing the Lacandone country," he enthused to Karl Hummel. "Maybe it is only a vision but I just can't help having them. I suppose I should stop afflicting you with them, however." Kelly contacted Major Herbert Dargue, a veteran of twenty-two years in the army, sixteen of them flying. Dargue reported back to Kelly that Townsend's "scheme to use an amphibian [was] most practical provided the expense can be met." He estimated they would need thirty thousand dollars for the airplane alone, an astronomical amount given the times and the state of faith mission finances. "Then one must be prepared to accept complete loss of the entire investment in a single crash," Dargue noted. Nevertheless, he thought it a "sound" idea. "The Indians will be won simply by the phenomenon of a big bird like that landing in their midst," he argued. "There is no doubt in my mind that the airplane will be one of the greatest assets to missionaries in their work and particularly so in Central and South America where terrestrial transportation is so difficult."[100]

Townsend naturally tried to recruit Major Dargue for his airplane project, but Dargue replied that it was "out of the question." He did, however, provide Townsend with a detailed breakdown of the costs of running an air operation such as he envisioned. In addition to the $30,000 for the airplane, Dargue estimated 15 percent of the total cost of the airplane annually for spare parts, with a complete replacement of planes or motors in from two to five years. A good pilot/mechanic would cost $6,000 per year, a cost that could be eliminated if Townsend could coax a missionary into the cockpit. Dargue thought it best if planes traveled in pairs for safety. With fuel, insurance, facility costs, hangars, three airplanes, two pilots, two mechanics, two radio operators, one laborer, and fifteen thousand gallons of fuel, Dargue estimated $134,000 for the first two years.[101] That Townsend did not appear to be fazed by such a figure is a tribute to his wild enthusiasm, his vision for what could be done for Indians, his faith in God, and perhaps his rapidly developing faith in Legters and even himself.

The CAM council was naturally reluctant to embrace the idea. "[I]t is possible that the future may hold something for us along [the airplane] line," Hummel wrote. "However, at the present writing I must confess that I had rather go over land, even if I had to walk." Hummel reported that another CAM missionary, a Mr. Butler, had suggested acquiring an airplane for traveling in Honduras. When the intrepid Anna Gohrman heard of it, she suggested Butler must be "backsliding," as to travel by air would be to lose the opportunity to pass out gospel tracts to all he met on the road. More important, the council was concerned about safety and the expense of the project. Townsend dismissed such concerns. From the beginning he felt it would be both safer and less expensive in the long run to reach jungle tribes by airplane. At any rate, he declared himself "willing to risk [his] neck in an effort to reach the Lacandones or the unexplored regions of Brazil with the Gospel by plane." Townsend argued that he could "reach" the Indians of South America with the gospel in ten years by air, and "without any greater loss of life than has already been incurred in efforts to reach those Indians by old methods of travel." "It's something to dream about any way," he concluded.[102]

On July 23, 1928, shortly before the Townsends arrived in California to resume translating in earnest, police arrested R. D. Smith in his home and deposited him in an asylum. His wife, it turned out, had requested his confinement. He was said to be "hopelessly insane," suffering from delusions and a persecution complex. "Psychopathic doctors" reported he had a contagious disease. He was confined for seven months, then spent two years on "psychopathic parole" under a restraining order to stay away from his home. Finally, in 1931 he was set free. Thereafter he lived in a cheap hotel on the one hundred dollars per month sent to him by his wife, a "fair proportion" of the family income, according to the board of the Bible House. The ardent proponent of the faith method of missionary service was reduced to begging laundry money from his friends.

A few years later, in November 1934, a committee that included Lewis Sperry Chafer, Charles Fuller, Charles Hurlburt (deposed founder of the Africa Inland Mission), and several CAM council members declared they found Smith in good health and petitioned his reinstatement at the Bible House. They argued Smith had never been insane but was the victim of a power grab by his wife and the Bible House board members. The committee reported, "No valid reason has ever been set forth by the Bible House Board to the committee as to why Mr. Smith could not be returned to service. Intimation as to his physical condition, *optional business methods as in contrast to methods now introduced,* and his domestic life, have been made." Did Blanche Smith and the Bible House board, in a desire to promote the work more aggressively, chafe against R. D.'s fanatical commitment to faith methods so much that they began to see such ideology as insane? We will never know, but that enigmatic phrase, "optional business methods as in contrast to methods now introduced," certainly invites such speculation. At any rate, as far as this author knows, Smith was never reinstated to the mission he loved and led for so many years.[103]

6
In Which Townsend Makes Everyone Nervous with Another Wild Idea and R. D. Smith Has a Nightmare

1929–1932

> We must be much in prayer that [Cameron] be delivered from anything that may be visionary.
>
> —Karl Hummel

In this chapter, which outlines the events leading to Cameron Townsend's departure from the CAM, perhaps it is fitting to pause first to reflect a bit on the man himself. Barely twenty-one when he sailed for Guatemala, Townsend was thirty-six when he left that country. Just what sort of man had he become? Why was the CAM simultaneously disappointed and relieved when he chose to depart?

Ask anyone who knew Cameron Townsend to describe him, and one of the first qualities they will mention is his vision. Townsend was a visionary, a dreamer, and a bit of a schemer. To read the letters stored under the heading "Idea Man" in the Townsend archive computer is to journey through an obviously fertile mind. Townsend was like a baseball player who swung at every pitch, convinced he could hit every one out of the ballpark. He struck out a lot, but when he got hold of one, and if the wind was blowing in the right direction, he hit it a long way. Most of his schemes were probably forgotten between the time it took for his letter to reach headquarters, Karl Hummel to think up a way to politely discourage the idea, and the letter to make its return sea voyage to Guatemala. Many were good ideas, if far ahead of their time. Some of these he worked on, but they died for lack of an organization to push them through, perhaps to reemerge in different form decades later. A few he clung to doggedly as part of his life vision, tenaciously pursuing them to ultimate success. In this last category was his commitment to Indian work in indigenous languages, Bible translation, a school of linguistics, and the use of modern technology, especially airplanes. As we shall see, it was this last vision that ultimately led to his departure from Guatemala.

Besides those visions already mentioned, Townsend was one of the first to push hard to establish a school for missionary children, reasoning that it would keep good people on the field and help recruit new ones. A letter that landed on Hummel's desk and began, "Another idea has come to my head. As usual it is a little wild," suggested a Guatemala cruise for American Christians that would culminate in a Bible conference to be held on Lake Atitlán. Townsend suggested Charles Trumbull and Charles Fuller as speakers. "Most Christian magazines would give the conference free publicity," he argued. "People who would go would probably be people of means [and] their interest would be aroused for missionary work in C[entral] A[merica] in a very special way." The Wycliffe Bible Translators would later be one of the first missions to conduct regular tours to link supporters more closely to the mission. Another time, he proposed making contributors to CAM honorary members of the mission so that they would feel more a part of the work. His model was the memberships given out by the National Geographic Society. He noted that people "owned" their denominational missionaries in ways they did not "own" the independent boards. They see "the rest of us as sort of outsiders," he complained. Townsend's proposal was meant to remedy that situation.[1] Such "clubs" and other associate "memberships" are common practice with missions today.

Another frequently remarked on trait of Cameron Townsend's was his driven single-mindedness, a characteristic that increased with age as his vision clarified. Much of Townsend's character stemmed from this characteristic. If, as Søren Kierkegaard said, purity of heart is to will one thing, Townsend had a very pure heart indeed. He had a one-track mind when it came to his most personal visions and simply would not be sidetracked, refusing to take no for an answer. Townsend was a salesman totally committed to his product, at times at the expense of other products. A close associate once confided that Townsend could be extremely persuasive when he wanted something done. He did not just wring your arm off, the elderly gentleman grinned, but he would wring it off and then hit you over the head with it. Townsend was a sincere sort; if he believed something, he believed it absolutely. His color palette did not incorporate much gray.

While he never could have accomplished what he did without such a trait, he was not necessarily an easy man to live with. He could be hardest on those closest to him, driving them to implement his vision. To outsiders, especially

Latin Americans, he was the sun, but to his lieutenants he could at times be the north wind. Another associate resorted to an old joke to describe Townsend's visionary management style: "Townsend took us polar bear hunting," he said. "One morning while most of us were still in bed, we heard a distant call, 'Open the door, open the door.' We jumped up and opened the door. Townsend appeared, running hard, with a polar bear hot on his heels. Townsend dashed in the front door, shouted, 'You fellows skin this one, I'm going after another one,' then fled out the back." Mention Townsend's visionary qualities to old Wycliffe hands today, and you're likely to get a wink and a remark such as, "Yes, but visionaries can be mighty hard to live with at times."

Townsend's single-mindedness sometimes expressed itself in intensely blunt speech. Townsend preferred clearness of expression over nuance, boldness over gentleness. Men such as R. D. Smith and Leonard Legters admired this trait. "I like Townsend's forcible way of bringing [things] to our attention," Smith once told Judge Scott. Such speech was not always welcome, of course, to those of more fragile disposition. Two of the women who worked closely with him at San Antonio almost quit, telling Townsend, "[M]any things that you have said have hurt us deeply until it did not seem possible to go on with the work." Townsend once asked Hummel to write some letters for him, remarking, "[Y]ou will be careful in your correspondence not to hurt anyone as I am so prone to do." Townsend, however, seemed to have the ability to be terribly blunt and yet not intend anything personal. Fences were mended as easily as he tore them down.[2]

Intensely emotional about the things that mattered most to him, he reacted strongly when they were threatened. He often overreacted. Many times reading letters in the archives, I was left shaking my head, rereading letters from Townsend's correspondents, searching for what in them occasioned such a strong reply. Often I was left baffled, as were his correspondents, who were forced to backpedal furiously to defuse the situation. Townsend perhaps diagnosed the situation best in a letter to Fred Lincoln at the height of the Indian-*ladino* controversy. "Down there under pressure we are all apt to get too intense," he acknowledged. "I've sinned that way more than anybody[,] but I'm sorry for it and hope to do better. . . . Even though we feel strongly we should never cease to love strongly too."[3]

This peculiar intensity and commitment to a vision was a quality found in Townsend's personal spiritual commitment as well. Indeed, this may well be the trait most often and most fondly remarked on by those who knew him. We have discussed Townsend's faith in an earlier chapter, so it suffices to remember here that even though his faith was not particularly nuanced or articulately defended, it was absolute. He went into most battles convinced that God was behind him and could be trusted to manage the details. When associates quailed at the enormity of a particular task or vision, Townsend would wink and say, "Once in a while I like to put God on the spot."

Townsend's faith did not always yield perfect results. When his mother fell ill in 1931, he wrote her, "I'm asking the Lord to bless the treatments and to quickly restore you. A sweet assurance has come into my soul that He will." He declared to his sister, "I have a conviction that [Mother] has been healed in answer to prayer. The conviction came as I was praying for her last Monday night and I trust that I'm not mistaken." Three weeks later his mother was dead. "I couldn't understand why He had refused me my petition when I had seemed to receive assurance of His having granted it," he wrote to his father. "I fear that I had been presuming on the Lord[,] and I must learn not to do that if He is to be able to use me to accomplish the things which need to be done among the Indians down here." When personality and belief system combine to create a person whose bent is to believe greatly and live large, however, such a lesson is never really learned. Townsend continued to "presume" on God throughout his life, and those inclined to believe that God admires the faith of his people agree that God came through for Townsend in remarkable ways.[4]

In many ways Townsend was the classic American evangelical entrepreneur, a combination of fierce piety with a burning evangelistic impulse, intuitive business sense, an instinctive embrace of the gadgets of modern science, and a bent toward empire building. Townsend was no fundamentalist, however. He had no patience for quibbles over theology, the "non-essentials," as he put it. He preferred the company of businessmen to that of pastors for just this reason. He admired "go-getters," men who built something, more than thinkers and pietists. In Christ's day he would have traveled with tax collectors rather than Pharisees. He never minded getting his robes dirty, so to speak, if to do so advanced his cause.

Townsend eventually became one of those rare larger-than-life figures capable of inspiring other humans to embrace his own idiosyncratic vision. A man who spent just ten minutes with him remarked privately that those ten minutes changed his life. Another, who first met Townsend in 1938, later wrote, "[M]y personal interview with him impressed me deeply—that here was a man with vision and tremendous drive, yet with remarkable personal interest in the individuals with whom he came into contact." A ninety-six-year-old man, who fifty years earlier left a good job to help Townsend found his jungle aviation service, remembered, when asked why he gave up so much for Townsend's vision, "You got the sense that here was a great man. It built me up that this man (the greatest I ever knew) would confide in me. He made me feel greater than I was."[5] The vision and commitment that such leaders possess was quite apparent to those who knew the young man in Guatemala, even if many more years of tempering were required to bring those qualities to their full maturity.

By the end of the decade the Cakchiquel Department of the Central American Mission had four stations and fourteen missionaries attached to it, including Elvira's brother, Carl Malmstrom, and his wife. Eighty "preaching points" were cared for by approximately twenty Indian evangelists. The Robinson Bible Institute in Panajachel trained Indian evangelists and pastors with a curriculum modeled after the Moody Bible Institute in Chicago. One hundred fifty children attended elementary school at the four schools in the department. In addition to the school in San Antonio, Townsend had established schools in Patzum, Palopo, and Balanya. Townsend trusted that many graduates would become "teachers in government Indian schools and there live Christ before their pupils."[6]

There were a few success stories, although by the early 1930s only eighteen children had remained in Townsend's schools through all six grades. Ten of the eighteen, however, were working in some form of Christian service. Joe Chicol assisted in the translation work and was now attending John Brown College in Arkansas. Elena Trejo was in California at Biola College planning to study to be a doctor. After six years with Townsend, she had completed her schooling at the Presbyterian school in Quezaltenango. Another graduate taught at the Robinson Bible Institute.[7]

The little band of San Antonio missionaries was depleted, however, by one when Fanny Becker decided she had seen enough of her husband's peripatetic megaphone ministry. She left her husband and returned home. A broken Dr. Becker asked Townsend to mediate. Townsend gently reminded Mrs. Becker, "You were informed of Dr. B's idiosyncracies [*sic*] before you married him." Just to make sure, Townsend had Becker checked out by a doctor, who assured him that "as far as he [could] tell there [was] no mental derangement." Mrs. Becker was not reassured.[8]

By late 1929 L. L. Legters was discouraged about the results of his labor for the Indians. He had raised thousands of dollars and sent missionaries out with several missions on behalf of the Indians, only to have most of them sidetracked into Spanish or Portuguese work. Missions still did not have a real commitment to following through on specialized Indian efforts. When a CAM couple supported by Legters decided to abandon the effort to learn an Indian language, Townsend raged, "If they are too old or incompetent so that they can not learn an Indian language they should take up Spanish work, [b]ut the ultimate responsibility is upon the mission. We must have a fixed purpose to specialize in behalf of the Indians." When the Guatemala field committee assigned the couple to Huehuetenango, Townsend fumed that it was a "terrible mistake." In disgust he asked Hummel to write to the committee for him, saying, "I . . . haven't got the grace or skill to word it nicely like you." Hummel's answer was that in a mission working among both Indians and *ladinos*, it was "practically impossible to draw the lines as regards the use of funds and workers" in the way Townsend and Legters wanted them drawn.[9]

When he finally left Guatemala for good, Townsend was still frustrated with the lack of missionary focus on indigenous-language work. In words not designed to win him many friends, he wrote, "How missionaries can be content to live among a people without learning their mother tongue is hard to understand. The ultimate explanation to which I am driven is that Satan, the enemy of the souls of mankind as a whole and particularly of the Indian race, has blinded most missionaries in a greater or less degree to the need."[10]

More than ten years after Townsend's departure, the problems of Indian ministry still troubled the CAM. Of thirteen missionaries in Indian fields, only three were using the Indian language "and that with difficulty." The author of a report on the issue wrote, "Has not our failure to reach large portions of our Indian fields been due to a lack of vision and an adequate and aggressive program on the part of the Mission as a whole?" He recommended the formation of a "permanent Indian Committee," which would survey the Indian field, present the facts, and formulate policy. The study suggested that the mission require new missionaries to Indian fields spend two years studying the language, with "the Indian language to be given first importance." Such missionaries should "live in a strictly Indian environment" and should "encourage reading and preaching in the Indian language."[11]

In 1950 the CAM was still reinventing the wheel. Edward Sywulka, one of Townsend's first students at the linguistics school Townsend eventually founded and a missionary to Guatemala, complained in a report to CAM headquarters that "comparatively few" missionaries "realize the importance of the Indian problem." He found "often a regrettable lack of interest in the need, due perhaps to lack of information or to the mistaken idea or ideal that work among the Spanish speaking people is what really counts." He continued, "In a candid criticism of our mission policy down through the years, we must admit that we have failed to make adequate provision [for working in the Indian languages.] [Learning Indian languages] has been the effort of the individual without the encouragement and backing that a planned program would have provided." He expended pages arguing that indigenous-language work was necessary. The reader who has spent time in Townsend's letters from the 1920s experiences a sense of déjà vu hearing Townsend's arguments repeated twenty-five years later by one of his students. Since Townsend's departure, no missionary had learned Cakchiquel. Sywulka acknowledged that there were "no adequate grammar[s]" for any of the Indian languages.

Perhaps the missionaries should not be judged too harshly. The Guatemalan government remained very ignorant of the problem. The 1940 census listed only five out of the eighteen Indian languages. In addition, Sywulka reported, "The majority of Indians themselves are discouragingly disinterested in learning to read." They lacked confidence in their ability to learn, could not see the advantage it would bring, and, it must be admitted, perhaps wanted no part of literate culture. The head of the government literacy campaign told Sywulka that "the whole problem of the Indian languages was so big and complex that for the present they were not considering it." "The burden, then," argued Sywulka, "rests upon the missions and upon the evangelical church with which they labor." The problem of *ladino* racism continued even in the churches. "We expect the Gospel to change and purify these relationships," Sywulka wrote, "and it does to the extent that its implications are clearly understood and accepted. How often, though, the feeling of superiority, consciously or unconsciously expressed, comes out into the open, just as it does, we confess, in the attitudes of 'we Americans' to those of other race or culture." With this in mind, the mission was still arguing over whether the two works ought to be separate. Sywulka, no doubt because of his training, favored separation as the most natural way to produce growth.[12]

In a sense it could be argued that Townsend failed in Guatemala. As we will see, he did not stay long enough to ensure that his own work would continue beyond him. But it could also be argued that an endeavor as radically removed from traditional mission efforts as Townsend envisioned required his removal to a country that by its very rejection of traditional missions was able to serve as an incubator for a startling new vision. Mexico in the 1930s would prove to be that country.

But now, in late 1929, Legters grew more and more frustrated as he sensed the council's irritation at his "butting in." Offended, he considered turning his support elsewhere. Townsend begged the council to be more supportive, even to invite Legters to associate with the mission as its Indian secretary. "Do you realize that Mr. Legters has indirectly been the means of our securing about as much financial support as we have received through the Mission?" he exclaimed. Also in his favor was the fact that three other couples working with the CAM in Indian fields had gained their support through Legters. "If any other man did that much I believe that you would offer him a place on the Council," Townsend complained. "If our coffers were full it wouldn't seem quite so suicidal."[13]

Karl Hummel thought the situation had been overblown. "Mr. Legters has some traits that are badly against him and they are what cause trouble," he informed Townsend. Apparently Legters's hyperbolic statements still bothered the council. In addition, Legters and the Pioneer Mission Agency associated too closely with missions that were tainted by modernism. Legters raised money and men to work with the Presbyterians, which irked conservatives in the CAM. Albert Bishop, for one, resisted the idea of "fundamentalist missionaries" going out under "the direction of an enemy of our Lord and of His Word." "To desire that sound in the faith young people should yoke up in a Mission Board with some who do not have the doctrine of Christ is serious," Bishop complained, "more serious than wishing that 1,000 saints should marry 1,000 worldlings." Still, Hummel assured Townsend that while the council did not favor associating too closely with Legters, they did "appreciate his fellowship and service and desire to cooperate in so far as they [could]."[14]

Townsend went to Dallas to try to clear up the situation in December 1929, and found the council members, many of whom he met for the first time, "exceptionally fine men." They declared themselves "unequivocally" for Townsend and Legters's method of Indian work. "I don't know how they could be any stronger for the Indians," he reported to Legters. "They would even be glad to cooperate in forward movements such as the one we propose for the wild tribes. I do hope that you can forget the past and cooperate with them."[15]

The Townsends spent 1929 in California completing their translation. On October 10, Townsend's mother and father symbolically inscribed the last two words of the Cakchiquel New Testament at a special service at the First Presbyterian Church of Santa Ana. Elvira finished typing the final copy a few days later, and they mailed the manuscript to the American Bible Society.

In early 1930 Cameron and Elvira moved to Chicago to expedite the proofreading of their Cakchiquel New Testament. They spent six months there in a forty-dollar-a-month two-room flat by the lake, broken up by one month on an uncle's Iowa farm undergoing "the milk cure" in an attempt to gain "more pep." In Chicago they met with Dr. Edward Sapir, a University of Chicago anthropologist. Sapir suggested that Townsend work with one of his graduate students to "clear up the phonetics of Cakchiquel, and to compile a dictionary of the language" under Sapir's "informal direction."[16]

Several years earlier, Townsend had completed a thirty-six-page Cakchiquel grammar textbook, of which he was quite proud. In 1926 he sent his grammar book to Sapir, who gave it a fairly favorable evaluation, calling it "an exceedingly valuable piece of work." Now, from Chicago, Townsend tried to sell his Cakchiquel grammar text to the Smithsonian, hoping they would publish it. A linguist there told him they "might be able to pay" three hundred dollars for it, but Townsend pleaded for more, offering a proposed Cakchiquel dictionary in advance. The dictionary work would require more funds, and, Townsend wrote, "being a poor missionary I have no funds to count on unless I can sell my Grammar at a good figure." The Smithsonian declined but suggested he get in touch with Franz Boas of Columbia University, the leading anthropologist in the country at the time. Boas asked how much he wanted for it, and Townsend asked for one thousand dollars, remarking, "[I]f you felt it was worth more after seeing what I've done[,] I would leave it to your sense of fairness to say." He had heard that a Quiché and a Mam grammar had each sold for one thousand dollars, and now he guaranteed Boas that "as far as going to the heart of the language is concerned, mine is ahead of them both." Eventually Boas refused the work, suggesting he submit it elsewhere. Townsend eventually tried to sell the grammar book elsewhere, including the University of Pennsylvania, but the Great Depression had gripped the country, and funds were limited. One scholar informed him that "most authors [were] lucky if they [got] theirs published without cost to them," as the market for linguistic manuscripts was very small. If Townsend was to work on a dictionary, "it would have to be done more or less for the love of science."[17] Regardless, these were new circles for Townsend, in which he would never have moved under normal circumstances, but the very task of translation drew Townsend into academic circles.

Townsend had better fortune with his New Testament. In May 1930 he mailed in the last corrected proofs. The American Bible Society had worked hard to make the Cakchiquel New Testament "an unusually satisfactory piece of work, one that will set a new standard for all of [its] productions for the Indians of Latin America." That goal proved to be "unusually expensive" and time-consuming. The typesetters were forced to proceed letter by letter because the language was so unfamiliar. The plates alone cost somewhere between five thousand and six thousand dollars. "Even the Indians who are inclined to be ashamed of their language will be proud over this New Testament," Townsend boasted to Eric North, general secretary of the ABS. Townsend planned to put out a first edition of the Cakchiquel-Spanish interlinear New Testament in a nice binding to introduce it to the "more well-to-do class," mostly Spanish speakers who might buy it out of curiosity. The Indians, who tended to take their cues from their Spanish-speaking neighbors, "would see the Spanish-speaking people buying it at a high price and it would gain a prestige in their eyes." He would then introduce a low-cost edition that they could afford. He thought it might be best to begin distribution through secular stores and peddlers "so as to free it from the prejudice attached to anyone connected with evangelical missions." He also ordered a specially bound copy for the Guatemalan president and national library, telling North, "I hope to be able to gain the favor of the educational authorities to the end of introducing the New Testament in the Indian schools on the ground that it would serve as a dictionary in learning Spanish."[18]

Although to his face the CAM council had assured Townsend they were right with him in his plans for the Indians, privately they were astounded at his ideas. They thought if perhaps they found "some untouched place" in their territory, that Townsend might expend his pioneering energy there and give up his crazy airplane-to-Amazonia crusade. When that tactic failed, they went over Townsend's head. "[W]e must be much in prayer that [Cameron] be delivered from anything that may be visionary," Hummel wrote. When God neglected to intervene, some hoped their old nemesis Elvira might persuade Townsend. They did not think she was fond of the idea of uprooting from her home on the lake to begin an "airplane project in Brazil." But by the dawn of the new decade, even Luther Rees saw the writing on the wall. "It seems we are going to lose Cameron," he reported. "If he is trying another door[,] he is likely to succeed."[19]

Indeed, by late 1929 the aviation part of the project had become a defining factor for Townsend. He began speaking specifically of "the aviation project for the wild tribes." He revealed his scheme to Legters in November 1929. Legters was quite discouraged about Indian work at the time, and it seems Townsend's notion perked him up. Townsend reported, "He had utterly given up his hopes for South America until I told him about my aviation project." The pair began negotiating to buy a biplane. Paul Townsend, once again playing the loyal little brother, owned some property in Long Beach that they hoped to exchange for the biplane. If they managed to obtain it, they planned to have someone teach Paul how to fly.[20]

After his encouraging meeting with the council in December 1929, Townsend tried to interest an assistant pastor from Moody Church, who seemed to be a "gifted executive," in heading up an "aeronautical department" in the

CAM. Legters was already working to interest wealthy Christians in the project. Townsend sent him copies of Dargue's estimates. "May God bless and direct you as you approach [a wealthy businessman] on the subject," he wrote.[21]

However, even Legters had difficulty raising funds for so visionary a scheme. In addition, he was getting reports from his contacts that the idea was not a sound one. He wrote a discouraging report to Townsend. But Townsend was only briefly thrown off his game by Legters's lack of enthusiasm. "After reading your letter I began to wonder if I have been mistaken about my leading toward the airplane project for those wild tribes," he admitted. Dispirited, he resurrected the blind finger-drop gambit. "I asked the Lord for an answer from Scripture," he informed Legters, "[and] as I opened the Bible my eyes fell immediately on the words 'Almighty God.' Then I opened again and the first words I read were, 'As thou hast believed, so be it done.'" Given such assurance, he determined to forge ahead. He begged Legters to catch his own expansive vision. "I am convinced that God is leading toward a big undertaking for the wild tribes of South Amer[ica]," he wrote. If they could fix the attention of the evangelical public on the Indians of Latin America "by a spectacular undertaking," Townsend believed, "the Indian work of the whole continent would be benefitted." "God likes to do marvelous things and He likes to use small instruments to do them," he reminded his partner.[22]

Townsend planned to attend the Moody Church mission rally in order to lay his plans before a group including the chairman of the missions committee, famed Bible teacher Donald Barnhouse, and various businessmen. Townsend argued that this meeting would be a "fleece," an evangelical technique for discovering God's mind in which the seeker threw out an idea to see if God would jump on the bandwagon. For evangelicals, "putting out a fleece" was several steps up the respectability scale from the blind finger-drop technique. In this case, if the businessmen were against Townsend's plan, it would indicate the idea was "not of the Lord." If the plan was God-directed, "some of them will become actively interested." Townsend planned to argue that since his undertaking was "so different and so big," a new organization would need to be formed. Townsend already had a plan. "A name that is different [and] appealing is desirable. How would 'Air Crusade to the Wild Tribes' or something like that be?" he enthused. "If the project is put before the public extensively and also in a striking way, 500,000 Christians can be secured to send in a dollar apiece [and] so become members of the crusade." He proposed that Legters be general secretary, with the field missionaries electing their own field secretary on a yearly basis. He had already written to Dr. Kelly asking him to accept the presidency of the new organization. Major Dargue, whom Townsend had sent a copy of the missionary classic *Borden of Yale* to give him "a real vision of service for God," was willing to cooperate in an advisory capacity.[23]

The meeting at Moody Church took place in pastor Harry Ironside's study. Townsend reported to Legters that it was "too short to really get any place." Apparently the men were cool to the idea. The general director of the Scandinavian Alliance Mission, who had spent twenty-five years in Venezuela, told of the "great obstacles" to be faced. "Of course it was not news to me," Townsend wrote, "but for a few minutes after we separated I began to feel that the project was not of God." This was, of course, the fleece that he himself had laid out. But fleeces, like finger drops, are easily discounted as a silly idea in the first place when one's mind is set, and Townsend was not about to let this bit of evangelical flimflammery stand in his way. Now, after thinking for a few minutes that the project must not be of God, "a calm contentedness" began to settle over him. "It seemed so good that we could stay on at Panajachel among the people whom we love so much and where our surroundings are so beautiful," he wrote. But this was a dangerous content. "Then I felt my ardor cooling off and a sense of unconcern over the lost take possession of me," he reported. "It was such a strange feeling—contentedness followed by a spiritual chill! I immediately cried to God, 'No matter how great the obstacles, I will go in quest of those hopelessly lost souls if it is Thy will.' Then warmth of spirit returned and I am satisfied that in His own time He will open the way."[24]

Meanwhile, in April 1930 the CAM council met and discussed Townsend's plans for Amazonia. With Townsend absent, they reversed their course. "The brethren want me to assure you of their keen interest and prayer fellowship, though at the same time they do not feel that it would be advisable for the CAM to sponsor the project, at least for the present," Hummel reported to Townsend. Hummel thought the divine financial weather vane might be pointing back to Guatemala. "If the Lord is leading you along the line that you have been figuring on, we do trust that means will be provided and the way opened," he told Townsend, "but if it is God's will for you to return to Guatemala to the routine which you perhaps do not relish, we do trust that you will not miss His leading in the matter." Albert Bishop was blunter. He lectured Townsend, "I believe when you accepted the direction of the territory allotted to you at the time of the visit of the Commission sent by our CAM that you took upon yourself an obligation that has not as yet been fulfilled. When that obligation has been met[,] if God leads you to Brazil I would say Amen from the depths of my soul."[25]

With no encouragement coming from any quarter, Townsend desperately wrote to Eric North at the American Bible Society. With his typical salesman's vision, he told North the truth—that Dargue had endorsed the project—but he did not tell him the whole truth, that many mission leaders were chary of the whole idea. "There are plenty of young men willing to cooperate with their lives," Townsend perhaps overstated, "but I am at a loss to know how to go about raising the necessary funds. . . . I have prayed over the plan for two years now[,] and God has given me perfect assurance that He is leading." Townsend claimed to have interested Pastor Ironside, as well as the Moody Bible Institute business manager, in his project. "There are a number of young men at MBI who would like to participate," he added. Townsend did not want to return to Guatemala but could feel his options narrowing, his expansive vision shutting down.[26]

In a long and carefully reasoned letter, North tried to gently let the air out of Townsend's balloon. He reminded him that Indian work in the past had been plagued by "marked unsteadiness." He implied that Townsend risked letting such a judgment apply to his labors. "[M]any years of service, and much money have . . . been practically wasted because the pioneer has opened territory faster than the builder could follow," he chided. "Or else the pioneer having opened territory has refused to settle down and build." North argued that Townsend should not spend an inordinate amount of money trying to reach small tribes when there was still so much work to be done with large and easily accessible tribes. In addition, the benefits of airplane use were still unproven; for now the risks far outweighed any perceived reward. "[T]he same amount of funds put into effective workers [would be] far more full of results on the conversion and Christianizing of the Indians than in investment in a plane, which a few moments failure of attention may entirely wreck," North pointed out. In an argument that must have stung, North returned to the divine weather vane: "Perhaps the fact that the Lord has given you so little leading upon the financial phases of the matter . . . has something to do with His leading upon the merits of the scheme itself." Point by point, North pushed Townsend inexorably in the direction he did not want to go. His work with the Cakchiquels, which he had pioneered so many years ago, now required his settling down for the long term to achieve the best results. "With the profound mastery which you have of the language, with the long years of understanding of the Indian life and ways of thought, and with this glorious new tool 'the complete New Testament' at your hand," North exclaimed, "what a marvelous work should be accomplished under your leadership among this large and important tribe!" North argued that the Cakchiquel work would be "crippled" without him, that effective distribution of the New Testament required the man who knew the tribe better than anyone else.[27]

Townsend refused to give up. He invested all his reserves of energy and passion. He tried once again to interest the CAM council in the project, wondering if they might experiment with the idea in a limited way just with the Lacandones in Mexico. If the attempt were a success, the resultant publicity might interest others to contribute. Hummel promised to bring up the idea at the June council meeting. When the council remained skeptical, Townsend talked the Pioneer Mission Agency into funding a small brochure advertising his airplane project. Dr. Kelly wrote an endorsement for publicity purposes, as did pastor Harry Ironside. The PMA, however, though they agreed to fund the brochure, refused to publicly endorse the project. Along with the CAM, they waited to see which way the wind would blow.[28]

For Townsend, the wind was always behind, filling his sails. Townsend launched his airplane project to the Lacandones. At his urging, Lynn Van Sickle, a graduate of the Moody Bible Institute, and at the time on the staff of the MBI radio station, began to take flying lessons. For fifty dollars, the cost of the expended fuel, a strapping twenty-three-year-old Christian pilot named Royal Woodchick camped with Van Sickle for two weeks in a remote area of northern Wisconsin and taught him to fly. Townsend reasoned that since Van Sickle was an auto mechanic, he ought to learn rapidly.[29]

While Van Sickle learned to fly, Townsend raised money. He prepared a circular that he sent out with the PMA-funded brochure to his personal mailing list. The circular was vintage Townsend—visionary, positive to a fault, stretching the facts just a bit, brazenly moving beyond the accepted parameters of a faith mission. "After much prayer and consultation a plan has been developed which one internationally known Christian layman [Dr. Howard Kelly] says 'WILL OPEN UP A NEW ERA IN MISSIONS,'" Townsend announced. "Surely we shall all agree that it is at least well worth trying." He wrote that the work initially would be carried on "under the auspices of the Central American Mission." (This prompted a note in the margin on the copy Townsend sent to Karl Hummel—"I probably stated this unwisely not having authorization from you. Sorry.") "The Pioneer Mission Agency . . . has promised to cooperate as far as it can," he went on. "However, in order to provide the special attention which will be required a committee is being formed here for more active promotion of the undertaking." The committee probably consisted of himself, Legters, and Van Sickle. "[T]he aviators have been secured," he promised, and then enthused, "Who ever heard of an aviator willing to labor midst dangers and hardships at a wage of fifty dollars a month! The spirit of SACRIFICE pervades this effort to fulfill our Lord's command." His final pitch made some concession to faith propriety: "We do not ask your financial support unless God puts it very definitely upon your heart[,] but we do beg for your help in prayer. . . .You can also help by trying to interest others." The brochure sent with the circular was titled "An Airplane Crusade to the Unevangelized Jungle-Lands of Latin America." The copy was similar but included an estimate of costs that demonstrated that approaching the Lacandones with an airplane ($33,500) would be cheaper than doing it the conventional way ($37,650). Townsend designated only $10,000 for the cost of the airplane, however, declaring that it would "be secured if possible as an advertising donation from factory manufacturers." The estimates could, of course, be manipulated however he desired.[30]

After sending out the circulars Townsend was enthusiastic. He told Hummel, "I trust to be able to forward remittances to you soon for the Crusade." The MBI business manager received one of the air crusade leaflets and published it in the *Moody Monthly,* at the time evangelicalism's widest-circulating popular journal. In addition, the October 11, 1930, issue of the *Sunday School Times* published a prayer request related to the air crusade. Townsend sheepishly wrote to Hummel, "I hope that these published statements assigning responsibility to the CAM for the project will not cause you trouble. I am hardly at fault since the Ex[ecutive] Committee assured me last Dec[ember] that if I could raise the support, they would sponsor the project at least for C[entral] A[merica]." He knew very well, of course, that the council would not be pleased to appear to be sponsoring the project before it was a viable concern. Hummel was forced to put out fires created by the articles, not least with the Guatemala missionaries themselves. He assured them that the publicity was "a little premature," and that the council was "insisting that a great deal more investigation be made" before undertaking such a step. The council, in turn, hastily summoned Townsend to Dallas.[31]

By November 1 twenty dollars had arrived from the PMA, gifts from two women; another five-dollar check came from a doctor in Southern California, five dollars from a lady in Baltimore, and four dollars from a woman in Ohio, for a grand total of thirty-four dollars, a bit short of the twenty-five thousand dollars Townsend figured he needed the first year. But he was just getting started. A businessman he knew pledged three hundred dollars and complimented Townsend's advertising sense. "He says that people like to back a going concern which is attempting bigger things all the time," Townsend informed Hummel. This adman sensibility appealed to Townsend; attempt something big, and the tide of publicity earned might just float all the rest of the boats in your flotilla as well. It worked in the life of faith as well as in fund-raising. The quiet piety of faith work, which seemed to clash so directly with the boosterism of American business culture, in the right hands actually meshed quite nicely as long as the piety of faith resolved to not remain quiet. If you were willing to attempt something big and let people know about it—like a string of orphanages, or the evangelization of China, or an air crusade to wild Indian tribes, really a crusade of any sort—then the vision of doing something with big numbers meshed with both a faith that believed in a big God and an American business culture that longed to create something of tangible size. The faith in God that was required fed the piety of both the agent involved and the supporters. All felt "faith-full," the givers as well as the receivers; all participated in a faith orthodoxy that favored those who publicly attempted great things for God.

Townsend had already recruited Woodchick and Van Sickle, Van Sickle's fiancée, and Vard Wallace, former Central America missionary, now airplane engineer and licensed mechanic. Thirty-five hundred dollars had been pledged, although many pledgers hedged their bets. They would contribute "if the project goes through." "Many" more people "manifested considerable interest," and Townsend expected to hear from them later. In addition to the Christian magazines, Charles Fuller was "giving the project publicity" on his radio program "almost every Sunday." Townsend thought a number of pastors were plugging his project in their churches. "All this is bound to yield results in time," he promised Hummel. He urged the council again to "definitely sponsor the project," at least for Central America and Southern Mexico. He wanted the crusade to be "an integral unit of the Mission" that would direct its own affairs like the field organizations in each republic. He asked that Van Sickle be accepted to the CAM to go to Guatemala to begin preparations. He also wanted Woodchick accepted and "assigned to further aeronautical training at the expense and under the direction of the Mission."[32]

Unfortunately, Townsend was unable to convince any significant Christian leaders to devote their time to helping him with the project. A written endorsement was one thing; active involvement quite another. Even Legters remained skeptical, as he got word from South American missionaries that rivers there were not friendly to airplanes. Because Townsend had no organization of his own to which he could turn, he was left trying to lead the project on his own, even as the Guatemala missionaries, the council, and most other Christian leaders he contacted clamored for his return to full-time Cakchiquel work. On top of that, he did not have the managerial skills to push the project through, a fact he recognized. "I am perhaps the one upon whom the Lord has laid the task of getting the undertaking started," he reflected, "yet I lack the executive ability required for a place of leadership.... I make a pretty good crank[,] but that is about as far as my gifts go in working with other missionaries."[33]

Still, he pushed himself to the point of ill health. Elvira reported privately to Hummel that Cameron was "as thin as a rail and for the most part looks as though he had been pulled [through] a knot-hole." He was not sleeping. And he was becoming bitter about American Christians who supported wealthy churches but would not give large sums to overseas projects. "The sum of the thing is," she wrote, "he has that project on his mind both night and day[,] and correspondence is piling up on us in this matter which is more than we are equal to." Townsend continued to believe that he had heard God clearly on the subject. "Every time something comes up to discourage I go to Him[,] and invariably He corroborates the leading and points me to Himself," he wrote. But all other signs were against him. He likened his situation to that of the disciples rowing across the Sea of Galilee at Christ's request. The winds against them were so strong that after many hours of rowing they were only in the middle of the sea, yet "they dared not [turn back,] for the Lord had ordered them to go to the other side." They only reached their destination after Christ appeared to them and entered the boat. "We have been constrained to take the Gospel to every creature," he wearily recorded. "The airplane is our one chance to reach some of them. The winds [and] waves are against us just now[,] but I for one dare not turn back."[34]

The naysayers were right, of course, at least in 1930. Townsend might have saved considerable energy if he had attended to his fleece. An enormously expensive air crusade in the midst of the Great Depression, when air travel was still unreliable, was a fool's errand, a grandiose project with no chance of getting off the ground. And indeed Townsend was desperately needed in Guatemala among the Cakchiquels. His departure did, in fact, cripple that work and in the long run may have seriously devalued the worth of his New Testament. But Townsend longed to "boldly go where no man had gone before." The CAM never had a realistic chance of holding him. It was probably good that for fifteen years he was shackled to the authority of a mission council, a steady responsibility in San Antonio and Panajachel, and an extremely debilitated and debilitating wife, or he might have spun off the wheel before undergoing the discipline himself of thoroughly learning an indigenous language and completing a New Testament translation.

The mistake Townsend's advisers made was that they failed to recognize how best to utilize his talent. They failed to appreciate that visionaries of this sort came along only once in a great while, and that although such visionaries might be very hard to live with, they needed to be turned loose to develop new projects, not tied down to those already begun, even if it meant training someone new to take over the visionary's old task. The restlessness felt by such leaders is a gift, not a liability, and the failure to recognize this can only lead to frustration on the part of all involved. It is as if Bill Gates were asked to sit at a computer all day and develop software. Undoubtedly he would be good at it, maybe better than anyone else, but grounding him at a computer would destroy the larger vision. The company might create a few terrific pieces of software, but it would never become the visionary giant that frightens even the U.S. government with the sweep of its power and influence. The Wycliffe Bible Translators under Townsend would become the largest and most innovative Protestant mission in the world, because a leader with a vision that leaped across established boundaries was given permission to innovate, even to fail, as Townsend undoubtedly would have done in 1930 had he been given approval to develop his air project. But as with most visionaries, his discouragement would have lasted for just a moment before his mind spun off new ideas, ideas that next time might have worked very well indeed.

The issue did not die an easy death. On December 11, 1930, Townsend, Van Sickle, and William G. Nyman, a retired and fairly well-to-do businessman who was on the council of the Bible House of Los Angeles, met with the executive committee. Townsend had managed to interest Nyman in his project, and Nyman promised to devote his energies to its promotion. That the council was nervous about challenging Townsend face-to-face over the issue is evident from a letter that circulated among them before the meeting. Karl Hummel wrote, "Whether it has been wise for Mr. Townsend to invite these brethren to meet with us here, I do not know." He threw out a fleece of his own. "My suggestion is that during these next few days we unite very definitely in prayer, asking the Lord to hinder these brethren from coming if it is not His will that they come. If the Lord is forcing us into an advance movement, we of course want to follow."[35] The temperamental difference between Townsend and the council could not have been clearer. For the council, "an advance movement" would require God to exercise "force" to get them on board. Townsend was already paddling hard across the sea, eagerly waiting for God to get on board with *his* "advance movement" so that they could make it to the other side and get started.

As they feared, Townsend was persuasive and talked them into at least "making a start" and "proceeding one step at a time." The council authorized Van Sickle to go to Guatemala to survey the need for airplane use. Hummel reassured the very skeptical Guatemala field committee that the approaching storm would be held in check. "It is of course understood that no funds for this project will be taken from current finances, and the plan will be pursued only in so far as it proves practical and as gifts are forthcoming, specially designated for it," he reported. The divine weather vane again! Still, Townsend had been very persuasive. The council now thought the airplane might be very useful in emergencies, as well as in pioneer work. Though they agreed that Townsend had a responsibility to the Cakchiquels, perhaps the primary concern of the field committee, Hummel now admitted that maybe Townsend had "the gift of a pioneer." If so, Hummel thought, "it would . . . be a mistake to confine him to an established work." "It is of course a serious matter," he added, "when a pioneer starts institutions that constitute a burden for others to carry on."[36]

Hummel indicated to the Pioneer Mission Agency that the CAM had decided to advance slowly on the project. "[I]f it can be used for the Lord's glory and is in His will, we do not want to show a lack of vision or faith," he wrote. "We do long to reach those inaccessible tribes of Indians." He encouraged the PMA to announce the project with them as Townsend had indicated they planned to do. It appeared, however, that Townsend had somewhat exaggerated the PMA's enthusiasm. They replied to Hummel that while they were "very much attached to [the Townsends] personally and admired their fine Christian spirit, . . . none of us felt that we were the ones who ought to be responsible for heading . . . up [the project]."[37]

A complicating factor for Townsend was that even as he desperately endeavored to enlist the CAM council in his air crusade, the council itself had for several years virtually ceased to function as an effective decision-making body. The longstanding rift between Lewis Sperry Chafer and several other councilmen boiled over into ugly accusations of immorality and crooked business dealings. The charges were proven to be totally unfounded, but all parties had a hard time letting go. The tension got so bad the council could not even meet together for prayer. Between 1928 and 1930 the council lost several members because of the feud, with Chafer eventually resigning in 1930.[38]

From his room in psychic rehab, R. D. Smith scrawled a handwritten note to Hummel. "I am very sorry CAM is lending its endorsement to this 'flying machine,' enormously extravagant, method of trying to evangelize the Indians of Cen[tral] America. Very spectacular but an invasion of the 'powers of the air' domain that may prove most disastrous."[39] In Smith's fevered dreams, he foresaw Satan, the "prince of the power of the air," according to Saint Paul, swatting gospel airplanes out of his sky.

Before anybody on the council could change their minds, the Townsends and Van Sickle departed for Guatemala. Hummel later remarked, "Van Sickle's hurried sailing was practically forced upon us, though he personally was very acceptable." Six months later Van Sickle was making progress in learning Spanish, but not much else. The circular and brochure failed to produce any funds. Townsend dashed off an article—"Shall the Hydro-airplane Project be Dropped?"—in an attempt to answer objections to the project and stimulate fund-raising. The council, however, did not want to publish it until they had more information. They felt it best to "quietly move on, letting the results answer all objections."[40]

The Cakchiquel New Testaments arrived in Guatemala in May 1931. "It was a glorious feeling to look at the beautifully bound volumes for which we have waited so long," Townsend announced. At 4:30 on the afternoon of May 19, 1931, Townsend, an American Bible Society representative, and Trinidad Bac were ushered into President Jorge Ubico's office. Townsend told him "of what the Bible had already done for Guatemala and what it will do." The ABS worker explained his work and about the Cakchiquel translation. He then handed the specially bound copy of the New Testament to Bac, who told Ubico what the Bible had meant to him. Bac then presented it to the president, who replied, "I congratulate you and thank you, for this is a forward step for our country." He urged Townsend to relocate to Coban and translate the New Testament into Quekchi, a suggestion taken by Townsend, who was desperately searching for direction, as possibly coming from God through the president. The picture of Ubico holding the New Testament made all the daily papers. The minister of education promised the government would buy a copy for "each one of its teachers." From the capital they journeyed to a conference at Patzum, where several hundred Indians waited. The group gathered under a leaky tent in an all-day rain to dedicate the New Testament. The festive gathering lasted well into the evening as many stood to speak of what it would mean to have the Bible in their own language.[41]

The visit to President Ubico resulted in a story that became one of Townsend's favorites over the years. It went something like this. The Indians in Comalapa appointed a certain man to carry a protest to the president. The president told the man that the trouble with the Indians in Comalapa was that they were "bound by too many old customs that were holding them back and keeping them poor." They needed progress. The president then took the Cakchiquel New Testament out of his pocket, handed it to the surprised Indian, and told him that "in that Book he would learn true progress." When the Indian returned home, he contacted some Protestant converts to learn more. Now, crowed Townsend, "he is very proudly telling that the President evangelized him!"[42]

The problem was that few Indians could read. Knowing that literacy was the key to widespread Scripture use, in the summer of 1931 Townsend set out to remedy that situation. He had developed a "simple Cakchiquel reader" and claimed that some Indians had learned to read in twenty lessons. After an eighteen-day campaign in one town, amazed government officials observed Indians who before knew nothing of the alphabet now reading a little from a Cakchiquel primer and the New Testament.

For Townsend, literacy and the gospel message were the key to the Indians' future. He once wrote of the Guatemalan Indians and literacy:

> As a people they have been exploited by the white man for four hundred years, and they can hardly conceive of any other motive than exploitation impelling him to approach them. Hence they are very cautious toward his approaches. Naturally, they are reticent regarding innovations. This might be counteracted if they were able to read and thus acquaint themselves with new ideas, but it will be a long time before their illiteracy is materially reduced. Although real ambition generally lies latent and undetectable beneath the miserable mien of the average descendant of the formerly great Maya race, so little is being done to quicken it and so very, very much to drown it in hopelessness that many a cycle will pass before the Indians as a people will become literate. In the meantime, the Gospel will continue to triumph even over this obstacle and will prove itself a most powerful force in counteracting Indian inertia and putting the race in motion in the march of progress.[43]

Consequently, Townsend dragged a government official to Patzum, where one hundred Indian men met them and requested that they reopen the school Townsend had begun there several years earlier. Townsend restarted the school in February 1932. He raised money from businessmen in Antigua and Guatemala City to support it before eventually turning it over to the government. During his literacy program there, approximately three hundred men and children took reading classes. "I wish that you could look in upon the evening school," he told his parents. "The Ladinos make fun and try to scare them by saying that they will turn 'evangelistas' [evangelicals] if they are not careful." Despite the opposition, the Indians continued to turn out in greater numbers than the literacy team could handle. "It's like the awakening of a race," Townsend mused. "How it touches one's heart to see how anxious they are to learn to read and how little interest anyone takes in helping them[,] and then you are filled with righteous indignation to see how successfully the enemies of the advancement of the Indians block the way of progress." He reported to Karl Hummel, "The whole Indian population came to look upon us as their protectors."[44]

By 1935 more than one thousand copies of the Cakchiquel New Testament were in circulation. Still, Carl Malmstrom reported, "The Cakchiquel translation is being used in many places in this territory, but not anywhere near as much as it ought to be used." In a sense Townsend's labor of love fell victim to his own ambition. Even as he conducted the literacy campaigns, he dreamed of moving on to the "wild tribes" in the Amazon. The Cakchiquel reading campaigns essentially died when the Townsends left Guatemala. The field committee argued strenuously that to leave when he did would largely waste his effort of the last decade, and that only he could "stir up the Cakchiquels to many times more use of the Testament." But in Townsend's mind he had already left the Cakchiquels, whom he genuinely loved, to others. His heart was in the Amazon, meeting a new people, learning a new language, and beginning the translation process all over again.[45]

In August 1931 Townsend and Van Sickle started for the Peten, the area they planned to survey for airplane use. Townsend hired an airplane to fly them into the area. He could not have been more excited. "We got into the plane a little after seven in the morning with our packs all made up for a month of hiking in the jungles," he reported. "After traveling over mountains for about 40 minutes one of the 3 motors developed trouble and we had to land. The pilot was able to get it in shape again[,] but in the meantime a dense cloud bank had come up so that he was afraid to continue the journey and we had to return." The intrepid Van Sickle hiked in on foot anyway with the secretary of the Nazarene mission. (The Nazarenes also planned to begin work in the Peten.) If the trails were passable, he would send for Townsend in late September.[46]

Van Sickle remained in the Peten until late October. His expenses were so heavy that Townsend was never able to join him. In addition, the Nazarenes were not supportive of Townsend's idea to enter their territory. Van Sickle reported that while the Nazarenes were "very nice," he did not feel he and Townsend were "wanted." Consequently, Townsend began wondering where else they might try the airplane project, and thought of Mexico. That the CAM council no longer played a large part in Townsend's decision-making process is indicated by the fact that he turned to Legters for advice as to what country he should enter. "May God lead you in advising us," he wrote.[47]

The Peten adventure ended definitively when Van Sickle abruptly returned home after hearing that his mother required his assistance because of "an emergency." He neglected to inform Townsend that he was leaving. The first Cameron heard of it was when he received word that Van Sickle had passed through Dallas. "Until then we were haunted with visions of his being laid away in a malaria grave," Townsend fretted to Hummel. Dr. Kelly was waiting for Van Sickle's report and was apparently ready to donate some money if the report was favorable. Van Sickle, however, never followed through. Apparently he was a bit of a fundamentalist and found it hard to get along with people. "Do you think that Lynn is going to make a leader for the new undertaking?" Townsend asked Hummel. "I've been praying desperately that he would[,] but my faith is waning. He can't cooperate very well with people that see things differently than he does."[48]

Meanwhile the CAM executive committee and the Guatemala field committee passed resolutions requesting that Townsend take over the superintendency of the Cakchiquel field while Carl Malmstrom and his wife went on furlough. Townsend agreed, even as he acknowledged that it was "a very bitter pill to us as we had expected to get into new work before that." Townsend's agreement did not last long. His mind was elsewhere, and the "bitter pill" simply proved unpalatable. In a transparent ploy, he used the field committee's decision on another subject as an excuse to back out of his commitment. Townsend's sudden decision naturally led to a good deal of bitterness, making his last few months of association with the CAM rather unpleasant. "The whole letter of his sounds to me like a 'if you don't do as I want, I won't play' spirit," grumbled one missionary. "Some of the rest of us have had to move, against our will, for the good of the work; why should he show such a spirit of independence, and think he is such a favorite!"[49]

Townsend's old friend Archer Anderson was now director of the field committee. Anderson urged Townsend to see the direction of God in the suggestion by both the field committee and the home council that they remain in the Cakchiquel work at least while the Malmstroms were on furlough. Perhaps not noticing the irony, he wrote, "I am sure we didn't take that step [make that suggestion] without prayer. We are told in Proverbs 11:14 and 24:6—'But in the multitude of counselors there is safety.'" Petards were a'hoisting all across Guatemala during Townsend's last few years with the CAM![50]

Townsend offered to spend half his time working with the Cakchiquels, but insisted that the other half be spent on the airplane project or beginning work with a new tribe. Beyond that he refused to budge. "[W]e are so firmly convinced that it is our Lord's will for us that we dare not disobey him[,] although we would far rather be obedient to the powers that be," he informed Anderson somewhat disingenuously. "We trust that in spite of this disobedience, both the Field Committee and the Council will consent to our following [our plans] for the ensuing year in full communion with the CAM which we love and esteem."[51]

At that point the field committee wondered if perhaps it were not better simply to let him go. "Should we keep him to [his agreement] and cause his dismissal from the Mission?" asked one missionary. "It is a question and it looks as tho[ugh] [it will] come to that, but if we cannot work in harmony are we better off without him? It would not be good for general discipline of the Mission to let him do as he pleases." Eventually, as "general discipline of the Mission" was essentially an oxymoron, the field committee washed its hands of the whole affair and turned Townsend over to Hummel and the home council.[52]

Hummel was disappointed in Townsend's stand. He engineered the passing of a resolution by the executive committee. The resolution first expressed "deep appreciation of the monumental work" of translating the New Testament, then continued, "[I]t is the conviction of the Executive Committee that Mr. and Mrs. Townsend should continue their labors with the Cakchiquel tribe, at least until adequate leadership is raised up to continue the work." The committee gave as reasons for their request that the Townsends were the only ones who knew Cakchiquel, that as the translators they were "the ones best fitted for bringing adequate returns on the large investment of time, effort and money," and that the "abundant fruitage of the past labors . . . demonstrate their aptness for this particular work, the great confidence that these Indians have in them, and the fact of divine blessing upon their ministry." The resolution concluded by throwing a small bone Townsend's way: "Be it further resolved that the Committee, recognizing Mr. Townsend's gift and vision for pioneer work, recommends that he exercise this gift in occasional exploration into unoccupied fields, at the same time continuing his directive leadership in the Cakchiquel work." Townsend was not much impressed. Indeed, by now his emotional ties with the CAM were almost entirely severed, and nothing the council could do would turn him from his plans. "I appreciate very much the resolution passed by the council regarding our work," he told Hummel, "but I pray God for the privilege of going into a new field." He continued to refuse to take any responsibility in Guatemala that would tie him down even temporarily as he desperately searched for someone to back his airplane project. He spent his last year with the CAM conducting literacy campaigns and working "zealously" to organize the indigenous churches among the Cakchiquels on a self-governing, self-supporting basis, knowing that the sooner he did so, the sooner he might feel free in his own mind to depart.[53]

Sometime in September 1931 Townsend met Moisés Sáenz, a chance meeting that would soon change the direction of his life. Sáenz, known in U.S. intellectual circles for his work developing the rural school system in Mexico, was from a prominent Mexican political family. He was also a Protestant, educated in the United States. Sáenz was in Guatemala as a representative of the Mexican government studying the "Indian problem." Townsend noticed him one day strolling beside Lake Atitlán with his camera. Townsend introduced himself and immediately recognized the gentleman's name. He invited Sáenz home and showed him his Indian work. Sáenz spent the night at the Townsend home, and the two talked late into the night about Indians, language, and literacy. The next day his visitor invited Townsend to come to Mexico and promised, "Our revolutionary leaders will back me." (He later sent a letter repeating the invitation.) He wanted Townsend to work with the Aztec Indians around Mexico City. He thrilled Townsend with stories of a town only four hours from the capital where the resident Indians spoke almost no Spanish. Townsend excitedly reported to Legters, "He said that they should have the New Test[ament] in their own language. . . . He said that it is a very large tribe. We are quite in the dark as to where God would have us labor[,] but when the need is so great and our desire to go to those who have no opportunity to hear is so impelling, He must want us to undertake a new field. . . . We want to go where there is no one else to handle the situation." Legters urged Townsend to see the Sáenz invitation as the direct leading of God. "It is a most difficult thing to get foreigners to begin work in Mexico," he wrote, "but through this man a door could easily be opened." Legters also reported that the climate in Mexico was "ideal" and would be excellent for Elvira, certainly much better than a South American jungle. He concluded, "I feel sure that the Lord has work for you besides just a supervisory work in Guatemala, and I know that He will guide you to His place."[54]

During the summer of 1932 Townsend came down with a serious lung infection, probably tuberculosis. When his doctor insisted he return to the United States, he decided it was time to make a clean break from his labors of the past fifteen years. Elvira reported to Hummel, "We have made the decision and the Lord has filled both of us with a great peace in the matter, so that we feel it is His seal on it." Despite the Sáenz invitation to Mexico, Townsend was still focused on his airplane project to South America. As soon as they reached the United States, Elvira planned to begin lining things up for the South American project. A doctor and his wife promised to go with them, as did Paul and Laura. "This all seems like a splendid beginning, to be sure!" Elvira declared. She hinted that she and Cameron would like to remain in the CAM, but by now all parties must have known the time had come for the Townsends and the CAM to part ways. Townsend gamely tried yet again to enlist the council. "We are anxious to know whether the CAM will back us in our project for reaching the wild tribes of S[outh] A[merica]," he wrote, "or if it will be necessary for us to resign. We would sure like to continue with the CAM but realize that our project is rather afield of the Mission's work." He tried the Pioneer Mission Agency again also. "Planes are very cheap now," he argued, "aviators are available who manifest a real love for souls[,] and if some organization like the PMA would really get behind this thing it could be given a fair trial."[55]

Unfortunately for Townsend, there was still little interest and fewer dollars for his scheme. When he sat down in August 1932 to write a letter to the Cakchiquel churches, he had no real idea what lay ahead for him. He knew, however, that he would never return to Guatemala as a CAM missionary. In his letter he metaphorically collapsed the events of the past several years into the space of a few months. He seems to have consciously sought to echo the tone of the apostle Paul's letters to his churches.

> For almost six months illness has kept us from the privilege of serving the Lord as before. The doctor orders us to go to the desert in California where consumptives are treated. When we heard this news we felt as if we were plunged into the dark. We asked the Lord, "Why?" As there is such a great need for workers, we found it strange that God should retire us through illness. After some weeks of perplexity the light came. The Lord told us, "Go forward and advance to new lands." We answered, "But Lord how can we leave the work here and the brothers we so long to serve?" The divine answer was, "If some man has a hundred sheep and one gets lost, would he not leave the 99 to search for the one that is lost?" We remember the Indians in the impenetrable mountains of Brazil and South America who have never heard the gospel. We have prayed a lot for them, and last Sunday we understood clearly that the Good Shepherd calls us to work for these unhappy people. We understood that He had allowed the illness to make us leave here and go there. As with Isaiah we answered to the Lord, "We are here, send us." Then came light and peace. So far everything is by faith. We don't know the way that the Lord will work or when, but we believe that he will raise up many companions and will provide airplanes and all that is necessary to go to the most inaccessible mountains to look for those abandoned souls. The Lord has given us the promise of Matthew 8:13: You go and as you believe it will be done unto you. . . . It gives us great pain to leave you, dear brothers, but God calls us and we can not disobey. . . . We will never forget you. . . . We will pray daily for you. Adelante, hermanos, siempre adelante! [Go forward, brothers and sisters, always go forward!] . . . Surrender completely to the hands

> of the Lord. Away with whatever is carnal, the lawsuits and all that hinders spiritual growth! Study the Bible more. Love. Forgive. Evangelize. Pray. Wait for Christ[,] who will soon come and cause you to rejoice. Perhaps we will be able to come at some time to visit one another, but if not, we will see each other in the sky. Glory to God! Greet affectionately all the brothers to whom we want this letter shown. . . . Your servant together in Christ.[56]

The rhetoric of this letter is instructive in several areas. In Townsend's conscious imitation of the apostle, especially in the closing litany of brief injunctions and the final sign-off, we see how the missionaries saw themselves in relation to the native church. The letter also provides an excellent example of interpreting life in reverse, how evangelicals saw the hand of God in the incidents and accidents of their lives. As Townsend collapsed time and narrated the story from an omniscient viewpoint, the interpersonal mess and failed projects dropped away, and the story tied neatly together. It now became in essence a brand-new story that would be constantly repeated until it became not only an altar to celebrate the past but a pillar of fire to point the way to a promising future.

"Adelante, hermanos, siempre adelante!" The words echo from a young man's journal fifteen long years ago. The excitement was building in Townsend. A pioneering time was once again just around the corner.

7

In Which Townsend Mixes Science with Faith, Writes an Audacious Letter, and Recruits a Few Geniuses along with More Than a Few Girls

1933–1945

> Our experience in Mexico the past 10 years shows us that [aggressive advance in missions] is absolutely possible and we have followed scientific methods plus faith. I guess that it wasn't necessary to add those last two words, for faith is the most scientific thing there is.
>
> —William Cameron Townsend

The winter of 1932 found the Townsends living in a small three-room house near Cameron's family in Santa Ana, California. Townsend's father dropped by regularly to make lunch, because Elvira had been ordered to bed with a heart "in rather bad condition." Townsend, not particularly healthy himself, was forced to be both housekeeper and nurse. He continued scheming, even as he chafed at the enforced inactivity. He worked on his idea for a cruise tour to Guatemala that would combine the study of missions with inspirational Bible studies by John Brown and Charles Fuller, both influential radio preachers. Both Brown and Fuller promised to promote the plan on their radio broadcasts, and Townsend thought he could sign up twenty-five "tourists" for an eighteen- to twenty-day trip in February 1933. As with many Townsend schemes, this one fell through for lack of anyone beside himself "to push it." But that was only one of several irons in the fire. He continued to avidly plan for his air crusade to the "wild tribes" of South America. "If funds were available next Spring I wish that we might visit some of the countries where these wild Indians exist and are yet unreached," he suggested to Hummel. "Gov[ernment] officials could be approached and if their reaction were favorable to the project, then the lay of the land could be spied out." He had a job all lined up for Legters. "[S]omeone . . . might be lining up young men (single and under 25 years of age) who were qualified to go. These would then be given a six months' training course in some swampy, wooded region in the USA."[1]

The CAM council agreed to "carefully and prayerfully consider the matter" yet again, but in the midst of the Depression it was simply too far afield from their commitments to think of sponsoring. They hoped Townsend would not organize another mission, as funds continued to be virtually impossible to raise. "There has been such multiplicity of independent missions in recent years that it is making it mighty hard on all concerned," Hummel reported. "Pastors frequently tell me that they have far more calls from faith missions speakers than they can give room to." The CAM was thinking of merging with the Inland South America Missionary Union and the Orinoco River Mission in order to lower overhead. If the merger went through, the new mission would cover some of the area Townsend was interested in exploring, and Hummel suggested that in that eventuality, the new mission might sponsor his air crusade.[2]

As winter dragged into spring and then summer, and the merger fell through, Townsend grew increasingly restless. "How I wish that we could be out on the field again!" he complained to Hummel. "We feel out of place here in the homeland." He consoled himself with the thought that "the Lord doubtless [had] a purpose in it all," including the tempering of his own character. "[W]e realize that there is an awful lot of dross to be removed before we can be used as He would like to use us," he groaned to Hummel. But the field was beginning to look farther and farther away. Elvira's doctor said it would be several years before she could go back, and even then she would not be permitted to take part in the work. Worse, Elvira had her heart set on returning to her lakeside home in Guatemala, the one place she had experienced a bit of peace. "Cameron cannot get settled to the thought of Guatemala's need of his life but rather feels the urge for the wild tribes," she confessed to a close friend. "That of course excludes me[,] for while I feel my life could count in a small measure among our people of Guatemala, I know full well that I do not have strength for pioneer work." Legters had an ambivalent view of Elvira's effect on Townsend's plans. "I thank God for a wife that can stay at home when necessary and not tie my hands," said the man who had left his cancer-stricken wife at home to pursue his Indian work. But he followed that remark with a bit of real wisdom. "But she may be the making of Him, while we think she is a hindrance."[3] Legters seemed to think Elvira might be God's dross remover for his good friend Cameron.

Casting about for some way to realize his vision, Townsend thought of bringing two educated Mayan Indians from the Yucatan to the United States to do a translation there, but decided the hurdles were too great. "I guess that I had better just relax to the pesky little duties that daily take my time but seem to be fruitless as regards the Lord's work," he moaned. "I realize that my time should be better utilized than by puttering around at house work."[4]

Legters, meanwhile, had been busier than ever. He turned his focus toward Mexico, working to get the Spanish-speaking churches interested in evangelizing the Indians around them. He spent virtually all of his time on the road, speaking more than five hundred times a year at various public gatherings. His aggressive approach continued to pay off, as funds arrived regularly at Pioneer Mission Agency headquarters in Philadelphia, even as other faith missions were desperately short. As one grateful missionary wrote to Legters, "I certainly do marvel at the way our special help for Indian work coming through the Pioneer Mission Agency has kept up during these times of depression." Legters himself reported, "During the past year or year and a half we have begun more new work than during any similar period in recent years. . . . It is a remarkable thing, from the human standpoint, that funds for carrying on the pioneer work have increased and not diminished during this time of depression."[5]

Townsend informed Legters that as soon as he and Elvira were healthy he was ready to pioneer in South America, but Legters told him it would be wiser to go to Mexico, "where the tribes were larger and much more accessible." Legters came to California to personally urge Townsend to consider Mexico as his next target of opportunity. Sometime during that meeting, Townsend suggested to Legters that they found a summer school "where candidates for pioneer missionary work could go for training in how to reduce languages to writing and to translate the Scriptures into them." He and Legters made a fateful bargain. Townsend agreed to postpone his air crusade to South America and spend a major portion of each year in Mexico if Legters would help him found such a school. Legters agreed.[6]

On August 10, 1933, Keswick USA was in the middle of a Victorious Life conference. Legters was one of the featured speakers, and he worked his audience with emotional pleas for Mexico and its Indians. He also mentioned Townsend's plan for starting a "linguistic training camp" for pioneer missionaries, although he did not push that as much, because it was still more Townsend's vision than his own. In addition, J. G. Dale and his wife, founders of the Mexican Indian Mission, "came to Keswick from Mexico with a great burden upon their hearts for the 43 Indian tribes of Mexico." Between Legters and Dale the conferees could think of little else.

Early that morning, Addison Raws, councilman for both Keswick and the Pioneer Mission Agency, rose early. He liked to wake the conferees for prayer by playing hymns on his cornet. Almost twenty-five years later, in a letter to an inquirer, he recalled what happened next as if it were yesterday. As he began to play, he noticed Legters and his wife walking toward him. Legters carried a flashlight and, more unusual, wore no necktie. His wife had a blanket wrapped around her. Both carried Bibles. Raws realized immediately that the Legterses had been up all night praying in the auditorium. After breakfast the group gathered at 9:00 for the Bible hour. Perhaps in response to the prayers of the Legterses, Raws reported that the group suddenly received a "new consciousness that the Lord, Himself, was in our midst and was wanting to do a new thing for His people." During the ten-minute break between the Bible and missionary hours, the leaders decided to cancel the rest of the morning's meetings and "turn it into a time of prayer and intercession that the Lord would again open the doors of Mexico to the Gospel." They all continued praying through lunch and till 5:00 p.m. Before the day was over the group felt assured that God had heard their prayers. Then a dramatic, if perhaps predictable, turn of events occurred. "Almost immediately the Lord revealed His will for Mr. Legters and Mr. W. C. Townsend of Guatemala to make a trip to Mexico City for the purpose of meeting with the Government to get permission for sending men into the Indian tribes to learn the languages and to translate the Bible into those Indian tongues."[7] How the Lord "revealed His will" Raws did not say. More than likely, someone, perhaps Legters himself, suggested the trip as an exploratory fleece, and everyone agreed it was a good idea. Nothing ventured, nothing gained. Given no dramatic objections, the group felt "at peace" about the decision, and, interpreting the event in retrospect twenty-five years later, and given the subsequent incredible success of the Legters-Townsend endeavor, Raws confidently asserted that the Lord had supernaturally revealed his will. For evangelicals, such leading was often as simple as that.

Legters immediately wrote to Townsend about the proposed trip. Someone had already offered a car and $160, which Legters saw as divine confirmation that now was the time. "We are going to Mexico for the express purpose of meeting with the authorities to see whether permission will be given to begin work among the Indians," he informed Townsend. "It seems to me absolutely necessary, or very necessary, that you go with us." He was breathless with excitement. Now was clearly the time! "I think that all our future plans for Mexico depend upon this one thing—whether the authorities will give us permission for work among those tribes. At this end God has worked in real power. I believe that He will work in the hearts of the authorities there and that the door will be opened." He promised Townsend they would start the summer linguistic training camp once they had someplace to send their graduates.[8]

In typical Legters fashion, he also dashed off a letter to his constituency seeking support for the "most important trip we have ever undertaken." "There are laws prohibiting the entrance of any new missionaries," he wrote. "[Nevertheless,] God can open the hearts and minds of men to do His will. . . . Will you also pray that as the Lord has opened the door for us to go to Mexico, He will lay it upon some hearts to provide the funds for the trip?"[9] His readers well knew what he was suggesting.

Townsend was naturally eager to accompany Legters. He carefully wrote out an official request to present to the Mexican government and sent it off to Moisés Sáenz for his review. Unfortunately, Sáenz was no longer in charge of Mexico's education program; in fact, he had publicly disagreed with the policies of his successor, Narciso Bassols. Nevertheless, he was still a very influential figure. The request was vintage Townsend, a grandiose work of salesmanship. That much of what he first outlined was eventually fulfilled makes the initial vision no less fantastic. As the request was typical of his later approach throughout Latin America, it deserves to be quoted in full.

> The undersigned, Leonardo L. Legters and Guillermo C. Townsend, the first a lecturer, explorer and humanitarian, the second an ethnologist and educator, both American citizens, respectfully come before you to state that after many years of working in the United States and in several countries of Latin America in favor of the cultural incorporation of the indigenous groups, we have ended up believing that there needs to be an organization in each nation where there are indigenous tribes to pursue the following ends: 1. To conserve for science a grammar and a dictionary of each indigenous language. 2. To translate the New Testament in each language and publish it in a bilingual edition.
>
> To achieve these ends the society would gather contributions from people and philanthropic organizations mainly in the United States to employ linguists and the necessary assistants. Of course no one will be used who would function as a bad moral example when living and working among the indigenous people. On the contrary, your employees would try to inculcate notions against alcoholism and other bad habits that brutalize the Indians. Knowing that Mexico is one of the countries where there is a great deal of enthusiasm for the cultural incorporation of the Indian, we want to form one of the first such societies here. It will be called the Mexican Society of Indigenous Translations. Together

> with other societies of a similar nature that we hope to form in Canada, the United States, Guatemala, Panama, Venezuela, Colombia, Ecuador, Peru, Bolivia, Brazil and Chile it will work in cooperation with a mother society that will be founded to procure funds and linguists. We hope to spend here in Mexico in this task no less than a million pesos during the next ten years, without taking out anything other than the satisfaction of having helped in the advance of the great indigenous race that has suffered so much and that has so much promise. We believe that the indigenous races will contribute in a great way to the enlargement of each nation where they live once they learn the native language and are set on the right track in the national culture.
>
> We are neither novices nor dreamers in this work. Mr. Legters lived and worked for many years among the indigenous groups in the United States before beginning his exploratory and philanthropic work among the indigenous tribes of Central and South America and Mexico. Mr. Townsend as a linguist has translated the whole New Testament into the Cakchiquel language of Guatemala and has formed a method to teach Cakchiquels how to read that was published less than two years ago by the Tipografía Nacional de Guatemala. With this method many learned how to read after only 15 days of study. As an educator he has founded several academies and schools in Guatemala for the indigenous groups, in which many children and adults have received an education which they would not have otherwise achieved. The following people will be able to provide information regarding the educational pro-native work of Mr. Townsend in Guatemala: [Townsend listed President Ubico among a number of other officials.] We will proceed to the organization of the society as soon as you assure us that our linguists will be able to settle down in the country. We promise that they will observe all the laws of the nation carefully.[10]

That all the two really had was a car and $160 mattered not a bit to Townsend. He tended to inhabit his dreams long before they actually arrived on the scene, which, an evangelical might point out, makes a good definition of faith.

It is important to make several initial observations here. First, the Mexican setting dictated several of the approaches that became standard operating procedure for the new mission. Mexico was a closed field at the time for missionaries, and several of the countries of Latin America were rapidly following its lead. Townsend's scientific approach was designed to gain access to closed fields, even as he genuinely wanted to use science to train better missionaries who would work in indigenous languages. Townsend sold his idea to Mexico as a service organization for both indigenous tribes and the Mexican government. Such a vision, when aggressively accepted and monitored by foreign governments, would force the new organization down unexpected paths, paths that few evangelical missionaries were, at least initially, comfortable taking. In the process an entirely new way of being an evangelical missionary was created. Indeed, new ways of being evangelical were envisioned. Second, it is important to note the degree to which Townsend was open with the Mexicans about his goal of Bible translation. Townsend has often been accused of deceiving Latin American governments about his real intentions. Legters, however, would have none of that. He wanted it clearly understood that the new society's goal was to translate the New Testament into indigenous languages. "Nothing ought to be underhanded," he ordered Townsend. The Mexican government must clearly "understand what we are doing."[11]

On October 18 Moisés Sáenz replied somewhat neutrally to Townsend's renewed overture. "I consider it very difficult that a foreigner could fit in with the government's programs in rural education or, in general, the programs related to the incorporation of the indigenous peoples," he wrote. The government had not been impressed with what Protestant missionaries had accomplished so far. "Missionaries in their various fields where there is Indian population could do a lot for the race, but concretely they are doing very little." Sáenz concluded on a more positive note. "All this is not to say, however, that I don't believe you could do an excellent work in Mexico, that I don't consider you qualified for it, or that I think it unnecessary that such work should be carried out. Do come to Mexico and see for yourself how things are, and then hopefully after your visit we can find a basis for you to stay."[12]

That was all Townsend needed to hear. He presented his official resignation to the CAM, because he did not want to "represent any religious organization." He hoped to find an individual to support him so that if Mexican officials asked how he made a living, he could avoid mentioning support from churches. "Having to be so careful makes me feel rather like a spy," he informed a friend, "but I'd be even that in order to get the Message to those poor Indian tribes." After packing Elvira off to her folks in Chicago, Townsend headed to Texas to meet Legters. Along the way he stopped in Wichita Falls, where the newspapers announced he would speak on the subject of the Latin American Indians at a service club luncheon. The local Episcopalian rector saw the notice and invited Townsend to his home. He gave Townsend a card of introduction to the Episcopalian dean in Mexico City.[13]

When Townsend first crossed the border in 1933, Americans were divided in their opinion of Mexico. Since the beginning of the Mexican Revolution in 1910, America had maintained a decidedly uneasy relationship with its southern neighbor. American meddling, both direct and indirect, added to Mexico's instability as one faction after another dominated Mexican politics. American oil companies, distressed by the revolutionary Constitution of 1917, which directly challenged capitalist interpretations of property rights, schemed constantly in Mexico and funded a barrage of negative press in America. The Catholic Church may well have been Mexico's most bitter critic. The Constitution of 1917 outlawed religious education, regulated religious worship, and prohibited priests from criticizing the government. During the administration of Plutarco Elías Calles (1924–1928) the bitterness between the government and church erupted into the bloody Cristero wars. The Catholic press in America vilified Mexico, and books such as Michael Kenny's *No God Next Door* suggested to Americans that Mexico was merely a "laboratory" for Moscow and its "relentless war against God and Christian civilization." Catholics were not alone in this view. The U.S. State Department was generally convinced that Mexico was going to become a staging ground for Marxist-Leninism in the Western Hemisphere. As John Britton noted, when Americans talked about their southern neighbor in the 1920s and 1930s, their conversations probably centered on the widely publicized hostility of the revolution to Catholicism and the "grossly exaggerated perception of international Communism in Mexico."[14]

By the time Lázaro Cárdenas came to power in 1934, perceptions had tempered somewhat. Economic problems at home and the rising international crisis in Europe turned American eyes elsewhere. When Americans thought of Mexico at all, it was viewed as a "troublesome nest of banditry and Bolshevism"—Cárdenas's unprecedented agrarian reforms, focus on socialist education, and the 1938 nationalization of foreign oil companies did little to enhance Mexico's international standing—but with the general weakening of the interventionist lobby, American rhetoric was often more smoke than fire. American ambassador Josephus Daniels, who agreed with a Scottish friend of his that too often for Americans a Communist was simply "any damn fellow you don't like," provided balance for Cordell Hull's anti-Communist bluster. The Catholic lobby was still active, but their efforts were often canceled out by the anti-

Catholic lobby. As Alan Knight noted, American politicians were well aware that the Catholic Church was "known as the Whore of Babylon in a good many American homes."[15]

Among certain segments of the public, Mexico was actually undergoing somewhat of a renaissance. The American left was fascinated by Mexico's revolutionary project, and a small colony of writers, artists, traveling professors, Communists, and bohemians contributed to a Greenwich Village atmosphere in Mexico City. Their rejection of bourgeois values and a fascination with all things Indian made them acceptable, even useful, to Mexican politicians and intellectuals.[16] By the 1930s their views of Mexico were beginning to have an impact on the popular media.

Frank Tannenbaum was typical of this group. As a young man, Tannenbaum had achieved minor celebrity as an anarchist and organizer for the Industrial Workers of the World (IWW), a left-wing labor union. He spent a year in jail after leading a small army of the unemployed into large churches and demanding sustenance as their right until they could find work. In jail he attracted some influential mentors—Upton Sinclair published a poem "To Frank Tannenbaum in Prison"—who got him into Columbia University. There he entered the mainstream of Progressive thought, and his articles about prison life brought about the dismissal of the warden of Blackwell Island. His affinity for labor and education first brought him to Mexico in 1922. He became quite enthusiastic about Mexico's prospects, writing, "there is a future in Mexico, a cultural future that may well prove the greatest Renaissance in the contemporary world." His publications earned him the high regard of Mexico's intellectuals and political leaders—his closeness to Cárdenas was legendary—and the suspicion of the U.S. State Department, which considered him part of the red cohort. When Townsend crossed the border in 1933, Tannenbaum had just published his influential study of Mexico, *Peace by Revolution,* and had become the "first major foreign interpreter of the [Mexican] Revolution."[17]

Religious liberals in the United States tended to side with their secular liberal brethren on the Mexico issue. Even during the oil confiscation crisis, the editors of the *Christian Century* maintained a balanced outlook. They sympathized with Cárdenas's efforts to free his country from foreign and Catholic domination.[18]

Evangelicals were probably more typical of the population at large. While their journals did not notice Mexico much during these years, except as one mission field among many, their attitude can be surmised from their indulgence in popular stereotypes and their increasing concern in the 1930s over the threat of international Communism. At a time when popular films such as *Viva Villa!* and children's books such as the Hardy Boys adventure *The Mark on the Door* depicted many Mexicans as swarthy, scheming bandits, it is not surprising that the influential evangelical *Moody Monthly* printed the following in a missionary's account of Mexico: "Of all the tramps that can be vile, and of all the generals that can be elegant and arrogant, Mexican tramps and Mexican generals take the prize.... No tramp is more vile, more forlorn, evil-looking and evil-smelling, than a pulque-soaked Mexican outcast." Evangelicals enjoyed the discomfiture of Catholicism in Mexico, which seemed to present an opportunity for Protestant missionaries. At the time, however, no Protestant missionaries who were not already residents were gaining access to the country. Many evangelical missions had recalled a good portion of their workers because so many restrictions had been placed on the kind of work they could do. More worrisome was how other countries in Latin America seemed to be taking their cue from Mexico. As Ed Haymaker once remarked to Legters, "Guatemala[,] like a number of countries[,] is developing an anti-missionary sentiment, as a kind of penumbra of their fight with Rome, and we must suffer vicariously for the sins of the 'Mother of Harlots.' The spirit seems to be permeating Latin America, doubtless radiating from Mexico[,] that is completely loco on the subject." Evangelicals were also concerned with Mexico's purported Bolshevist leanings. Magazines such as *Our Hope* kept up a constant anti-Communist drumbeat, but perhaps since Mexico did not fit into any prophetic scenarios, they spent the bulk of their time focused on Europe. Elvira probably expressed evangelicalism's general opinion of Mexico when she wrote to a friend while her husband was trying to gain entrance to the country, "I am afraid that Mexico is not far from going Communistic and in that case we can hope for very little at this time."[19]

Granted permission to cross the border on November 11, 1933, so long as he did not preach or study Indian languages, Townsend spent hours in the waiting rooms of government offices trying to find someone to listen to him. Officials at the border had been very suspicious of the duo's missionary intent, but the letter from Moisés Sáenz paid off, eventually getting them into the country on a restricted passport. The prospects for initiating work in Mexico, however, appeared grim. Townsend tracked down books on indigenous languages in old bookstores, jotted notes whenever he ran across Indians, and wrote to President Ubico in Guatemala asking for assistance, all the while waiting to hear word of his petition. After several weeks spent casting about Mexico City, Legters decided to return home, as he had pressing speaking engagements. Townsend thought of returning with him to look for Sáenz, who was currently in the United States on a lecture tour. He thought if he returned "under Sáenz' wing" he would get a passport with fewer restrictions. But after receiving an encouraging letter from Elvira, he decided to stay in Mexico a bit longer.[20]

Exactly one month after crossing the border, with a cold so bad he could barely speak above a whisper, Townsend found himself being feted in an upscale restaurant by a new group of acquaintances, including Bernard Bevins, an English writer he had met at an Episcopal church bazaar (the card of introduction from the Episcopalian rector in Wichita Falls had paid dividends); the British vice consul; an iron manufacturer; and Miss Reh, an American archeologist and writer. A fascination with Mexico's Indians and an interest in hearing about Townsend's proposed project brought the group together. Frank Tannenbaum happened to wander in, and they invited him to join them. Before the meeting broke up, Tannenbaum gave Townsend a note of introduction to Rafael Ramírez, the director of rural education. Townsend's blood rushed up. This sequence of circumstances was entirely too incredible. God must be pulling the strings.[21] Any evangelical worth their salt would have felt the same.

When Townsend tracked down Ramírez in Monterrey, he discovered that the director had already heard of him. "You . . . presented a petition regarding bringing in men to translate the Bible," he told Townsend. "We don't want Indians to get the Bible. That is what has been the trouble with them ever since the Conquest." Townsend argued that the real trouble was that the Catholic Church had *not* given them the Bible, an argument that, according to Townsend, changed Ramírez's attitude "completely." While it was undoubtedly not nearly that simple, Townsend could be very persuasive, and the combination of Townsend's salesmanship and the endorsement by Tannenbaum eventually softened Ramírez. While not permitting Bible translation or "any religious propaganda," he took the other restrictions off Townsend's passport and gave him permission to freely travel the country. He could study the problem of the incorporation of the Indians into the broader culture and examine the rural school system, which the Mexicans had inaugurated to deal with the issue. Townsend was now traveling a path already well worn by the American left and the Mexican government. Mexican officials, knowing the country's image in America needed help, used "techniques of hospitality" (interviews, tours, favors, friendships) to "reinforce the favorable predispositions of the leftist visitors." A tour of rural schools was a familiar technique, as education was frequently of great interest to the left. John Dewey had been personally escorted on such a tour in 1926 by vice minister of education Moisés Sáenz. The visitors in turn shared their insights with the American public through their publications. Dewey wrote three articles for the *New Republic* after his trip.[22]

Unfortunately for Townsend, when he checked back in with Ramírez in Mexico City, he did not find the director nearly as accommodating. Ramírez had dug up Townsend's original request and had rethought his position. He decided that Townsend would probably wind up being a missionary of no unique flavor after all. As Legters later reported, "[T]he Government . . . saw in our project only a subterfuge for bringing missionaries into the country." Ramírez permitted him to make his planned trips and studies but denied the railroad passes, apparently deciding from their official application that they were already backed by significant funds from the United States. Refusing to become discouraged, as he had a sense that he was being used by God "in opening doors which have well nigh shut," Townsend wrote to Elvira, "Now it means that I must win the confidence of the officials fully before leaving Mex[ico] and that our young men must be willing to come in merely to learn the languages and make personal contacts until such time as the officials have been won over to the wisdom of giving the poor Indians the Bible." He upped the ante with Ramírez by suggesting the founding of a "pan-American, pro-indigenous institution" that would raise contributions "from altruistic people around the world in the great program of the redemption of the Indian." Such an organization might finance a trip by Mexican educators "experienced in the incorporation of the Indian into the culture" to other American countries, "fomenting interest in the problem and exposing the methods that are giving such good results in Mexico." He asked Ramírez to study the matter, concluding, "I don't doubt for a moment that I will be able to demonstrate to you that I don't deserve the suspicion that unfortunately has relapsed onto me."[23]

As he set out on his travels, Townsend knew full well that he had a short window of opportunity in which to win the confidence of the Mexican officials if his overall project was to have any hope of success.[24] The articles he wrote about Mexico after his initial trip must be read in that light. Townsend was a pragmatist, willing to shed preconceived notions and ideologies in pursuit of his central vision of Bible translation and the salvation of the lost. But for Townsend, what began in pragmatism usually ended in passion. As he traveled the back roads of Mexico alone, a passion for the country and its revolutionary idealists was kindled.

For the next two months Townsend traveled almost five thousand miles through rural Mexico visiting schools and surveying local languages. Armed with introductions from Ramírez, education officials welcomed and aided him at every turn. "You would think that I were a big gun for sure," he crowed to Elvira and went on to tell her how struck he was with the "spirit of sacrifice" manifested by the rural schoolteachers. He was genuinely impressed by the educational accomplishments of the revolutionary government.[25]

February and March found Townsend back in the States tending to Elvira's health and writing articles about Mexico. Ramírez kept him supplied with Department of Education publications to provide background and answer questions. Although Townsend felt "lost" trying to write "secular articles," he managed to place three with the *Dallas News* and another with the education journal *School and Society.* While it is difficult to judge their effect in America, in Mexico they passed from Ramírez to Narciso Bassols, the Marxist secretary of education, and Townsend was on his way to being a well-recognized "fellow traveler."[26]

The Mexican education project was a massive undertaking, in reality a cultural mission in which the rural schoolteachers sought to impact almost every aspect of peasant life from literacy to sanitation, agriculture, athletics, and religion. Echoing themes in Tannenbaum's *Peace by Revolution,* Townsend's article in *School and Society* (which Ramírez called "extremely complete and written with the deep sympathy which characterizes you") outlined the massive undertaking, praising the dedication of the rural schoolteachers as "itinerant apostles of learning." One article for the Dallas paper opened with the question, "Why is it that we hear so much about the Russian Revolution and so little about a movement right next door to us which is quite as interesting and potentially of far more significance to the Western Hemisphere?" In case this question alarmed his readers, Townsend emphasized the positive effect the Mexican Revolution had on the formerly exploited "common people," and assured his audience that as far as he could tell, the "Mexican Revolution will continue to be Mexican," not heading down a Russian path.[27] Although Townsend honestly laid out the reality of land redistribution and other socialist measures, much of his language (exploitation by capital, class privilege, human betterment, cooperatives, public control of private business) would have been recognizable to an older generation steeped in Populist politics. Populist ideas, as well as Mexico's puritanical streak—several Mexican states enforced total prohibition and attempted to enforce other moral reform measures—might well have appealed to older conservative Protestants who could still remember the evangelical crusades for moral reform and the days when evangelicals embraced many Populist ideals. Townsend, with his solid conservative credentials, had a ready, if somewhat grudging, audience.

Townsend left nothing to chance. In one article he referred to the secretary of education as "one of the brainiest men in Mexico," prompting Ramírez to remark that Bassols "wishes to express his sincere thanks for the appreciation you extended him, for which he feels undeserving."[28]

Over the next year and a half Townsend continued to travel in and write about Mexico. As he grew more comfortable, he began to address the two most ticklish issues between the United States and its southern neighbor: Communism and religious persecution. Calling a scene he had witnessed in southern Mexico "an experimental test of unadulterated communism," he went on to describe "the formation of a new town of dreamy ideals." This experiment in cooperative living, what Townsend called "the saner principles of communism," worked in Mexico where it failed in Russia, because while Russia "coerced" its peasants into "accepting the dictates of an industrial proletariat," Mexico was gradually educating its peasants to "take their place willingly beside industrial labor in establishing the new order." Furthermore, Mexican leaders were not "slaves of theory" and would travel only so far as experiment showed to be wise.[29]

There are at least three reasons why Townsend wrote so candidly in the mid-1930s about socialism/Communism in Mexico. First, he was still writing with one eye firmly fixed on the reception of his work by Mexican politicians. Second, at this point he was not yet the leading spokesman for a new mission and was not addressing a specifically religious audience. He did not have to worry about alienating a constituency (not that Townsend ever particularly worried about that anyway, but eventually others in the organization would worry about it for him). Finally, he was genuinely impressed with the *ideals* of the leaders of the revolution. For Townsend, the self-sacrificing commitment of the rural schoolteachers, the devotion by many in the Department of Education to the Indians and the rural poor, and the attempts at moral reform were all very Christlike activities. This idealism, which he shared, let him see past the rhetoric and the violence (both of which frightened many Americans) to a common ground that he felt true Christians shared with Mexico's idealistic revolutionaries.

In two 1934 articles Townsend described in detail the war in Mexico between church and state. After disclosing some of the harsh measures taken against organized religion, Townsend wrote, "Such an indictment of all religions seems incredible[,] and one wonders if the men who make it are not of a disreputable type . . . are not frightful red demons with pronged forks ready to catch up all Mexico and throw it into hell." To this point in the article Townsend could be almost any fundamentalist railing against the forces of Satan. But the next few sentences turn in an astonishing direction. After acknowledging that he initially carried with him to Mexico such prejudiced attitudes, he declared, "[W]hen I came to know them I found that most of them are sincere, zealous men aflame with a desire to uplift their Fatherland. They feel that religion has played the traitor and like Moctezuma has let down the bars before the invasion of avarice, exploitation, political injustices, foreign imperialism, ignorance, superstition and even immorality. You look almost in vain over the annals of Mexican history for material with which to refute their accusations and then are forced to admit that they are not as unreasonable as you had supposed." Townsend did not place the blame solely at the feet of the Catholic Church. The evangelical missions, although of more recent advent and in a favored position with Mexican liberals, squandered their opportunity by squabbling "among themselves over matters of dogma and discipline when they should have thrown themselves unitedly [with the revolutionaries] into the campaign for social betterment." The problem for Mexico's leaders, as Townsend saw it (and here his eyes were definitely on his Mexican readers), was to find a way to foster personal Christian piety and morality, much needed in a society based on collective living, while combating "ecclesiasticism." After all, Townsend said, the Christ who called the religious leaders of his day a "generation of vipers" and who blessed the poor while ordering the rich to sell all they had was clearly an ally, not an enemy, of the revolution. The solution to Mexico's problem was to find a way to get the Bible to the people that would be unencumbered by self-interested interpreters. He suggested a "Bureau of Morals and Religion within the Department of Education," which would distribute portions of the Bible as a "textbook on right living" and an "effective antidote to fanaticism." With Bible reading would come honesty, a hunger for knowledge, a diminishment of class prejudice, and a "keener sense of the public weal." Townsend concluded, "If the educators find this transformation going on in its early stages before it has been crystalized in ecclesiastical molds[,] they can guide it so as to greatly aid them in their program of social uplift." In reawakening the echoes of the possibility of governmental reform combining with religious endeavor to create a truly Christian nation, Townsend was applying a uniquely American vision to the Mexican context.[30]

The themes developed here, the positive outlook on Mexico's socialist agenda, the Christlike ideals of at least some facets of the revolution, and the duty of Americans, particularly American Christians, to find a compatible way to both evangelize and be of assistance to America's closest neighbor, would recur again and again in Townsend's public life in the ensuing years.

Over the next decade, Townsend and Legters's plan developed along three fronts. The foundation was Camp Wycliffe, the linguistic training camp founded in the summer of 1934. From Camp Wycliffe, essentially Townsend's dream, novice linguistic missionaries first trickled, then flooded, into Mexico, fulfilling Legters's dream of reaching the Indian tribes of Mexico with the gospel. The third front was initially almost entirely a Legters operation in the United States, as he raised funds for the linguists in Mexico through the Pioneer Mission Agency. Eventually, when the PMA decided that Townsend and Legters had essentially created a new mission board, the two went ahead and founded a new mission, the Wycliffe Bible Translators, to promote the work at home. Consequently, what is popularly known today as the Wycliffe Bible Translators is in reality a somewhat unwieldy merger of three different organizations: (1) Camp Wycliffe, founded to train missionaries with *any board* to undertake pioneer work in Indian languages; (2) the Summer Institute of Linguistics, initially founded to provide an organization for translators from Camp Wycliffe who were not already committed to other boards and chose to join "the Townsend group" in Mexico; and (3) the Wycliffe Bible Translators, which took over promotion and fund-raising for both Camp Wycliffe and the Summer Institute of Linguistics when the PMA decided the work was getting too large for them to handle. We will review the development of the new organization in that order.

As we have seen in earlier chapters, practical training for conservative evangelical missionary candidates was practically nonexistent before Townsend inaugurated his training schools. Missionary candidates, often not even high school graduates, studied the Bible for a few years at a Bible institute, then, upon obtaining the institute's seal of approval upon their Christian character, were accepted after a brief interview by a faith mission and sent overseas with little practical orientation. Townsend's decision to train prospective missionaries for the difficult pioneer work of reaching indigenous groups in their own languages changed the face of evangelical missionary education, essentially linking evangelical missions closely with the broader culture's twentieth-century embrace of both education and technology. Such linkages would eventually be a key factor in bringing evangelicalism out of whatever cultural ghetto its fundamentalist side might have longed for.

As far back as October 1922, when Townsend had been in Guatemala for only a few years, he wrote about the need of missionary recruits for more training before immersing themselves in work in a foreign country. He dreamed of founding a training school for new missionaries at Panajachel on Lake Atitlán. His vision was to create a school that would be staffed by and open to candidates from all the missionary boards. Such a school remained a Townsend pipe dream until he left the CAM. Missionaries were too desperately needed on the front lines to take time out to train them.[31]

Once freed from his CAM responsibilities, and with Legters on board to help promote the work, Townsend was finally able to found his dream school. May 1934 found Townsend hard at work in Sulphur Springs, Arkansas, where they had gone to get special treatments for Elvira from an osteopath. It was believed that the hot springs contained potent curative power, so while Elvira soaked, Townsend planned his first summer training camp in the hills above Sulphur Springs. He decided to risk the summer heat in Arkansas, because, like the traditional boards, he coveted trained seminary men, and he wanted them to be able to attend on their summer break. Backed by the Pioneer Mission Agency, he rented seven acres and a barn and stocked a small camp library with material on Indian languages and culture, and biographies of David Brainerd, George Müller, Hudson Taylor, and other famous missionaries. He secured the endorsement of Robert McQuilkin, founding president of Columbia Bible College, who wrote, "I believe that you are beginning a work that might form the model for many such camps, not simply for the work of translation, but for other training in pioneer missions."[32]

Townsend sent out a small flyer to Christian colleges and seminaries announcing a "Summer Training Camp for Prospective Bible Translators." Life at the camp was to be "uncomfortably simple," because its purpose was "to eliminate all who cannot stand up to hard living conditions." The flyer proposed an ambitious class schedule. Legters would teach "Indian Customs and Psychology," "Indian Evangelization and Spiritual Development," "Indian Distribution and Tribal History," "How to Get Guidance," and "How to Work with Others." Joe Chicol, the young Cakchiquel Indian who had spent the past few years at John Brown Bible College, would give lessons in Spanish and in "Indian Orthography and Pronunciation" and "Indian Superstitions, Vices and Religions." Townsend planned to teach "Economic and Cultural Status of the Indians," "Governmental Programs Regarding the Indians," "Indian Translation—Field Problems," "Indian Philology," and the "Why and How of Reading Campaigns." Paul Townsend would instruct students in "The Indian Workers' Practical Living Problems." The brochure assured, "Some notions will also be given regarding the geography and history of Latin America." All this was to be covered "as time permits."[33]

The first Camp Wycliffe, named after John Wycliffe, the legendary translator of the English Bible, began on June 7, 1934. Two students attended that first summer, although Joe Chicol both taught and sat in on classes, and a local high school boy, Oral Van Horn, helped out around camp. Richmond McKinney was a graduate of the University of Tennessee and had completed his first year of seminary at the Evangelical Theological College in Dallas (what would become

Dallas Theological Seminary). Edward Sywulka was a child of missionaries from Africa and a graduate of McQuilkin's Columbia Bible College in South Carolina. The men were given tools and lumber to construct their own furniture. They cut wild oats for mattresses and prepared and cooked all of their own meals. They rose at 6:00 a.m. for "private devotions," then had breakfast at 7:00 and a prayer meeting at 8:30. The rest of the morning was spent in classes. Townsend's classes amounted primarily to telling tales of his Cakchiquel work and presenting a detailed delineation of Cakchiquel grammar. Three times a week the group undertook a ten-mile hike around Sulphur Springs. Dinner was at 6:00 p.m., and evenings were free for study. In July the students drove to California for lessons in phonetics from Dr. McCreery at Biola. (Phonetics is the study of the sounds of a language. Students learn how to reproduce the sounds orally and how to create an alphabet that incorporates all the sounds made by native speakers.) The entire camp cost Legters and the PMA two hundred dollars. Each of the men also chipped in five dollars per month for room and board.[34]

After that first Camp Wycliffe, Ed Sywulka went to Guatemala with the CAM, where for many years he proved to be a Townsend-like voice, agitating for a greater focus on Indian-language work. Legters raised his support. After a brief exploratory trip into Mexico with Townsend, McKinney returned for his second year of seminary in Dallas. He came back for a second summer's training at Camp Wycliffe in 1935, and eventually went with Townsend to Mexico, where he worked for many years with the Othomi tribe. He proved to be somewhat of a thorn in Townsend's side, as did several of the early seminary men, who found it hard to submit their wills to a college dropout with a farmer's demeanor, especially when he insisted on radical departures from accepted evangelical missionary methods.

For his part, Townsend continued to study in and write about Mexico. He had planned to return to Guatemala to help Sywulka get settled and to assist the Cakchiquel missionaries in distributing his New Testament, but that plan fell through when the CAM missionaries asked him to leave Elvira behind. As his focus turned toward Mexico and his new training camp, his aviation plans came into perspective. He told a prospective aviator that it would be three or four years before he had enough linguists trained to "tackle the Amazon problem on the proper scale." When he was not in Mexico, he worked to promote the second session of Camp Wycliffe. Sywulka wrote a long letter endorsing the training, which Townsend sent to seminaries. He wanted announcements posted in every Christian college and Bible school in America. Although he professed to prefer only about a dozen students the next summer, he wanted to get students thinking about the challenge so that the numbers would be there when he had the facilities to train them. He printed five hundred posters advertising the camp, and the PMA distributed them.[35]

The second session of Camp Wycliffe opened in June 1935 with five students. Richmond McKinney was back for a second summer of training. Bill Sedat, a German, eventually spent his missionary career in Guatemala. Legters's son, David Brainerd Legters, and Max Lathrop, both Westminster seminary graduates, would go with Townsend to Mexico.

But the best thing that ever happened to Cameron Townsend was when a skinny, insecure China Inland Mission reject named Ken Pike hitchhiked his way to Camp Wycliffe that summer. Pike had a master's degree in theology from Gordon-Conwell Theological Seminary and had majored in Greek in college. He had washed out from the CIM because of his health. He was so frail that he had to nap after class every afternoon, and sometimes even during Townsend's lectures. A bit out of sorts socially, he hitchhiked to camp in order to practice talking to people. (When Legters first saw him, he was perched in a tree in Arkansas, where he had gone to try to overcome his fear of heights and to gather firewood. Legters is reported to have muttered, "Dear God, when will you send us better material?") Pike was devastated when he was rejected by the CIM, but he decided to persevere in his goal to be a missionary. He was a scholar and wanted to work at Bible translation, so he wrote to every mission he could think of asking if they were interested in such work. Legters, writing for the PMA, was the only one to reply in the affirmative. Although upon laying eyes on him, Legters did not have high hopes for Pike, the young man proved to be a rugged fieldworker and an extremely talented linguist. Later, after receiving his PhD in linguistics from the University of Michigan in 1942, he was a professor there from 1948 to 1977 while building Townsend's fledgling organization into the most important agency of descriptive linguistics in the world.[36]

But all that was in the future. The summer of 1935 remained a time of small steps forward. The owner of the farm refused to charge the group rent that second year. The osteopath was providing free care for Elvira, and neighboring churches stopped by with pies and ice cream. A local hardware company donated construction materials and supplied the Townsends with a house trailer to take to Mexico. In addition, John Brown College provided free airtime for Townsend to give a weekly missionary message over its radio station. Townsend's father was the camp cook, and Townsend, Legters, and McCreery once again made up the faculty. This time McCreery came to camp, rather than vice versa.[37]

10. Evelyn and Ken Pike. Courtesy Townsend Archives.

A few mission secretaries and heads of other religious institutions visited the camp that second summer, and Townsend picked up a few more endorsements. "I consider [Camp Wycliffe] the fourth great missionary movement of the past half century," said one on a radio broadcast. "In order they are: the Moody schools for training missionaries, the Student Volunteer Movement, the Layman's Missionary Movement, and now Camp Wycliffe and its plan to train men for translating the Bible into all the languages of the earth." Another prominent Bible teacher wrote, "This is the most practical thing I have seen for preparing people to be missionaries." The superintendent of an Indian mission said, "This effort, if properly guided and developed, will prove to be the greatest thing for the evangelization of primitive peoples which our generation has seen."[38]

That summer, the small band set aside a day to pray for a permanent opening to be secured into Mexico. While Townsend's publication efforts had met a positive reception, he as yet had no official invitation to bring in workers on other than tourist visas. Shortly after the day of prayer, Legters "came to Camp with the startling information that [President Cárdenas] . . . had dismissed the most outstanding anti-Christian leaders from his Cabinet." While Cárdenas's cabinet reorganization had nothing to do with his staff's religious position,

Townsend saw the shakeup, in conjunction with the day of prayer, as a sign that perhaps the climate in Mexico might be more hospitable to his approach.[39]

And indeed that fall, with the help of Mexican university men and others interested in Indian languages and in the Indians themselves, Townsend finally secured the permission of the Mexican government to enter the country on a more permanent basis and begin work with indigenous groups. While the next chapter will tell that story, suffice it to say here that the Townsends located in Tetelcingo, a small Aztec village just south of Mexico City. Richmond McKinney, although he returned first for his final year of seminary, began work with the Othomis. Ken Pike began analyzing the Mixteco language. David Brainerd Legters went to the Yucatan to work with the Mayas. Thus a pattern was born. Townsend lived most of the year in Mexico but spent the summers in the United States at Camp Wycliffe. At the close of camp he journeyed to Mexico with the new recruits and helped them get settled before returning to Tetelcingo. As the group grew, he spent more and more time in administrative work, until in the early 1940s other recruits took over the Tetelcingo work.

The foundation of the work continued to be Camp Wycliffe. In its third year Townsend moved the summer training camp to Siloam Springs, where the doctor treating Elvira had relocated his practice. Eight new recruits for Mexico came out of the camp in 1936, the most significant being Eugene Nida. Nida was a tremendously gifted linguist, a graduate of UCLA who had been offered a scholarship to a PhD program in Germany. Although he was sickly and a bit of a hypochondriac, so never made good at being a pioneer missionary, he eventually joined Pike at the University of Michigan, earning a PhD in linguistics and anthropology in 1943. He and Pike oversaw the development of Camp Wycliffe for the next decade. That he does not deserve as much credit as Pike for turning the Summer Institute of Linguistics (SIL) into a world-renowned linguistics organization stems from the fact that at Townsend's urging he took a position with the American Bible Society in the 1940s. He worked for both organizations for a period of years before his duties at the ABS took him out of SIL's orbit. While penning numerous books, Nida also oversaw translation efforts all over the world during his years with the ABS. He pioneered the principle of "dynamic equivalence," one of the most important developments in the history of translation theory. Between Pike and Nida, Townsend had seen two remarkably gifted linguists literally drop into his lap in the first three years of his fledgling institute. Apart from them SIL may never have been much more than a pseudoscientific new approach to missionary work.[40]

Both Nida and Pike were already on the faculty of Camp Wycliffe in 1936.

It was Nida's first year there, but Townsend recognized his gifts and immediately placed him on the faculty. Nida taught comparative philology and morphology, while Pike, after just part of one year in Mexico, taught Indian phonetics. (Morphology, the study of the patterns of word and sentence formation, became Nida's specialty.) McCreery taught general phonetics again, while Legters and Townsend, with their roles already drastically reduced, gave general insight into Indian life and work. When Pike and Nida took over, Camp Wycliffe quickly got much more technical. Generic personal experience courses such as those taught by Legters disappeared in a blizzard of linguistics. Even McCreery was quickly phased out, with 1937 his last year. Pike took over his courses.

Pike spent a good bit of his first year in Mexico reading as much technical linguistic work as he could get his hands on. "Townsend has his plan of action here in Mexico upon the basis of scientific research for and with the government," he wrote to his mother. "In the bargain we will of course plan to do the translating which is our goal. But we do not want to masquerade as linguists and be anything else but that. The only answer then is to become linguists, in fact, not theory, and deliver the real goods." Or as Townsend put it, "Why should not missionaries do a more scientific piece of work than the linguists themselves?" Now, alone deep in the heart of Mixteco country, Pike ordered linguistics books and trained himself in their practical application. At Townsend's urging, Pike began investigating where he could get advanced training in phonetics and linguistics as it pertained to Indian languages. He was told by a source in the English department at Harvard that the best place to study was with Edward Sapir at Yale. His source informed Pike that the "best book in linguistics which has appeared in many years is Language by Leonard Bloomfield."[41]

Pike attended a special linguistics institute sponsored by the University of Michigan in the summer of 1937 at which Sapir, Bloomfield (whose book Pike claimed to have "memorized"), and other prominent Americanist linguists taught. Although the institute was open only to PhDs, an introduction from Sapir and some pages from his initial efforts in phonetics earned him a tuition fellowship. Sapir reviewed the first two chapters of his phonetics book and was "quite impressed." Pike reported, "Later I had a talk with him beginning in his office, going to lunch, and then in his room until midnight. He skipped a reception to do it, but said the reception was work . . . and the language restful!" Sapir consented to write an introduction to Pike's book when it was completed. When the Yale professor heard how many people Camp Wycliffe had already sent into the field and the extent of their goals, he remarked "that in a little time [SIL] might dominate the American Indian linguistic field." Pike earned A's in all of his courses, and Sapir designated him "one of the two 'finds' of the year in the field of Indian linguistics." For their part, Mexican linguists with whom Townsend established a close relationship were delighted with Pike's progress, because they believed it "intimately tied" *them* into the international linguistics community as well. They hoped Townsend and Pike could encourage graduate students in linguistics to conduct their research in Mexico.[42]

The summer of 1937 saw nine new students attend Camp Wycliffe. The camp was beginning to round into its eventual shape. The statement of purpose read: "The classes of the Summer Institute of Linguistics serve Camp Wycliffe . . . as its linguistic department and special rates are extended to its students." Townsend made a careful distinction between SIL and Camp Wycliffe, because he did not want other mission boards to think Camp Wycliffe was merely a recruiting organization for SIL in Mexico. He genuinely wanted all the boards to send their recruits to Camp Wycliffe for training. So he carefully explained that SIL merely provided the teachers to Camp Wycliffe as a service. Every piece of publicity material stated explicitly that all boards were welcome to send their candidates for training. The PMA was also part of the somewhat confusing equation. The PMA sponsored Camp Wycliffe out of its interest in promoting pioneer missions. The SIL provided experienced linguists from Mexico to teach the courses. All the organizations received credit, although by 1937 SIL dominated the brochures.[43]

Nine new students was not enough for Townsend, who felt they could have profitably handled at least twenty-five. He pushed the PMA and his own Mexico recruits to increase their promotional efforts. Townsend sent out a letter under his and Charles Trumbull's signatures urging mission boards and "Christian Educators" to send candidates to Camp Wycliffe. (Trumbull lent his signature as an officer of the PMA, but he was widely known as the editor of the popular evangelical magazine *The Sunday School Times.*) The letter advocated a new kind of missionary: "linguistic missionaries." "The career as such has not existed except as individual missionaries linguistically gifted saw the need for Bible translation and applied themselves to it," Townsend wrote.[44]

Initially there was some confusion over how recruits joined the Mexico organization. Did they send an application to the PMA, or did they just become members of SIL after graduating from Camp Wycliffe? Essentially, attending Camp Wycliffe became the essence of the application process. The faculty voted on applications after all the grades were in and they had an indication of an applicant's linguistic ability.[45] A problem developed, however, when Townsend's old-school sense of urgency clashed with Pike's and Nida's academic sensibilities. In many ways Townsend did not fully comprehend the reforms he had himself unleashed. He remained a faith missionary who longed to hurry as many recruits to the field as quickly as possible so that the world would be evangelized and Christ would return. His vision for Camp Wycliffe was that it be a training organization to steer such missionaries into pioneer Indian work and to give them a few tools to assist them with indigenous-language learning and Bible translation. At the same time, he genuinely sought scientific legitimacy, but he valued it more as a stamp of approval for his organization than for its own sake. However, for men like Pike and Nida, whose feet were daily in both the academic and the missionary communities, the issue became much more complex. Their lives were devoted to missions, but not at the expense of illegitimacy in the academic world.

By mid-September 1937 Camp Wycliffe was in an uproar. The students were very discouraged. Most of them simply could not keep up with the demands placed upon them by the faculty. Two had decided to quit, and others refused to recommend the camp to their friends. The strain of turning prospective missionaries into linguists was beginning to show. Nida had instituted a grading system based on college standards rather than those normally used by Bible institutes, and grades were very low. He and Pike grumbled that Bible school transcripts were meaningless as indicators of student ability, because their "grades [did] not indicate mental acumen." "[P]erhaps most serious of all," Townsend told Legters, "[was] the attitude of Kenneth and Eugene toward the members of the class who have not had adequate background, which made them feel as though it was a hopeless proposition for them to ever do translation work." Townsend was forced to intervene. "Gene and Ken promised to be a little more moderate about pouring on the work and are taking a better attitude toward the ones who don't have the proper background to enable them to keep up," he reported to Elvira. Adopting faith mission logic, Townsend insisted, "I feel that it is very important in the future for all of us to take the stand that the men and women whom God sends here should be helped, whether we feel that they are properly gifted or not."[46]

Someone scrawled in the margins of one of Townsend's letters, "Mr. T[ownsend] . . . takes any who show the Lord's leading." This was the perceived view of his stand, and there was a lot of truth to it. Townsend pointed to some in the group who lacked sterling educational qualifications but who were nevertheless doing decent linguistic work in Mexico. He believed that with the proper training just about anyone could be made useful. Therefore, he approved the ideal of seeking highly qualified applicants, but in the meantime, until their stature and publicity guaranteed that better applicants were inquiring, he wanted to admit all the hopefuls he could. In this regard he clearly showed his faith mission upbringing. He did not want to delay the work in Mexico by rejecting under-educated but eager applicants. "Personally, I would rather accept five failures, [if we get one or two] 'unqualified' workers [who actually work out]," he argued, "than accept the responsibility of denying God's Word to a single tribe on account of standards which God has laughed at and utterly disregarded time and again."[47]

But whether Townsend agreed with it or not, a new standard for prospective missionaries had been set. The goal of the emerging institution was not simply to rubber-stamp whomever God happened to send along. The seal of God's favor was no longer simply cash in hand, a willing heart, and a little Bible knowledge. An academic standard had been set, and while it could be lowered, there was no turning back without abandoning the entire vision and becoming just another faith mission. Apart from rigorous linguistics training, SIL would be just another mission, with only pretensions toward serious scholarship. Their Bible translations would have been second rate, and SIL linguists would never have provided any work of note to the academy. Legters saw the inevitable direction the new mission would turn before Townsend did. He did most of the recruiting while he was alive, and he refused to encourage applicants he thought were inadequately prepared. About one trip, he reported to Townsend, "There were a number of men at the [Moody Bible Institute] who spoke to me about Camp, men who had not had high school. I did not encourage them." It was simply difficult at the time to find qualified people from a typical evangelical constituency; a very small percentage attended college.[48]

The struggle over the issue is highlighted in Camp Wycliffe's recruiting brochures. It is suggestive that an early application blank asked about the applicant's educational qualifications *before* ascertaining how long the person had been a Christian. A 1936 ad for the camp put out by the PMA listed as admission requirements, "Single men between the ages of twenty and thirty who have had some Bible and language study, college and seminary training preferable. A very limited number will be accepted; no modernist need apply." Despite aggressive recruiting in seminaries, in itself a radical departure from faith mission methods, few well-trained students applied. Gradually the organization was forced to lower its sights, even as it increased the rigor of its training. The requirements in 1937 made no mention of seminary. Instead the brochure offered a more detailed statement: "The Summer Institute of Linguistics is not interested in the development of the swivel-chair type of linguist, but rather in the type which at the cost of hardship and privation is willing to settle among primitive people and thoroughly learn their languages. . . . The Institute will be able to receive only 25 students this summer so that it reserves the right of selection. Character, brains, brawn, and the fortitude of a pioneer as well as a college diploma are desired in candidates." Another brochure stated, "Applicants should be college graduates with some systematic training in the Bible. A working knowledge of Greek is particularly desirable."[49]

In 1937 the staff discussed whether to send out "linguistic helpers" as well as linguists. They decided to accept the first twenty-five who had a university degree, some "systematic Bible training, a physique able to stand up under living conditions met with in Indian villages, a willingness to sacrifice and live in such a village, and a spiritual experience fitting them for the work." If fewer than twenty-five of that type applied, they would begin admitting those who did not have as much academic training as "linguistic helpers," or "workers who could help introduce the New Testament among the various tribes after the translation had been put out, but who were not linguistically talented for the actual translation themselves." Although such a category was rarely used, it demonstrates Townsend's attempt to balance faith mission objectives with the educational background needed for the type of work his new mission had in mind.

By 1945 the requirements were stated as follows: "High school and Bible training are required of our candidates, and of course college work is always a great help. We do not accept candidates definitely until they have completed satisfactorily the linguistic course given at Camp Wycliffe." With experience, the mission decided to place the barrier at the application to the Wycliffe Bible Translators (WBT) after camp rather than with the application to the linguistics training offered by SIL. The initial requirements were lowered so that more people could at least attempt the training. Of course those under appointment with other boards had always been assured a spot. Those who chose to go overseas with WBT/SIL had to complete the courses satisfactorily.[50]

In 1939 the American Bible Society publicly endorsed SIL and Camp Wycliffe. That summer the society contributed five hundred dollars to the work. Gradually, evangelical mission boards warmed to the idea of sending their recruits to SIL. Veteran missionaries began to attend during their furlough years. Some, such as the New Tribes Mission, founded their own training programs based on the Camp Wycliffe model.[51]

In addition, Pike began to notice a good deal of interest at the University of Michigan in SIL's work. Something of a pipeline developed between SIL and the university. The university gave scholarships to SIL's best graduates to follow in Pike's footsteps and attend the linguistics institute's summer sessions, because they knew the SIL students would put what they learned to practical use. Charles Fries (director of the linguistics institute and professor at the University of Michigan), Leonard Bloomfield (University of Chicago), Sapir (who died early in 1939), and Morris Swadesh (University of Wisconsin) all supported at least the scientific aspects of SIL's work. As Edgar Sturtevant (head of the Department of Linguistics at Yale and associate director of the linguistics institute) said, "Of course none of us are interested in the religious phase of your work, but we all are very much so in the linguistics part." Pike felt pressure from these scholars to make sure SIL genuinely contributed to linguistic knowledge. He remarked to his parents, "We and our group [have] become definitely earmarked as being in the missionary business. Now we have to deliver the goods, or the Lord's name will surely be brought into reproach." Fortunately, they didn't face much competition at the time. Pike had a difficult time finding any articles or books on the Indian languages of Mexico other than what was being produced by SIL. Pike's first major contribution to linguistics was his dissertation on the problem of tonal languages, which were notoriously difficult to analyze. After reading his work, Fries told him it was sufficient for a PhD dissertation. Fries set up a committee that included Bloomfield, Swadesh, and himself. Townsend crowed to the president of Mexico, "Pike won a great victory lately at the University of Michigan when he gave a conference on the problem of the tones of the indigenous languages from Mexico to the sages of the Linguistic Institute that meets there every summer. They want to give him the doctorate in philosophy."[52]

Bloomfield remarked of Pike's dissertation that it was a "big thing, important [and] highly original," although he admitted it was "all new to me." When Pike's book was published in 1943, Bloomfield wrote, "The book is . . . the first thing on intonation that I have read with any interest or profit. . . . You are adding to human knowledge in this field . . . and adding at a tremendous rate of speed." Evelyn, Pike's wife, was not as impressed. "You see[,] a lot of these things are mere guesses," she told friends, "but everybody's guess is just as good as anyone else's, if the reasoning is acceptable."[53]

Guesses or not, Camp Wycliffe's reputation was building, and slowly the number of students began to increase, and with it the number of recruits for Mexico. The summer of 1938 saw fifteen new students at Camp Wycliffe, and an additional nine returned for a second year of study. Some brought Indians back with them to receive help from Pike and Nida in cracking a difficult language. Between first- and second-year students and faculty, Camp Wycliffe entertained roughly thirty people. Eighteen first-year students attended the summer of 1939.[54]

In April 1940 applications were coming in so fast for the camp that Legters was growing alarmed. He did not think the camp would have enough room for them all. "I shall be suggesting to some of the applicants that they do not come this year," he reported to Townsend. "Each one will not be accepted unless they have something of preparation." He proposed enlisting a camp director to oversee the entire affair, including the hiring of cooks and other camp help. Eventually, forty new students representing ten mission boards attended the 1940 session.[55]

That summer James Boyd from the ABS and Dr. John Harrington, senior ethnologist at the Bureau of American Ethnology at the Smithsonian, visited camp. Harrington gave two lectures on ethnological problems and their relationship to linguistics. Both men were impressed. In an article for the *Bible Society Record,* Boyd observed, "The ministries of science have in recent years increasingly come to the aid of Christian missionaries. . . . The sharpest impression, however, left on a visitor to Camp Wycliffe was the unusual combination of scientific devotion and of old-fashioned Biblical piety manifest alike in teachers and taught." He quoted from a letter from Harrington, which read, "[These young people are doing] much better and more scientific [work] than we had been doing. These men really know. They are gifted experts."[56]

In 1941, after Camp Wycliffe's last summer in Arkansas, the staff undertook a thorough review of the first eight years of the new training institution. Camp Wycliffe, or as it was now more often referred to, SIL, had trained 142 missionary linguists—64 men and 78 women from twenty-six different states and Canada. Twenty different denominations were represented in the student body, although half were either Presbyterians or Baptists. They had even trained 6 missionaries from Pentecostal denominations, an example of the enforced bedfellows created by a scientific approach. More than half the students had some college or university training, although only 63 had earned a bachelor's degree. The number who had attended college demonstrates remarkable success at appealing to educated evangelicals. They had managed to recruit only 20 with seminary degrees, although 9 had some other type of graduate degree. As might be expected, 91 had been to Bible school, but only 55 graduated. Forty-two graduates of SIL had gone with Townsend to Mexico, and were officially listed under the PMA. That only roughly 30 percent had done so demonstrates Townsend's success at promoting the school with other missions. The rest were scattered about with other missions, including 7 with the CAM, 6 with the South American Indian Mission, 5 with the Assemblies of God, 4 with the C&MA, 4 with AIM, and 4 with Presbyterian boards.[57]

Also in 1941 two events of tremendous historical import for the history of SIL took place. First, Townsend ceded control of the academic side of the work to Ken Pike. Townsend always favored the pioneering aspects of the work in Mexico or elsewhere in Latin America to the academic training at home. But as it was primarily his vision, he had maintained control for the first few years of its existence. But in 1941 what had long been obvious in practice became true in fact. Townsend wrote, "In view of the great stress which must be placed upon the scientific part of the work, and in view of the fact that I am not only lacking in training along that line but also feel that my special calling is pioneer work on the mission field itself, I am asking the Institute staff to elect Dr. Kenneth L. Pike to be director of the Summer Institute of Linguistics in my stead." For the next three decades the two men steered the organization together, Pike taking charge of the academic side of the work and Townsend the oversight of the work on the field, particularly its expansion into new territory. Never the best of friends, but always deep admirers of each other's gifts, the two men shared a general vision for the work, even as they often argued bitterly over the details.[58]

The organization received an enormous boost in 1941 when the University of Oklahoma at Norman invited SIL to begin holding its summer sessions on its campus. Della Brunsteter, a faculty member at Oklahoma, met Pike at Michigan, then visited Camp Wycliffe in Arkansas and was so impressed that she insisted the university extend the invitation. Townsend was initially reluctant because of the ramifications of moving the operation to a major secular university. He also worried that the accommodations would hinder the "training in hard knocks" he so valued for his pioneer missionaries. "We are very hesitant . . . about going to the University," he reported to the PMA, "and are only considering it because they have been so insistent that we begin to think that perhaps God has a purpose in it."[59] (Townsend solved his "hard knocks training" problem by founding a jungle training camp in Chiapas in southern Mexico in 1944.)

Pike and Nida both visited the university in the fall of 1941. The president of the university seemed "quite interested." Nida offered them three hundred hours of teaching to their students and SIL's help to foster interest in linguistics and in native American cultures on campus in exchange for housing, dining, and classroom facilities, and access to the library and athletic building. He also requested college credit for "those of collegiate standing." The ABS was in favor of the move, and Nida also noticed that the Oklahoma invitation "seemed to carry considerable weight" with the mission boards. By December they had decided to accept the offer. The university offered to help in publicity as well, although that suggestion made even more delicate the problem of how to explain the relationship between the secular university and the missionary organization. The SIL seems to have worried about this more than the university, however, and in 1949 the university asked to be explicitly named in SIL's publications. "It is my understanding that this has not been done in the past because you have felt that it would be presumptuous on your part," the university president wrote to Pike. "May I assure you that the University would be only too pleased and would be highly honored to have its name associated with your scholarly publications."[60]

That first summer at the University of Oklahoma, the student body more than doubled. One hundred and thirty students attended SIL's Camp Wycliffe as sponsored by the university. Pike and Townsend were forced to recall SIL members from Mexico in order to help with the teaching. More than twenty mission boards were represented. Townsend managed to recruit almost forty new translators for Mexico from the student body. The high-profile move to a university campus, the closing of many missionary fields as a result of the world war and the consequent number of missionaries forced to remain at home, and Townsend's constant promotion of the institute for a decade combined to produce the explosive growth.[61]

Although the army took over Oklahoma's campus for the next two summers, SIL remained in Oklahoma at Bacone College in Muskogee, where it continued to enjoy large numbers. One hundred and forty-five students attended classes at Bacone in 1944; twenty-six mission boards were represented, including the China Inland Mission. When the war ended, SIL moved back to the campus at Norman, where it continued to prosper. In 1949 more than 225 students attended the summer session.[62]

In 1943 Oswald Smith, pastor of the large and influential Peoples Church in Toronto, who had become an important supporter of the new mission, urged Townsend to open a summer linguistics camp in Canada. He gave notice that his church would support all the Canadians from Camp Wycliffe who were accepted by SIL for work in Mexico.[63] Townsend, who had long wanted to expand the work, needed no second invitation. The first Canadian SIL was held at Briercrest Bible Institute in 1944 with forty students, the first year in which SIL operated schools in two locations. The Canadian SIL was just the first of many such expansions.

Women had long played a major role in the missionary enterprise, even as mission leaders treated them with a degree of condescension. Women could function as wives at mission stations and could undertake educational work and outreach to other women. But the evangelistic trips, street preaching, and church planting had always been left to the men. Single women were under a double burden to prove their worth. They had no husbands to give them automatic entrée to the field, and as women, unless they were exceptionally thick-skinned and rugged, their work would be limited in scope. The faith missions had cracked open the door, permitting women more freedom than the traditional boards, but even there, as we have seen, they were viewed with a certain ambivalence.

Townsend's vision for training rugged pioneer missionaries had little room for women, at least initially. Legters did not approve of single women "doing that kind of work"—that is, living alone or in pairs in rugged Indian country. Camp Wycliffe was designed for men. When a married couple attended the second summer session, he attended classes at camp while she took some of the courses at home. Early advertisements called for "single men between the ages of twenty and thirty" to apply.[64]

Still, with so much against them, women hammered down the door to get into SIL. In many ways Camp Wycliffe served as a vehicle for empowering women who longed to serve as missionaries. The classrooms at Camp Wycliffe established an empirical, rather than ideological, basis for judging their capabilities, and as quickly as they could earn A's and B's in linguistics classes they poured into Mexico and challenged Townsend to send them to remote areas along with the men. Women as well as men came back from Mexico to teach at sessions of Camp Wycliffe, served as translation consultants and literacy administrators, and earned PhDs in linguistics.

Elvira was the first woman to take a class at Camp Wycliffe. She sat in on McCreery's phonetics classes in 1935. That same year a "prominent Bible teacher" urged Townsend to establish a similar training camp "for young ladies." In 1936 Camp Wycliffe accepted its first "girls" into its girls' camp, a few miles removed from the men's camp. Townsend explained that the girls' camp was "undertaken only after many requests had been made for us to provide the same opportunity for young women who desired to enter pioneer missionary work as we did for young men." The recruiting focus remained on men, however. "The opening of a young women's section of Camp was highly satisfactory," Townsend informed Elvira's brother. "I feel that the section should be continued another year, though, in view of the greater lack of men volunteers than of women, the emphasis should be placed upon raising men recruits[,] while the number of women accepted should be considerably smaller than that of the men."[65]

Rafael Ramírez, Mexico's director of rural education, may have been the first to actually suggest that single women work in Indian villages. In 1936 he offered salaries with his department to Townsend's niece and a friend if they "were to go to an Indian town to work." That fall Townsend brought three single women graduates of Camp Wycliffe to Mexico. Eunice Pike (Ken's sister and, like her brother, a gifted linguist) and Florence Hansen were the first single women to reside in an Indian village and take up linguistic work. Townsend permitted them to go only after they suggested he lacked the faith that God could protect women as well as men in rugged living conditions. They settled with the Mazatecos, a full day by horseback from the nearest railroad station.[66]

Townsend's acquiescence to the will of the single women caused a good deal of controversy in the early years of the new mission. Miss Yost, the director of the girls' Camp Wycliffe in 1936, was opposed to "girls so young and untrained" going to Mexico. She informed Legters that Florence Hansen was "too good looking to be a missionary." Ken Pike also mentioned in a letter the "trouble" Townsend faced, "what with some objection to the girls." Townsend, however, held true to faith mission ideas of discovering God's will. Who was he to tell Hansen and Pike they could not go if they were convinced it was God's will for them? "Those of us who have wondered just what place single lady missionaries might have in our project have learned from this lesson that God has heroines today," he informed the Pioneer Mission Agency. The decision was hard on Legters. "I have fear about some of the girls which have been sent out," he grumbled to Townsend. "When I left Camp I took my hands off them and left it to the Lord, but personally I have fear for their future. It may be old age creeping upon me."[67]

Once women had been accepted, however, and had excelled in their studies and avoided disaster in Mexico, there was no compelling reason to turn back. The flyer advertising 1937's Camp Wycliffe offered positions to "men and women," if still somewhat grudgingly. "A Girl's Camp operated a few miles from the Men's Camp, but with classes together, makes it possible to take in a few young women." The next year all talk of a separate girls' camp ceased. By 1940 all mention of men or women dropped out of the publicity material. "All persons are invited to apply who are going to pioneer fields where the language work is not yet finished," read the brochure.[68]

By the fall of 1940 there were five pairs of single women in their early twenties living with Indians in Mexico. In February 1941, out of 37 linguists in Mexico with SIL, 11 were single women. Overall, 22 of 37 members were women. An organization that had been founded only seven years earlier as an all-male affair was now 60 percent female. The ratio of women to men held steady as the mission grew. With 122 members in the fall of 1944, one-third were single women, and overall, two-thirds were female. Some single women spent months alone when a partner was forced to leave the village, and the mission was even considering allowing single women to live alone in a village before finding a partner.[69]

At the 1940 camp, Eunice Pike assisted her brother in teaching phonetics; Florence Hansen assisted Nida in teaching linguistics; Elvira taught Spanish; and Mrs. Legters taught archeology. By 1952 the faculty at SIL numbered twenty, ten of whom were women.[70]

8
In Which Townsend Goes Pioneering, Makes Some Strange Bedfellows, and Starts an Odd New Mission

1935–1945

I know each of you must feel as we do—that you have the best location, the finest people to work with, and that you have been of all people most signally blessed.

—David Brainerd Legters

In the fall of 1935 an old Buick pulling a small house trailer parked in the dusty square in the small Indian village of Tetelcingo, sixty miles south of Mexico City. It was two years after Cameron Townsend and L. L. Legters first crossed the border, and Townsend had been writing articles about Mexico ever since. It was one year after the first Camp Wycliffe. Ken Pike had just attended the second Camp Wycliffe that summer. It was only a few months after President Lázaro Cárdenas received the resignation of his cabinet, prompting prayer at Camp Wycliffe that the door might be opened to Mexico. In what Townsend certainly saw as an answer to that prayer, government officials had finally granted him permission to enter the country for the purpose of studying an Indian language. He deliberately picked Tetelcingo, knowing its reputation for being the most primitive ("backward" was the word more often used) "Aztec" settlement in the state of Morelos. Here he could be certain of hearing the indigenous language; only the mayor spoke Spanish. And here he could demonstrate to Mexican officials that true religion would aid, not hinder, the revolution's attempt to better the lives of the Indians. "It's a miserable little town," he told Karl Hummel, "but we hope, by God's grace, to change it."[1]

Before long Townsend had put together a literacy primer in the local language, and the Department of Education printed five thousand of them to be used throughout the state. An avid amateur farmer (his journals and letters are filled with horticultural notes), Townsend planted a vegetable garden and began to introduce the villagers to lettuce, radishes, celery, and beets. Soon flowers decorated the village square, and fruit trees, donated by Ramírez, shaded a makeshift park. By the end of the year word had reached President Cárdenas about the "backward" village in Morelos where a gringo, with the help of several of his own officials, had launched precisely the kind of makeover envisioned by the Department of Education.[2]

"Yesterday [January 21, 1936] we had a surprise," began Elvira's report to Moody Church in Chicago. "None other than the President of Mexico himself . . . came here to our humble, little makeshift home. We had a delightful visit with President Cárdenas, a most pleasant man to know. He was so interested in what we were doing for the betterment of the town."[3] Cárdenas spent an hour looking over the Townsends' work, and each man came away thoroughly impressed by the other. A lifelong friendship formed immediately.

Townsend was thrilled to have as a benefactor the "peasant president," widely known for his genuine commitment to the welfare of those in Mexico who had been exploited for so long, primarily the Indians. On his legendary travels through Mexico's backcountry, for hours at each stop, and unprotected by bodyguards, he patiently listened to the needs of the people. They returned his affection, as the title of a recent book about Cárdenas, *As if Jesus Walked on Earth,* accurately reflects. Cárdenas's integrity, his commitment to the poor, his refusal to profit personally from his political position, and his opposition to the liquor trade and gambling houses, all had immense appeal for a conservative Protestant. Townsend wrote, "I don't know whether [Cárdenas] is a Christian or not[,] but I do wish that my life were as Christlike." Townsend's admiration for the man heightened his passion for Mexico and the ideals of the revolution. A few days after their meeting in Tetelcingo, Townsend wrote to Cárdenas, "If before having the pleasure of knowing you, I loved and admired the revolutionary work of Mexico, now, upon knowing its highest representative personally I feel more intimately identified with her and more resolved and determined in service."[4]

As for Cárdenas, he found in Townsend a hands-on ally in his program for the Indians who was willing to actually live in a remote village and oversee a program of "social betterment." In the years ahead Cárdenas would apply to Townsend a word often used of himself, a word that resonated in the idealistic circle of Mexican politics. The word was *desinteresado,* or "disinterested," as in "the disinterested efforts that the Townsend family is developing in behalf of

11. Mexican President Lázaro Cárdenas. Courtesy Townsend Archives.

the town." The word seemed to have much the same meaning for Mexicans of the revolutionary generation as it did for the leaders of the American Revolution. It implied a certain noblesse oblige, the giving of oneself to public service with no intention of self-aggrandizement, and no better word could be applied to anyone in Mexico during the presidency of Cárdenas. At any rate, a responsible, experienced, on-site overseer was simply too good to pass up. Cárdenas seems to have decided on the spot to make Tetelcingo a model community. He ordered up two hundred more fruit trees for immediate delivery and virtually gave Townsend a blank check with several government agencies to rebuild the town. As Elvira wonderingly reported to Moody Church, "He . . . promise[d] . . . everything needed to make this backward village an example for others."[5]

What was more, Townsend wanted to recruit other Americans for the same work. Upon assurances from Townsend that any others he might bring would engage in the same type of social service, Cárdenas gave him free rein to bring in as many workers as he could recruit, pledging his administration to give them "every aid which might be necessary." Cárdenas himself oversaw the placement of some of the recruits and took a personal interest in their work, providing throughout his administration a small stipend as "rural school teachers" for the majority of the early recruits. Often the incoming recruits were feted at the presidential palace before departing to their assigned villages. The nine-course dinners left the rather humble evangelicals "walking on air," even as the presence of alcohol put more than a few fundamentalist consciences into a tizzy.[6]

It is also quite possible that Cárdenas was genuinely interested in SIL's religious work. Townsend seems to have convinced him at some point that the Bible might have a positive moral effect, and he presented his work as both scientific and socialistic. As Marjorie Becker has shown, eventually the *Cardenistas* had to come to terms with the religiosity of Mexico's peasants, who were simply not willing to part with their syncretic Catholicism. Cárdenas may have been persuaded by Townsend's argument that the Bible would provide a religious antidote to the peasants' obscurantism, superstition, and fanaticism. Anything that distanced them from the Catholic Church was seen as a positive influence by the *Cardenistas.* Cárdenas could relax the anti-clericalism of his predecessor Calles, a popular move internationally, while still encouraging a counter to what was seen as the backward fanaticism of the Catholic Church. In addition, Townsend and SIL provided an antidote for the argument that Mexico was against religion. A decade later, when Manuel Gamio, the prominent Mexican anthropologist, attended a reunion at Columbia University, he found himself forced to defend Mexico's stand on religion. While agreeing that Calles had fallen into "certain unnecessary exaggerations," he mentioned the work of SIL as the kind of religious effort the Mexican government could embrace. He told Townsend that he was pleasantly surprised to find that "many people knew something of what you do[,] and those that were unacquainted with your work expressed their approval when I explained to them the religious but nonsectarian nature of your work, the scientific and at the same time practical and constructive program of the Institute." His audience was also impressed to hear of how Cárdenas had embraced SIL.[7]

The Cárdenas-Townsend friendship continued to grow over the years. Cárdenas frequently invited him to join his traveling party. (Townsend got to know Frank Tannenbaum, another frequent Cárdenas invitee, quite well on these trips.) Cárdenas's wife, Amalia, befriended Elvira, and on several occasions the couples vacationed together. Always concerned about the Townsends' health, Cárdenas often offered one of his homes as a vacation spot, insisting they get away from the pressures of Tetelcingo. At one point Cárdenas sent them twenty-five hundred pesos to build a nice house in Tetelcingo, a significant gift in a village where two hundred pesos could build a decent home. The Townsends used the money to build ten small houses for the caretakers of the five-thousand-tree orange grove recently planted, at Cameron's request, along the federal highway.[8]

What Townsend accomplished in just the next six months, with the considerable help of several government agencies, is quite remarkable. His report to Cárdenas in June 1936 listed forty-three completed and ongoing projects, including a better road to the town (the residents did not want the president to suffer so many bumps the next time he visited), a siphon irrigation system for the new park, literacy campaigns, new crops introduced to the region via a model farm, the school repaired and resupplied, several dairy cows and pigs purchased, a barber shop constructed and supplied, new uniforms for the town basketball team, a truck donated, a large clock placed on the square (so that the school could follow regular hours), and other improvements. Within a year better drinking water had been secured, a laundry built, and two small houses for a community center donated by American ambassador Josephus Daniels. Unfortunately, Townsend had to be gone during the summers, and inevitably when he returned, he found things in disrepair. Without continual supervision, Townsend learned (as have so many with good intentions through the years) that it is much easier to build someone a house than to convince him he really ought to use it. Still, Townsend continued working. In 1938 he was trying to get silkworms established in Tetelcingo. The town continued to be a model community long after Cárdenas left office. SIL members all contributed from their own funds to keep projects going there, as it was close to Mexico City and a place frequently visited by officials. They operated co-ops to sell supplies at reasonable rates to the villagers, and instituted a "little mail-order mercantile service for isolated Indians, in cooperation with the Mexican Government."[9]

In his town Pike juggled all sorts of projects, including agriculture, digging wells, and, one of the community's favorites, sign painting for municipal offices so that people would know what went on there. After painting a few, he soon had everyone asking him to make a sign for them. Pike found the Mexican officials to be extremely grateful for the work SIL members did in the villages. "They do not demand, but are excessively pleased (according to our standards) by a little in the way of manual things we can do for the people. . . . They are happy to see us wrap up people's stubbed toes, and start a little garden, add a little bit of culture, or carpentry, or music, or anything at all." Many of the revolutionary leaders had Indian blood, so "to work with the Indian [was] to work with their folks." As the Mexican leaders found it very difficult to get their own

12. Townsend on his front porch in Tetelcingo, Mexico, studying the Aztec language. Courtesy Townsend Archives.

people to live in Indian villages, it "seemed to them a miracle" that Americans, "carrying legends of fabulous wealth and jobs in their own country," would do what few of them would do themselves.[10]

When the novelist and somewhat jaundiced adventurer Max Miller visited Tetelcingo in 1936, after hearing in a bar that there he would "have a sight of the true primitive," he was disappointed to discover that he could drive right to the spot and that an American had already been living there for a year. Although "William Thompson" was not there, Miller decided it was obvious the people loved the "Professor of Languages" because of the "hallowed way they spoke of him." He figured his own pleasant reception was "probably due to the fact I was coasting on the crest of his wave."[11]

Townsend quickly set about impressing the Mexicans with his serious linguistic intentions. By the fall of 1935 he was already using *Instituto Linguistico de Verano* (Summer Institute of Linguistics) stationery. Although it would be another year before an official field organization became necessary when the PMA desired a responsible organization in Mexico to which it would relate as fundraiser, Townsend needed a home organization that sounded both academic and nonthreatening. The "linguistic institute" impressed Mexican officials with his genuine desire to undertake serious linguistic work, while "summer" was chosen over "international" because it sounded less pretentious. While Cárdenas was most interested in the village development work, Mexican academics were eager to enlist SIL's help in investigating the numerous Indian languages. A Mexican linguistic society, the *Instituto Mexicano de Investigaciones Lingüisticas* (IMIL), had recently been organized, and the Ministry of Education requested that it prepare primers to teach the Indians to read in their own languages. The director, Dr. Mariano Silva y Aceves, asked Townsend to cooperate in the effort. He was also elected to membership in the society. "The secretary delivered quite an oration . . . welcoming me to membership [and] upon concluding crossed the room and threw his arms around me in a warm embrace," Townsend reported to Legters. "He . . . said that I was no longer a foreigner but a brother Indian."[12]

Most of the early Mexico recruits were forced to interact with the Mexican academy on a fairly regular basis. Genaro Vásquez, the secretary of labor, gave Ken Pike a commission to conduct a study regarding the living conditions of indigenous workers. A letter from Vásquez asked the civil and military authorities to grant him all necessary assistance. He also traveled with a letter from Dr. Aceves authorizing him to study Mixteco and make a "summary of linguistic materials" to be published in the magazine put out by the IMIL. Aceves also asked the civil and military authorities to lend Pike the necessary facilities "given the scientific character of this commission." In April 1936 Townsend, introduced as "the distinguished philologist and North American Indianista," gave a series of seminars sponsored by the IMIL on his Cakchiquel work. At times he, Pike, and others taught courses at the Mexican National University. The SIL and the IMIL jointly published several linguistic journals and sponsored linguistic conferences. Many of the translators assisted the government in Indian literacy campaigns. Most at one time or another translated Cárdenas's speeches addressed to indigenous groups. Elvira, of all people, authored a book on "Latin American Courtesy," which was published by the IMIL in conjunction with SIL.[13] All of these activities occurred in just the first decade of SIL's existence in Mexico.

In many ways the Mexicans themselves were responsible for giving shape to the new mission. They took Townsend at his word and employed SIL's missionary linguists in their own interests. The pressure that men like Pike, Townsend, and Nida felt from Mexican and American academics to produce solid academic work prompted them to increase the pressure on their recruits to "publish or perish." If SIL had been founded in a country with a less interested or less developed academy, it may quickly have devoted itself entirely to Bible translation and neglected serious linguistics. As it was, SIL's leaders had to push new recruits hard, often literally forcing them to produce linguistic material. Richard

Pittman, Townsend's associate director in Mexico for many years, admonished the group, "[Our motto should be]: 'Prepare to Publish.' By that, I am not thinking primarily of our Scripture publications, but scientific publications."[14] Most recruits, even after graduation from Camp Wycliffe, had dreams of converts, rather than of grammatical analyses, dancing in their heads. It would require several generations, and the development of a more educated evangelical constituency in the United States, before recruits with a genuine interest in linguistics for its own sake began applying to SIL.

Townsend found that if SIL upheld its end of the bargain, the government officials tended to look benignly on Bible translation. "The President of the Republic is well informed of our spiritual objectives," Townsend reported to the PMA. "He even told me that the agencies which should undertake the liberation of the Indians of South America are the Gospel Missions. Many of the officials consider us missionaries. This does not seem to affect their friendship toward us in the least." An official in the Ministry of Education remarked to Townsend, "I hope the day will come when there will be a Protestant pastor among all the Ind[ian] tribes of Mex[ico] so as to give the Indians a more decent religion."[15]

Townsend had more trouble with his own group than he did with the Mexicans. Pushing recruits trained at places like the Moody Bible Institute to radically transcend their ideological boundaries remained a problem for Townsend and SIL for several more decades. Joining SIL was a far cry from the "evangelism only" missions they heard from in chapel. Townsend did not even permit his recruits to engage in open evangelism until they had thoroughly learned the indigenous languages; even then they were not to take part in church services. A number of the early recruits, especially the seminary-trained men, balked at cooperation with a "heathen" government. On that point they stood with most evangelical missions. The Africa Inland Mission, for example, felt it had to be constantly "vigilant against government control and the diluting of its commitment to evangelism."[16] Some left SIL because of its policies and joined other missions; others simply made Townsend's life miserable over the issue. After the first year receiving the government salaries as rural schoolteachers, Townsend did not reapply for the stipends as the law required, because of the objections of some of his men over receiving such funds. When the government renewed the stipends anyway, the grumbling quieted briefly.

Townsend continued to insist on his policy of cooperation with governments and scientific organizations until it became standard operating procedure for SIL. Townsend declared he intended to work with "worldly men and even atheists," as long as the cooperation with them was constructive to his program of "linguistic research and unselfish service." Such cooperation," he argued, "has never been destructive to our faith or morals." When the Mexican congress proposed a new law opposing religious schools, the issue flared up again. Townsend pleaded with his people not to openly oppose government policies, arguing that they should at least remain neutral if they could not cooperate. "Why should we be alarmed over a law which may be passed which will prohibit religious schools?" he wrote to the group. "Did any of us go to Mexico to found religious schools? Of course not.... We are in Mexico to serve and not to dictate policies to the Government." Townsend put his typical positive spin on the issue. "If [the congress] wants to teach the children of Mexico to share with one another as sincere socialists should, that is Mexico's lookout and not ours. We should be more anxious than ever to give the word of God to the people, for it is the best preparation in the world for sharing." He concluded, "If the policy of cooperation leads me a little further afield from the direct task of Scripture translation than the rest of you, please be lenient in judging me, for I have prayed carefully over each step and am confident that He has led me to do it for your sakes and the gospel's."[17] While Townsend could be naive at times about the actions and motives of Latin American governments, his sincerity and genuine affection for Latin Americans gave him access and influence far beyond most, if not all, missionaries before him.

Each fall the new recruits from Camp Wycliffe entered Mexico with Townsend. Residency papers awaited them at the border courtesy of the Mexican government. Often their first few days in Mexico City included trips to the presidential palace and to the residency of American ambassador Josephus Daniels. The entire group, including those who had spent the past year in an Indian village, then met for conference. The new workers were given their assignments, or rather, an assignment was negotiated between God, Townsend, the executive committee, and the new recruit. Although Townsend was sensitive to an individual's leading from God, he well knew the problems such leading could generate. Notes from a meeting in 1939 read, "It was suggested that it be drawn up definitely as a policy of our organization that obviously in Christian work the Lord leads the individual, but for the sake of binding the whole together the individual should be subject to the group." This was an especially acute problem for SIL, which had a tenuous position in Mexico and was embarking on a unique project. One member who refused to follow the rules could jeopardize the position and the legitimacy of the entire group. The SIL was a mission with multiple constituencies, both religious and secular. It had to communicate legitimately to both; hence its unique corporate culture.[18]

Whenever submitting to leadership presented a problem for a young recruit, as, being evangelicals weaned on faith mission models, this did from time to time, Townsend pointed the new missionary to New Testament passages that urged Christians to "obey them that have the rule over you." If the recruit continued to push, he often replied with some version of the following question, which for an evangelical proved very difficult to answer. "If we are so much in error," he asked, "why does God bless us so much?" A successful, growing, and prosperous organization was prima facie evidence that a leader had heard the voice of God and therefore was more than likely someone who ought to be listened to.[19]

Once all agreed on God's will in the matter, an experienced worker took the young couple or two single women into Indian country, where they began the process of finding a suitable village in which to live. It took some as much as a week of travel by train, bus, truck, horseback, or on foot to reach their proposed village. The new missionary might find the indigenous group welcoming, hostile, fearful, or indifferent. "More of the Indians are friendly though the majority still think we're there to kill [and] eat them!" reported one fresh recruit.[20] Once settled, the recruits waved good-bye to the experienced worker and spent their first night alone in an Indian village where no one spoke English and few knew Spanish. Accommodations were usually extremely primitive. The arduous, lonely, and at times tremendously rewarding process of learning an unwritten language began.

Initial enthusiasm usually carried fresh workers through the first few months at least. Giddy letters poured into headquarters, and Elvira extracted the most interesting quotes and typed them into a circular that made the rounds of the entire group. The young missionaries argued about who had landed among the "cream of the tribes." David Brainerd Legters spoke for most when he wrote, "I know each of you must feel as we do—that you have the best location, the finest people to work with, and that you have been of all people most signally blessed." Many found they even enjoyed the struggle to learn a new language. Ken Pike's letters, as might be expected, were filled with linguistic notes, but others with less aptitude expressed similar sentiments. "As for the language, I love it!" wrote Florence Hansen. "[T]he plaza, on Sunday, which is the market day here, sounds like a continual nasal song."[21]

Inevitably the work turned out to be much more difficult than anticipated. Townsend always woefully underestimated the time required to complete a translation of the New Testament, but even Pike initially thought the process would require about ten years in each tribe.[22] It was probably good that no one at the time knew that most translators would require closer to thirty years. That Townsend had completed his Cakchiquel translation in ten was more an indication of its poor quality than his genius. As SIL increased its linguistic expertise, quality control on translation work became much more exacting.

Few young evangelicals ever dreamed of missionary work being this difficult. The missionary stories they had heard in their youth were of preaching, teaching, and conversions. To find themselves stuck at a desk learning a tonal language filled with sounds their mouths simply could not make was not their idea of missionary work. In addition, Townsend asked them to refrain from sharing their faith until they could do it adequately in the Indian language. They were not ever to conduct public meetings or work openly in churches. They were scientists and were expected to conduct themselves as such. Open proselytizing might jeopardize the position of the group with the Mexican government. At least one translator was briefly jailed for witnessing in Spanish. Furthermore, Townsend did not want his recruits forcing the new believers into denominational modes. He wanted to give indigenous groups the Bible and then let them affiliate as they wished, and he wanted the translators to be free to move on to another group when they finished one translation.[23]

As the initial enthusiasm wore off, letters to headquarters often sounded a more realistic note. "At times we confess we wished for relief, even if it were to go home to Heaven," wrote one. "It was not a happy existence to be forbidden from telling others of Christ, or singing hymns so no one could hear, or camouflaging our purpose among the Indians." Some found their souls "withering from lack of fellowship" with other Christians. Perhaps more typical of a first-year translator was a sobering outline of early accomplishments that indicated a dawning understanding of just how long and difficult the process was going to be. A report to the PMA stated: "What God has accomplished through us may be summarized briefly. We believe that we have the main outlines of the tonal system. Our alphabet is complete except for half a dozen doubtful letters. We can hold a five minute's conversation besides knowing the common expressions of greeting, etc."[24]

By the second or third year the young missionaries had developed a fairly extensive catalog of words, which they turned into a dictionary. Often these early linguistic discoveries were published in Mexico, although Pike, mindful of the group's reputation at home, generally did not permit publication in English until the work was more polished. Many began translation work by the second or third year. It was good practice, even if the finished product was much too rough to be useful. The SIL worker usually hired a native speaker to help with the work. They communicated in broken Spanish until the American knew the Indian language. A portion of text might be read in Spanish; then the translator would try to help the "informant" understand what was being said. Once the Indian understood, he or she would interpret the text back to the translator in the indigenous language. (Bloomfield remarked that the process sounded like "trying to write Latin prose with a few peasants for helpers.") The process could be excruciating, especially the passages that dealt with theological topics. Eunice Pike remembered trying to find a word to use for "worship." She posed a series of questions to the Indian woman working with her: "Why do the people go to church? It is the fiesta of Saint So-and-So. What feeling do the people have toward the witch doctors? They are afraid. Why do the people use the parrot feathers? To cure them from sickness. How do we feel toward God? A look of bewildered longing comes over her face as she answers, I don't know."[25]

Translators continued to use informants even after learning the language fluently themselves. Often they checked their work with several informants, both men and women, to ensure their translation was correctly understood. The choice of informants was obviously critical, and the translators often went through several before finding one who enjoyed the work enough to stick at it. Dealing with drunk or otherwise unreliable informants was a frequent complaint.[26] Often, however, the informant became the first convert in the indigenous group and subsequently a leader in the fledgling church. They were also often the first to see the benefits of literacy.

By the third or fourth year, those translators who had not washed out early had settled into their new homes, and the tone of their letters, though not as giddy as in the first few months of their tenure, often expressed a real satisfaction in the work and a love for their new home and neighbors. One couple described how their front porch was a gathering place for the Indians, who were surprised when the missionaries now understood a "particularly savory piece of gossip." She conducted knitting and reading classes. They were known as "the gringos who speak our language," and people came from throughout the region for medical help "simply because we understand them." The Mexican government kept them supplied with quinine, and they used their own funds to add to their medical stores. By this time many had completed rough drafts of entire books. The way was led by the two single women, Florence Hansen and Eunice Pike, who finished a rough draft of I John and the Gospel of John in 1938. They finished a first draft of the entire New Testament in 1941.[27]

Townsend did not have to hide his light under a bushel in Tetelcingo as much as SIL members did elsewhere in Mexico. He was able to be much more open about his faith there because of the protection of President Cárdenas. He reported to the PMA, "We were able to teach the Word in a private, personal way with more liberty since President Cárdenas evidently had told his representative in the region that he wanted us to have a free chance to demonstrate the working power of the Gospel." Early converts were appreciative. One rewarded the Townsends with a large dish of cooked tadpoles. Within three years a former town mayor was pastoring a church of significant size in the small village.[28]

Elvira, too, adapted well to life in Tetelcingo. Townsend's niece, who lived with them for a time in Mexico, reported that Elvira was a "splendid hostess," with a well-appointed table and a house that was neat to a fault. She kept the family accounts meticulously. Her circulars to the new recruits were a model of encouragement and piety. Townsend's niece remembered that although she was usually pleasant, "every once in a while, unexpectedly or with very little warning, she would become very angry and lash out at people. I think she never lashed out at me physically, but she did toward Uncle Cam with fists and kicks." She thought that Cameron was "very attentive" to Elvira, although candidly admitting, "Now I do know that Uncle Cam, with his singleness of purpose and relentless drive, wasn't always easy to live with. Any one of us working with him knew that; we had to modify our actions accordingly."[29]

As busy as Townsend was with his projects in Tetelcingo and Camp Wycliffe, and with administrative work for his growing mission, he always found time for idealistic schemes to promote better relationships between Mexico and the United States. Bound for the States for the first time since meeting the Mexican president, Townsend wrote Cárdenas that he was going to tour eight southern states, "speaking in some Universities and informing the newspapers about the vast program that you are developing in favor of the masses." He requested literature and photographs taken on Cárdenas's most recent tours, which were immediately provided. A pattern was established. Whenever Townsend traveled in America, he combined recruitment and fund-raising for SIL and Camp Wycliffe with advocacy for Cárdenas and Mexico. On this trip he contributed a long editorial to the *Tulsa Daily World* responding to accusations that ex-president Calles had recently made during a trip to that city. The editorial, awkwardly titled "Commoner, Not Communist, Is Cárdenas," stressed the themes that Townsend enunciated wherever he went—how Cárdenas's personal qualities of honesty, fairness, and compassion had turned Mexico into a more democratic society. Cárdenas was not a Communist, simply a man doing everything possible to right the wrongs that the centuries had exacted of Mexico's indigenous population. He was a man of the people, traveling and meeting them incessantly, without ostentation, hardworking, the "Lincoln of Mexico." Townsend also wrote an article to promote Mexican tourism. In glowing terms he outlined Mexico's many "enchantments" and "low rates." Describing the descent from the air into Mexico City, he wrote, "[T]he winged monster crosses over [the mountains'] shoulder and glides down to rest upon the broad valley, once a lake, where lies Mexico City, the Paris of America." He turned serious in closing, chiding Americans who criticized Mexico, not "appreciating that Mexico is now vibrant with plans to uplift her underprivileged classes and to amalgamate them into the culture of the nation." The Mexican Revolution "too often goes uncomprehended," he wrote, and pictured it as the "rumbling and roar of an irresistible forward surge of humanity, the crusade of a people such as history seldom records." Townsend argued that good neighbors "refuse to meddle in family affairs. . . . The first step in neighborliness is to get acquainted, so come on, ye million tourists! See Mexico, study her and really come to know her."[30]

During the summer of 1937, Elvira was the one on the road, recruiting for SIL and speaking about Mexico. She concentrated on SIL's natural evangelical constituency, speaking in churches, schools, and over the radio. Townsend's strategy was to focus on Cárdenas's "personal qualities and humanitarian goals," ideals much admired by evangelicals. He reported that everywhere his wife went "[h]er favorite topic was . . . THE PRESIDENT OF MEXICO," and the reaction she received was "very favorable."[31] The Townsends had the potential to reach an untapped audience for Mexico. Rhetoric such as the Townsends' was used in the 1930s only by the American left. Cárdenas knew he would need more than the left on his side in the difficult days ahead.

On a Saturday late in February 1938 Cárdenas and Townsend relaxed on folding chairs in the shade behind the Townsends' trailer in Tetelcingo. They had just finished lunch with Cárdenas and his wife, and now the president seemed to want to talk. (Cárdenas had sent an aide the day before to request that Townsend do Cárdenas "the favor [as the aide put it] of inviting him to dine with you tomorrow.") The president explained at length the trouble he had been having with the American and British oil companies, who refused to come to terms with the Mexican labor unions, even defying a Supreme Court–mandated wage increase. He seemed to suggest to Townsend that if the oil companies did not comply, drastic action would be taken. He clearly hinted that while he had confidence in the people of America, he needed help reaching them with the facts of the case. Before leaving that evening, the reflective president told Townsend how much his friendship had meant to him and that he hoped it would continue when he was out of office. Cárdenas then gave Townsend the ceremonial fountain pen with which he had signed all of his documents and decrees since becoming president. He told Townsend that the pen had given away more land to the poor than any pen in Mexican history.[32]

A few weeks later Townsend was in the national palace overlooking the *Plaza de la Constitución,* where hour after hour thousands of Mexicans in a patriotic frenzy marched beneath the balcony where Cárdenas stood. The previous Friday, March 18, Cárdenas had electrified the nation by nationalizing the oil companies, igniting patriotic fervor in Mexico and the most serious crisis with its northern neighbor since the early days of the revolution. Cárdenas's expropriation marked the "first major act of its kind," the first time foreign oil companies had been expelled from an underdeveloped country in the name of national sovereignty. Townsend was at a desk in a room off the balcony frantically writing an article in support of Mexico's sudden move. In the United States articles were also being written. In the months and years ahead the Mexican situation would be hashed and rehashed in the nation's papers. The oil companies poured a great deal of money into a propaganda offensive arguing that Uncle Sam should compel the return of their property, to "teach the Greasers 'Thou Shalt Not Steal.'" Standard Oil published and distributed a free paper called "The Lamp," which tried to inflame public opinion against Mexico and "degenerated to . . . abuse of all things Mexican." The *Atlantic Monthly* devoted an entire issue in July to "Trouble below the Border," an issue that Ambassador Daniels recalled was "devoted to misrepresentation and slander and hate," and in which "[e]very page smelled of oil."[33]

Moisés Sáenz warned Cárdenas that "the situation requires neutralization abroad, especially in the United States." He offered to go immediately to the States and begin a two-pronged offensive. The first would "attack the question head-on . . . not avoiding polemic if the situation calls for it." The second would "present Mexico in non-controversial aspects (tourism, education) to promote good will toward the country."[34]

Given this climate, Cárdenas readily accepted Townsend's offer to travel to the States on a similar mission. Armed with funds from Cárdenas to purchase a new car (Elvira was a heart patient, and Cárdenas did not want her riding trains) and a letter from Ambassador Daniels to Roosevelt's appointment secretary, the Townsends set off for the United States. While Townsend worked the East, Elvira and a friend (another heart patient) worked the Midwest. At some point, Townsend's activity on Mexico's behalf brought him to the attention of the FBI, and agents began tailing him around the country. Eventually, after ascertaining that he was a loyal citizen, they contemplated attempting to turn him into an agent to gather information about Cárdenas and Mexico. There is no indication that anyone ever contacted Townsend for that purpose, and he certainly would not have agreed if asked.[35]

Elvira made up a one-page flyer complete with Mexican flag and newspaper headlines as talking points. With Mrs. Cárdenas keeping her occasionally supplied with new material, she spoke up to five times a week at places like John Brown College in Arkansas, Christian conferences, women's clubs, and churches throughout the Midwest. Combining her missionary experiences in Mexico with personal stories about the Cárdenases, she undoubtedly presented a compelling case for Midwestern Protestants to support Mexico in its current troubles. She reported that "most of our people" take a "sympathetic stand" once they understand the true facts. Members of SIL traveling in other parts of the country reported similar sentiments.[36]

Townsend had a more discouraging trip. Unable to see Roosevelt, he had to settle for writing the president and secretary of state Cordell Hull long letters complaining of America's treatment of Mexico and beseeching the government to turn a deaf ear to the "monied interests" and their "hog-it-all-or-cut-your-throat" tactics. He managed to get an audience with a Standard Oil executive, who listened politely then responded that Standard Oil intended to continue fighting to get its property back.[37]

Townsend also spoke to evangelical audiences wherever he could. By the end of the summer he figured he and Elvira had spoken more than eighty times to religious audiences. Handwritten notes allow us to reconstruct some of what Townsend may have said. His notes begin, "Christian travelers and missionaries often find it necessary to correct false reports published by unscrupulous newspaper correspondents concerning foreign lands where they journey or live. In fact, it is hard to see how they could call themselves Christian if they did not, for to remain silent when one hears his neighbor falsely spoken of is hardly loving others as one's self." Citing the *Atlantic Monthly* issue devoted to an attack on Mexico, he went on to complain of the hypocrisy of pretending a "Good Neighbor" policy in the midst of such unfriendly activity. Mexico, he said, has been patient, "realizing that selfish trusts were behind it all," and that when the American public learned the facts they would "react in a friendly way." He then challenged his audience, saying it was time for evangelicals in the United States to demonstrate Christlike friendship to Mexico, where "for centuries selfish exploitation both in religion and economics" has left such friendship in short supply. Essentially, he was asking evangelicals to support the interests of a foreign country over the interests of their own. He closed with personal reminisces about Cárdenas. Townsend's message was a brilliant mix of populist sentiment, devotion to fair play and the underdog, and an appeal to Christian and missionary idealism.[38]

Townsend continued to write articles, although as he wearily reported to the secretary of the American Bible Society in Mexico, "some [have] been published[,] but most . . . have been rejected due to the fact that the editors feel that I simply cannot be right in view of the tremendous amount of literature they read from other sources which tells another story." Frustrated, Townsend wrote to Cárdenas that he felt that if he could just get the information to them, 80 percent of Americans would agree that Mexico was in the right. "But how can one inform them of the truth," he complained, "when the press is capitalistic and twists the news?" Townsend's solution was to suggest publishing a magazine to send to congressmen, university presidents, libraries, and prominent individuals. Townsend's "magazine" turned into an eighty-five-page booklet, *The Truth about Mexico's Oil.* Friends helped him publish one thousand copies; every congressman received one. The booklet was a remarkably thorough airing of the history of the entire conflict, the expressed purpose being to "tell the American people [Cárdenas's] side of the story." Raising echoes of the Teapot Dome scandal of the early 1920s, Townsend's theme was that the "history of the oil industry in the United States is full of pages stained black." He sought to convince his readers that Mexico's quarrel was with the unscrupulous oil companies, not with the American people.[39]

One ally Townsend recruited on this trip was Dr. Howard Kelly, the renowned Johns Hopkins University surgeon and gynecologist, who had been supporting Townsend's work since 1921. Townsend kept Kelly informed about events and urged him to use his good name to influence U.S. lawmakers. Kelly in turn offered to fund the printing in pamphlet form of an article on Mexico that Townsend had published in the evangelical journal *The King's Business.* Later, after Cárdenas retired from office, Kelly offered to put up some money to bring the Cárdenases and Townsends to the United States on a goodwill trip. While the Cárdenas trip never came about, and the resolution of the pamphlet idea is unclear, that Townsend was able to bring a man of Kelly's stature to his point of view on Mexico is an indication both of Townsend's legendary powers of persuasion and of the success, at least among evangelicals, of his efforts on Cárdenas's behalf.[40]

Perhaps Townsend's most long-lasting effort on Mexico's behalf was his biography of Cárdenas published in 1952, still the only full-length biography in English. Townsend's experience during the oil crisis convinced him to refocus his efforts on the biography he had first conceived, and suggested to Cárdenas, at SIL's "state dinner" with the president in 1936. His initial vision was to highlight Cárdenas's work in behalf of Mexico's Indians. As he told Cárdenas's secretary, "The sincere, self-denying and powerful friends of the poor are so scarce that it is imperative to make them well known to the world." Townsend had spent months on the work (aided by stacks of information, newspaper clippings, and copies of Cárdenas's speeches sent to him by subsecretary of foreign relations Ramón Beteta), and considered the biography essentially complete when in 1938 the oil crisis necessitated additional chapters and a whole new dimension for the work. Townsend plugged away at the biography during the 1940s, but as SIL grew and his work expanded into Peru and other Latin American countries, he never seemed to have the time to see to its final completion.[41]

Finally, in 1948, having been reviewed for accuracy by both Beteta, now secretary of the treasury, and the retired Josephus Daniels, the biography was ready for publication. Harold Bentley, head of the publishing department at Columbia and a friend of Townsend, managed to interest Harper's Publishing in the book. Townsend agreed with their request to have Anita Brenner review his work and put it in shape for their needs. A prominent figure among the fellow travelers in Mexico City during the 1920s, Brenner had gone on to earn a doctorate in anthropology at Columbia. She was well known as an author and interpreter of Mexico in American intellectual circles. Brenner was enthusiastic about the project, but thought it was too long. She promised to give Townsend two days a week to assist with the editing and revising. Despite the revisions, however, Harper's declined to publish the biography, because it still "sounded too much like propaganda."[42]

At this point the Cárdenas biography had become too important to Townsend, Cárdenas, and the Mexican government to let it wither on the vine. Despite having been out of office for a decade, Cárdenas was still a prominent figure and was again being accused of Communist tendencies, a disturbing charge in the postwar world. Although Cárdenas never responded publicly, his friends in the Mexican government, who did not appreciate having the reputation of the most prominent living figure from the revolution tarnished, spoke up for him. They clearly saw Townsend's biography as one way of doing so. With Beteta offering to provide twenty-five thousand pesos to expedite the book's publication, Townsend turned to a small press in Ann Arbor, Michigan. Eventually, with an additional two thousand dollars from the Mexican government funneled through the national oil company PEMEX, the biography (with a foreword by Frank Tannenbaum) was published in 1952 by George Wahr Publishing. With the help of Arnold Kruckman of the Kruckman News Service in Washington, D.C., Townsend managed to get the book favorably reviewed by several major newspapers, including the *New York Times,* the *Christian Science Monitor,* the *Chicago Tribune,* and the *Washington Post.* Kruckman also got a copy of the book to Nelson Rockefeller, Walter Lippman, and other significant journalists, including members of the Overseas Writers (a once-flourishing group of diplomatic journalists) with a particular interest in Mexico. Kruckman was completely convinced of Cárdenas's greatness, writing, "I have never known of another ruler so utterly selfless." He compared Cárdenas's qualities to Jesus, the Duke of Windsor, and Soviet-spy-turned-anti-Communist Whittaker Chambers![43]

Townsend sent out twenty-five thousand letters urging the purchase of the book for friends, libraries, and local congressmen. He sent the book to every congressman in Washington and every state governor himself, albeit with the help once again of the Mexican government through PEMEX. University presidents and public libraries throughout the Southwest received copies as well. Though many congressmen replied with a form letter, those with a particular interest in Mexico or Latin America seemed genuinely thankful and eager to read the book. A Texas congressman from a district that bordered Mexico indicated he had heard of the book and had "been wanting a copy." Several years later Townsend's biography of Cárdenas could still be found in Washington. While visiting then-Senator John F. Kennedy to lobby for increased U.S. aid to Latin America, the senator mentioned to Townsend that he had his book.[44]

While the Cárdenas biography may have had some influence in secular and official circles, the consistent advocacy by Townsend and other SIL members for Mexico through prayer letters, personal letters, and public appeals undoubtedly had its greatest impact among his natural constituency, American evangelicals. Townsend vigorously promoted the book to SIL's constituency (helped by another one thousand dollars from Beteta), a constituency that by now, as Townsend noted, probably remembered General Cárdenas every night in their prayers. Townsend's constituency numbered in the thousands; by 1952 SIL had more than three hundred members, and their supporters numbered more than twenty thousand.

A few snapshots provide a point of entry into a world impossible now to retrieve through statistics. We glimpse eight young people, recruited by Townsend and paid by Cárdenas, working in community development in Mexico for an Inter-American Service Brigade. In California an old man, the beginning (and the end, as it turned out) of another Townsend dream, the International Association of Friends of Mexico, travels with his box of letterhead, beating the drum for inter-American goodwill. The governor of Arkansas agrees at Townsend's insistence to sponsor an official reception for a Mexican government official. Townsend's sister publishes an article in the *Enid Morning News* celebrating the "work of the Mexican Revolution." An evangelical pastor in Texas promises to give Cárdenas land he owns in Mexico for distribution among the peasants and offers to visit schools and clubs in America "showing movies of the work that Mexico is carrying out, fomenting in this way not only tourism but better understanding between the two people."[45]

Our final snapshot takes us to a "Good Neighbors Picnic" near the Mexican-American border. At the height of the oil crisis Townsend convinced more than two hundred friendly evangelicals to meet with Cárdenas. On a hot July day in 1939 dozens of newly washed and waxed Fords and Chevys wound their way from cities in Southern California to the Mexican border town of Agua Caliente, where, in the parking lot of an old casino, they disgorged more than two hundred sharply dressed evangelical Protestant pastors, businessmen, doctors, schoolteachers, farmers, and their assorted family members. While the men pulled heavy picnic baskets from the trunks of their cars, their wives, clutching tickets to a "Good Neighbors Picnic sponsored by the Summer Institute of Linguistics," haltingly garnered directions to the patio. There, in what Townsend modestly billed "one of the most unusual picnics . . . in the history of the world," they spent the afternoon dining and conversing with Cárdenas, three members of his cabinet, and other high officials of the Mexican revolutionary government. After dinner and an exchange of impassioned speeches, President Cárdenas shook hands and signed autographs, while Townsend mused that "keen observers . . . realized another Lincoln was in their midst." After the meal some who had thought Townsend was perhaps too enthusiastic in his portrait of Cárdenas expressed glowing praise. One lady told Townsend, "Cameron, you did not tell us half." Two snapshots linger—Ramón Beteta, undersecretary of foreign affairs, passionately exhorting his audience, "You Christians at least should be able to understand our burning desire to help the masses who have suffered for so long," and Cárdenas, encouraged with how the day had gone, exclaiming, "Townsend, you will see how when I go out of office I am going to work together with you in matters of the spirit."[46]

And yet to leave the analysis of Townsend's impact with such glimpses still sells it short. As Joel Carpenter has recently shown us, evangelicals by 1950 had built up a tremendous network of agencies through which they kept in contact and disseminated their message.[47] The list of Townsend confidants reads like a roll call of leading evangelical power brokers of the era. We can be confident that all of them felt at one time or another the force of Townsend's personality on Mexico's behalf, and most more than likely influenced some in their own constituencies.

Elvira Townsend's home church was the Moody Church in Chicago, called by Carpenter a "pocket-sized denomination." She exchanged "newsy" letters and collected foreign stamps for pastor Harry Ironside, whom Carpenter called "perhaps the preeminent dispensationalist spokesman of his day." Ironside had once exclaimed to Elvira, "Your experiences with high officials—both Mexican and

American—are amazing to a simple man like myself who never gets a chance to associate with the great or near great," and he now hoped to see the Townsends and Cárdenases together on his platform, vowing to show the president "a little courtesy around the Moody Church." He promised to display a Mexican flag on the platform and to "drape a number of chairs with the Mexican colors."[48] Townsend's home church was the Church of the Open Door in Los Angeles (another of Carpenter's "pocket-sized denominations"), and his pastor, Louis T. Talbot, visited the SIL work in Mexico at Townsend's invitation. Dawson Trotman, founder of the Navigators, served on SIL's board and visited Townsend in Mexico. Radio evangelist Charles Fuller, founder of *The Old-Fashioned Revival Hour*, served briefly on the board and voiced the introduction for SIL's first promotional film. Townsend communicated regularly with Oswald J. Smith, pastor of the Peoples Church in Toronto, keeping him informed of his activities with Cárdenas. Smith also visited the work in Mexico. R. G. LeTourneau, millionaire evangelical businessman, agreed to assist Cárdenas in the giant Tepalcatepec River Basin project. Clarence Jones, founder of HCJB Radio, broadcasting across the world from Ecuador, distributed Elvira's book on Latin American courtesy over the air. Townsend also had close ties with Torrey Johnson and Jack Wyrtzen of Youth for Christ; Dr. Edman at Wheaton; Henry Crowell at Moody Bible Institute; Clarence Erickson, successor to Paul Rader as pastor of the Chicago Gospel Tabernacle; Robert McQuilkin, president of Columbia Bible College; and Louis Sperry Chafer at Dallas Theological Seminary. Through these men and others like them Townsend's impressions of Cárdenas and Mexico had at least the potential of reaching a vast audience.

Some of Townsend's constituency, however, were concerned that his biography of Cárdenas did not present a strong "testimony." One writer bemoaned the fact that something that had taken so much effort would not "come through the fires which are to 'try every man's work.'" He went on to accuse Townsend of becoming "ashamed of Jesus" in his effort to "be popular among atheistic intelligentsia." Some in SIL, concerned about just this sort of reaction, urged Townsend to publish the book on his own with no public SIL connection. Townsend would not hear of it. "I think that you realize how much I've tried during the years our Institute has been operating in Latin America to defend these countries against misunderstandings and the avarice of monied interests in the U.S.A," he replied furiously. "I can't think of our Institute going back on that stand now."[49]

By the end of 1938 the "Townsend group," as it was known in Mexico, had grown to thirty-two linguists working in thirteen Indian tribes. There were still thirty-eight "untouched" tribes in Mexico, however, and Townsend was impatient to expand. In addition, there was still his dream of reaching the "wild tribes" of the Amazon to consider. For the next several years the group continued to grow at a pace of about ten per year. In early 1941 Elvira wrote to Harry Ironside that the group had grown to the point that they were beginning to think of themselves "as a mission."[50]

In 1941 Mexican officials asked Townsend to send someone to the Lacandones and Seres, two very small Indian groups numbering in the hundreds. Although some argued that it was a waste of manpower to devote years to such a small number, Townsend could think of no valid reason not to honor the request. If Christ had pursued one lost sheep, so would he. Eager to get workers in each tribe, he decided to publicly pray for fifty new workers by the following fall. He asked each member to be responsible for recruiting one new worker. As usual, his faith in God was readily exercised, and he publicly stated that he believed God would honor his request. It was a staggering number to expect for a small, if growing, new mission. It would mean more than doubling the mission's size in one year. The challenge was made in November 1941.[51]

The subsequent story has become something of legend in SIL circles. Townsend's official biography states, "By the end of 1942 Cam had his fifty new volunteers for Bible translation, plus one more for good measure." Indeed, the mission was flooded with a remarkable number of recruits in the next year, as Townsend's prayer coincided with the move of Camp Wycliffe to the University of Oklahoma. However, the actual number of new recruits in the next year was thirty-five. Townsend, however, perhaps jealous of God's honor, cooked the books to reach fifty, and a legend was born. Townsend added the ten who had joined SIL in the fall of 1941 to the thirty-five new workers in 1942. But that still only came to forty-five. In November 1942 Townsend was clearly disturbed that the entire fifty had not materialized. He wrote to the membership, "I sometimes wonder if a mistake hasn't been made somewhere along the line by those of us whom you have placed in positions of leadership. If we did err and for that reason the fifty workers needed haven't materialized, do pray, please, that God will overrule our error even yet." It was not until the following summer that Townsend thought of a way to reach fifty. He counted the Nymans and their secretary, who manned the newly organized home office of the Wycliffe Bible Translators, and Elaine Mielke, who had recently arrived but could perhaps be said to have joined earlier (she at least expressed interest in joining in 1942), and came up with fifty-one new workers "added to our force in one year." "Of course some have left, one died, etc.," he wrote, "but other organizations have brought out or soon will bring out new workers to Indians tribes here too." Regardless, it was a remarkable growth spurt for the new mission.[52]

The mission continued to grow rapidly, and by the fall of 1945 SIL had more than 135 members working in forty-five locations in Mexico. In ten years Townsend's band of missionary linguists had grown to be almost twice as large as the CAM, which had recently celebrated its fiftieth year.[53]

After President Cárdenas retired from office, he and Townsend continued to see each other fairly regularly. Cárdenas, who was placed in command of Mexican defenses during World War II, requested that Townsend supply Bibles and spend time working with the troops under his command. In the spring of 1942 Townsend spent five weeks with Cárdenas in Ensenada conducting services, organizing athletic events, and engaging in other work. He served as sort of a social and spiritual director for the troops. Cárdenas himself distributed two hundred New Testaments to his officers. The ex-president once asked Townsend to help him draw up a plan for a "New Life Movement" in Mexico similar to what had been done in China. He wanted to raise the level of morals in Mexican society. "The Bible of course will be the official textbook," Townsend told his friends. "Carefully chosen selections from it will be kept before the people in the press, over the radio, on posters located in public places and in pamphlets." The plan was more than likely suggested by Townsend to the general; he then presented it to his constituency as a request from Cárdenas. During World War II Townsend asked Cárdenas to lead a "world campaign of love" (*campaña mundial de amor*). With the world convulsed by hate, Townsend felt the need to "regiment the forces of love." He declared there would be "more than enough" recruits, but they needed a leader like Cárdenas. What exactly Townsend had in mind is not clear. At approximately the same time, Townsend apparently attempted to organize a military battalion composed of equal numbers of American and Mexican men to supplement the Mexican armed forces. He proposed his project to U.S. Army officials. The FBI got wind of his plans, knew he was in touch with Cárdenas, and began monitoring his phone calls. The agent in charge reported, "[T]he proposed project of organizing a military battalion composed of young college students from the United States and Mexico [was] to act as a home defense for Mexico." The report stated that Townsend had "discussed the matter with an officer attached to the Western Defense Command, who has submitted the proposed organization to Lieutenant General [the name was blacked out]." The report unearthed "no indication of any subversive activities on the part of the Subject," but advised that the proposed battalion had arisen "due to the Subject's intense desire for closer relations between the United States and Mexico, which according to [again blacked out] had been materially improved as a result of the Subject's missionary work." As with many of the schemes hatched in Townsend's tremendously fertile mind, these never got off the ground.[54]

A great deal of the credit for the mission's rapid expansion must go to Leonard Legters. His unceasing and aggressive promotion laid a solid foundation for the work in the United States and kept sufficient funds flowing to the field to keep food on the table for the early recruits. Legters felt a personal responsibility for the field missionaries at a level unheard of in most faith missions. Where the home council of the typical faith mission felt called to pray, Legters felt a burden to pray and then beat the bushes to find the money to keep *his people* alive. Both he and Townsend defined faith in a very aggressive manner, one of the primary reasons SIL expanded so rapidly. "I have been speaking each month through the entire month[,] taking no rest," he told Karl Hummel in 1938, "that I might have enough to care for those for whom we had made ourselves responsible. . . . We have 9 folks who have gone out without support, [and] I . . . feel personally responsible to them."[55]

Legters's support for the SIL group in Mexico was forwarded through the Pioneer Mission Agency for most of the first decade of SIL's existence. The PMA, which had a mailing list of four thousand names in 1937, channeled funds to missionaries and national workers around the world, wherever Legters could entice someone into pioneer Indian work. The SIL group in Mexico and Camp Wycliffe were only two works for which it felt responsible. Legters routinely spoke as many as five hundred times in a calendar year, at Victorious Life conferences and churches, always challenging Americans to support pioneer missions. In the middle of the Great Depression the PMA's receipts continued to climb, while other missions desperately struggled. From summer 1933 to summer 1934, the PMA took in $1,000 more than the previous year; its total receipts were $7,552.66. The next fiscal year the PMA increased its income by another $2,500.[56]

As early as 1935 Legters had suggested the formation of the "American Linguistic Society" to operate under the PMA to handle the business of the SIL group in Mexico. He envisioned that the linguistic society would operate out of the PMA offices in Philadelphia. The American Linguistic Society would essentially provide nothing more than letterhead. Legters simply thought it "would be wise to have a non-religious name" in countries such as Mexico. Better that checks came from the American Linguistic Society than from the Pioneer Mission Agency. Townsend vetoed the idea. "The conviction grows on me that the organization you suggest would be premature as regards the situation here," he told Legters. "Things are developing far more satisfactorily than we had expected here and it has been entirely in an informal way."[57]

The PMA and Legters continued to handle the funds, although by 1938 Legters was arguing that they needed a full-time fund-raiser and recruiter. For one thing, as the linguistic profile of the group grew, Legters began to feel intellectually inadequate as its representative. "I realize my helplessness to do this work which you think I am able to do," he complained to Townsend. "I hide my face in shame when I must talk with men who have even a smattering of information about the work we seek to do." He and Townsend decided to use Eugene Nida as their primary recruiter, and Nida began to spend as much as half the year traveling for the group around the country.[58]

Although the new mission was clearly more aggressive in its promotion than the typical faith mission, the official financial policies continued to reproduce standard faith mission rhetoric. In 1938 Townsend wrote to the parents of a prospective female recruit, "[N]either our organization nor the Pioneer Mission Agency assumes any responsibility further than to forward any funds that may come in for the support of workers." He did, however, expect a single woman to have ninety dollars in hand before he would send her to Mexico, to be used for travel money and two months' living expenses. Recruits were "expected to keep their friends informed of what they [were] doing," but they were not permitted to "solicit funds." He informed the concerned parents that thus far "no one has failed to receive a sufficient supply for his or her needs. Mrs. Townsend and I have found the faith basis to be satisfactory throughout our twenty-three years of missionary experience."[59]

Quotas were established at seventy dollars per month for a married couple, thirty-five dollars for a single person. Quotas were designed, however, to help the office parcel out undesignated funds, not as a support level to be reached before leaving for the field. When Townsend exhorted the troops, he sounded very much like a leader of any other faith mission. "All of you came out [on the faith] basis, though some of you seem to have different conceptions of what it means," he once admonished the group. He was proud of those who, when they got low on funds, "pared down living expenses to the limit" and even "went without food until God provided." But he chastised members who overdrew their accounts at the office to maintain their standard of living. "An overdraw constitutes a loan," he chided, "and borrowing doesn't sound like George Müller. If God doesn't send money, there must be some reason for it." Hitting all the faith tropes, Townsend said that everyone would be glad to share with those in need, "provided that by doing so we are not thwarting some plan God has for you in letting you be without funds. . . . Lean on the Lord and be ready to get along on beans and tortillas if He so wills."[60]

By 1943 the group in Mexico was made up of two categories, those with minimum support pledged and those without. Those without were cared for from a "sharing fund," which tried to bring everyone up to quota. As long as the sharing fund remained full, the tensions such a system was bound to cause remained muted. Nevertheless, new recruits inevitably began to feel pressure to bring support with them to the field so that they would not be totally reliant on the sharing fund.[61]

As each year began to see dramatic increases in numbers, the need for funds mounted. Slowly God's financial weather vane began to be applied *before* recruits came to the field. It began to be seen as God's sign or seal of approval on a prospective recruit that someone offered to support them. This was in many ways the first real point of emphasis in faith mission history for recruits to begin to undertake their own individual deputation. "I do think that one of God's seals upon your work is this, that He lays you personally upon the heart of some people who make you a special charge of their own," Legters informed a member in 1939. "I am asking Him that if He would have you remain in the work then that He puts it upon someone to very personally give for your support." It would be many years, however, before such a standard would be strictly applied. As Legters told the same person, "[Still,] as long as you are with us in Mexico we shall do all possible to see that you have the funds you need."[62]

The PMA formalized the suggestion in 1941 that all new recruits were to "have the promise of their support before they go to the field." The suggestion came as the PMA was feeling the pressure of caring for the rapidly expanding group. There is no sign the suggestion was officially adopted at the time, although it certainly contributed to the rapidly changing faith culture. Elvira was sympathetic, writing to the treasurer of the PMA, "Personally, I do think it would be a fine thing for new ones going out, [to have] some sort of support from friends or their home churches, for each year with new ones added there must needs be a heavier burden on the general support fund there at Philadelphia, unless new ones come to the field with some kind of provision." The suggestion, of course, went quite against standard faith mission procedure, as to have guaranteed support negated trust in God. But the culture was changing. In 1941, of the forty-six people in the "Wycliffe Translation Group," thirty-seven were at least partially supported by various churches, anywhere from five to forty dollars per month. Forty-two were partially supported through gifts of friends, but only two were completely supported through such gifts. Only twenty-five needed support from the PMA general fund.[63]

In November 1939 Legters cleared his calendar for the following summer, refusing all engagements. He could not promise Townsend he would even attend

Camp Wycliffe. "The Lord has given me no freedom to make any plans for after April 1," he informed Townsend. "Many invitations have come in, enough for two years, but I am saying no to every one, even to W. C. Townsend about next year." In May 1940 Legters suffered a heart attack while on vacation in Northern California. He died a few hours later.[64]

The loss of Legters pushed Townsend even further to the edge of standard faith methods. He now had no one at home who shared his passion, who made the welfare of Cameron Townsend and his group his primary concern. "Will you make it a vital thing in your life to help [the new recruits]?" he begged his constituency that summer. "Please pardon the frankness of this letter. It is provoked by the recollection of Mr. Legters' do-or-die attitude toward vital things. Casting aside all 'pious piffle' and secondary issues[,] let us all press forward until every tribe has heard the Story of infinite love." The "pious piffle" might possibly have referred to theological arguments that prevented Christians from working together, but in context it seems more likely to refer to the pious restraints and niceties of faith solicitation.[65]

In November 1940 word reached Townsend from David Brainerd Legters that the PMA felt that with Legters gone the group had grown too large for them to continue to handle. Townsend stalled for time, but admitted, "[P]erhaps it is time that the translators themselves complete the maturity of their growth by forming an organization in the States to act as their representative." The PMA continued to handle the group's funds for the next year and a half, but when Townsend prayed for fifty new recruits, the PMA had had enough. They requested that Townsend meet with them in the spring of 1942 to go over plans to form a "regular mission board."[66]

As a consequence of those meetings, Townsend asked William G. Nyman if he would become the home secretary of the organization. Nyman had had considerable experience on mission councils during his years as a businessman in Chicago. In 1930 he joined the board of the Bible House of Los Angeles. He served on the mission committee at Church of the Open Door and was chairman of the board of trustees of Biola. He had known Townsend for at least a decade, and had offered to assist him in his "air crusade to the wild tribes"; he and his wife visited the Townsends in Mexico early in 1941. He was precisely the sort of man Townsend admired, a self-made businessman who had faith in God but also knew how to get things done. Now retired, Nyman accepted the position and opened the first home office in his house in Glendale, California. They considered several names, including Bible Translation Movement and Pioneer Translation Agency, before settling on the Wycliffe Bible Translators.[67] Initially, then, the Wycliffe Bible Translators (WBT) simply took over from the PMA as the sponsoring organization for Camp Wycliffe and the Summer Institute of Linguistics in Mexico.

Townsend desperately tried to avoid "getting stuck" being general director of the new organization. He did not want to spend his time doing deputation work and publicity in the United States. He wanted to be foreign secretary, directing advances around the world. The members and the PMA, however, refused to let him off the hook, and he indeed became Wycliffe's first general director, a post he held for the next several decades. He usually managed, however, to assign publicity duties to someone else, although he agreed to return to the United States for deputation if Nyman needed help—that is, if too many missionaries got behind financially. Incorporation papers for both WBT and SIL were authorized by the state of California in the fall of 1942. On September 11, 1942, a letter went out from the PMA requesting that donors for the Mexico translators begin sending their donations to Glendale and the WBT.[68]

While Townsend was named general director of WBT, Nida became president, Pike was named vice president, and Nyman was chosen as secretary-treasurer. Townsend immediately aimed high for his board of directors. Dawson Trotman, founder of the Navigators, was a very active member of the first board. Townsend asked radio evangelist Charles Fuller, but it was several years before Fuller agreed to closely associate with the new mission. Townsend avoided the tension between home and field that was so common in the CAM by incorporating SIL as the field organization. "In general," Pike reported, "the home branch governs itself and the field branch governs itself." The new mission adopted the China Inland Mission doctrinal statement word for word.[69]

Today the Summer Institute of Linguistics includes both the linguistic training schools and all the overseas organizations, while the Wycliffe Bible Translators is an organization based in numerous countries that channels recruits and money to SIL. Technically, today, applicants to the WBT are trained by the SIL, accepted by the WBT, then seconded by the WBT to an SIL organization in whatever country they conduct their work, thus perpetuating the organizational structure that the mission has found useful in marketing itself both at home and on the field. But while it has definite historical precedent and allows members to move comfortably in both missionary and secular academic circles, this structure continues to be somewhat unwieldy and confusing to many. However, the charge made by some that the organization intentionally obfuscates the relationship between the two organizations has little historical precedent and in this Internet age overstates the case, as the integral connection between the two organizations is obvious to anyone interested in sorting out the matter.

Nyman was an excellent businessman and well respected in mission circles. As his time was donated, he managed to keep office expenses quite low. The largest expense was publicity, which the new mission engaged in energetically. The Mexico group helped out by publishing *Translation* magazine, a newsy, picture-filled journal that kept supporters in touch with the organization and its needs.

While nobody got rich, the new mission prospered by faith standards. Its first December in business in 1942, the office sent more than $3,000 to Mexico. The master mailing list included more than ten thousand names. Three years later there were thirteen thousand. Between Nyman's letters, *Translation* magazine (fourteen thousand copies were printed in January 1944), individuals writing letters to their friends, flyers and brochures relating to special projects, regular deputation by members of the group, and the recruitment of "name" supporters such as Trotman, Fuller (who plugged the group on his radio program), Oswald Smith (who volunteered to support all Canadian recruits through the Peoples Church), Clarence Erickson of the Chicago Gospel Tabernacle (who became an aggressive supporter and sent the group $350 a month from his church, besides funding numerous individuals), Louis Talbot (pastor of the Church of the Open Door, who held WBT rallies at the church), Jack Wyrtzen, and Torrey Johnson (who gave WBT speakers special slots to speak at Youth for Christ rallies), the group's constituency remained informed and growing. When the group doubled in size that winter, the allowance for each worker continued to be met regularly.[70]

Townsend believed it was critically important to keep his backers directly engaged with the fieldwork. Consequently, he pestered them to visit Mexico. When Oswald Smith and Jack Wyrtzen visited, Townsend begged his best people to be available to conduct personal tours. "A man as important as Dr. Smith should have [Pittman or Pike] with him on his trip," Townsend ordered. "He is a missionary minded pastor with a far reaching ministry[,] and more will be accomplished, I believe, by getting him properly indoctrinated with pioneer missions, the linguistic approach and other Wycliffe specialties than by holding many deputation meetings." After receiving the executive tour of Mexico, Louis Talbot, pastor of Church of the Open Door, offered to travel the country on behalf of WBT. "Nothing would give me greater pleasure than going over this country in behalf of that Mission," he told Nyman. "I feel that I could raise $25,000 or more a year for it." It is unclear what came of this offer. Talbot was an enthusiastic supporter, but more than likely was not able to get out of his positions with Church of the Open Door and Biola.[71]

From the beginning, Townsend pushed the board of WBT out of its comfort zone. He was determined to avoid becoming just another faith mission. He fought to ensure that WBT would not encroach on the radical methods adopted by SIL in Mexico. The WBT and SIL directors—WBT's concerned with relating to conservative evangelicals at home, SIL's with Latin Americans and academics—did not always see eye to eye. One of Townsend's first clashes with the WBT board was over the acceptance of Pentecostals. The board balked at such a step, but Townsend refused to back down. He insisted that his organization was not "dedicated to the propagation of some special system of theology, practice or discipline as the denominational missions are (and even most faith missions)." To accomplish SIL's special task of Bible translation, Townsend needed "to harness the consecration and energies of all who genuinely love the Lord and are vitally concerned about the Great Commission." "If some who want to help us are afflicted with what you and I consider to be doctrinal errors whether of the nature of those held by John Wesley, A. B. Simpson, J. C. O'Hair or any other saint of God, that should not be given too much consideration," he instructed the board.[72]

The board naturally worried that it would cost them support. The PMA and other conservative mission leaders had already threatened to refuse membership on WBT's advisory councils over the issue. Townsend would have none of it. "If God be for us, who can be against us?" he argued. "What we know, or think we know, about [the Bible] . . . should not be the mold we pass on to the world, but rather the Book itself." Townsend admitted that he did not care much for certain Pentecostal practices. "I didn't want other folks praying out loud while I was praying any more than I wanted the pipe organ to be playing while I was speaking or praying," he said. But he had found the Pentecostals who attended Camp Wycliffe to be "perfectly proper," and he did not see why they would not continue to be so as Bible translators. They already had members who "probably believed in healing through the atonement" and one couple who had worked for many years at Angelus Temple with Aimee Semple McPherson. "I wish that we had a hundred more missionaries like them," Townsend wrote. Besides, a scientific society should not prohibit membership based on theological differences. "In the scientific world, we are supposed to accept facts even though they go against our theories," he noted, "but in spiritual things we tend to discount all the virtues a man has . . . if we hear that his connections are under ostracism." Townsend insisted that acceptance or rejection be based on performance at Camp Wycliffe, a startling new method indeed for passing judgment on missionary candidates. That did not bother him. "We are . . . building something new and there are many points where we have found it necessary to diverge from old methods," he concluded. "[W]ithin fifteen years we'll have a thousand members in all parts of the unevangelized world. . . . Let's not limit our sphere of service by officially condemning . . . pet theories."[73]

Townsend also pushed the board constantly to focus on rapid growth, again a radical departure from standard faith methods. If the number of recruits after camp each fall did not meet his goal, letters piled up in Nyman's in-tray demanding an explanation. They were usually filled with a list of projects that would enhance publicity, or with information about major contacts Townsend had made that he wanted Nyman to follow up with his own special charm. In a typical letter from 1943, Townsend wrote, "I have suggested to Pike [and] Nida that we open a camp in Calif[ornia], one on the Atlantic coast, and another one in Canada besides the main one in Okla[homa]. The four camps could take care of 500 students, and God seems to give me faith to believe that He can raise them up, if the different boards become enthusiastic about it." And he wanted the camps up and running immediately. He presented a detailed outline for who would teach each course at the different camps, and suggested staggered start times so that Pike and Nida could spend time at each. He included suggestions for "effective publicity" to all the mission boards. He wanted someone to visit "evangelical Russian churches" to present the challenge to them "of a hundred tribes in Siberia . . . without the Bible." "As soon as the war is over, we should have a large number of young Russian Christians ready to go to those tribes," he argued. Reading Townsend's letter at the time, the plans must have seemed preposterous, and indeed they were. Eugene Nida wryly remarked, "I rejoice in your continued expanding vision[,] but if we have 500 students at Camp Wycliffe, we are going to have to kick out an awful lot of walls." But without Townsend's vision and the constant pressure he inflicted on his top executives, the mission would not have expanded as rapidly as it subsequently did. Although opening three new camps for five hundred students in one year was perhaps a ridiculous idea, the organization did begin a new school in Canada and before too many years opened several others around the world.[74]

"All of this [must be done] on top of prayer," Townsend concluded at the end of one particularly frenetic letter. For Townsend, prayer was a cry in the midst of a whirlwind, not a leisure-time activity. Townsend understood how faith worked. When the Moody Church sent a check for one thousand dollars, he wrote to Nyman, "God is faithful! . . . I suppose that the committee acted in response to your letter as well as prayer." Or as he once put it, "[W]e have followed scientific methods plus faith. I guess that it wasn't necessary to add those last two words, for faith is the most scientific thing there is."[75]

As Mexico filled up with translators, and it seemed all the indigenous groups had workers, Townsend began to turn his eyes once again to South America. Mexico was "just a training field" for Latin America, Siberia, the Philippines, and wherever else translators might be needed, Townsend informed his supporters. He thought perhaps he would lead an initial expedition of twenty-five or so in the fall of 1944 into whatever country opened up. He planned to secure graduates of Camp Wycliffe in the summer of 1943, give them a year's training in Mexico, and another summer at Camp Wycliffe in 1944, before departing for South America. Unfortunately, 1943's Camp Wycliffe did not yield the bonanza of recruits that Townsend had hoped for. It was full, but most of the students were already committed to other boards.[76]

Townsend was inclined to grumble, but a piece of good news forestalled his impatience. That summer the American Bible Society asked Pike to go to South America to provide leadership in some key decision making about indigenous alphabets. Literacy pioneer Frank Laubach planned to mount an extensive campaign in Bolivia, and the ABS wanted the alphabet problem solved before Laubach started printing primers. In Peru, Pike lectured for a week to Peruvian high school teachers of English at the invitation of the minister of public education. "While speaking with the Minister of Education about English, the subject of Indian linguistic work also came up," Pike later reported. "When I told him about Mexico, [our] linguistic activities plus some social or practical work, and spiritual and translation work, he suggested we do the same in Peru. . . . I requested it in writing for Mr. Townsend, and he granted it."[77]

Townsend eagerly accepted the official invitation. He informed Enrique Laroza, the minister of public education, that he would begin putting together a team immediately and that they would need permission to live in the jungle with the Indians. Townsend informed Laroza that it would be 1945 before SIL would be able to bring recruits to Peru, after providing them some training at a jungle training camp he was constructing in Chiapas, Mexico. (Several months at Jungle Camp became the required second step, after graduating from Camp Wycliffe, for SIL recruits.) Another reason Townsend wanted to wait until 1945 to take in the first group of SIL translators was that he thought the New Tribes Mission might be entering the country in January 1944. He did not want to go to Peru too soon after that, "for I don't want our work to be confused with theirs in the eyes of the Gov[ernment]."[78]

Townsend was never happier than when faced with a pioneering expedition, although this opportunity was bittersweet because of the absence of Legters. "It will seem strange to make [the] expedition to another land without Mr. Legters's companionship," he wrote. Elvira reported that Cameron was "in a daze these days." "I suppose he is walking in another world a good bit of the time," she said, "thinking of his trip to South America." Elvira was not at all pleased with the prospect; in fact, she was bitterly opposed to her husband leading the expedition to Peru. She argued that it required all of his time and energy to oversee the work in Mexico. The Mexican government considered him responsible for the group there, and if he went down to Peru, then that government would also look to him as the responsible party. She did not think one man should be in charge of both countries. To the Nymans, she grumbled, "Cameron's going there now, would heap on work for me, for you know well, I'm sure, that behind the scenes it is Elvira Townsend who takes care of all the detail work." Of course she also hated leaving her home in Tetelcingo, even as she had not wanted to leave Panajachel in Guatemala. She most definitely did not share her husband's enthusiasm for pioneering. During one of her "episodes," she is supposed to have screamed at her husband that he would go to Peru over her dead body.[79]

In late December 1944 the Townsends were in California attending WBT board meetings. Their Christmas letter closed, "The Lord enabling us, we would like to go on to South America—some time next year should the Lord tarry—our lives be spared—and should all doors open for such a move. His will be done!" Before most of their friends read the letter, Elvira was dead. Her heart had been giving her trouble for some time, but in her last few days she had felt better and had been in "unusually high spirits" as Christmas approached. At 10:15 on Saturday night, the twenty-third of December, she was sitting up in bed opening Christmas presents. After admiring them, she laid her head back to rest with Cameron beside her. Suddenly she said she needed air. This was not unusual, so Townsend placed her on a lounge between two windows. She asked for more covers. She asked him to turn on the lights, but as they were already on, Townsend realized something serious had happened. They called a doctor, who "pronounced it a cerebral hemorrhage" and stroke. She died without ever regaining consciousness at 3:00 p.m. the next day, Christmas Eve.[80]

At Elvira's funeral Dawson Trotman read a statement written by Townsend. "If I have permitted hardships, dangers, pleasures, and the powerful chords of human love to swerve me at times from full obedience [to God], henceforth 'none of these things shall move me,'" Townsend wrote. "This pledge is not taken lightly. It has been burned into my soul, and . . . the pain now seems like nothing as I visualize the fruit and joy of a truly all-out effort for my Savior and the unevangelized tribes that need Him so." Indeed, Townsend could now visualize an all-out effort without the encumbrance of a sick wife. Although he genuinely loved her—no one can read their letters and deny that—she had been a burden as well as a real help in the work, but now he could go to the Amazon with no dissenting voices. Townsend penned perhaps his greatest tribute to his sick and cantankerous wife in a letter he wrote to the members of the mission shortly after her death. "Please never forget this closing sentence!" he wrote. "When you are tempted to quit, think of Elvira and stick on the job."[81]

A few months after Elvira's death, the now forty-eight-year-old Townsend was sitting on the deck of a riverboat deep in the Peruvian jungle. The minister of aviation had given orders that he be provided free travel in a military airplane to an outpost in the jungle. From there he secured a berth on the *Ancon*, which plied its way up and down the Ucayali River. Hammocks hung loosely across the deck, and it was difficult to find a spot to sit down away from the fifty other passengers. He passed the time by writing to the Nymans. "What is BAD is the utter lack of cleanliness about the preparation [and] serving of food," he groaned. "Dish-washing is a revelation of indifference to germs. I commit myself to the care of God [and] eat without concern—also without much relish." Regardless, he was having the time of his life. "The capitan [and] passengers are nice to me," he reported, "so I'm enjoying myself and wouldn't trade places with anyone." He had "the sensation of launching forth on a new undertaking that is humanly impossible." He would not have wanted it any other way. "There is a tremendous job to be done here," he reported, "[and] in spite of what some leaders think, it <u>can be done.</u> Modern means of travel [and] LINGUISTICS are essential though."[82]

Townsend visited Indian villages to ascertain how many language groups needed linguistic work. He jotted word lists and took notes on appearance, settlements, and food. He meticulously noted the materials a center in the jungle would require, including long lists of tools and supplies. In addition, he talked up SIL and its innovative program with everyone he met. Deep in the jungle he stayed with a family working with the South American Indian Mission. Townsend gave their teenage son three hundred dollars to attend Camp Wycliffe. He had convinced the young man of the importance of linguistic work and wanted to get him trained before he lost his enthusiasm. He met the consul general of Colombia and sold him on SIL's methods. He reported to Nyman that the man "has become greatly interested and suggests that we begin work in his country." He concluded, "What a joy it is to serve [God]! Surely, my cup runneth over. The only 'flies' in it are the multitudinous [and] vicious insects here."[83]

Before leaving Peru, Townsend signed an agreement with the Ministry of Public Education on June 26, 1945. Townsend signed the accord as the "General Director of the Summer Institute of Linguistics Inc., of the University of the State of Oklahoma." The contract stipulated that SIL would undertake a "program of investigation" comprising "the study of languages [and] the gathering of anthropological data." In addition, SIL would render "practical service," including "assistance as interpreters, . . . linguistic courses for . . . school teachers who teach in Indian communities, . . . the formulation of bilingual . . . primers, . . . the translation into the native tongues of laws, sanitary advice, handbooks dealing with agriculture, the tanning of leather, and other crafts, as well as books of great moral and patriotic value, and . . . the uprooting of vice by all means possible." The ministry, in turn, would provide a fully equipped office in Lima and would mediate with other government agencies to make sure SIL personnel obtained all the needed permissions to bring equipment into the country duty free. The ministry would also help SIL acquire land to establish a center in the jungle and grant the group permits to bring in airplanes and radios, "it being understood that the aforementioned apparatuses shall also be available to the Peruvian Government for the transmission of such information as it may desire."[84]

The contract was obviously carefully worded. Such contracts, as well as WBT/SIL's dual identity, have led to the criticism that SIL duped Latin American countries into gaining entry as linguistic scientists, when in reality they were just missionaries. (The FBI appeared to agree. One of their reports on Townsend stated, "His personal card bears the inscription 'Director General del Summer Institute of Linguistics, University of Oklahoma,' although apparently this is a cover under which he operates in order to minimize opposition from a Catholic country."[85]) The Mexican government, of course, knew what they were getting, and Townsend's relationship with Cárdenas allowed the group a great deal of flexibility. Townsend was certainly much more cautious in his approach to other Latin countries.

However, this critique of Townsend and SIL seems to take a very dim view of the intelligence of Latin American government officials. These men were not dupes. As a Brazilian missionary, not from SIL but who had "drunk deep at Camp Wycliffe," once warned a friend, "I appreciate the standing that a scientist has with governments and all who are in authority. But . . . you don't get to be a scientist just overnight. Either the name is a hypocritical sham or else it represents long periods of painstaking study. And these people know in five minutes of conversation whether you are the sham or the scientist." Most governments thoroughly researched SIL, which was, after all, a high-profile North American institution, before extending an invitation. There is evidence in the Townsend archives that countries such as Brazil sent officials to their neighbors to check on SIL's work. Such governments knew the quality of SIL's scientific work, as well as its desire to translate the Bible into Indian languages.[86]

Finally, the wording of the contracts downplaying Bible translation as "translating books of great moral value" often had its impetus in Latin American government circles. As most were Catholic countries, they simply could not risk explicit statements in a public contract that clearly outlined that this group had Protestant missionary intent. Peru was a very different setting than Mexico. The Catholic Church was not in disfavor as in Mexico; in fact, Peru operated under a *Patronato* agreement with the Vatican. Although the Church had not had state support since 1856, it still wielded a great deal of influence. It was recognized as the official church of the country and protected accordingly. The vast majority of government officials were Catholic, and the Church exercised a great deal of influence over them. Even while he was negotiating with SIL in 1945, a group he clearly understood to be Protestant, President Manuel Prado canceled all Protestant propaganda among the indigenous groups in Peru, saying, "The Constitution protects the Catholic religion. The nation spends large sums for the development of Catholic missions . . . and their activities should not be vitiated by diverse forms of religious propaganda." The secretary of the American Bible Society warned Townsend that he would be "walking a tightrope," trying to achieve SIL's and the Peruvian government's goals for indigenous groups, without bringing down the wrath of the Church on them both.[87] Often the agency involved with SIL, which desperately wanted their services (they could not get their own academics to go out and live for decades with jungle tribes, a point made years later by a Peruvian general when SIL was publicly criticized), knew implicitly that they had to downplay the missionary intent of SIL if they hoped to get the contract ratified. In short, they went into the relationship with their eyes open and were willing to accept SIL's missionary aspect as perhaps unwelcome baggage in order to gain SIL's scientific expertise. Later, when the newspapers figured out what SIL was, they often published an exposé. Such articles have informed much of the criticism that SIL has received. But it should be remembered that what was a surprise to a nationalistic reporter was no surprise to the government, even if a few politicians had to act surprised to save their jobs.

It is also important to mention that in the early days, SIL often had more requests for its services than it could handle. The mission was not always out banging on doors. Many, perhaps most, of the Latin American countries where SIL eventually worked made overtures to the mission before it was ready to expand.

Having said that, there were some within SIL itself who felt they were not being above board with their intentions, who wanted terms spelled out explicitly in contracts, who wanted to be able to publicly evangelize like other missionaries, and so forth. Some, including Ken Pike, accused Townsend to his face of not being entirely honest. Some, especially in the early days before the SIL schools established a solid reputation, felt they were stretching the truth to call themselves linguists. Others thought that Townsend overplayed the connection to the University of Oklahoma in order to impress government officials, despite the fact that he regularly cleared the language of official documents with the president of the university. The university was always delighted with the prestige it gained in Latin countries through the SIL connection.

Townsend could appear to want it both ways, desiring his recruits to be called missionaries when seeking support from churches or getting his men out of draft status during World War II, but not wanting to be called missionaries when dealing with wide publicity in Latin America. He argued that SIL was not a mission, because it "did not build up ecclesiastical organizations on the field but turned over the fruits of its labors to the mission boards or national churches." He liked to compare SIL to the American Bible Society. They were both service organizations. He did not want other missions whose territory SIL might enter to feel threatened, and did not want any organization to feel that if it gave public support to WBT it was slighting other missions. "[A]ny assistance rendered us is a service to all," he insisted. Probably the fine line here was more obvious to Townsend than to anyone else, but given the historical development of the organization in Mexico, the radical nature of his program, and the petty theological and methodological disputes to which evangelicalism was prone, his perspective can perhaps be understood.[88]

After securing the Peruvian contract, Townsend promptly sent a telegram to headquarters. "Agreement signed today envisioning linguistic investigation translations service Indian Tribes. Twenty-five competent students hundred thousand dollars needed first year." His audacious new undertaking, an undertaking he had envisioned for several decades, was just beginning. He hurried back to Camp Wycliffe to find recruits for Peru. At the Day of Prayer chapel service, he gave a message from Job 42:10: "And the Lord turned the captivity of Job, when he prayed for his friends: also the Lord gave Job twice as much as he had before." Obtaining "twice as much" would not be easy. He asked Charles Fuller to "come to our rescue by preaching a good strong missionary sermon over your world-wide broadcast." He hoped Fuller would reach a number of ex-servicemen who already had jungle training. "We are going to have to have an airplane . . . and a helicopter as well as radio communications and good medical service," he reported to Fuller. "We must go at this job in a scientific way."[89]

In November 1945 he sent a letter to his constituency. The letter was titled simply—"Help!" "Can a 'faith' organization utter such a cry and be consistent?" Townsend asked. Clearly, for Townsend, that was a rhetorical question. "When Peter had caught more fish than he could handle[,] he called for help and his companions came to his assistance," he wrote. "There is scriptural basis then for us to cry, 'Help!' to missionary-minded people upon certain occasions, and this seems to be such an occasion." And then Townsend outlined his version of the faith method—"Our expectation is in Him and in Him alone . . . but His Word teaches us to share our opportunities with others of a like mind, and so I want to tell you why help is urgently needed." His letter was an ingenious nod to faith sensibilities. "[R]eviewing [the list of past accomplishments] has made me so confident of the Lord's continued help in the big problems that lie ahead, that I don't feel any more like crying, 'HELP!' to you dear friends," he concluded. "If the Lord of the Harvest, however, should prompt you to enquire, I shall be glad to write you the details." Those who responded received a staggering list of needs, including an airplane pilot and mechanic, radio technician, doctor, ten more translators, several helicopters, "one amphibian airplane, one small hydroplane, two way radio equipment, clinic equipment for the jungle, one jeep, one commander car, one tractor with log puller, saw mill, etc., tents, sleeping bags."[90]

Nyman faithfully sent the letter to their entire donor list. "We are using almost all of the list you gave us," he reported, "and though it staggers our faith to ask so much of our Lord, we nevertheless are not wavering, but expecting Him to supply every need for Peru." So far that day, he wrote, they had received twelve hundred dollars in the Glendale office. Not all of Townsend's supporters approved, however. A lawyer from Chicago sent twenty-five dollars but "took exception [to the notion] that Faith Missions can call for help." Townsend reported to Nyman, "I replied that we do not ask for funds but that we are willing to make our needs known, when requests come in" (even if he solicited those requests). The distinction, of course, was arbitrary, but it was the sort of semantic gymnastics forced on a missionary leader operating within the faith mission tradition. In the years ahead, Townsend would find other, even more ingenious ways around the rules that straitjacketed those who were forced to deal with a constituency that had been weaned on the faith basis.[91]

That fall the horizon seemed limitless to Townsend. Good things were happening. Shortly after Elvira's death, he had written to a close friend in the organization, "I'm sure that I'll never have a home of my own again, but I'm also sure that all your homes will be mine." Townsend's prophecy was short-lived. In October 1945 he proposed to Elaine Mielke, a young woman who had captured his heart that spring. She was a schoolteacher from Chicago who had joined the group to work on literacy projects and to teach missionary children. President Cárdenas served as best man. Elaine was the perfect companion for the second half of Townsend's life. Twenty years his junior, she had the energy to keep up with him. She happily bore him four children and provided a home in whatever outpost he happened to be stationed. For the foreseeable future, their home would be in the jungle of Peru, where in 1946 the Townsends led twenty-three raw recruits. Townsend's dream of reaching the "wild tribes" had begun.[92]

Epilogue

In Which Townsend Decides Catholics Are Okay After All and the Reader Gets a Glimpse of the Future

> Don't talk to me about Protestants and Catholics. The truth of the matter is that if the Lord Jesus Christ came to Peru today as He did to Palestine, He would select Townsend to be one of his apostles.
>
> —Peruvian congressman

In Peru, Townsend finally realized his vision of an "Air Crusade to the Wild Tribes" when he founded the Jungle Aviation and Radio Service (JAARS) in 1948. The use of airplanes bypassed weeks of hard travel through the jungle and, together with radios, made the daily life of missionaries much safer. To raise the funds necessary to support his air force and now global organization, Townsend twisted the arms of Christian businessmen, shook the tree of every philanthropic organization he could think of, struck deals with airplane companies, became the first missionary organization to get into the movie business, got gigs for converted headhunters on *This Is Your Life* (the biggest TV show of its time), built an enormously expensive exhibit at the World's Fair (headhunters were involved there as well), and by so doing contravened just a few faith rules, even while he smiled and insisted he was a faith missionary. But these are stories for another day.

Even as Townsend rewrote the rules for how to be a faith missionary, he was throwing out the rulebook for how to be evangelical. His policy of nonsectarian service to all placed him in the orbit of folks that most American evangelicals simply could not abide. Primarily this meant Catholics, and Townsend may have been the first evangelical to decide they were not so bad after all. At least they were not always the enemy.

Townsend had seen his policy of nonsectarian service to all work in Mexico.

In one Mexican village an SIL translator helped the villagers build a water mill to grind their wheat into flour. This saved them a three-day trip to a larger mill town. He also helped them construct a sawmill and a primitive electricity-generating station. Eventually the priest in charge of the area tried to get the translator evicted by telling the people he was a heretic. The village officials replied, "Father, he may be a heretic, but he is the only one who knows how to fix our machinery." The translator stayed.[1]

But his policy would have to take on new meaning in many Latin American countries where the Catholic Church still exercised enormous influence. In Peru, Townsend decided to make himself and SIL so useful to the Catholic Church that they would have a very hard time getting rid of him. This usefulness first came into play far out in the Amazon jungle. As SIL had the best flight service in the jungle, Townsend made it a policy that despite inconvenience and cost, a pilot could not overfly certain Catholic mission stations without dropping in to see if he and his airplane could be of service. SIL saved the Catholic missionaries weeks of hard travel by flying priests and nuns to their stations, brought in mail and newspapers, and sometimes just dropped in to chat. All SIL members were to address priests as "Father," nuns as "Mother" or "Sister." Townsend invited them to his home at every opportunity and encouraged SIL members to do likewise. Townsend's basic policy was that if "you want to win [over] a member of the opposition . . . or nullify their opposition to you, give them a lift in your auto or airplane or show them some other kindness. . . . If you are unkind to them, you will not win them and you give them a strong argument to use against you." It was against SIL rules to attack the Catholic Church at any level. "Love," he instructed his recruits, "is the weapon of Wycliffe's warfare. . . . Call on them. Give them presents. Give them a lift . . . and give them their customary titles while graciously standing up for your faith, should it be called into question. This is the Christian way, the way of Wycliffe Bible Translators, the way of victory over wrong."[2]

Townsend pursued this policy aggressively. Although his approach rarely worked with the Jesuits, who would "walk ten days through the [jungle] rather than ride ten minutes" on an SIL airplane, he had better luck with the Franciscans and Dominicans. Townsend worked on one group of Dominicans for three months, and after the government tried to fly them into a new mission station in a DC-3 and almost crashed, they finally agreed to fly with SIL. Of course, Townsend made sure the pilot took a photograph of the event and filed it away for time of need. After finally coaxing into his airplane one priest who had criticized SIL, Townsend wrote that "we finally . . . succeeded in lassoing him . . . with cordiality." He demanded that his pilots give him an account of how much flying they were doing for Catholics, and if the numbers were too low, he pushed them to find ways to get the Catholic missionaries back on the planes. Townsend found ways to get priests involved in other SIL programs as well. He managed to get a Franciscan onto the platform at the first graduation ceremony of the jungle teacher's training course in Peru. Afterward the priest remarked wryly that Townsend was "more anxious to have me there than the president of the Republic."[3]

The priests and nuns in the jungle often returned these favors, providing hospitality, including meals, overnight stays, boat rides, rescue operations, and at times hospital care. Many friendly letters and gifts were exchanged on both sides. When an SIL member sent a Capuchin monk recently assigned to a jungle station two grafted grapefruit saplings as a housewarming gift, the monk returned the favor with "a bottle of sweet, muscatel Spanish wine." There is no record of how the teetotaling evangelical disposed of the gift! A law of the frontier prevailed, wherein both sides recognized the dangers of jungle living and the size of the task if the indigenous groups were to be reached. As one Franciscan told an SIL member, "Let's not let petty differences cause us to fight among ourselves in an area that demands our combined efforts." One bishop told Townsend privately that it was "better for the Indians of the jungle to be Protestants than . . . pagans," a gracious concession to be sure.[4]

Townsend was the first to admit that all this jungle camaraderie began as a pragmatic stratagem to keep SIL in the country. His letters to fundamentalist detractors were filled with metaphors of warfare. Rome was the enemy, and SIL's acts of "love" were intended to "pour water on Rome's gunpowder." He talked of "dropping atom bombs of love" on the priests and nuns. It was "warfare on the most refined level."[5]

It was not long, however, before something rather extraordinary began to happen in the jungle. These ancient antagonists began to discover that they liked each other. Despite their doctrinal differences, they found that in the Amazon basin there was much in life that could be shared. As one SIL member wrote, "We certainly have more in common with Catholics than with godless atheists, agnostics, and even religious liberals." It might be sitting on the veranda listening to a sermon over HCJB with a Franciscan priest. It might be the discovery that a priest liked to preach D. L. Moody's sermons to his congregation. It might be the realization that despite real differences they shared an interest in the welfare of the indigenous people. It might be a long discussion of the intricacies of a complex Indian language. It might be the shared intensity of fighting a jungle smallpox epidemic, searching for a downed airplane, or bringing a sick comrade to a hospital. Or it might simply be the enjoyment of the company of an educated man or woman deep in the Amazon jungle. Whatever the reason, Townsend was able to write, "We sure don't find it hard to love these lovely people." "I think," Townsend recorded another time, "that I speak for most of my colleagues when I say that we want to serve the monks and nuns in love—not just to get an advantage over them."[6]

For many the new approach became a profoundly spiritual experience as old prejudices were broken down. Dr. Richard Pittman once told the author, "I never realized that evangelicals could have these kind of attitudes toward Catholics until I met Cameron Townsend." A member from Scotland wrote of visiting the "Mother Country" and viewing the graves "of the Old Faithfuls, who gave their lives rather than yield to the domination of the R. C. Church." Deeply resisting Townsend's approach, he recorded that while in prayer "the Lord asked me, 'Is that the love wherewith I loved you?' It broke me down in tears before Him[,] and I know that the unseen barrier was swept away. I could love an R. C. priest into the Kingdom now whereas previously I could not have done so." Another member wrote to Townsend, "Your teaching, by precept and example, that the 'best way to fight the machine is to love the individual' has been the most inspiring thought which has entered my head since I found Christ." He concluded, "I am not blind to the fact that, had it not been for your . . . effort, I would have been a very poor, mean man."[7]

His nonsectarian policy, however, caused Townsend and SIL a great deal of grief. Other evangelical missionaries in Latin America deeply resented the fact that SIL went out of its way to "fellowship" with and even aid "the enemy." The conflict was especially intense in Ecuador, where the first SIL translators to enter discovered that it was the "custom of the evangelical missionaries to ignore, shun, and otherwise avoid any direct contact with the [Catholic] clergy." The Ecuador branch director reported that he had to be "extremely careful" in his relationship with Catholics "because of the extreme antagonism (which borders at times on hatred) of the clergy by the American missionaries." Needless to say, when SIL began flying the priests and nuns into the jungle, things became extremely tense. The ill feeling toward SIL became a contributing factor in the famous murder of five missionaries by the Waorani (Auca) Indians. The missions involved deliberately kept SIL in the dark about their intention of contacting the Waorani, when SIL might have been their best source of Wao language data.[8]

Field missionaries naturally relayed such stories to their constituencies at home. Over the years, Townsend and other SIL officials fought a running battle with evangelical leaders in the United States over such tactics. Many believed SIL was guilty of aiding in the spread of false doctrine. Bob Jones Jr.

called Townsend's use of Scripture to support his position "devious and illogical" and "worthy of the Jesuits." He "determined to expose [SIL's] betrayal of those Bible-believing Protestants who support them under the delusion that they are a ministry of Scriptural and Protestant evangelism."[9] Such men were upset when Townsend called Catholic missionaries "heroic" or praised the famous antislavery crusader Bartolomé de Las Casas (although some had no idea who Las Casas was, thinking Townsend was praising a current Latin American priest). Every Townsend argument was countered Scripture verse with Scripture verse. Meetings were held, position papers exchanged, theologians called in as referees, all to no avail. Some churches stopped supporting SIL. Schools such as Bob Jones University and Prairie Bible Institute directed their students to other missions. In 1959 SIL withdrew from the Interdenominational Foreign Missions Association to avoid further controversy and possible expulsion.

For Townsend, problems with the "rut-riders" (as he called them) were simply par for the course. He told his followers, "We do what we feel is the right thing and don't worry about what people will say." He also used such letters to his own advantage. He enjoyed sending his Catholic friends copies of them so that they would be well aware of the price he paid at home for the service he gave the Church. In a letter to the Peruvian minister of public education, in which he enclosed copies of articles written against SIL, he remarked, "Some preachers are so narrow that five of them could sleep in a 'cama de una plaza' (a single bed)." Despite the problems, to the surprise of some, recruitment and fund-raising continued stronger than ever. It seemed there were enough new evangelicals out there to support a mission charting a bold course. Many pastors were persuaded by Townsend's arguments. Others, while not fully convinced, appreciated the accomplishments of SIL and decided to live and let live.[10]

There had always been critics of Townsend's nonsectarian policy within the organization as well. Townsend's approach was so radical so often, and he so frequently made decisions without consulting his board of directors, that some did not "regard 'Uncle Cam' as synonymous with 'WBT/SIL.'" As one member reported to Townsend, "They think of you as being far ahead of the organization—almost out of sight, and are, therefore, hesitant to follow you." In a sense, Townsend was a victim of his own promotional genius. SIL grew so fast that entire branches had little if any contact with him. New members were not adequately indoctrinated into SIL's unique policies, and, without the opportunity to personally see Townsend in action (an event that most found powerfully persuasive), many recruits found they were only superficially persuaded of his approach. In addition, in most countries outside Latin America there was not the vital need to work closely with Catholics. Without the intimate interaction with the Church that some Latin countries provided, many SIL members continued to entertain standard evangelical views of Catholics. Others took a pragmatic view, reasoning that the potential loss of support from their constituency outweighed the benefits of following Townsend on his most radical ventures. It is safe to say that many members never really understood what "nonsectarian" meant to Townsend.

They found out in 1966 when a young Maryknoll seminarian named Paul Witte mailed in his application. It may have been only at this moment that Townsend himself fully realized what nonsectarianism meant to him. In 1960 Ken Pike had warned Townsend that his views on nonsectarianism did not lead to "any foreseeable . . . stopping point, short of full integration . . . in outlook, membership, and service." Townsend had scrawled in the margin—"Absurd!"[11] When the absurd happened, Townsend embraced it. He probably fought harder to secure Paul Witte for SIL than for anything else he ever did. He pushed the issue to the point of ill health. Witte's membership would be the crown jewel of nonsectarianism, the final proof that Christians of all persuasions could lay aside their differences to bring the Scripture to "every tongue." Witte's membership would also be the final proof in Latin America that SIL was completely "scientific" and nonsectarian. Though the move was eventually rejected by the membership, it is a monument to Townsend's personality and policies that such an audacious move was seriously considered in the mid-1960s by an evangelical organization such as SIL. The debate was heated, and the final vote was close. In general, the motion was supported by individuals within the organization who had close local contact with the Catholic Church or close supervision from Townsend. It was opposed by those with little local contact with the Church or little supervision from Townsend.

Townsend did not take defeat particularly well. He tried to secure a position for the Wittes through the Colombia branch, but the corporation blocked that move. He arranged for the Wittes to be employed by a friendly Colombian bishop and channeled funds to them through the bishop and the branch. He helped them raise funds in the United States. He even founded an entirely new organization intended to promote Bible translation societies in all the denominations, including the Catholic Church. Unfortunately, one of the founding board members of FAST (Final Advance for Scripture Translation) was a confirmed anti-Catholic, and the organization accomplished little. Eventually, Paul Witte and a friend founded their own Catholic translation society, Logos Bible Translators, which continued in fits and starts for some time.[12]

With the advent of Vatican II and the subsequent prominence of the Catholic charismatic movement, SIL found itself working more closely with Catholics than ever before. A Catholic priest sat in on a JAARS board meeting. Invited by some friendly nuns to a retreat, a woman from SIL, at the insistence of the nuns, celebrated mass. "Never," she wrote, "have I been to a more meaningful communion service. . . . [Although] I could never embrace the Catholic religion . . . this I know, we have to accept the fact that they belong to Christ just as much as we do." She now regretted her vote on the Witte issue, and told Townsend that she finally realized "what a great man of faith you are." In Guatemala a Catholic priest and a Protestant toured together selling Townsend's Cakchiquel New Testament and sold out so quickly they had to reprint it. In Peru, where the charismatic movement deeply affected both the Catholic Church and SIL, members found themselves attending bishops' conferences and helping to organize Catholic Bible studies. One translator decided that soon "there will be . . . an evangelical branch of the R. C. Church, just like there is in the Lutheran, Anglican, etc. And all evangelicals will fellowship whether R. C. or Protestant." Another translator wrote to say she had spent so much time with Catholics while in SIL that she was resigning to "worship and serve [God] within the framework of the Catholic Church."[13]

Perhaps the most startling result of Townsend's policies occurred in the mid-1970s, when the governments of Peru, Colombia, and Ecuador came under pressure to expel SIL. By then the world had changed dramatically. Now the political left, represented by anthropologists, linguists, educators, and nationalistic students, which had once welcomed SIL, sought to terminate their contracts. The lineup supporting SIL included leaders of indigenous communities, conservative political leaders, and the bishops of the Catholic Church.

As for Townsend, he was on to new challenges, determined to obtain a contract from the Soviet Union to undertake Bible translation. He warned those who were interested in joining him to expect radical developments. "In all probability," he warned, "I shall employ Moslems . . . and even atheists."[14]

Townsend's vision for nonsectarian service to all and his pragmatic adaptability laid the foundation for the emergence of SIL as perhaps the most influential North American Protestant mission in the world. Both SIL members and Catholics overcame powerful religious and cultural attitudes in order to view each other "with better eyes." Clearly Townsend and those recruits who followed his example were profoundly affected by an idea. Once convinced of this idea and immersed in a local context that reinforced the positive values of the idea, strongly conservative individuals were enabled to act in ways usually deemed liberal, years before their liberal brethren caught up with them. Townsend's story demonstrates that fundamentalists and evangelicals can transcend the boundaries of the box into which scholars frequently place them, if and when environment and personal allegiance coincide to overpower deeply ingrained theological and cultural beliefs.

From Peru, SIL entered Guatemala in 1952, Ecuador and the Philippines in 1953, Bolivia in 1955, then Colombia, Brazil, and Indonesia in rapid succession, until today SIL linguists operate in virtually every country of the world. The mission now includes approximately six thousand members. In addition to attracting one-third of its members from developed countries outside the United States, the movement has spawned indigenous Bible translation organizations. In some countries SIL linguists operate only as consultants to national Bible translators. The mission recently celebrated the completion of its five hundredth New Testament, and work is ongoing in more than eleven hundred other languages. Still, more than one thousand languages remain without any Christian Scripture.

Over the years SIL's schools have trained a staggering number of linguists, probably somewhere between thirty and forty thousand. At one time or another Camp Wycliffe has seen descendant institutes in Oklahoma, North Dakota, Washington, Oregon, Texas, England, Australia, Germany, New Zealand, Canada, Japan, France, and Singapore, many of them connected with various universities and colleges. The University of Texas at Arlington eventually took over the role played for many years by the University of Oklahoma. At Texas, SIL adopted a year-round training schedule. SIL currently trains between two hundred and three hundred linguists every year. The organization includes approximately 340 PhDs and nearly 2,000 people with masters' degrees. It probably has trained more PhDs in linguistics than any other organization in the world. Its publishing bibliography now contains more than twenty-two thousand entries. SIL is currently "accepted by many as the world's leading organization in the fields of language survey, language development and minority language literacy."[15]

Currently there is some discussion within the organization of whether it ought to continue such an academic focus. The pressures to be a more normal mission still rear their head. One member recently explained, "Because of the difficulty of attracting young recruits, we are tempted to modify our core program to interest new members by offering them easier assignment options, reduced training requirements, more immediate spiritual results, [and] more identity as a 'religious' organization." The author of the piece argued against such a position, because he did not want the organization to lose its attractiveness to the "best and brightest young people."[16]

The mission has seen its constituency parallel its own intellectual growth.

More than 90 percent of the readers of WBT's popular magazine, *In Other Words,* have attended at least some college. More than 60 percent have a college degree, with 30 percent holding a graduate degree.[17]

SIL continues to operate in the faith mission tradition, although the tradition bears little resemblance to the faith missions of old. Official policy states that WBT "is a faith work, dependent under God on faithful giving by Christians. The organization does not pay its missionaries a salary or guarantee them an income. Each person is expected to look to God for all material needs, including basic living expenses, while serving with Wycliffe. God supplies these needs through gifts from churches and individual Christians[,] creating a bond which results in blessing to both missionary and donor." Today, however, developing an adequate network of faithful givers is one of the first tasks facing a prospective missionary; no missionary departs for the field without their full quota of support promised. The mission assists new members by "conducting Partnership Development workshops with trained consultants." As recruits visit their friends and prospective supporting churches, the policy that governs their presentation is "discretion and good taste." Missionaries are permitted to be flexible according to the audience. Prayer letters mention percentages of support raised rather than direct dollar amounts. If you ask a missionary why he or she continues to be discreet in their fund-raising practices, you rarely get an answer touching on faith mission ideology. As mentioned in an earlier chapter, they usually reply that they do not want to be like the televangelists, a legitimate answer to be sure, but one lacking in historical understanding of their roots. A recently amended bylaw (as of 1998) now reads: "The needs of the work are laid before God in prayer and may also be presented to constituencies, to each in a way appropriate to its interest in the work, with sensitivity and propriety, in a spirit of dependence on God."[18]

The relaxing of faith standards, coupled with the affluence of evangelicals in general, has certainly paid off. In 1994 forty-five thousand churches and more than two hundred thousand individuals were listed as regular financial partners of the mission. Four hundred thousand people received WBT's magazine, *In Other Words.* In 1947 WBT's income was $163,907. The total income for WBT in 1996 was $95,302,000. More than half of the missionaries regularly receive more than 99 percent of their support quota. Two-thirds receive more than 90 percent; only 10 percent receive less than 60 percent of full quota.[19]

Perhaps the evangelical missionary movement can be said to have matured through its contact with modernity in the twentieth century. Education has had a powerful impact, even to the tempering of religious zeal. Much more is required now of missionaries than a simple longing to serve God and a belief that he is calling them to the missionary life. Indeed, the very discovery of

God's will is now a matter for organizations, as much as individuals, to decide. Evangelistic technique has graduated from tract distribution and street preaching to indigenous-language translations and extensive literacy efforts. Mission tools have progressed from megaphones to computers and airplanes. Insights gleaned from the study of anthropology and linguistics guide mission strategy. American missionaries now place the nurturing of local leadership as a first priority, even to the point of limiting their own involvement in indigenous life. Missionaries have led the way for evangelicals from isolation to cooperation, from cultural naiveté to sophistication. In all of this it is hard to avoid seeing the hand of Cameron Townsend.

Next to Townsend's grave just outside Waxhaw, North Carolina, stands the Mexico-Cárdenas Museum, constructed by Townsend during the final decade of his life, which ended in 1982. It was a fitting tribute to a lifelong friendship that united two very different men in the idealistic pursuit of a better life for Mexico's indigenous people. Townsend was able to find enough common ground between two divergent ideologies—evangelical Protestant and secular socialist—to make them, however briefly, allies in the program of Mexico's most well-regarded revolutionary. Motivated by gospel imperatives and immersed in contexts forcing the reevaluation of ideologies learned at home, perhaps a missionary was the only one who could have pulled off the reconciliation of such incongruities.

Townsend never forgot the lessons he learned from Cárdenas. He vigorously promoted Latin American causes throughout his life. Within a year of moving to Peru, he was lobbying the American ambassador, complaining that it was "disgraceful and dangerous for a wealthy and powerful nation to pose as a 'good neighbor' while doing little or nothing to help its less fortunate sister nations." When President Eisenhower raised tariffs on Peruvian lead and zinc, Townsend lobbied the administration, arguing that any discomfort caused American miners was outweighed by America's duty to be "good neighbors" to Peru. When Guatemala was accused of "going communist," Townsend sent an article to *Reader's Digest,* hoping to demonstrate to Americans that those impressions were wrong. But even if a country did embrace Communism, Townsend never countenanced American intervention, particularly to rescue American business interests. He opposed Kennedy's Cuba policy on those grounds. And when a young SIL operative, frustrated in his attempts to work out a contract with the Venezuelan government, suggested entering as scientists under the aegis of the American oil companies, Townsend's chief lieutenant in Latin America replied in words that undoubtedly echoed his boss: "[W]e should not link ourselves up with any large American corporation, for the type of power they wield has been the traditional reason that Latin Americans have accused the United States government of imperialism. Such association of ours with powerful groups should be the furthest from our thoughts since our mission is to serve and not to command."[20] SIL never entered Venezuela.

It is ironic that the man who once wrote to Cárdenas that he could not sleep at night thinking "of the crimes against humanity being committed by the oil companies" is often accused of being in league with them or the CIA in meddling in Latin American affairs and promoting the genocide of the Indians. Such yellow journalists choose precisely the wrong man against whom to level such charges.

Richard Pierard and others have noted that "fortified by the national mood . . . many evangelicals uncritically aligned their efforts with civil religion and capitalism."[21] Missionaries were often the first to recognize the fallacies of this alignment. Living in underdeveloped countries and working intimately with nationals from all social strata, missionaries observed America through foreign eyes and consequently recognized the ambiguities of American political and economic involvement abroad. That evangelical leaders at home thought critically about such issues may be in some measure owing to their contact with missionaries such as Townsend.

Townsend was a visionary maverick in many ways. He was not a typical evangelical missionary. But Townsend's story suggests that missionaries may have been leaders at home more often than followers. Operating on the frontiers of religious and cultural interaction, missionaries were placed in ideal positions to reanalyze, reinterpret, and perhaps even discard facets of their worldview in favor of startling new paradigms. The ease with which Townsend moved through disparate political worlds illustrates this fact. SIL members often found themselves caught between the realities of their frontier experience and the need to relate to a constituency that was often oblivious to such conditions and decades behind them in outlook. In the process of resolving that tension, many at home found their own vision inadequate. Scholars studying evangelicalism point to Billy Graham and certain influential schools such as Fuller Seminary as key players in the emergence of a "new evangelicalism" out of the more traditional evangelical movement. Townsend's story indicates that evangelical missionaries may have exercised significant influence in the moderation of evangelicalism.

There are many puzzles in religious history. Why did America become so Christian after secularism was given a strategic boost with the separation of church and state? Why did African slaves embrace the religion of their American masters? Why, in the last half of the twentieth century, have Latin America and Africa become so Protestant when Catholicism, Islam, and tribal religions had prior claim? Why do reports out of China echo similar themes? Evangelicalism is the answer to all of these conundrums. The story of Cameron Townsend and faith missions provides clues to the astounding success of this religious movement. If at times one is tempted to despair of the evangelical mind, other facets of the movement remind us that perhaps in the area of religion, success in numeric terms, at least, depends little on that organ most favored by evangelicalism's cultured despisers. What evangelicals have always had in abundance is passion, aggressive adaptability, pragmatic creativity, and the adamantine conviction that they are right and everybody else is wrong. Furthermore they inhabit a world in which being wrong has terrible consequences. The history of religion would appear to suggest that such qualities are essential if a religious movement hopes to triumph over its rivals.

Notes

Unless otherwise indicated, "Townsend" refers to Cameron Townsend. Some names of correspondents were incomplete or unavailable.

Chapter 1

1. Unless otherwise indicated, general information about Townsend's early life is taken from James Hefley and Marti Hefley, *Uncle Cam: The Story of William Cameron Townsend, Founder of the Wycliffe Bible Translators and the Summer Institute of Linguistics* (1974; Huntington Beach, CA: Wycliffe Bible Translators, 1995), 12–27.

2. Townsend to "home folks," 29 December 1939, Townsend Archives (hereafter TA), Waxhaw, North Carolina, [document number] #02423; Hefley interview (hereafter HI) with Ethel Townsend, undated, p. 7, TA. The interview would have taken place sometime in the early 1970s.

3. Transcript of a tape recording made by Paul Townsend, p. 2, TA; HI with Ethel Townsend, p. 8, TA; William Cameron Townsend's Student Volunteer blank, Student Volunteer Movement Archives, R6 42, Yale Divinity School Library.

4. HI with Cameron Townsend, pp. 6–7, TA.

5. HI #2 with Cameron Townsend, p. 6, TA.

6. Mama to "My Dear Children," 9 November 1924, TA #01017.

7. HI with Ethel Townsend, p. 18, TA; HI with Paul Townsend, p. 11, TA.

8. HI with Cameron Townsend, "High School and College Days," p. 2, TA #43637.

9. Townsend academic transcript, copy in author's possession; *La Encina* (Occidental College yearbook, 1915), 51; Robert Glass Cleland, *The History of Occidental College, 1887–1937* (Los Angeles: Ward Ritchie Press, 1937), 56, 46, 33, 79. The Mott observation about the size of the SVM band at Occidental is from Townsend to Robert McQuilkin, 12 May 1947, TA #04720.

10. *La Encina* (1918), 65; *La Encina* (1917), 53.

11. President John Willis Baer, "The Ultimate Occidental," in *La Encina* (1917), 7; W. D. Ward, "The Occidental Idea," in *La Encina* (1915), 11.

12. Townsend, "The Southern California Farmer," 23 April 1915, TA #00113; Hugh Steven, *A Thousand Trails: Personal Journal of William Cameron Townsend, 1917–1919, Founder of Wycliffe Bible Translators* (White Rock, BC: CREDO Publishing, 1984), 22; Townsend, "Genius and Physique," 11 January 1916, TA.

13. *The Occidental,* 3 October 1916, p. 7; *La Encina* (1917), 62; *La Encina* (1918), 69, 57, 64, 94, 33.

14. HI #2 with Cameron Townsend, p. 9; Townsend's Student Volunteer blank, Yale University; Townsend academic transcript; Cal Hibbard to Williams Kahn, 29 November 1961, TA #19753; Hefley and Hefley, *Uncle Cam,* 25.

15. HI #2, p. 5; HI with Evelyn Pike, TA; Townsend's Student Volunteer blank, Yale University; Michael Parker, *The Kingdom of Character: The Student Volunteer Movement for Foreign Missions (1886–1926)* (New York: University Press of America, 1998), 15, 18.

16. Townsend, "Be a Foreign Missionary at Home," 12 October 1915, TA #00110.

17. Parker, *Kingdom of Character,* 76–80, 143; Steven, *Thousand Trails,* 21.

18. *La Encina* (1918), 33; *Occidental,* 23 May 1917, 3.

19. HI #2, p. 14; *La Encina* (1917), 51.

20. HI #2, pp. 5 and 17.

21. HI #2, p. 15; Townsend Journal (hereafter, Journal; this is Townsend's personal journal, upon which Steven's *Thousand Trails* is based), 18 August 1917, TA #00135.

22. Hibbard to Williams Kahn, 29 November 1961, TA #19753; HI with Cameron Townsend, TA.

23. Townsend academic transcript.

24. HI with Paul Townsend, TA, p. 14.

25. HI #2, p. 5.

26. Journal, 2 October 1917, TA.

27. Jim Elliot quoted in Elisabeth Elliot, *Through Gates of Splendor* (1956; rpt., Wheaton, IL: Tyndale House, 1981), 14; Townsend quote from "For the Tribes of Mexico," *Moody Monthly,* February 1942, 356.

28. Joel A. Carpenter and Wilbert R. Shenk, eds., *Earthen Vessels: American Evangelicals and Foreign Missions, 1880–1980* (Grand Rapids, MI: W. B. Eerdmans, 1990), xii–xiv.

29. "What Next in Missions?" *The Institute Tie,* July 1910, 872; John R. Mott, *The Evangelization of the World in This Generation* (1900; rpt., New York: Arno Press, 1972), 165.

30. George Marsden, *Fundamentalism and American Culture: The Shaping of Twentieth-Century Evangelicalism, 1870–1925* (New York: Oxford University Press, 1980), 4.

31. A good example of a *Moody* article is "Marvels Told by the Doctor of Cameroun," *Moody Bible Institute Monthly,* November 1924, 107–08; Arthur T. Pierson, *The New Acts of the Apostles; or, the Marvels of Modern Missions* (London: James Nisbet and Co., 1896), 51, 84.

32. Dorothy Westrom VanKampen, "Why I Want to Be a Missionary," *Moody Monthly,* August 1940, 669.

33. Elisabeth Elliot, *The Savage My Kinsman* (1961; Ann Arbor: Servant Publications, 1966), 13–14.

Chapter 2

1. Journal, 17, 18, 19, 24, 26, 29 September 1917, TA; HI #2, p. 40, TA; Townsend to "home folks," 21 September 1917, TA; Robert Harkness, *Reuben Archer Torrey: The Man, His Message* (Chicago: Bible Institute Colportage Association, 1929), 55.

2. Virginia Garrard-Burnett, *Protestantism in Guatemala: Living in the New Jerusalem* (Austin: University of Texas Press, 1998), 47–50.

3. Ciro F. S. Cardoso, "Central America: The Liberal Era, c. 1870–1930," in Leslie Bethell, ed., *The Cambridge History of Latin America*, vol. V, c. 1870–1930 (Cambridge: Cambridge University Press, 1986), 220–21.

4. Garrard-Burnett, *Protestantism*, 10–20.

5. Ibid., 21–46.

6. The term "spiritual manifest destiny" is Garrard-Burnett's; ibid., 46; C. I. Scofield, "The Central American Mission Field," *The Missionary Review of the World* (New York: Missionary Review Publishing Co., March 1898), 184–89.

7. This historical sketch was taken from the following pamphlets: "Bible House of Los Angeles: Foundation and Methods," 1952; "Bible House of Los Angeles Anniversary Bulletin," 1953; "An Open Door: Report of the Bible House of Los Angeles," 1909; "Secretary's Report to the Board of Trustees of the Bible House of Los Angeles, October 1, 1914." The latter two were written by R. D. Smith. All of these reports can be found in the archives of the American Bible Society, New York.

8. Hefley and Hefley, *Uncle Cam*, 29; Townsend to "home folks," 28 October 1917, TA.

9. Journal, 10 October 1917, TA #00183.

10. Journal, 3 October 1917, TA.

11. Journal, 14 October 1917, TA #00189.

12. Journal, 14, 21, 23, 24 October, 18 November 1917, TA.

13. Lewis Sperry Chafer to R. D. Smith, 16 December 1924, Central American Mission Archives, Dallas (hereafter CAM); Steven, *Thousand Trails*, 56; Journal, 3 October 1917, TA.

14. Journal, 30 November, 3 December 1917, TA.

15. Garrard-Burnett, *Protestantism*, 44–45; Dorothy Martin, *100 . . . and Counting: The Story of CAM's First Century* (Dallas: CAM International, 1990), 28, 34, 100.

16. Lois Boyd and R. Douglas Brackenridge, *Presbyterian Women in America: Two Centuries of a Quest for Status* (Westport, CT: Greenwood Press, 1983), 165; *Moody Bible Institute Annual Report, 1931–1932* (Chicago: Moody Bible Institute Archives), 12; Gordon J. Bishop, "Needed: Men for Missions," *Moody Monthly*, March 1948, 487–89.

17. Townsend, "History of the Work of the Central American Mission among the Cakchiquel, Zutigil, and Quiche Indians from 1919 to 1935," TA #946084.

18. Journal, 17 October 1917, TA.

19. HI, "Early Reminiscences by WCT," unmarked pages, TA; Steven, *Thousand Trails*, 71; Journal, 20 October 1917, TA #00200.

20. Journal, 11, 22 October 1917, TA.

21. Journal, 23 October 1917, TA #00207–08; Steven, *Thousand Trails,* 77–79.

22. Steven, *Thousand Trails,* 90.

23. Journal, 25 October, 27 November 1917, 22 January 1918, TA.

24. Journal, 22 November 1917, TA #00273.

25. Journal, 23, 24 October, 19 November 1917, TA #00211; Townsend to "folks," 28 October 1917, TA; Steven, *Thousand Trails,* 105.

26. Journal, 21 July, 28 November 1918, TA.

27. Steven, *Thousand Trails,* 83; Journal, 8 November 1917, 28 January, 7 February 1918, TA.

28. HI #3, p. 27, TA; Journal, 28 October 1917, TA #00222; Steven, *Thousand Trails,* 88; Townsend to "home folks," 17 May 1918, TA #00599.

29. Journal, 22 November 1917, TA #00273.

30. Journal, 26 November 1917, TA #00280.

31. Journal, 24 November 1917, TA.

32. Scofield, "Central American Mission Field," CAM.

33. A. E. Bishop, "Special Bulletin No. 3," 22 January 1918, TA #00613; Luther Rees to William Pettingill, 21 November 1921, CAM.

34. Journal, 12, 14 October 1917, TA.

35. Journal, 26, 27 October, 6, 17 November 1917, TA.

36. Journal, 28 October 1917, TA #00222.

37. Journal, 1, 7, 22 November 1917, TA.

38. Townsend to "home folks," 22 January 1918, TA #00610.

39. Steven, *Thousand Trails,* 198; Journal, 18, 19 December 1917, TA; Townsend to "home folks," mid-July 1918, TA.

40. Townsend to "home folks," 1 February 1919, TA #00651; Townsend to "home folks," 17 May 1918, TA #00599; Townsend to Paul, 7 July 1918, TA #00591; Steven, *Thousand Trails,* 198, 200.

41. Townsend to "home folks," 19 July 1918, TA #00583.

42. Journal, 26 November 1918, TA #00537.

43. Journal, 16, 23 November 1917, 16 July, 23, 28 August 1918, TA; Steven, *Thousand Trails,* 150.

44. Journal, 21 May 1918, TA #00404.

45. Journal, 31 October 1917, TA #00229–30; Steven, *Thousand Trails,* 151.

46. Allan Figueroa Deck, "The Challenge of Evangelical/Pentecostal Christianity to Hispanic Catholicism," in Jay P. Dolan and Allan Figueroa Deck, eds., *Hispanic Catholic Culture in the U.S.: Issues and Concerns* (Notre Dame, IN: University of Notre Dame Press, 1994), 422.

47. Journal, 25 October, 14 November 1917, TA.

48. Journal, 18 August 1918, TA #00462.

49. Journal, 21 August 1918, TA.

50. Journal, 10 May, 4, 5, 13 August 1918, TA.

51. The statistics are from Garrard-Burnett, *Protestantism,* 45, 162.

52. Journal, 20 November 1917, TA #00268.

53. Journal, 23 October 1917, TA #00208; Steven, *Thousand Trails,* 191; Townsend to "home folks," 13 June 1918, TA #00596; Townsend to "home folks," 14 October 1918, TA #00571.

54. HI, "Devotional Life and Doctrinal Stand," pp. 2–3, TA.

55. Townsend to "home folks," March 1919, TA #00642.

56. Journal, 12, 14, 15 November 1918, TA; Townsend to "home folks," 13 November 1918, TA #00574.

57. Townsend to "home folks," 24 April 1918, TA; Townsend to "home folks," 17 May 1918, TA #00599; Steven, *Thousand Trails,* 186–87.

58. Townsend to "home folks," 19 July 1918, TA #00583.

59. Steven, *Thousand Trails,* 200; Townsend to "home folks," 3 November 1918, TA #00575; Journal, 31 December 1918, TA.

60. Townsend to "home folks," 31 December 1918, TA; Townsend to "home folks," 16 February 1918, TA; Townsend to "folks," 22 August 1918, TA; receipt from U.S. National Museum, 13 August 1918, TA; Townsend to "home folks," 3 November 1918, TA #00575.

61. Townsend to "home folks," mid-July 1918, TA; Townsend to "home folks," 14 October 1918, TA #00571.

62. Judge Scott to R. D. Smith, 28 January 1919, CAM; Smith to Scott, 21 January 1919, CAM.

Chapter 3

1. Townsend to "home folks," 17 February 1919, TA; Townsend to "home folks," March 1919, TA #00642.

2. Elvira to Joe Malmstrom, 19 November 1917, TA #900124; Elvira to Joe, 11 June 1918, TA #900597; Elvira to Joe, 30 July 1918, TA.

3. Townsend to "home folks," 1 February 1919, TA #00651; Garrard-Burnett, *Protestantism,* 35.

4. Townsend to "home folks," 20 January 1919, TA #00647; Townsend to "home folks," 1 February 1919, TA #00651; Townsend to "home folks," 10 February 1919, TA.

5. Townsend to "home folks," 20 January 1919, TA #00647; Townsend to Paul, 26 January 1919, TA #00646.

6. Elvira to Scott, 30 August 1919, TA #00634.

7. HI, TA #43653; Scott to Townsend, 19 June 1919, TA; Scott to Jones, 3 June 1919, CAM; Scott to Townsend, 9 June 1919, TA.

8. Rees to Scott, 27 May 1919, CAM; Townsend to Scott, 7 March 1921, TA #00794.

9. Elvira to Scott, 30 August 1919, TA #00634; Townsend to Carl, 5 September 1919, TA #00631.

10. Townsend to "home folks," 15 December 1919, TA #00620; Elvira to Scott, 30 August 1919, TA #00634.

11. Marybeth Rupert, "The Emergence of the Independent Missionary Agency as an American Institution, 1860–1917," PhD dissertation, Yale University, 1974, 111.

12. Parker, *Kingdom of Character,* 116.

13. Rowland V. Bingham, "Seven Sevens of Years and A JUBILEE! The Story of the Sudan Interior Mission," in Joel A. Carpenter, ed., *Missionary Innovation and Expansion* (rpt., 1943; New York: Garland, 1988).

14. Quoted in Rupert, "Emergence of the Independent Missionary Agency," 136, 144.

15. Dana Lee Robert, "Arthur Tappan Pierson and Forward Movements of Late-Nineteenth-Century Evangelicalism," PhD dissertation, Yale University, 1984, 172–75.

16. Arthur Judson Brown, *The Foreign Missionary: An Incarnation of a World Movement* (1907; New York: Fleming H. Revell, 1932), 67.

17. Valentin Rabe, "Evangelical Logistics: Mission Support and Resources to 1920," in John K. Fairbank, ed., *The Missionary Enterprise in China and America* (Cambridge: Harvard University Press, 1974), 75; Harold R. Cook, "Missions at the Grass Roots," *Moody Monthly,* August 1950, 832; Dean of the Education Office, *Annual Report, 1933–1934* (Chicago: MBI Archives), 8.

18. Joel A. Carpenter, "Propagating the Faith Once Delivered: The Fundamentalist Missionary Enterprise, 1920–1945," in Carpenter and Shenk, *Earthen Vessels,* 101; Ed Cook, "How Shall We Introduce the Theme of Missions in the Sunday-school?" *Christian Workers Magazine,* December 1917, 300; Robert Niklaus, John Sawin, and Samuel J. Stoesz, *All for Jesus: God at Work in the Christian and Missionary Alliance over One Hundred Years* (Camp Hill, PA: Christian Publications, 1986), 104.

19. *AIM Mission Manual* (Wheaton, IL: Billy Graham Center Archives), No. 81, 10–11, p. 16; Kenneth J. Johnston, *The Story of New Tribes Mission* (Sanford, FL: The Mission, 1985), 29; AIM file (Wheaton, IL: Billy Graham Center), No. 81, 8–61; Bob Jones to Ralph Davis, 6 March 1950, AIM file.

20. William Culbertson, "Should You Go to a Bible Institute?" *Moody Monthly,* June 1950, 736; Dean of Education Office, *Annual Report, 1919–1920* (Chicago: MBI Archives), 20.

21. Valentin H. Rabe, *The Home Base of American China Missions, 1880–1920* (Cambridge: Harvard University Press, 1978), 88; C. T. Studd, "An Original Plea for Missionary Workers," *Christian Workers Magazine,* February 1915, 365; Robert Ekvall, recorded interview (Wheaton, IL: Billy Graham Center), CN 92 T1; Dean of Education Office, *Annual Report, 1931–1932* (Chicago: MBI Archives), 12.

22. Andrew Walls, "The American Dimension in the History of the Missionary Movement," in Carpenter and Shenk, *Earthen Vessels,* 14.

23. Rabe, "Evangelical Logistics," in Fairbank, *Missionary Enterprise,* 75; Parker, *Kingdom of Character,* 34–35.

24. Dana Robert, "Pierson and Forward Movements," 272–80.

25. Roger Steer, *George Müller: Delighted in God* (Wheaton, IL: Harold Shaw, 1981), 30–39.

26. J. Hudson Taylor, *Hudson Taylor* (Minneapolis: Bethany House, n.d.), 13–22, 128, 143.

27. Hudson Taylor quoted in Daniel W. Bacon, "The Influence of Hudson Taylor on the Faith Mission Movement," thesis, Trinity Evangelical Divinity School, 1983, 29.

28. Carpenter, "Propagating the Faith," 55.

29. C. I. Scofield, "The Indians of Central America," in *Missionary Review of the World* (New York: Missionary Review Publishing Co., March 1896), 186–92; Scofield, "Central American Mission Field."

30. Scofield, "Central American Mission Field."

31. Scofield, "Indians of Central America."

32. The slogan comes from Edward Erny and Esther Erny, *No Guarantee but God: The Story of the Founders of the Oriental Missionary Society* (Greenwood, IN: Oriental Missionary Society, 1969).

33. See Martin, *100 . . . and Counting,* for an overview of CAM's history.

34. Bingham, "Seven Sevens of Years," in Carpenter, *Missionary Innovation;* Garrard-Burnett, *Protestantism,* 43.

35. Quoted in Dick Anderson, *We Felt Like Grasshoppers: The Story of Africa Inland Mission* (Nottingham, Eng.: Crossway Books, 1994), 31; Karl Hummel to Archer Anderson, 8 August 1929, CAM.

36. "Central American Mission: Application for Appointment as Missionary," CAM; R. D. Smith to Hummel, 16 April 1926, CAM.

37. Hummel to Townsend, 27 March 1933, TA #01759.

38. L. L. Legters to Townsend, 16 August 1927, TA #01284.

39. Elvira in the *Central American Bulletin* (hereafter *CAB*), TA #00636; Townsend, "A Glimpse of Central America," in *Moody Church News,* January 1926, TA #01236; *CAB,* 15 March 1922, CAM.

40. R. D. Smith to "friend," 5 October 1921, CAM.

41. Townsend to "home folks," March 1919, TA #00642; Townsend to Mrs. Greenleaf, 7 March 1927, TA #01344.

42. Rees to Pettingill, 18 March 1922, CAM; R. D. Smith, "Secretary's Report to the Board of Trustees of the Bible House of Los Angeles, October 1, 1914" (New York: American Bible Society Archives).

43. Townsend to Judge Scott, 24 November 1919, TA #00627.

44. Townsend to "home folks," 20 January 1919, TA #00647; Townsend to Paul, 26 January 1919, TA #00646.

45. Townsend to Carl Malmstrom, 5 September 1919, TA #00631; Elvira in *CAB,* TA #00619.

46. Scofield, "Central American Mission Field" and "Indians of Central America."

47. "Preparations for the Establishment of Presbyterian Work among the Indians of Guatemala," TA #46090; H. C. Dillon, "Document II: Indians of Guatemala and Yucatan," TA #46090.

48. Scofield, "Indians of Central America."

49. "Pioneer Mission Agency," Keswick Archives (hereafter KA), Whiting, New Jersey.

50. Scofield, "Central American Mission Field"; Garrard-Burnett, *Protestantism,* 52; Edward Haymaker to Townsends, 10 November 1920, TA #00657.

51. Garrard-Burnett, *Protestantism,* 52, 68, 70.

52. Townsend, "History of the Work of the Central American Mission among the Cakchiquel, Zutigil, and Quiché Indians from 1919 to 1935," TA #946084; Townsend to Judge Scott, 24 November 1919, TA #00627; HI, TA #43617; Diane Langmore, *Missionary Lives: Papua, 1874–1914* (Honolulu: University of Hawaii Press, 1989), 133.

53. Elvira to Scott, 8 March 1920, TA #00693; Townsend, "The Guatemalan Indian," TA #46143; Townsend to "home folks," 26 January 1920, TA #00701.

54. Townsend, "The Corn-stalk House," TA #946085.

55. Townsend to Mr. Jordan, 20 December 1924, TA #01011.

56. Townsend to "home folks," 21 June 1920, TA #00681.

57. Elvira to Scott, 1 October 1920, TA.

58. Scott to Townsend, 7 August 1920, TA #00674; Townsend to Scott, 21 August 1920, TA.

59. Scott to Townsend, 3 July 1920, TA #00678; Townsend in *CAB,* 3 May 1920, TA #00685; Townsend to Scott, 13 September 1921, TA #00725.

60. Townsend, "The Cakchiquel New Testament," TA #946100.

61. Elvira in *CAB,* 10 May 1920, TA #00683; Townsend, "Guatemalan Indian," TA #46143; Townsend to Scott, 27 September 1920, TA #00667; Elvira in *CAB,* 31 May 1920, TA #00683.

62. Townsend, "Guatemalan Indian," TA #46143.

63. Elvira to Scott, 1 September 1920, TA #00669; Townsend to Scott, 27 July 1920, TA #00675; Scott to Townsend, 7 August 1920, TA #00674; Elvira to Scott, 8 November 1920, TA #00658; Elvira to Scott, 14 February 1921, TA #00798.

64. Townsend to Chafer, 22 October 1923, TA #00952; see the memorial pamphlet, "Dr. Howard A. Kelly: The Beloved Christian Physician," copy on file with the author; Carl Bode, *Mencken* (Carbondale: Southern Illinois University Press, 1969), 149–51.

65. Scott to Townsends, 5 June 1920, TA #00682; Townsend to Scott, 27 July 1920, TA #00675; R. D. Smith to Scott, 16 November 1920, TA.

66. Elvira to Scott, 11 March 1920, TA; Elvira in *CAB,* 21 August 1920, TA #00672. There is an excellent discussion of the ideals of missionary prayer letters in Jeffrey Swanson, *Echoes of the Call: Identity and Ideology among American Missionaries in Ecuador* (New York: Oxford University Press, 1995), 133, 136.

67. Elvira to Scott, 1 October 1920, TA.

68. Letterhead from 1922, TA #00894; rough draft of copy for *The National Cyclopedia of American Biography,* 6 July 1926, KA.

69. "The First Day at a Victorious Life Conference," *Christ Life,* November 1929, KA; Townsend on Legters from HI, TA #43539, 43540.

70. Legters to PMA board of directors, December 1932, TA #901671; Townsend to Mr. Beets, 5 November 1943, KA.

71. For a good popular history of Keswick, see J. C. Pollock, *The Keswick Story: The Authorized History of the Keswick Convention* (London: Hodder and Stoughton, 1964). The Englishman's quote about Pearsall Smith is found on page 14.

72. "The Conference and Its Message," in *The Victorious Life: Messages from the Summer Conferences* (1918; New York: Garland, 1988), 1–6; McQuilkin quoted in "The Aim and Message of the Conferences at America's Keswick," KA.

73. Robert C. McQuilkin, "The Conference at Whittier," in *Victorious Life*, 7–11; Philip Howard, "The Conference at Princeton," in *Victorious Life*, 15.

74. J. Harvey Borton, "A Business Man's Victory," in *Victorious Life*, 338; Pollock, *Keswick Story.* For the links between Keswick and the Student Volunteer Movement, see Parker, *Kingdom of Character*, 36–42.

75. "Aim and Message," KA; Howard, "Conference at Princeton," in *Victorious Life*, 14; Charles Gallaudet Trumbull, "The Conference at Cedar Lake," in *Victorious Life*, 22, italics mine.

76. Hummel to CAM missionaries, 22 May 1928, TA; Elvira to Scott, 30 August 1919, TA #00634; Townsend to Hummel, 10 May 1926, TA #01227.

77. Townsend in *CAB*, 3 January 1921, TA #00807.

78. Howard Dinwiddie notes, KA.

79. Dinwiddie to Townsend, 29 January 1923, TA #01006.

80. Townsend to Scott, 7 March 1921, TA #00794.

81. Townsend to Dinwiddie, 14 February 1921, TA #00797.

82. Anna Marie Dahlquist, *Burgess of Guatemala* (Langley, BC: Cedar Books, 1985).

83. Anna Marie Dahlquist, *Trailblazers for Translators: The Chichicastenango Twelve* (Pasadena, CA: William Carey Library, 1995); Conference minutes, 23 January 1921, KA.

84. Ibid.

85. Dahlquist, *Trailblazers*, 34–54.

86. Townsend to Dinwiddie, 5 September 1921, TA #00728; Dahlquist, *Trailblazers*, 34–54; Dahlquist, *Burgess of Guatemala*, 97–99; Dinwiddie to Townsend, 23 August 1921, TA #00734.

87. Townsend to Scott, 31 January 1921, TA #00800.

88. Scott to Jones, 9 February 1921, CAM; R. D. Smith to Scott, 18 May 1921, CAM.

89. Rees to R. D. Smith, 14 February 1921, CAM; R. D. Smith to Rees, 19 February 1921, CAM; Rees to Chafer, 20 May 1922, CAM.

90. R. D. Smith to Rees, 19 February 1921, CAM; R. D. Smith to Townsend, 19 February 1921, CAM; Townsend to R. D. Smith, 2 May 1921, TA #00777.

91. Dinwiddie to Townsend, 30 April 1921, TA #00781; Albert Bishop to Dinwiddie, 9 June 1921, CAM; see also Dahlquist, *Trailblazers*, 50–54; Townsend on Legters from HI, TA #43539, 43540.

92. Howard B. Dinwiddie, "The Voice of Blood: What Does the White Man Owe His Red Brother?" KA.

93. Dinwiddie to Townsend, 24 March 1921, TA #00789; Dinwiddie to Townsend, 23 May 1921, TA #00768; Dinwiddie to Elvira, 27 June 1921, TA #00756; Dinwiddie to Townsend, 29 July 1921, TA #00740.

94. L. L. Legters, "Missionary Survey of Guatemala Indians," May 1921, KA; HI with Townsend, TA #43602, 43539, 43540.

95. Townsend to Scott, 7 March 1921, TA #00794.

96. Dinwiddie to Townsend, 23 May 1921, TA #00768; Dinwiddie to Townsend, 1 July 1921, TA #00747.

97. Townsend, "Co-pastors," TA #946090; Townsend to council, 18 July 1925, TA #01119.

98. Townsend in *CAB,* 15 May 1921, TA #00779; Townsend to Scott, 15 May 1921, TA #00771.

99. Townsend, "Part of St. Mark Published in 1921," TA #946101; Townsend, 10 July 1921, TA; Townsend, "What Won the Mayor," TA #946102.

100. Bingham, "Seven Sevens of Years," in Carpenter, *Missionary Innovation,* 34, 58, 60; Dahlquist, *Trailblazers;* Carey to Kingston, 1 September 1986, TA #43283; Townsend in *CAB,* 5 April 1922, TA #00917.

101. Townsend, "Methods of Reaching the Indians," TA #01903; italics mine.

102. Townsend in *CAB,* 31 April 1921, TA #00779.

103. Townsend to Paul, 26 January 1919, TA #00646; Townsend to Scott, 26 May 1921, TA #00767.

104. Townsend to Scott, 26 May 1921, TA #00767; Townsend to Scott, 13 September 1921, TA #00725; Townsend, "Guatemalan Indian," TA #46143.

105. Wilkins Bowdre Winn, "A History of the Central American Mission as Seen in the Work of Albert Edward Bishop, 1896–1922," PhD dissertation, University of Alabama, 1964, 121.

106. Townsend in *CAB,* 25 July and 17 August 1921, TA #00751.

107. Townsend to Scott, 25 April 1921, TA #00782; Elvira to Scott, 14 June 1921, TA; Elvira to Scott, 5 May 1921, TA #00776; Townsend to Dinwiddie, 20 June 1921, TA #00757.

108. Dinwiddie to Elvira, 27 June 1921, TA #00756; Elvira to Scott, 27 June 1921, TA #00755.

109. Elvira to Scott, 4 April 1921, TA; Elvira to Scott, 27 June 1921, TA #00755.

110. Elvira to Scott, 30 August 1921, TA; Elvira to Scott, 13 September 1921, TA; Elvira to Scott, 5 October 1921, TA #00717; R. D. Smith to Scott, 5 October 1921, CAM.

111. Dinwiddie to Townsend, 30 April 1921, TA #00781; Townsend to Scott, 26 May 1921, TA #00767.

112. Dinwiddie to Townsend, 29 July 1921, TA #00740; Dinwiddie to Townsend, 23 August 1921, TA #00734; Dinwiddie to Townsend, 27 September 1921, TA #00722; Dinwiddie to Elvira, 1 October 1921, TA #00719.

113. Samuel Moffett to "friend," 28 November 1921, CAM; "Minutes of the Meeting of

the Conference Regarding the Indians of Central and South America and Mexico, September 13 and 14, 1921. Friends' Arch Street Center, Phila.," KA.

114. Journal, TA #00812–39.

115. Blanche Smith to Rees, 23 November 1921, CAM; Townsend to Beets, 5 November 1943, KA; "Pioneer Mission Agency," KA; Legters, "Pioneer Mission Agency," KA; "The Pioneer Mission Agency: What and Why?" *Sunday School Times,* 25 February 1922, KA.

116. Dinwiddie to Townsend, 6 June 1922, TA; Rees to Pettingill, 8 February 1922, CAM; *CAB,* 15 March 1922, CAM; Scott to R. D. Smith, 1 October 1921, CAM.

117. Dahlquist, *Trailblazers,* 72–79; Dinwiddie to Townsend, 29 January 1923, TA #01006.

118. Dahlquist, *Trailblazers,* 16–18, 56; Legters to Townsend, 6 September 1928, TA #01376; Townsend to Rees, 11 August 1922, TA; Townsend to Rees, 11 September 1923, TA #00967.

119. Blanche Smith to Rees, 29 December 1921, CAM.

120. Blanche Smith to Rees, 21 October 1921, CAM; Blanche Smith to Rees, 23 November 1921, CAM; Blanche Smith to Rees, 25 December 1921, CAM.

121. Townsend to Rees, 14 December 1921, TA #00711.

122. Blanche Smith to Rees, 25 December 1921, CAM; Blanche Smith to Rees, 29 December 1921, CAM.

123. Blanche Smith to Rees, 31 December 1921, CAM.

124. Townsend to Rees, 14 December 1921, TA #00711; Rees to Townsend, 11 January 1922, TA #00930; Rees to Pettingill, 11 January 1922, CAM; Paul Townsend to Chafer, 13 November 1923, CAM.

125. Blanche Smith to Rees, 28 January 1922, CAM.

Chapter 4

1. PMA to "Mr. Editor," 24 October 1923, KA.

2. Townsend to Rees, 25 January 1922, TA #00928.

3. Blanche Smith to Townsend, 28 January 1922, TA #00927; Townsend to Rees, 11 February 1922, TA; Townsend to Rees, 1 March 1922, TA #00922; Townsend to Rees, 5 April 1922, TA; Rees to Townsend, 7 March 1922, TA #00921; Blanche Smith to Rees, 25 March 1922, CAM; Blanche Smith to Rees, 1 February 1922, CAM.

4. Townsend to Rees, 21 March 1922, TA #00918; Blanche Smith to Rees, 17 March 1922, CAM.

5. Elvira to Rees, 18 March 1922, TA #00919.

6. Blanche Smith to Rees, 25 March 1922, CAM; Elvira to Rees, 29 March 1922, TA; Rees to Townsend, 18 April 1922, TA #00904; Townsend to Dinwiddie, 16 May 1922, TA #00890.

7. Elvira to Rees, 18 March 1922, TA #00919; Townsend to Rees, 5 April 1922, TA.

8. Dana Robert, "The Crisis of Missions," in Carpenter and Shenk, *Earthen Vessels,*

32, 41; Rupert, "Emergence of the Independent Missionary Agency," 136; quoted in David P. Sandgren, *Christianity and the Kikuyu: Religious Divisions and Social Conflict* (New York: Peter Lang, 1989), 19; Scofield, "Central American Mission Field," 184–89.

9. Frank F. Ellinwood, *Questions and Phases of Modern Missions* (New York: Dodd, Mead and Co., 1899), 83–84, 98.

10. Mott, *Evangelization of the World*, 15.

11. Carl Schumacher, "Class Notes on the Subjects in the Missionary Course: September 1924–August 1926" (Chicago: Moody Bible Institute Archives), 585–86.

12. Rees to Townsend, 30 March 1922, TA #00913; Rees to Pettingill, 13 March 1922, CAM; Rees to Pettingill, 21 July 1922, CAM.

13. Townsend to Scott, June 1921, TA #00753; Rees to Frank Gillingham, 27 January 1922, CAM.

14. Rees to Pettingill, 19 April 1922, CAM.

15. Townsend to Rees, 11 August 1922, TA.

16. J. D. Hannah, "Chafer, Lewis Sperry (1871–1952)," in Daniel G. Reid et al., eds., *Dictionary of Christianity in America* (Downers Grove, IL: InterVarsity Press, 1990), 237–38.

17. Chafer to Rees, 4 July 1922, CAM; Chafer to Rees, 11 February 1925, CAM; Chafer to R. D. Smith, 1 November 1924, CAM.

18. For details, see HI, TA #43649, and Townsend to Dr. Francis, 28 June 1922, TA #00869.

19. Elvira to Rees, 22 May 1922, TA #00886; copy of *Moody Monthly* article in TA #00874; Elvira to Rees, 27 June 1922, TA #00870.

20. Elvira to Rees, 13 July 1922, TA #00862; Elvira in *Moody Church News*, March 1923, TA #01002.

21. Townsend to Dinwiddie, 16 May 1922, TA #00890; Townsend to Dinwiddie, 6 October 1922, TA #00848; Dinwiddie to Townsend, 6 June 1922, TA #00880; Townsend to Dinwiddie, 8 July 1922, TA #00865; Dinwiddie to Townsend, 9 September 1922, TA #00850.

22. Townsend to Rees, 2 May 1922, TA #00897.

23. Dinwiddie to Townsend, 29 January 1923, TA #01006.

24. Dinwiddie to CAM, 20 March 1923, CAM; Chafer to Dinwiddie, 31 March 1923, CAM; see Dahlquist, *Trailblazers*, 107–08.

25. Chafer to Dinwiddie, 7 June 1923, CAM; Dinwiddie to Chafer, 22 June 1923, CAM.

26. Townsend in *CAB*, 17 January 1923, TA #00841; Townsend to "Uncle Tom," 16 March 1923, TA #01004.

27. Townsend to Chafer, 3 May 1923, TA #00995; Townsend to Chafer, 19 June 1923, TA #00984; Townsend to Thomas Jones, 2 April 1923, TA #01001.

28. Chafer to Townsend, 2 May 1923, TA #00997; Chafer to Townsend, 7 May 1923, TA #00994; Chafer to R. D. Smith, 5 May 1923, CAM.

29. Townsend to Chafer, 19 June 1923, TA #00984.

30. Alvyn J. Austin, "Blessed Adversity: Henry W. Frost and the China Inland Mission," in Carpenter and Shenk, *Earthen Vessels,* 53.

31. Scofield, "Central American Mission Field," 184–89.

32. Hummel to council, 23 November 1927, CAM; Hummel to council, 12 July 1926, CAM.

33. Hummel to council, 22 January 1927, CAM; Dinwiddie to Townsend, 2 July 1925, TA #01127.

34. Scott to Jones, 9 February 1921, CAM.

35. Chafer to R. D. Smith, 15 June 1923, CAM; Chafer to Rees, 7 July 1922, CAM.

36. Chafer to Pettingill, 2 March 1923, CAM; Chafer to R. D. Smith, 2 March 1923, CAM.

37. Chafer to R. D. Smith, 5 May 1923, CAM; Chafer to R. D. Smith, 15 June 1923, CAM.

38. Townsend to Chafer, 19 June 1923, TA #00984; Chafer to R. D. Smith, 13 December 1923, CAM.

39. Chafer to R. D. Smith, 15 June 1923, CAM.

40. Townsend to Chafer, 26 October 1923, TA #00951.

41. Chafer to Townsend, 8 November 1923, TA #00948; Townsend to Chafer, 19 November 1923, TA #00943.

42. R. D. Smith to Chafer, 18 December 1923, CAM; R. D. Smith to Hummel, 15 April 1925, CAM.

43. R. D. Smith to Chafer, 18 February 1924, CAM; Rees to Chafer, 17 April 1924, CAM.

44. Townsend to "Uncle Tom," 18 March 1923, TA #01004; Elvira to Chafer, 9 February 1925, TA #01171.

45. Townsend to "home folks," 19 May 1923, TA #00992; *Cakchiquel News,* 10 May 1923, TA #46141; *Cakchiquel News,* 1 July 1923, TA #46139; Anderson to Chafer, 25 March 1924, CAM.

46. Anderson to Chafer, 10 June 1923, CAM.

47. Townsend to Chafer, 25 April 1923, TA; Chafer to Townsend, 7 May 1923, TA #00994.

48. R. D. Smith to Rees, 22 August 1922, CAM; Townsend to "Uncle Tom," 16 March 1923, TA #01004; Townsend to Chafer, 25 April 1923, TA; Townsend to Dinwiddie, 31 March 1923, TA #01003; Townsend to Chafer, 14 May 1924, TA #01066.

49. Townsend to "home folks," 19 May 1923, TA #00992; Laura and Paul Townsend to "home folks," 10 June 1923, TA #00987.

50. Chafer to Rees, 26 July 1922, CAM.

51. Chafer to Pettingill, 2 March 1923, CAM; Chafer to Dr. John Harrington, 30 July 1923, CAM; Pettingill to Chafer, 6 July 1923, CAM; Chafer to Pettingill, 9 July 1923, CAM.

52. Quoted in Chafer to Pettingill, October 1923, CAM.

53. Henry Frost to Chafer, 10 October 1923, CAM; Chafer to Pettingill, October 1923, CAM.

54. Harrington to Chafer, 18 July 1923, CAM; Chafer to Pettingill, 19 June 1923, CAM.

55. R. D. Smith to Townsend, quoted in Smith to Chafer, 4 October 1923, CAM; Townsend to Chafer, 21 August 1923, TA #00973; Townsend to Rees, 11 September 1923, TA #00967; Paul Townsend to Chafer, 13 November 1923, CAM.

56. Townsend, "Water Baptism and the Biblical Mode," TA #01008.

57. Townsend to Chafer, 30 March 1924, TA #01079; Chafer to Townsend, 21 April 1924, TA #01074; Paul Townsend to Chafer, 20 May 1924, TA #01060.

58. Signe Norrlin to Chafer, 24 September 1923, CAM.

59. Fannie Becker to Rees, 14 October 1923, CAM; Fannie Becker to Rees, 26 April 1924, CAM.

60. Paul Townsend to Chafer, 6 August 1923, CAM; Paul Townsend to Chafer, 6 September 1923, CAM.

61. R. D. Smith to Chafer, 11 September 1923, CAM; Chafer to Rees, 4 September 1923, CAM; Rees to Elvira, 3 October 1923, TA #00959.

62. Elvira to Rees, 13 October 1923, TA #00956; Townsend to Hummel, 6 January 1936, TA #01990.

63. Rees to Chafer, 10 November 1923, CAM.

64. Townsend to Chafer, 22 October 1923, TA #00952; Townsend to Chafer, 26 October 1923, TA #00951; Paul Townsend to Chafer, 13 November 1923, CAM; Townsend to Chafer, 19 November 1923, TA #00943; Chafer to R. D. Smith, 28 March 1924, CAM.

65. Townsend, "St. John Published in 1923," TA #946103; Townsend to Chafer, 21 August 1923, TA #00973; R. D. Smith to Townsend, 9 February 1927, TA #01354; Chafer to Townsend, 8 January 1925, TA #01180.

66. Townsend to Chafer, 12 November 1923, TA #00945; Laura to "folks," 18 February 1924, TA #01084; Townsend to Chafer, 30 March 1924, TA #01079.

67. R. D. Smith to Chafer, 3 December 1923, CAM; Chafer to R. D. Smith, 8 December 1923, CAM; R. D. Smith to Chafer, 1 April 1924, CAM.

68. Townsend to Chafer, 3 October 1924, TA #01023; Townsend in *CAB*, 14 October 1924, TA #01020; Laura to "folks," 18 February 1924, TA #01084; Paul Townsend to Chafer, 6 September 1923, CAM; *Cakchiquel News*, 15 June 1924, TA #46136.

69. Chafer to Townsend, 30 April 1924, TA #01072; Chafer to Townsend, 6 October 1924, TA #01022.

70. Townsend in *CAB*, 14 October 1924, TA #01020.

71. *Cakchiquel News*, 1 July 1923, TA #46139; *Cakchiquel News*, 15 December 1924, TA; *Cakchiquel News*, 15 December 1925, TA.

72. Townsend to Hummel, 28 January 1930, TA; Townsend, "Guatemalan Indian," TA #46143.

73. Townsend to Chafer, 5 May 1924, TA #01070; Chafer to Townsend, 22 May 1924, TA #01059.

74. Townsend to Fred Lincoln, 21 August 1924, TA #01030; Paul Townsend to Hummel, 30 June 1925, CAM; Don Arturo Borja to Paul Townsend, 5 July 1925, CAM.

75. Townsend to Lincoln, 14 July 1924, TA #01045.

76. Bishop to Townsend, 31 July 1924, TA #01037; Lincoln to Bishop, 2 August 1924, TA #01036.

77. Townsend to Jordan, 20 December 1924, TA #01011.

78. Townsend to Chafer, 30 March 1924, TA #01079; Anderson to Mildred Spain, 5 May 1924, CAM; Townsend to Chafer, 23 April 1924, TA #01073.

79. Anderson to Chafer, 25 March 1924; Anderson to Chafer, 12 April 1924, CAM; Paul Townsend to Chafer, 20 May 1923, CAM.

80. Chafer to Townsend, 21 April 1924, TA #01074; Chafer to Anderson, 16 April 1924, CAM.

81. Anderson to Spain, 5 May 1924, CAM; Townsend to Chafer, 5 May 1924, TA #01070; Townsend to Rees, 14 May 1924, TA #01064.

82. Chafer to Townsend, 13 May 1924, TA #01069.

83. Townsend to Anderson, 10 May 1924, CAM.

84. Anderson to Townsend, 11 May 1924, CAM.

85. Townsend to Anderson, 13 May 1924, TA #01067.

86. Statements dated 13 May 1924, TA #01068.

87. Antonio Bac to Chafer, 15 May 1924, TA #01063; Townsend to Chafer, 14 May 1924, TA #01066.

88. Mr. Dunlop to Chafer, 14 May 1924, TA #01065.

89. Rees to Fannie Becker, 15 May 1924, CAM; Chafer to Rees, 23 May 1924, CAM; Chafer to Townsend, 22 May 1924, TA #01059.

90. Chafer to Rees, 24 May 1924, CAM.

91. R. D. Smith to Rees, 27 May 1924, CAM.

92. Rees to Chafer, 28 May 1924, CAM.

93. Rees to Townsend, 28 May 1924, TA #01056.

94. Cameron, Elvira, Paul Townsend, Anderson to Rees, 30 May 1924, TA #01055; Anderson to Rees, 4 June 1924, CAM.

95. R. D. Smith to Rees, 14 August 1924, CAM; Chafer to R. D. Smith, 1 November 1924, CAM; Elvira to Rees, 11 September 1924, TA #01028; Elvira to Rees, 8 August 1925, TA #01109; Elvira to Rees, 22 June 1925, TA #01134; Townsend to Chafer, 24 November 1924, TA #01016; Townsend to Chafer, 3 October 1924, TA #01023; Townsend to Chafer, 3 October 1924, TA #01023.

96. Becker to Chafer, 30 December 1924, CAM; Becker to Jones, 25 December 1923, CAM; Becker to Chafer, 12 November 1923, CAM; Becker to Chafer, 30 October 1923, CAM; Townsend, "Dr. and Mrs. H. A. Becker," TA #946093.

97. Scott to Jones, 9 February 1921, CAM.

98. Rees to Mr. Sutcliffe, 16 May 1925, CAM; "Central American Mission: Application for Appointment as Missionary," CAM.

99. Rees to Chafer, 20 May 1922, CAM; Chafer to Townsend, 16 April 1924, TA #01075;

Townsend to Chafer, 5 May 1924, TA #01070; Townsend to Chafer, 9 April 1924, TA; R. D. Smith to council, 7 July 1922, CAM.

100. R. D. Smith to Scott, 25 February 1920, CAM; R. D. Smith to Rees, 6 July 1922, CAM.

101. Gladys Wright, No. 284, T1, and Paul Stough, CN 89, T1 (Wheaton, IL: Billy Graham Center); AIM (Wheaton, IL: Billy Graham Center), No. 81, 10–10 and 14–11; Martin, *100 . . . and Counting,* 114; Carpenter, "Propagating the Faith," 116–17.

102. Chafer to R. D. Smith, 17 September 1924, CAM.

103. Sandgren, *Christianity and the Kikuyu,* 22; Anderson, *We Felt Like Grasshoppers,* 58–65.

104. Anderson to Chafer, 11 November 1924, CAM; Chafer to Rees, 15 October 1924, CAM; Anderson to Hummel, 19 March 1932, CAM.

105. Anderson, *We Felt Like Grasshoppers,* 34; Rees to Chafer, 17 April 1924, CAM; Ernest Powell to R. D. Smith, 10 June 1925, CAM.

106. Anderson, *We Felt Like Grasshoppers,* 24–28.

107. "What Next in Missions?" 872; Schumacher, "Class Notes," 585.

108. R. D. Smith to Scott, 25 February 1920, CAM; R. D. Smith to Rees, 15 March 1927, CAM; Hummel to R. D. Smith, 27 June 1925, CAM.

109. Hummel to Gillingham, 17 September 1926, CAM.

110. Rees to Scott, 27 May 1919, CAM; Pettingill to Rees, 14 March 1922, CAM; Paul Townsend to Hummel, 26 September 1925, CAM.

111. Chafer to R. D. Smith, 10 April 1924, CAM.

112. Pettingill to Rees, 10 July 1922, CAM; Rees to R. D. Smith, 5 July 1922, CAM; Rees to Blanche Smith, 11 January 1922, CAM.

113. Chafer to R. D. Smith, 29 September 1923, CAM; Paul Townsend to Hummel, August 1928, CAM.

114. Charles Hurlburt to AIM Council, 20 December 1919, CAM.

115. Chafer to Townsend, 26 March 1924, TA #01080.

116. R. D. Smith to Rees, 27 May 1924, CAM.

117. Hummel to Townsend, 28 February 1929, TA #01472; Hummel to Townsend, 27 March 1933, TA #01759.

118. Judge Scott to R. D. Smith, 28 January 1919, CAM.

119. Paul R. Clifford, "Grubb, Kenneth George," in Gerald H. Anderson, ed., *Biographical Dictionary of Christian Missions* (New York: Macmillan Reference, 1998), 265; Kenneth Grubb to Hummel, 23 March 1935, CAM.

120. Townsend to Chafer, 20 December 1924, TA #01010; Chafer to Townsend, 8 January 1925, TA #01180.

Chapter 5

1. Quoted in R. D. Smith to executive committee, 17 April 1923, CAM; Hummel to council, 30 May 1925, TA #01141; Rees to council, 21 May 1925, CAM.

2. Quoted in Townsend to Scott, 13 September 1921, TA #00725; Chafer to R. D. Smith, 1 November 1924, CAM; Chafer to R. D. Smith, 28 March 1924, CAM; Chafer to R. D. Smith, 10 April 1924, CAM.

3. Quoted in R. D. Smith to executive committee, 17 April 1923, CAM; Chafer to R. D. Smith, 15 June 1923, CAM; Rees to Chafer, 28 April 1924, CAM; Rees to council, 21 May 1925, CAM.

4. Rees to Hummel, 21 May 1925, CAM; Hummel to council, 30 May 1925, TA #01141.

5. Gillingham to Hummel, 10 April 1925, CAM; Gillingham to Hummel, 6 May 1925, CAM.

6. R. D. Smith to Hummel, 27 April 1925, CAM; Gillingham to Hummel, 14 May 1925, CAM.

7. Rees to council, 21 May 1925, CAM; Hummel to Gillingham, 23 April 1925, CAM.

8. Rees to council, 21 May 1925, CAM; Powell to R. D. Smith, 10 June 1925, CAM.

9. Chafer to Townsend, 21 April 1924, TA #01074.

10. Townsend to Rees, 13 April 1925, TA #01153.

11. R. D. Smith to Rees, 27 June 1924, CAM; R. D. Smith to Chafer, 18 December 1923, CAM.

12. Chafer to Rees, 23 May 1924, CAM.

13. Townsend to Chafer, 16 February 1925, TA #01170.

14. Townsend to council, 16 February 1925, TA #01169.

15. Paul Townsend to R. D. Smith, 15 April 1925, CAM; R. D. Smith to Paul Townsend, 5 May 1925, CAM.

16. Hummel to Townsend, 3 March 1925, TA #01165.

17. R. D. Smith to council, 3 March 1925, CAM; R. D. Smith to Hummel, 2 April 1925, CAM.

18. R. D. Smith to Townsend, 3 March 1925, CAM.

19. Townsend to R. D. Smith, 24 March 1925, TA #01158.

20. R. D. Smith to Townsend, 27 March 1925, CAM; R. D. Smith to Rees, 7 April 1925, CAM; R. D. Smith to Hummel, 15 April 1925, CAM; R. D. Smith to Hummel, 16 April 1925, CAM; Gillingham to Hummel, 10 April 1925, CAM.

21. Statement quoted in Rees to Hummel, 26 June 1925, CAM.

22. R. D. Smith to Hummel, 22 May 1925, CAM.

23. Rees to Gillingham, 16 June 1925, CAM; Rees to Hummel, 18 April 1925, CAM; Rees to council, 21 May 1925, CAM.

24. Hummel to R. D. Smith, 16 April 1925, CAM; Hummel to council, 30 May 1925, TA #01141.

25. Gillingham to Hummel, 6 May 1925, CAM; R. D. Smith to Hummel, 1 June 1925, CAM; Townsend to Hummel, 5 November 1925, TA #01093; Townsend to council, 2 July 1925, TA #01129.

26. Rees to Townsend, 3 May 1925, TA #01149.

27. Powell to R. D. Smith, 10 June 1925, CAM; Rees to Gillingham, 16 June 1925, CAM.

28. Rees to council, 3 May 1925, CAM.

29. Paul Townsend, as executive secretary of the Cakchiquel Department, to "Colaborers," 26 May 1925, CAM.

30. Lincoln to Paul Townsend, 12 June 1925, CAM.

31. Paul Townsend to Hummel, 26 September 1925, CAM.

32. Elvira to Chafer, 9 February 1925, TA #01171; *Cakchiquel News,* 15 December 1925, TA.

33. Paul Townsend to Lincoln, 26 June 1925, CAM; Paul Townsend to Borja, 15 July 1925, CAM.

34. Paul Burgess testimonial, 12 June 1925, CAM.

35. Paul Townsend, "The Unity of the Church and the Manifestation of That Unity," July 1925, CAM; Rees to R. D. Smith, 16 August 1925, CAM.

36. Letters collected by Paul Townsend and forwarded to the CAM council, CAM.

37. Townsend to Hummel, 3 July 1925, TA #01125; Townsend to Rees, 9 July 1925, TA #01123.

38. Undersigned to council, 8 October 1925, TA #01099; Fern Houser to Hummel, 7 October 1925, TA #01100.

39. Hummel to council, 29 October 1925, CAM; Townsend to Hummel, 28 November 1925, TA #01091.

40. Townsend to Barret, 15 April 1940, TA #02609; see Townsend to Legters, 18 July 1927, TA #01299.

41. "Report of the Deputation to Guatemala Representing the Council of the Central American Mission, December–January, 1925–26," TA #01241.

42. Townsends to "friends," 30 January 1926, TA #01238.

43. Townsend to Rees, 1 March 1926, TA #01234; Townsend to Hummel, 21 April 1926, TA #01232.

44. Quoted in Townsend to Hummel, 5 November 1925, TA #01093.

45. "Report of the Deputation to Guatemala."

46. Townsend to Hummel, 21 April 1926, TA #01232; R. D. Smith to Hummel, 22 June 1925, CAM.

47. Hummel to council, 3 May 1931, CAM; Martin, *100 . . . and Counting,* 102 and 113.

48. Elvira to Hummel, 1 June 1925, TA #01139; Paul Townsend to Stella Zimmerman, 13 July 1925, CAM.

49. Paul Townsend to Hummel, 5 October 1925, CAM; R. D. Smith to Jones, 25 August 1925, CAM; Hummel to Paul Townsend, 10 September 1925, CAM; R. D. Smith to Hummel, 26 September 1925, CAM.

50. Chafer to R. D. Smith, 1 November 1924, CAM.

51. Chafer to Rees, 24 November 1924, CAM.

52. Jones to R. D. Smith, 22 December 1926, CAM.

53. Townsend to Dinwiddie, 12 May 1925, TA #01145; Legters to "Fellow-helpers," 27 July 1924, KA; Legters to Ralph Davis, 18 May 1924, TA #01061; Dinwiddie, "Voice of Blood," KA; Dinwiddie to Townsend, 10 June 1925, TA #01138.

54. Victorious Life Testimony and Pioneer Mission Agency to "friends," January 1926, KA.

55. Legters to Townsend, 13 January 1925, TA #01179.

56. R. D. Smith to CAM council, 11 February 1925, CAM. Apparently Dinwiddie wanted to transfer some Christian and Missionary Alliance missionaries from Spanish work in Argentina and Chile to Indian work in Ecuador and Colombia.

57. R. D. Smith to Hummel, 11 September 1925, CAM.

58. Townsend to Hummel, 11 May 1925, TA #01147; *Cakchiquel News,* 15 June 1928, TA #46117; *Cakchiquel News,* 15 January 1929, TA #46114; *Cakchiquel News,* 15 June 1928, TA #46117; Townsend to Hummel, 29 November 1929, TA #01445.

59. Townsend to Chafer, 20 December 1924, TA #01010; Townsend to Chafer, 16 February 1925, TA #01170; Dinwiddie to Townsend, 2 July 1925, TA #01127; Townsend to Greenleaf, 7 March 1927, TA #01344; Elvira in *CAB,* 15 June 1927, TA #01309.

60. Townsend to Legters, 19 October 1927, TA #01267.

61. Townsend to Dunlop, 22 December 1927, TA #01245.

62. L. L. Legters, "Report of the Second Exploratory Trip into Brazil, 1926," TA #01198.

63. Townsend to Mrs. Vandever, 14 February 1927, TA #01351.

64. Legters, "Report of the Second Exploratory Trip"; Hummel to Sutcliffe and Philpott, 2 December 1927, CAM; "Minutes of Special CAM Council Session, December 19, 1927," CAM.

65. Townsend to Hummel, 11 May 1925, TA #01147; HI with Townsend; A. E. Forbes to Townsend, 3 August 1927, TA #01290; Paul Townsend to Hummel, August 1928, CAM; Paul Townsend to Hummel, 24 September 1928, CAM; Carl Malmstrom to Townsend, 30 July 1930, TA; Elvira to Hummel, 6 January 1932, TA #01709.

66. Martin, *100 . . . and Counting,* 66, 77.

67. Hummel to council, 25 June 1926, CAM; Hummel to council, 9 October 1926, CAM; Hummel to council, 23 November 1927, CAM; Hummel to Bishop, 23 November 1929, CAM.

68. Alvyn Austin, "No Solicitation: The China Inland Mission and Money," in Larry Eskridge and Mark A. Noll, eds., *More Money, More Ministry: Money and Evangelicals in Recent North American History* (Grand Rapids, MI: W. B. Eerdmans, 2000), 207–34.

69. Hummel to missionaries, 12 May 1927, TA #01323; R. D. Smith to Hummel, 11 September 1925, CAM; Martin, *100 . . . and Counting,* 28; R. D. Smith to Hummel, 12 May 1927, CAM.

70. Charles Hurlburt to AIM council, 20 December 1919, CAM.

71. Anderson, *We Felt Like Grasshoppers,* 32.

72. R. D. Smith to Hummel, 27 April 1925, CAM.

73. Hummel to R. D. Smith, 5 February 1927, CAM; Hummel to council, 25 June 1926, CAM; Davis to "friends," 10 July 1924, TA #01061.

74. Herbert Mackenzie to Hummel, 28 June 1926, CAM; italics are mine.

75. R. D. Smith to Hummel, 30 July 1926, CAM.

76. Hummel to R. D. Smith, 19 February 1927, CAM; Hummel to R. D. Smith, 25 July 1927, CAM.

77. Hummel to council, 23 May 1927, CAM; Central American Mission to "Prayer-Helper," May 1927, CAM.

78. R. D. Smith to CAM, Western Union cable, CAM; R. D. Smith to Hummel, 31 May 1927, CAM.

79. Hummel to Townsend, 29 August 1934, TA #01858.

80. Hummel to missionaries, 28 September 1927, TA #01271; Paul Townsend to Hummel, 31 July 1927, CAM; Hummel to Townsend, 24 October 1929, TA #01449.

81. McConnell to Rees, 22 November 1921, CAM.

82. McConnell quoted in R. D. Smith to council, 24 August 1925, CAM; R. D. Smith to Jones, 25 August 1925, CAM.

83. Townsend to Hummel, 15 January 1930, TA #015??.

84. Hummel to Townsend, 7 February 1930, TA; "To Save China by Saving America: Protestant Missionary Internationalism and the Sino-Japanese War, 1937–1941," 18, unpublished paper in author's possession.

85. Mrs. W. C. Townsend to "My Dear Children," 15 May 1926, TA #01223; italics mine.

86. Hummel to Townsends, 25 January 1933, TA; Mildred Spain to Elvira, 21 August 1933, TA.

87. Spain to council, 28 July 1933, CAM; Richmond McKinney to Spain, 31 July 1933, CAM.

88. See Anderson, *We Felt Like Grasshoppers.*

89. Anderson, *We Felt Like Grasshoppers,* 24–28.

90. Legters to Townsend, 20 December 1927, TA #01246; Townsend to Legters, 1 February 1930, TA; Townsend to Legters, 21 December 1929, TA #01440; Townsend to Carl Malmstrom et al., 15 July 1935, TA #01932.

91. Legters to Townsend, 20 December 1927, TA #01246; Legters to Hummel, 5 April 1927, CAM; Legters to Townsend, 5 July 1927, TA #01301; Legters to Townsend, 23 March 1927, TA #01334; Legters to Townsend, 18 May 1927, TA #01319.

92. Townsend to Hummel, July 1927, TA; Hummel to Townsend, 26 September 1929, TA; Hummel to R. D. Smith, 14 May 1927, CAM; Hummel to Townsend, 24 October 1929, TA #01449.

93. Barrows to Townsend, TA; Townsend to Annie Esdon, 16 February 1928, TA #01422; Hummel to Townsend, 27 March 1928, CAM.

94. Paul E. Pretiz and W. Dayton Roberts, "Positioning LAM for the Twenty-first Century," *International Bulletin of Missionary Research,* October 1999, 155; Legters, "Report of the Second Exploratory Trip"; Johnston, *Story of New Tribes Mission,* 33.

95. Townsend to Hummel, 12 May 1928, TA #01406.

96. Ibid.; Frank Toms to Townsend, 20 May 1928, TA; Hummel to Townsend, 12 June 1928, TA #01397.

97. Townsend to Legters, 23 July 1928, TA #01390; Townsend to Bishop, 30 July 1928, TA #01388; Townsend to Hummel, 2 August 1928, TA #01385.

98. Townsend to Hummel, 27 October 1928, TA #01367; *Cakchiquel News,* 15 January 1929, TA #4611?; Elvira to Hummel, 27 March 1929, TA #01469; Elvira to Rees, 12 July 1929, CAM.

99. Townsend to Beets, 5 November 1943, KA; Townsend to Albert Stradling, 17 April 1928, TA #01413.

100. Townsend to Hummel, 24 July 1928, TA #01389; Major Herbert Dargue to Dr. Howard Kelly, 19 June 1928, TA #01395.

101. Dargue to Townsend, 11 April 1929, TA #01415.

102. Hummel to Townsend, 27 September 1928, TA #01375; Townsend to Hummel, 27 October 1928, TA #01367.

103. Italics mine. See Blanche Smith to Hummel, 11 March 1930, CAM; Hummel to Blanche Smith, 20 March 1930, CAM; Blanche Smith to Hummel, 27 March 1930, CAM; Blanche Smith to Hummel, 29 August 1930, CAM; "A Statement Regarding Ralph D. Smith and the Bible House Board of Los Angeles . . . by . . . a Committee of Investigation," November 1934, CAM.

Chapter 6

1. Townsend to Chafer, 19 November 1923, TA #00943; Townsend to Hummel, 16 May 1930, TA #01525; Townsend to Hummel, 12 March 1930, TA #015??.

2. R. D. Smith to Scott, 20 July 1920, TA; Lavanchie Barrows to Townsend, TA; Townsend to Secord, 6 February 1925, TA #01172; Townsend to Hummel, 6 January 1936, TA #01990.

3. Townsend to Lincoln, 14 July 1925, TA #01120.

4. Townsend to "Mother," 10 April 1931, TA #01664; Townsend to sister Oney, 22 January 1932, TA #01705; Townsend to "Father," 26 February 1932, TA #01698.

5. Kenneth Weathers, "Some Intimate Observations Relating to the Short-Lived Inter-American Service Brigade," draft copy in author's possession; personal interview with Lawrence Routh.

6. Letterhead, Townsend to Hummel, 16 September 1929, TA #01455; Townsend to Legters, 26 February 1927, TA #01348; Townsend, "A Glimpse of Central America," in *Moody Church News,* TA #01236; Townsend to Vandever, 14 February 1927, TA #01351; Townsend, "New Educational Tactics," TA #946116.

7. Pamphlet, TA #00650.

8. Townsend to Fannie Becker, date uncertain, CAM.

9. Townsend to Hummel, 29 November 1929, TA #01445; Townsend to Hummel, 4 February 1930, TA #01541; Hummel to Townsend, 2 December 1929, TA #01444.

10. Townsend, "The Language Project," TA #946120.

11. "Preserving the Pioneer Outlook: A Candid Criticism of Ourselves and Our Missionary Program," date uncertain (probably 1945), CAM.

12. Edward Sywulka, "The Challenge of the Indian Field of the Central American Mission in Guatemala," June 1950, CAM.

13. Townsend to Hummel, 16 September 1929, TA #01455.

14. Hummel to Townsend, 26 September 1929, TA; Bishop to Townsend, 4 May 1930, TA.

15. Townsend to Legters, 21 December 1929, TA #01440.

16. Townsend to Hummel, 15 January 1930, TA #015??; Townsend to Eric North, 19 February 1930, TA #901540; Dr. Edward Sapir to Townsend, 17 March 1930, TA #01597.

17. Townsend to Abbot, 20 August 1930, TA #01503; [unknown] to Townsend, 4 September 1930, TA #01560; Townsend to Franz Boas, 22 October 1930, TA #01492; Townsend to Boas, 29 November 1930, TA #01488; Mason to Townsend, 22 December 1930, TA #01547.

18. Townsend to North, 18 March 1930, TA #901537; Townsend to North, 12 May 1930, TA #901527; North to Stockwell, 12 September 1930, TA #901622.

19. Hummel to Rees, 12 July 1929, CAM; Hummel to Anderson, 8 August 1929, CAM; Hummel to Rees, 18 October 1929, CAM; Rees to Hummel, 11 October 1929, CAM.

20. Townsend to Hummel, 29 November 1929, TA #01445; Paul Townsend, "Paul Townsend Reporting on Townsend's Dream of Using Planes in the Amazon Area," TA #01181.

21. Townsend to Legters, 21 December 1929, TA #01440; Townsend to Hummel, 2 April 1930, TA #01532.

22. Townsend to Legters, 5 April 1930, TA #01531; Townsend to Legters, 24 April 1930, TA #01529.

23. Townsend to Legters, 24 April 1930, TA #01529.

24. Townsend to Legters, 12 May 1930, TA #01527.

25. Hummel to Townsend, 9 April 1930, TA #01593; Bishop to Townsend, 4 May 1930, TA.

26. Townsend to North, 12 May 1930, TA #901526; Townsend to Legters, 20 May 1930, TA #01523.

27. North to Townsend, 6 August 1930, TA #01566.

28. Hummel to Townsend, 23 May 1930, TA #01579; Townsend to Spain, 6 August 1930, TA #01505; Hummel to Townsend, 26 September 1930, TA #01557; Townsend to Legters, 16 September 1930, TA #01500.

29. Townsend to Legters, 16 September 1930, TA #01500.

30. Townsend to "friends," 11 October 1930, TA #01494; "An Airplane Crusade to the Unevangelized Jungle-Lands of Latin America," TA #01478.

31. Hummel to Guatemala Executive Committee, 19 November 1930, CAM.

32. Townsend to Hummel, 1 November 1930, TA.

33. Townsend to J. Harvey Borton, 29 November 1930, TA #01487.

34. Elvira to Hummel, November 1930, TA #01489; Townsend to Borton, 6 November 1930, TA #01550.

35. Hummel to Townsend, 15 November 1930, TA #01551; Hummel to council, 3 December 1930, CAM.

36. Hummel to Guatemala Field Committee, 22 December 1930, CAM.

37. Hummel to Borton, 15 January 1931, CAM; Borton to Hummel, 17 February 1931, CAM.

38. Richmond McKinney to Hummel, 20 March 1930, CAM; Rees to Hummel, 21 November 1927, CAM; Hummel to Townsend, 24 April 1930, TA; Dahlquist, *Trailblazers for Translators,* 19.

39. R. D. Smith to Hummel, 1930, CAM.

40. Hummel to Anderson, 13 February 1932, CAM; Hummel to Townsend, 19 August 1931, TA #01647.

41. Elvira to Ms. Guelph, 22 May 1931, TA #01660; Townsend to "home folks," 21 May 1931, TA.

42. *CAB,* 15 March 1932, TA #01694.

43. Townsend to Hummel, 15 November 1931, TA #01666; 4 November 1931, TA; Townsend to Legters, 16 July 1931, TA #01650; Townsend, "Language Project," TA #946120.

44. Townsend to Hummel, 18 January 1932, TA #01708; Townsend to "home folks," 9 February 1932, TA #01701; Townsend to Hummel, 9 March 1932, TA #01696.

45. Malmstrom to Frank Toms, 21 October 1934, CAM.

46. Townsend to Vandever, 24 August 1931, TA #01646.

47. Townsend to Legters, 21 October 1931, TA #01633.

48. Townsend to Hummel, 18 January 1932, TA #01708.

49. Townsend to Hummel, 24 August 1931, TA #01645; Townsend to Anderson, 26 August 1931, TA #01644; Anderson to Houser, 31 August 1931, TA #01643.

50. Anderson to Houser, 15 September 1931, TA #01636.

51. Townsend to Anderson, 4 September 1931, TA #01641.

52. Houser to Anna Gorman, 21 September 1931, TA #01635; Anderson to Hummel, 8 October 1931, CAM.

53. Hummel to Anderson, 23 October 1931, CAM; Townsend to Hummel, 18 January 1932, TA #01708; Anderson to Hummel, 19 March 1932, CAM.

54. HI, TA #43657; Townsend to Legters, 11 November 1931, TA #01630; Legters to Townsend, 21 January 1932, TA #01706.

55. Elvira to Hummel, 22 August 1932, TA #01687; Townsend to Hummel, 11 September 1932, TA #01682; Townsend to Legters, 11 November 1931, TA #01630.

56. Townsend to "Congregación Evangélica," 24 August 1932, TA #01684.

Chapter 7

1. Elvira to Hummel, 1 December 1932, TA #01486; Townsend to Hummel, 26 January 1933, TA #01767; Townsend to Hummel, 14 October 1932, TA.

2. Hummel to Townsend, 12 October 1932, TA #01679; Hummel to Townsend, 22 November 1932, TA #01673; Townsend to Hummel, 1 December 1932, TA #01486.

3. Townsend to Hummel, 11 April 1933, TA #01757; Elvira to Spain, 27 August 1933, TA #01740; Legters to Hummel, 29 October 1934, CAM.

4. Townsend to Spain, July 1933, TA #01750.

5. Legters to Pioneer Mission Agency board of directors, December 1932, TA #901671.

6. Townsend to Beets, 5 November 1943, KA.

7. Addison Raws to Grossman, 3 June 1959, TA #17641. See also Townsend, "A Long Prayer Meeting at Keswick," TA #01743.

8. Legters to Townsend, 29 August 1933, TA #01739.

9. Legters to "those who are interested in the evangelization of the Indians," 1 September 1933, CAM.

10. Townsend and Legters to Soto, TA #02077.

11. Legters to Townsend, 11 November 1935, TA #01916.

12. Moisés Saénz to Townsend, 18 October 1933, TA.

13. Townsend to Will and Etta Nyman, 8 April 1934, TA #01882; Townsend to council, 7 November 1933, TA #01733.

14. Arthur J. Drossaerts, Archbishop of San Antonio, "Foreword," in Michael Kenny, *No God Next Door: Red Rule in Mexico and Our Responsibility* (New York: William J. Hirten Co., 1935), iv; John A. Britton, *Revolution and Ideology: Images of the Mexican Revolution in the United States* (Lexington: University Press of Kentucky, 1995), 96.

15. Alan Knight, "The Rise and Fall of Cardenismo, c. 1930–c. 1946," in Leslie Bethell, ed., *Mexico since Independence* (Cambridge: Cambridge University Press, 1991), 422; Josephus Daniels, *Shirt-Sleeve Diplomat* (Chapel Hill: University of North Carolina Press, 1947), 66; Alan Knight, *U.S.–Mexican Relations, 1910–1940: An Interpretation* (San Diego: Center for U.S.–Mexican Studies, 1987), 98.

16. See Britton, *Revolution and Ideology.*

17. Quoted in Charles A. Hale, "Frank Tannenbaum and the Mexican Revolution," *Hispanic American Historical Review* 75, no. 2 (May 1995): 232, 215.

18. See, for example, "Who Threatens Liberty in Mexico?" *Christian Century,* 13 February 1935, 206–08.

19. Britton, *Revolution and Ideology,* 171; "Over the Mexican Border," *Moody Monthly,* February 1933, 269; Haymaker to Legters, 12 June 1933, CAM; Elvira to Hummel, 28 December 1933, TA.

20. Townsend to "friends," 11 November 1933, TA #01729; Townsend to Cabrera, 5 December 1933, TA; Townsend to Elvira, 10 December 1933, TA #01718.

21. Townsend to Elvira, 13 December 1933, TA #01717; Townsend to Elvira, 20 December 1933, TA #01716; Journal, 28 December 1933, p. 986, TA #01791.

22. Townsend to Elvira, 20 December 1933, TA #01716; Britton, *Revolution and Ideology,* 66–71, 94.

23. Legters to PMA, 8 October 1934, TA #901852; Townsend to Elvira, 20 December 1933, TA #01716; Townsend to Rafael Ramírez, 29 December 1933, TA #01712.

24. TA #01716.

25. Townsend to Elvira, 23 January 1934, TA #01897; Townsend's travel inventory, TA #01892.

26. Townsend to Nymans, 8 April 1934, TA #01882; Ramírez to Townsend, 15 March 1934, TA #01886.

27. Ramírez to Townsend, 4 June 1934, TA; Townsend, "Mexico's Program of Rural Education," *School and Society,* 30 June 1934, 848–51, TA #901866; Townsend, "The Guardians of the Mexican Revolution," TA #42602.

28. TA #01886.

29. Townsend, "How Far Will Mexico Go with Communism?" TA #42601.

30. Townsend, "Is Religion Doomed in the Land of Cuauhtemoc?" TA #42599.

31. Townsend to Dinwiddie, 6 October 1922, TA #00848.

32. Legters to PMA, 8 October 1934, TA #901852; Townsend to Legters, 24 May 1934, TA #01874; Townsend to Nymans, 8 April 1934, TA #01882; Townsend to "friends," 27 May 1934, TA #01873.

33. "Summer Training Camp for Prospective Bible Translators, June 7–September 7, 1934," TA #43073.

34. Legters to PMA, 8 October 1934, TA #901852; Edward Sywulka to "friends," 27 June 1934, TA #01865; Townsend to Nyman, 16 July 1934, TA #01864.

35. Sywulka to "the fellows at Westminster Seminary who are interested in Indian evangelization," 9 February 1935, TA #01958; Townsend to Walter, 23 February 1935, TA #901955; Townsend to Borton, 23 February 1935, TA #01955.

36. Ken Pike to Hibbard, 19 December 1986, TA #39527.

37. Townsend to Vandever, 1 November 1935, TA #01918.

38. Legters to PMA, 1 September 1935, TA #901924.

39. Townsend to Beets, 5 November 1943, KA. Gerard Colby and Charlotte Dennett, in their 1995 book, *Thy Will Be Done, the Conquest of the Amazon,* make a great deal of this fairly innocuous event. The book is an unintentionally humorous nine-hundred-page diatribe that attempts to indict Townsend as a coconspirator with big oil to wrest land away from Latin American Indian groups. If their work had not received so much attention from anthropologists and others with a chronic distaste for missionaries, it would scarcely be worth mentioning in a serious work of scholarship. I will let what Colby and Dennett make of this prayer meeting and cabinet shakeup exemplify their scholarly technique. Colby and Dennett claim that Townsend knew about this 1935 cabinet shakeup in advance, and manipulated the prayer gathering so that he could seem to announce the shakeup as an answer to prayer, thereby pointing the impressionable young evangelicals toward Mexico as God's will for their lives. They write: "And no sooner had they risen [from prayer] at noon for lunch than 'someone arrived from town to report' that the local radio station had announced that President Cárdenas had fired his entire cabinet. Elated, the students were eager to follow 'Uncle Cam' into Mexico that autumn. God, it seemed, had answered their prayers with a miracle. . . . Cam did not tell the youths that the news was only late in arriving at Sulphur Springs. Cárdenas, in fact, had fired his cabinet weeks before, in early June, and one of his officials had already written Townsend of the turn of events. The news had already been printed in the national press. Why it was not reported in Sulphur Springs until that miraculous day of prayer was never discovered." (See Gerard Colby and Charlotte Dennett, *Thy Will Be Done, the Conquest of the Amazon: Nelson Rockefeller and Evangelism in the Age of Oil* [New York:

HarperCollins, 1995] 65–66.) As proof, Colby and Dennett cite a letter to Townsend from Rafael Ramírez dated June 4, 1935, which they claim to have discovered in the Townsend Archives.

Unfortunately the Colby-Dennett attempt at character assassination collapses on every level. In the first place there is no letter from Ramírez to Townsend dated June 4, 1935, in the Townsend Archives. There *is*, however, a letter from Ramírez to Townsend dated exactly one year earlier, June 4, 1934. The letter simply informs Townsend that Ramírez's boss, Narciso Bassols, had "left the post of Secretary of Education in order to take charge of that of Government." He went on, "Our new Secretary, Lic. Eduardo Vasconcelos, who has taken charge of this Ministry just recently, is inspired by the very finest desires to encourage the education of the Indians" (Ramírez to Townsend, 4 June 1934, TA.) Clearly the letter had nothing to do with the cabinet shakeup of 1935. But Colby and Dennett also failed to simply check the history books for the dates of the actual shakeup in 1935. On June 12, 1935, Plutarco Elías Calles (Cárdenas's mentor and former Mexican strongman) challenged Cárdenas's policies (specifically toward organized labor) in the Mexican press. It seemed to indicate Calles's willingness to perhaps take part in the formation of a new government. In response to this, on June 15, 1935, Cárdenas requested and received the resignations of his cabinet, testing their loyalty. This may have been a somewhat private affair, as it was not until three days later, on June 18, 1935, that the public announcement was made of the cabinet's reorganization. At any rate there is no reason to believe that *any* letter from Ramírez (who was a lower-level political functionary, not a political appointee and not a member of Cardenas's cabinet) on June 4 of 1934 *or* 1935 could possibly have contained any clue about future events. Calles had not even challenged Cárdenas at that point.

The reader is left with two choices. In their rush to paint Townsend as a charlatan, Colby and Dennett either intentionally falsified archival data and ignored the actual history of the event, or their scholarship is so slipshod that they both mistranslated and misdated the letter from Ramírez and never bothered to check the actual dates of the Calles-Cárdenas encounter. Either choice is unpleasant, and, as the book is filled with such faux scholarship, one questions its championing by serious scholars in anthropological journals. Anthropologists have much to teach missionaries, and there are issues of great import around which constructive dialog can be built. But for anthropologists to support work such as *Thy Will Be Done* is to open the discipline to the ridicule of broad-minded scholars of all persuasions, and to divert attention to ridiculous arguments that simply cannot be won, once the facts are known. Perhaps the final word can be left to Michel de Montaigne, who once wrote of such authors and arguments in his essay "Of Books," "I have also noted this, that of so many souls and actions that he judges, so many motives and plans, he never refers a single one to virtue, religion, and conscience, as if these qualities were wholly extinct in the world; and of all actions, however fair in appearance they may be of themselves, he throws the cause back onto some vicious motive or some profit. It is impossible to imagine that among the infinite number of actions that he judges there was not a single one produced by the way of reason. . . . This makes me fear that his taste was a bit corrupted; and it may have happened that he judged others by himself."

40. Townsend to Hummel, 16 August 1936, TA #01978; Eugene Nida to Siebeen, 19 September 1936, TA #02069.

41. Pike to "Mom," 14 January 1937, TA #02266; Townsend to North, 15 September 1937, TA #02094; Hanby to Pike, 24 August 1936, TA #02070.

42. Townsend to Hummel, 12 February 1937, TA #02151; Pike to "Mom," 5 July 1937, TA #02248; Townsend to PMA, 8 September 1937, TA #02102; de la Vega to Townsend, 3 August 1937, TA #02176; Dr. Mariano Silva y Aceves to Townsend, 20 August 1937, TA #02173.

43. "Announcement of the Fourth Annual Session of the Summer Institute of Linguistics," TA #02241; "Call to Camp Wycliffe," 1937, TA #43063.

44. Trumbull and Townsend to "Christian Educators and Missionary Leaders," 26 April 1938, TA #02306; Townsend to PMA, 8 September 1937, TA #02102.

45. Nida to Townsend, 3 August 1943, TA #03554.

46. "Basis of Acceptance, 1949," TA #42998; Townsend to Legters, 20 September 1937, TA #02089; Townsend to Elvira, 18 September 1937, TA #02092.

47. Townsend to Max Lathrop, 27 January 1939, TA #02478.

48. Legters to Townsend, 3 January 1938, TA #02369.

49. "Application Blank for Entrance to Camp Wycliffe," 1936, TA #43069; "Camp Wycliffe," 1936, TA #43067; "Announcement of the Fourth Annual Session of the Summer Institute of Linguistics," TA #02241; "Call to Camp Wycliffe," 1937, TA #43063.

50. "Minutes of Faculty Meeting Held on August 31, 1937, at Camp Wycliffe," TA #43064; Nyman to Loper, 17 October 1945, TA #04113.

51. Townsend to Hummel, 19 October 1939, TA #02440; Johnston, *Story of New Tribes Mission.*

52. Lathrops to PMA, "Annual Report," September 1938, TA #902380; Pike to "folks," 10 July 1938, TA #02405; Pike to "folks," 14 July 1938, TA #02403; Charles Fries to Pike, 22 July 1938, TA #02399; Townsend to Lázaro Cárdenas, 25 July 1938, TA #02296.

53. Leonard Bloomfield to Pike, 24 June 1940, TA #02691; Bloomfield to Pike, 27 January 1943, TA #03645; Bloomfield to Pike, 29 January 1945, TA; Evelyn Pike to "friends," 16 July 1939, TA.

54. Pike to Fries, 25 July 1938, TA #02398; Townsend to Marroquín, 25 July 1939, TA #02452; Elvira to "Camp Wycliffians," 27 March 1940, TA #02615.

55. Legters to Townsend, 4 April 1940, TA #02657; Townsend to "friends," 25 June 1940, TA.

56. James Oscar Boyd, "Camp Wycliffe," *Bible Society Record,* October 1940, TA #942266.

57. "Detailed Analysis of Information Regarding Students of Camp Wycliffe," TA #43046.

58. Townsend to PMA, 10 September 1941, TA #902724.

59. Ibid.

60. Nida to Townsend, 11 September 1941, TA #02863; Pike to Nida, 4 December 1941, TA #03043; President Cross to Pike, 1 October 1949, TA #43000.

61. Pearce et al. to "friends of the PMA" et al., 18 June 1942, TA; Pike to PMA, 20 August 1942, TA.

62. "Student Census of Summer Institute of Linguistics, 1944," TA #43025; "1949 Camp Wycliffe Statistics," TA #42999.

63. Oswald Smith to Townsend, 11 August 1943, TA #03551.

64. Hummel to Townsends, 21 December 1934, TA; Townsend to Walter, 23 February 1935, TA #901955; "Camp Wycliffe," 1936, TA #43067.

65. Legters to PMA, 1 September 1935, TA #901924; Townsend, "Camp Wycliffe's Activities during Past Years," fall 1936, TA #43066; Townsend to Carl Malmstrom et al., 15 July 1935, TA #01932.

66. Townsend to Hummel, 5 March 1936, TA #01988; Townsend to Hummel, 11 August 1936, TA #01980.

67. Florence Hansen to "family," 2 February 1937, TA; Pike to Townsend, 29 March 1937, TA #02198; Townsend to PMA, 8 September 1937, TA #02102; Legters to Townsend, 2 November 1939, TA #02500.

68. "Call to Camp Wycliffe," 1937, TA #43063; "Camp Wycliffe," 1940, TA #43056.

69. Pittman, "Marooned," 1940, TA #02677; "Summer Institute of Linguistics Workers with Their Addresses," 26 February 1941, TA #02823; Pike to executive committee, 10 May 1941, TA #03059; "Workers," fall 1944, TA; "Detailed Analysis of Information Regarding Students of Camp Wycliffe," TA #43046.

70. [Unknown] to Legters, 7 May 1940, TA #02607; "The Summer Institute of Linguistics," 1952, TA #429??.

Chapter 8

1. Townsend to Hummel, 8 October 1935, TA #01922.

2. Townsend to Legters, 14 November 1935, TA; Hefley and Hefley, *Uncle Cam,* 92.

3. *Moody Church News,* June 1936, TA #01983.

4. Townsend to Pike and Nida, 20 February 1937, TA #02157; Townsend to Cárdenas, 29 January 1936, Archivo General de la Nación (hereafter AGN), Mexico City, Fondo Lázaro Cárdenas (hereafter FLC), 710.1/1598.

5. Telegram, Cárdenas to Uranga, 1 March 1938, AGN; *Moody Church News,* June 1936, TA #01983.

6. Cárdenas to Townsend, 28 March 1936, AGN; Townsend to Karl Hummel, 19 September 1936, TA #01976.

7. Marjorie Becker, *Setting the Virgin on Fire: Lázaro Cárdenas, Michoacán Peasants, and the Redemption of the Mexican Revolution* (Berkeley: University of California Press, 1995); Manuel Gamio to Townsend, 27 May 1948, TA #05521.

8. Elvira to Cárdenas, February 1938, TA #2311.

9. Townsend to Cárdenas, 26 December 1936, AGN; telegram, Townsend to Cárdenas, 2 February 1938, AGN; Townsend to "friends," 20 April 1945, TA #04015.

10. Pike to "folks," 26 April 1937, TA #02253; Pike to Townsend, 20 March 1941, TA #03013.

11. Max Miller, *Mexico around Me* (New York: Reynal and Hitchcock, 1937), 287–94.

12. Borton to Townsend, 29 September 1936, TA #02024; Townsend to Legters, 11 October 1935, TA #01920.

13. Genaro Vásquez to *las Autoridades Civiles y Militares de la República,* 18 December 1935, TA #01909; Aceves to Pike, 20 December 1935, TA #01907; Vega to Van Slyke, 28 April 1936, TA #02074; Townsend to "folks," 12 November 1941, TA #02716.

14. Pittman to "linguists," 18 February 1942, TA #903353.

15. Townsend to PMA, 8 September 1937, TA #02102; Townsend to Hummel, 12 April 1937, TA #021??.

16. Sandgren, *Christianity and the Kikuyu,* 23.

17. Townsend to "fellow-workers," 29 November 1939, TA; Townsend to "fellow workers," 4 December 1939, TA #02432.

18. "Meeting May 20, 1939—Mrs. Hull's," copy in author's possession.

19. Dean Pittman to Townsend, 29 August 1945, TA #904057; Townsend to Nikkel, 13 December 1943, TA #03453.

20. [Herbert?] Lemley to Vandever, 16 September 1939, TA #02568; Lemley to PMA, 9 September 1940, TA #902684.

21. Legters to "fellow members," 15 January 1937, TA #02265; Florence Hansen to "friends," 1 November 1936, TA #02015.

22. Pike to Townsend, 31 March 1938, TA #02357.

23. Townsend to "fellow-workers," 14 November 1941, TA #02715.

24. Lathrops to PMA, June 1938, TA #902407; Otis and Mary Leal to PMA, 17 August 1938, TA #902391.

25. Eunice Pike to "friends," February 1939, TA #02579.

26. Harold Bentley to Elvira and Cameron Townsend, 8 February 1939, TA #02552.

27. Lathrops to PMA, "Annual Report," September 1938, TA #902380; Hansen and Pike to PMA, September 1938, TA #902371; Elvira to Bessie, 17 April 1941, TA.

28. Townsends to PMA, 7 September 1938, TA #02283.

29. Evelyn Pike to Hibbard, 6 February 1994, TA #946599.

30. Townsend to Cárdenas, 7 April 1936, AGN, FLC, 710.1/1598; Vásquez to Sanchez, 15 April 1936, TA #02075; Townsend to Vásquez, 25 June 1936, AGN; "Cárdenas es Proletarista no Comunista," AGN (published as "Commoner, Not Communist, Is Cardenas," *Tulsa Daily World,* 21 June 1936); Townsend, "Many Paths to Mexico's Enchantments," TA #42596.

31. Townsend to Cárdenas, 30 October 1937, AGN.

32. Townsend to "Father," 6 June 1938, TA #02309; Hefley and Hefley, *Uncle Cam,* 105; Townsend, "The Truth about Mexico's Oil," SIL, 1940, p. 15.

33. George Philip, *Oil and Politics in Latin America: Nationalist Movements and State Companies* (Cambridge: Cambridge University Press, 1982), 224; Townsend, "Mexico Confiscates the Oil Industry," TA #42593; Daniels, *Shirt-Sleeve Diplomat,* 227, 258.

34. Sáenz to Cárdenas, 21 March 1938, AGN, FLC, 577/10.

35. Elvira to Hummels, 31 March 1938, TA #02308; Josephus Daniels to McIntyre, 4 April 1938, TA #02415; letters to and from J. Edgar Hoover from an undisclosed source, dated 6 May 1943 and 27 May 1943, in Townsend file #100-135694, author's copy through Freedom of Information Act Request.

36. "Flyer," TA #02271; Elvira to Marroquín, 1 May 1938, TA #02302; Elvira to Mrs. Cárdenas, 3 May 1938, TA #2301; Amalia Cárdenas to Elvira, 17 May 1938, TA #02350.

37. Townsend to Cordell Hull, 10 September 1938, TA #02287; Hefley and Hefley, *Uncle Cam,* 107.

38. "Report of Mr. and Mrs. W. C. Townsend for the Year Sept. 1937–Sept. 1938," TA #02283; "Justice to Mexico," TA #42594.

39. Townsend to Marroquín, 15 September 1938, TA #0228?; Townsend to Cárdenas, September 1938, TA #902284; Townsend, "Truth about Mexico's Oil," pp. II, 1, copy in author's possession.

40. Townsend to Dr. Howard Kelly, 28 March 1940, TA #02614; Townsend to Ramón Beteta, 27 December 1939, TA #02425; Townsend to Kelly, 13 December 1942, TA #02703.

41. William Cameron Townsend, *Lázaro Cárdenas: Mexican Democrat* (1952; Waxhaw, NC: International Friendship, 1979); Townsend to Rodríguez, 27 September 1936, AGN, FLC, 710.1/1598; Townsend to Beteta, 7 September 1937, TA #02104.

42. Daniels to Townsend, 20 November 1947, TA #04795; "Report of General Director—Board of Directors' Meeting—August 1948," TA #05248; Townsend to Bentley, 22 October 1948, TA #05234; Townsend to Applequist, 11 November 1949, TA #05847.

43. Townsend to Kenneth and Evelyn Pike, 23 October 1948, TA #05232; Townsend to Bermudes, 9 July 1951, TA #06922; Wells to Dean, 29 August 1951, TA #907213; Townsend to Beteta, 1 January 1952, TA #07791; Arnold Kruckman to Townsend, 13 January 1952, TA #07175; Kruckman to Townsend, 11 February 1952, TA #08141.

44. Townsend to Nymans, 26 December 1951, TA #6790; Townsend to Friends, TA #06841; Townsend to J. G. Dale, 29 January 1954, TA #10344; sample copies of responses from congressmen on file with the author; Townsend to George McGhee, 12 December 1961, TA #19729.

45. Numerous documents, including Kenneth T. Weathers, "Some Intimate Observations Relating to the Short-Lived Inter-American Service Brigade," draft copy in author's possession; "*Proyecto de Trabajo,*" AGN, FLC, 710.1/1598; Townsend to Cárdenas, 25 April 1939, AGN, FLC, 463.1/18; Beteta to Townsend, 19 October 1939, TA #2504; Townsend to Cárdenas, TA #02272; "*Ante-Proyecto Para La Organizacion de Una Asociacion Internacional de Amigos de Mexico,*" TA #02076; Townsend to Cárdenas, 13 September 1937, TA; Vásquez to Townsend, 8 January 1937, TA #02212; TA #02381.

46. Townsend to "friends," 5 August 1939, TA #2450; Townsend to Karl Hummel,

13 June 1939, TA #02459; Townsend to Mildred Spain, 15 July 1939, TA #02455; Townsend to "friends," 5 August 1939, TA #02450.

47. Joel A. Carpenter, *Revive Us Again: The Reawakening of American Fundamentalism* (New York: Oxford University Press, 1997).

48.Ibid., 46, 112; Harry Ironside to "My dear sister," 11 January 1938, TA #02367; Ironside to Elvira, 7 March 1938, TA #02359; Ironside to Elvira, 7 July 1939, TA.

49. Fischer to Townsend, 4 February 1952, TA #10294.

50. Townsends to "friends," Christmas 1938, TA #02275; Elvira to Ironside, 2 March 1941, TA #02821.

51. Townsend to "fellow-workers," 14 November 1941, TA #02715.

52. Hefley and Hefley, *Uncle Cam,* 119; Townsend to "fellow workers," 1 September 1942, TA #03123; Townsend to "fellow workers," 27 November 1942, TA #03105; Townsend to Nyman, 30 June 1943, TA #03419.

53. Nyman to Loper, 17 October 1945, TA #04113.

54. Townsend to Pittman, 24 April 1942, TA #03148; Townsend to PMA, 1 September 1942, TA #03123; Townsend to "friends," 18 March 1941, TA #02819; Townsend to "friends," 2 May 1941, TA #02806; Townsend to Cárdenas, 18 October 1941, TA #02718; File #100-135694, FBI report, 26 August 1942, author's copy through Freedom of Information Act.

55. Legters to Hummel, 10 October 1938, CAM.

56. Legters to Townsend, 29 September 1937, TA #02167; Legters to PMA, 8 October 1934, TA #901852; "Annual Report of the Pioneer Mission Agency, 1933–1934," TA #901836; "Annual Report of the Pioneer Mission Agency, September 1, 1934–August 31, 1935," TA #901925.

57. Legters to Townsend, 11 November 1935, TA #01916; Townsend's reply was written on the back of Legters's letter of 11 November 1935, TA #01915.

58. Legters to PMA, September 1938, TA #902373; Legters to Townsend, 14 February 1939, TA #02551; Legters to PMA, September 1939, TA #902372.

59. Townsend to Slocums, 1938, TA #02274.

60. Townsend to "fellow workers," 27 November 1942, TA #03105.

61. Townsend to "fellow workers," 13 January 1943, TA #03511; Nida to Townsend, 3 August 1943, TA #03554.

62. Legters to Christiansens, 9 March 1939, TA #02577.

63. Borton to Townsend and Nida, 17 June 1941, TA #02980; Elvira to Blatchley, 9 August 1941, TA #02767; "Detailed Analysis of Information Regarding Students of Camp Wycliffe," through 1941, TA #43046.

64. Legters to Townsend, 9 November 1939, TA #02498.

65. Townsend to "friends," 25 June 1940, TA.

66. Townsend to PMA, 28 November 1940, TA #02587; Pearce to Townsend, 18 February 1942, TA #03253.

67. Townsend to Nyman, 10 May 1942, TA #03099; Nyman to Townsend, 12 May 1942,

TA #03077; Townsend to Pittman, 16 May 1942, TA #03142; Pearce et al. to "friends of the PMA" et al., 18 June 1942, TA.

68. Townsend to Borton, 17 August 1942, TA #03126; Townsend to PMA, 1 September 1942, TA #03123; Townsends to "friends," 27 October 1942, TA #03116.

69. "Extract of the Minutes of the Mexican Branch of the Wycliffe Bible Translators and Summer Institute of Linguistics," September 1942, TA #03268; Pike to Nida, 24 September 1942, TA #03298.

70. Nyman to Townsend, 19 July 1945, TA #03890; Townsend to "Mexico group," December 1942, TA #03100; William Nyman, "Why Is God a Stranger in the Land?" TA #03068; Townsend to Nyman, 20 January 1944, TA #03721; Townsend to "fellow-workers," 30 April 1943, TA #03493; Nyman to Townsend, 20 January 1943, TA #03387; Townsend to Nymans, 21 March 1945, TA.

71. Townsend to George Cowan, 15 December 1944, TA #03736; Townsend to Pittman, 30 November 1944, TA #03738; quoted in Nyman to Townsend, 12 March 1945, TA #03897.

72. Townsend to Nyman, 23 February 1943, TA #03506.

73. Ibid.

74. Nida to Townsend, 25 January 1944, TA #03853; Townsend to Nyman, 31 July 1943, TA #03414; Townsend to Nymans, 22 March 1945, TA #03951; Townsend to Nymans, 26 March 1945, TA; Townsend to Pike and Nida, 3 August 1943, TA #03473; Townsend to board, 2 December 1943, TA #03393.

75. Townsend to Dr. Edman, 5 February 1944, TA #03786; Townsend to Nymans, 9 July 1945, TA #03926.

76. Townsend to board of directors et al., 21 July 1943, TA #03476; Townsend to Church of the Open Door board, 17 February 1943, TA; Nida to Townsend, 3 August 1943, TA #03554.

77. Pike to Townsend, 22 August 1943, TA #03548; North to Townsend, 31 August 1943, TA #03543; Pike, "General Report on South American Trip," 21 February 1944, TA #03875.

78. Townsend to Enrique Laroza, 8 March 1944, TA #03781; Townsend to board, 2 December 1943, TA #03393; Townsend to Nyman, 6 December 1943, TA #03392.

79. Townsend to Borton, 16 March 1944, TA #03779; Elvira to Etta Nyman, 30 March 1944, TA #03708; Elvira to Nymans, 30 November 1943, TA #03395.

80. Cameron and Elvira to "friends," Christmas 1944, TA; Nyman to Pittman, 2 January 1944, TA #03878.

81. Townsend, "Statement of Purpose Made at Elvira's Funeral," 28 December 1944, TA #03731; see also Elvira's memorial pamphlet, TA #03862; Townsend to members of the Wycliffe family, 12 January 1945, TA #04032.

82. Townsend to Nyman, 13 May 1945, TA #03937; Townsend to Nyman, 1 May 1945, TA; Townsend to Nymans, 23 May 1945, TA #03935.

83. Townsend to Nymans, 21 May 1945, TA #03936; Townsend to Nymans, 2 June 1945, TA #03934.

84. TA #04069.

85. Townsend file #100-135694, obtained through Freedom of Information Act, copy in author's possession.

86. Neill, 31 October 1945, TA; documents in author's possession.

87. Jeffrey Klaiber, "The Church in Peru, Ecuador, and Bolivia," in Enrique Dussel, ed., *The Church in Latin America, 1492–1992* (Maryknoll, NY: Orbis Books, 1992), 289; John J. Considine, *New Horizons in Latin America* (New York: Dodd, Mead and Co., 1958), 254; Townsend to Clarence Church, 8 February 1947, TA #04763.

88. Pike to Townsend, 19 July 1943, TA; Townsend, "Wycliffe Bible Translators, What Are We?" July 1943, TA #03474.

89. Townsend telegram, 29 June 1945, TA #03927; notes for "Day of Prayer," 16 August 1945, TA #41896; Townsend to Charles Fuller, 11 July 1945, TA #03989.

90. Townsend to "friends of a like mind," November 1945, TA #03962; "Help," 30 October 1945, TA #03911.

91. Nyman to Townsend, 23 November 1945, TA #03881; Townsend to Nyman, 28 November 1945, TA #03908.

92. Townsend to Pittman, 29 December 1944, TA #03730; Elaine Mielke to "friend," 6 October 1945, TA #03972; Townsend to Winans, 26 October 1945, TA #03970.

Epilogue

1. Townsend, "SIL/WBT Policy of Service," February 1971, TA #28410.

2. Townsend, "Notes on Spiritual Work," 28 April 1948, TA #05317; Townsend, "Wycliffe's Attitude toward Antagonistic Religious Leaders," 1952, TA #07478.

3. Townsend, "Overcome Evil with Good," 1968, TA #50001; Townsend to Henry Crowell, 24 December 1956, TA #11929; 23 April 1959, TA #16726; Townsend to JAARS pilots, 1967, TA #924758; "W. C. Townsend Answers the Second Ketcham Article," January 1961, TA #918174.

4. 17 May 1957, TA #13979; Burns to Townsend, 23 June 1955, TA #11625; Townsend to Benavides, 5 July 1957, TA #12811.

5. Townsend to Newman, 7 January 1954, TA #10383.

6. 17 January 1963, TA #21641; Townsend to Nyman, 6 April 1954, TA #09825; Townsend to Crowell, 26 November 1958, TA #14350.

7. 31 July 1965, TA #23206; 5 August 1974, TA #30433 and 3 November 1974, TA #30156.

8. 8 November 1954, TA #10436; 23 June 1955, TA #11625.

9. Jones to Montano, 6 December 1958, TA #16819.

10. Townsend to George Cowan, 3 October 1966, TA #23522; Townsend to Lopez, 16 June 1960, TA #18264.

11. 1 November 1967, TA #25280; Pike to Townsend, 17 November 1960, TA #18077.

12. Summary based on documents in the author's possession too numerous to mention.

13. Boni to Townsend, 11 March 1970, TA #27849; 2 April 1969, TA #26949; 22 May 1967, TA #25400; 7 March 1977, TA #33825.

14. 29 August 1970, TA #27196.

15. "Historical SIL Enrollment Data," October 1987, TA #42519; "The Summer Institute of Linguistics, Catalog of Courses, 1996–1997."

16. Stephen L. Walter, "Is SIL an Academic Organization? A Question of Core Values," *InterCom* (January–March 2000), 9–12.

17. *Team Spirit,* January 1999, 10.

18. "Wycliffe Bible Translators: Financial Principles and Practices."

19. *Beach Blurb,* 21 March 1994; "WBT-USA Delegate Conference," June 12–16, 1998.

20. Townsend, "Memorandum for Ambassador Cooper," 24 October 1946, TA #04261; Townsend to Sam Rayburn, 5 August 1957, TA #12761; William T. Cormack, "How Communistic Is Guatemala?" TA #942716 (Townsend used his mother's surname to avoid involving SIL); TA #06488, 06675.

21. Richard Pierard, "*Pax Americana* and the Evangelical Missionary Advance," in Carpenter and Shenk, *Earthen Vessels,* 179.

Bibliography

Sources on the Summer Institute of Linguistics and the Wycliffe Bible Translators

Capa, Cornell, and Dale Kietzman, eds. *Language and Faith.* Santa Ana, CA: Wycliffe Bible Translators, 1972.

Colby, Gerard, and Charlotte Dennett. *Thy Will Be Done: The Conquest of the Amazon: Nelson Rockefeller and Evangelism in the Age of Oil.* New York: HarperCollins, 1995.

Cowan, George M. *The Word That Kindles.* Chappaqua, NY: Christian Herald Books, 1979.

Dahlquist, Anna Marie. *Trailblazers for Translators: The Chichicastenango Twelve.* Pasadena, CA: William Carey Library, 1995.

Hartch, Todd. *Missionaries of the State: The Summer Institute of Linguistics, State Formation, and Indigenous Mexico, 1935–1985.* Tuscaloosa: University of Alabama Press, 2006.

Hefley, James, and Marti Hefley. *Uncle Cam: The Story of William Cameron Townsend, Founder of the Wycliffe Bible Translators and the Summer Institute of Linguistics.* 1974. Huntington Beach, CA: Wycliffe Bible Translators, 1995.

Huxley, Matthew, and Cornell Capa. *Farewell to Eden.* New York: Harper and Row, 1964.

Hvalkof, Søren, and Peter Aaby, eds. *Is God an American? An Anthropological Perspective on the Missionary Work of the Summer Institute of Linguistics.* Copenhagen: International Work Group for Indigenous Affairs (IWGIA), 1981.

Kingsland, Rosemary. *A Saint among Savages.* London: Collins, 1980.

Pike, Eunice V. *Ken Pike: Scholar and Christian.* Dallas: Summer Institute of Linguistics, 1981.

Steven, Hugh, ed. *A Thousand Trails: Personal Journal of William Cameron Townsend, 1917–1919.* White Rock, BC: CREDO, 1984.

———. *Wycliffe in the Making: The Memoirs of W. Cameron Townsend, 1920–1933.* Wheaton, IL: Harold Shaw, 1995.

——. *Doorway to the World, the Mexico Years: The Memoirs of W. Cameron Townsend, 1934–1947.* Wheaton, IL: Harold Shaw, 1999.

——. *Yours to Finish the Task: The Memoirs of W. Cameron Townsend from 1947–1982.* Wheaton, IL: Harold Shaw, 2004.

Stoll, David. *Fishers of Men or Founders of Empire? The Wycliffe Bible Translators in Latin America.* London: Zed Press, 1982.

Wallis, Ethel Emily, and Mary Angela Bennett. *Two Thousand Tongues to Go: The Story of the Wycliffe Bible Translators.* 1959. Huntington Beach, CA: Wycliffe Bible Translators, 1964.

Walter, Stephen L. "Is SIL an Academic Organization? A Question of Core Values." *Inter-Com* (January–March 2000).

Wycliffe Bible Translators. *Pass the Word: 50 Years of Wycliffe Bible Translators.* Huntington Beach, CA: Wycliffe Bible Translators, 1984.

Sources on Missions

Anderson, Dick. *We Felt Like Grasshoppers: The Story of Africa Inland Mission.* Nottingham, Eng.: Crossway Books, 1994.

Anderson, Gerald H., ed. *Biographical Dictionary of Christian Missions.* New York: Macmillan Reference, 1998.

Austin, Alvyn. "No Solicitation: The China Inland Mission and Money." In Larry Eskridge and Mark A. Noll, eds. *More Money, More Ministry: Money and Evangelicals in Recent North American History.* Grand Rapids, MI: W. B. Eerdmans, 2000. 207–34.

Bacon, Daniel W. "The Influence of Hudson Taylor on the Faith Mission Movement." Thesis. Trinity Evangelical Divinity School, 1983.

Boyd, Lois, and R. Douglas Brackenridge. *Presbyterian Women in America: Two Centuries of a Quest for Status.* Westport, CT: Greenwood Press, 1983.

Brown, Arthur Judson. *The Foreign Missionary: An Incarnation of a World Movement.* 1907. New York: Fleming H. Revell, 1932.

Carpenter, Joel A., and Wilbert R. Shenk, eds. *Earthen Vessels: American Evangelicals and Foreign Missions, 1880–1980.* Grand Rapids, MI: W. B. Eerdmans, 1990.

Carpenter, Joel A., ed. *Missionary Innovation and Expansion.* New York: Garland, 1988.

——. *Modernism and Foreign Missions: Two Fundamentalist Protests.* 1921. New York: Garland, 1988.

Clymer, Kenton J. *Protestant Missionaries in the Philippines, 1898–1916: An Inquiry into the American Colonial Mentality.* Chicago: University of Illinois Press, 1986.

Dahlquist, Anna Marie. *Burgess of Guatemala.* Langley, BC: Cedar Books, 1985.

Ellinwood, Frank F. *Questions and Phases of Modern Missions.* New York: Dodd, Mead, and Co., 1899.

Elliot, Elisabeth. *No Graven Image: A Novel.* 1966. Westchester, IL: Crossway Books, 1982.

——. *The Savage My Kinsman.* 1961. Ann Arbor, MI: Servant Publications, 1996.

———. *Through Gates of Splendor.* 1956. Wheaton, IL: Tyndale House, 1981.

Erny, Edward, and Esther Erny. *No Guarantee but God: The Story of the Founders of the Oriental Missionary Society.* Greenwood, IN: Oriental Missionary Society, 1969.

Fairbank, John K., ed. *The Missionary Enterprise in China and America.* Cambridge: Harvard University Press, 1974.

Flemming, Leslie A., ed. *Women's Work for Women: Missionaries and Social Change in Asia.* Boulder, CO: Westview Press, 1989.

Garrard-Burnett, Virginia. *Protestantism in Guatemala: Living in the New Jerusalem.* Austin: University of Texas Press, 1998.

Goffin, Alvin M. *The Rise of Protestant Evangelism in Ecuador, 1895–1990.* Gainesville: University Press of Florida, 1994.

Hill, Patricia Ruth. *The World Their Household: The American Woman's Foreign Mission Movement and Cultural Transformation, 1870–1920.* Ann Arbor: University of Michigan Press, 1985.

Hunter, Jane. *The Gospel of Gentility: American Women Missionaries in Turn-of-the-Century China.* New Haven, CT: Yale University Press, 1984.

Hutchison, William R. *Errand to the World: American Protestant Thought and Foreign Missions.* Chicago: University of Chicago Press, 1987.

Johnston, Kenneth J. *The Story of New Tribes Mission.* Sanford, FL: The Mission, 1985.

Langmore, Diane. *Missionary Lives: Papua, 1874–1914.* Honolulu: University of Hawaii Press, 1989.

Martin, Dorothy. *100 . . . and Counting: The Story of CAM's First Century.* Dallas: CAM International, 1990.

Mott, John R. *The Evangelization of the World in This Generation.* 1900. New York: Arno Press, 1972.

Niklaus, Robert, John Sawin, and Samuel J. Stoesz. *All for Jesus: God at Work in the Christian and Missionary Alliance over One Hundred Years.* Camp Hill, PA: Christian Publications, 1986.

Parker, Michael. *The Kingdom of Character: The Student Volunteer Movement for Foreign Missions (1886–1926).* New York: University Press of America, 1998.

Pierson, Arthur T. *The New Acts of the Apostles or the Marvels of Modern Missions.* London: James Nisbet and Co., 1896.

Pretiz, Paul E., and W. Dayton Roberts. "Positioning LAM for the Twenty-first Century." *International Bulletin of Missionary Research* 23 (October 1999): 153–55.

Rabe, Valentin H. *The Home Base of American China Missions, 1880–1920.* Cambridge: Harvard University Press, 1978.

Robert, Dana Lee. "Arthur Tappan Pierson and Forward Movements of Late-Nineteenth-Century Evangelicalism." PhD diss. Yale University, 1984.

———. *American Women in Mission: A Social History of Their Thought and Practice.* Macon, GA: Mercer University Press, 1996.

Rupert, Marybeth. "The Emergence of the Independent Missionary Agency as an American Institution, 1860–1917." PhD diss. Yale University, 1974.

Sandgren, David P. *Christianity and the Kikuyu: Religious Divisions and Social Conflict.* New York: Peter Lang, 1989.

Sanneh, Lamin O. *Translating the Message: The Missionary Impact on Culture.* Maryknoll, NY: Orbis Books, 1989.

Steer, Roger. *George Müller: Delighted in God.* Wheaton, IL: Harold Shaw, 1981.

Swanson, Jeffrey. *Echoes of the Call: Identity and Ideology among American Missionaries in Ecuador.* New York: Oxford University Press, 1995.

Taylor, J. Hudson. *Hudson Taylor.* Minneapolis: Bethany House, n.d.

Varg, Paul A. *Missionaries, Chinese, and Diplomats: The American Protestant Missionary Movement in China, 1890–1952.* Princeton, NJ: Princeton University Press, 1958.

Winn, Wilkins Bowdre. "A History of the Central American Mission as Seen in the Work of Albert Edward Bishop, 1896–1922." PhD diss. University of Alabama, 1964.

Sources on Latin America

Baldwin, Deborah J. *Protestants and the Mexican Revolution: Missionaries, Ministers, and Social Change.* Urbana: University of Illinois Press, 1990.

Becker, Marjorie. *Setting the Virgin on Fire: Lázaro Cárdenas, Michoacán Peasants, and the Redemption of the Mexican Revolution.* Berkeley: University of California Press, 1995.

Bethell, Leslie, ed. *The Cambridge History of Latin America.* 11 vols. Cambridge: Cambridge University Press, 1984–1995.

———. *Mexico since Independence.* Cambridge: Cambridge University Press, 1991.

Britton, John A. *Revolution and Ideology: Images of the Mexican Revolution in the United States.* Lexington: University Press of Kentucky, 1995.

Brown, Jonathan C., and Alan Knight, eds. *The Mexican Petroleum Industry in the Twentieth Century.* Austin: University of Texas Press, 1992.

Camp, Roderic Ai. *Mexican Political Biographies, 1935–1993.* 3rd ed. Austin: University of Texas Press, 1995.

Considine, John J. *New Horizons in Latin America.* New York: Dodd, Mead and Co., 1958.

Cronon, E. David. *Josephus Daniels in Mexico.* Madison: University of Wisconsin Press, 1960.

Daniels, Josephus. *Shirt-Sleeve Diplomat.* Chapel Hill: University of North Carolina Press, 1947.

Delpar, Helen. *The Enormous Vogue of Things Mexican: Cultural Relations between the United States and Mexico, 1920–1935.* Tuscaloosa: University of Alabama Press, 1992.

Dussel, Enrique, ed. *The Church in Latin America, 1492–1992.* Maryknoll, NY: Orbis Books, 1992.

Hale, Charles A. "Frank Tannenbaum and the Mexican Revolution." *Hispanic American Historical Review* 75, no. 2 (May 1995): 215–46.

Hinshaw, Robert E. *Panajachel: A Guatemalan Town in Thirty-Year Perspective.* Pittsburgh: University of Pittsburgh Press, 1975.

Kenny, Michael. *No God Next Door: Red Rule in Mexico and Our Responsibility.* New York: William J. Hirten Co., 1935.

Knight, Alan. *U.S.–Mexican Relations, 1910–1940: An Interpretation.* San Diego: Center for U.S.-Mexican Studies, 1987.

Martin, David. *Tongues of Fire: The Explosion of Protestantism in Latin America.* Oxford, UK: B. Blackwell, 1990.

McConnell, Burt M. *Mexico at the Bar of Public Opinion: A Survey of Editorial Opinion in Newspapers of the Western Hemisphere.* New York: Mail and Express, 1939.

McCreery, David. *Rural Guatemala, 1760–1940.* Stanford, CA: Stanford University Press, 1994.

Miller, Max. *Mexico around Me.* New York: Reynal and Hitchcock, 1937.

Oakes, Maud. *Beyond the Windy Place: Life in the Guatemalan Highlands.* London: Victor Gollancz Ltd., 1951.

Philip, George. *Oil and Politics in Latin America: Nationalist Movements and State Companies.* Cambridge: Cambridge University Press, 1982.

Smith, Carol A., and Marilyn M. Moors, eds. *Guatemalan Indians and the State, 1540 to 1988.* Austin: University of Texas Press, 1990.

Stoll, David. *Is Latin America Turning Protestant? The Politics of Evangelical Growth.* Berkeley: University of California Press, 1990.

Stoll, David, and Virginia Garrard-Burnett, eds. *Rethinking Protestantism in Latin America.* Philadelphia: Temple University Press, 1993.

Tannenbaum, Frank. *Peace by Revolution: An Interpretation of Mexico.* New York: Columbia University Press, 1933.

Townsend, William Cameron. *Lázaro Cárdenas: Mexican Democrat.* 1952. Waxhaw, NC: International Friendship, 1979.

Weyl, Nathaniel, and Sylvia Weyl. *The Reconquest of Mexico: The Years of Lázaro Cárdenas.* New York: Oxford University Press, 1939.

Sources on American Religion

Ahlstrom, Sydney E. *A Religious History of the American People.* New Haven, CT: Yale University Press, 1972.

Balmer, Randall. *Mine Eyes Have Seen the Glory: A Journey into the Evangelical Subculture in America.* New York: Oxford University Press, 1989.

———. "Mine Eyes Have Seen the Glory: Program Two, The Making of a Subculture." Gateway Films, 1992, WTTW Chicago and Isis Productions Ltd.

Bederman, Gail. "'The Women Have Had Charge of the Church Work Long Enough': The Men and Religion Forward Movement of 1911–1912 and the Masculinization of Middle-Class Protestantism." *American Quarterly* 41, no. 3 (September 1989): 432–65.

Brereton, Virginia L. *Training God's Army: The American Bible School, 1880–1940*. Bloomington: Indiana University Press, 1990.

Carpenter, Joel A. *Revive Us Again: The Reawakening of American Fundamentalism*. New York: Oxford University Press, 1997.

"The Conference and Its Message." In *The Victorian Life: Messages from the Summer Conferences*. 1918. New York: Garland, 1988.

Dolan, Jay P., and Allan Figueroa Deck, eds. *Hispanic Catholic Culture in the U.S.: Issues and Concerns*. Notre Dame, IN: University of Notre Dame Press, 1994.

Hamilton, Michael S. "Awash in a Sea of Fundamentalism: Problems in the Literature on American Fundamentalism, 1925–1960." Unpublished paper.

———. "The Fundamentalist Harvard: Wheaton College and the Continuing Vitality of American Evangelicalism, 1919–1965." PhD diss. University of Notre Dame, 1994.

Harkness, Robert. *Reuben Archer Torrey: The Man, His Message*. Chicago: Bible Institute Colportage Association, 1929.

Lundin, Roger. "Whose Emily Dickinson?" *Books and Culture* 2, no. 4 (July–August 1996): 12.

Marsden, George. *Fundamentalism and American Culture: The Shaping of Twentieth-Century Evangelicalism, 1870–1925*. New York: Oxford University Press, 1980.

———. *Reforming Fundamentalism: Fuller Seminary and the New Evangelicalism*. Grand Rapids, MI: W. B. Eerdmans, 1987.

Marty, Martin, and R. Scott Appleby, eds. *Fundamentalisms Observed*. Chicago: University of Chicago Press, 1991.

Noel, Napoleon. *The History of the Brethren*. Denver: W. F. Knapp, 1936.

Pollock, J. C. *The Keswick Story: The Authorized History of the Keswick Convention*. London: Hodder and Stoughton, 1964.

Reid, Daniel G., et al., eds. *Dictionary of Christianity in America*. Downers Grove, IL: InterVarsity Press, 1990.

General Sources

Bode, Carl. *Mencken*. Carbondale: Southern Illinois University Press, 1969.

Cleland, Robert Glass. *The History of Occidental College, 1887–1937*. Los Angeles: Ward Ritchie Press, 1937.

La Encina. Occidental College Yearbook, 1915–1918.

Traxel, David. *1898: The Birth of the American Century*. New York: Knopf, 1998.

Periodicals Regularly Cited

Central American Bulletin

The Christian Century

The Christian Workers Magazine
The Institute Tie
Missionary Review of the World
Moody Bible Institute Monthly
The Sunday School Times

Archives Visited

Archivo General De La Nación, Mexico City, Mexico
Billy Graham Center Archives, Wheaton, Illinois
Central American Mission Archives, Dallas, Texas
Keswick Archives, Whiting, New Jersey
Mexico Branch (SIL) Archives, Mexico City, Mexico
Moody Bible Institute Archives, Chicago
Summer Institute of Linguistic Archives, Dallas, Texas
William Cameron Townsend Archives, JAARS, Waxhaw, North Carolina

Index